"This book is about
making money in the
fitness industry, with
the application of real
business principles
while maintaining
your integrity."

... from the Introduction

contents

LESSONS FROM LIFE

Acknowledgements

A MAN DOESN'T BECOME the man he is without contributions from others he has met in his life. Much of the success I've enjoyed over the years is the result of patient teaching and faithful guidance from people who have passed through my life as friends, employers or simply as role models.

This list could be longer and include many more characters I've encountered in my 45 years, but the people listed below are the ones who have had the most positive influence on my life and my career. I would personally like to thank everyone on this list for being part of my life, and I apologize for listing everyone here, but this might be the only book I ever write, so I tried to get you all in at once:

• Barry Lehane: Thank you for very patiently taking the time to teach me how to treat people, be creative in my approach to business, and remain true to my integrity. Your caring attitude and personal involvement with your clients is a model I've tried to follow my entire career. Thank you for being such a great teacher.

• Chuck "Coach" Hawkins: Thank you for being a role model at the time in my life when I most needed one. I am proud to think that someday I could live up to the standard you set for me, and that I could become even half the friend, person and teacher that you are. Thank you for being my "Coach."

• Mark Steinfield: There would be no Thomas Plummer and Associates without you, and this book would have remained a dream without your work and faith that we could make a difference in the fitness industry. Thank you for being my friend.

• Jim Bottin: Thank you for your friendship, faith and support at a time when you might have been the only person in the industry who had heard of me. You were our first associate and you opened the door for the rest of our team by being the first to stand behind us. Thank you for your quiet support and guidance over the years we've been together.

• Al Dilegge: Good and bad, success and failure, great years and days to be forgotten, we've seen it all as friends. Thank you for being there for all these years.

• Dave Levy: Thank you for your quiet faith and behind-the-scenes support during my career. We were rookies together at a time when anything was possible, and our secret goals were to be the best in the industry. You've achieved that success, and thank you for carrying me along with you on that journey.

• Jan Dennis: We've been friends for over 25 years and I still believe that there are more good times ahead. Thank you for the encouragement, and for never giving up on me during my more creative years as your friend.

• Steve Parker: Watching you grow has been one of the highlights of my life. You've given me too much credit for your success; it's simply been our mutual quest for living a better life that has kept us on the road together. Thank you for your friendship and faith that anything in my life was possible.

• Bill Clark. You were the first person who ever hired me in the fitness industry. Some of the most creative ideas I've ever had, I can happily say I stole from you. I miss your spontaneity and your belief that all things in anyone's life are possible if they simply set goals. Thank you for taking a chance on me early and for your friendship.

• Robbie Colasurdo: You laughed, you cringed and you even said it might work, and then you let me experiment in your businesses. I'm glad it worked and I'm glad you're my friend.

• Grand Master H. U. Lee: Thank you for showing me how to create a vision others could believe in and follow, and for teaching me how to lead by setting a personal example. I miss our friendship and your inspiration in my life.

• Robin Dyche: You've survived tough times and smiled, because your core values never changed. Thank you for taking the time to listen, and for always keeping an open door when I needed to talk to someone.

• Ken Reinig: They said you could never do it on your own, and did you ever show them. Thank you for making me laugh and for keeping the whole thing in perspective, and thanks for being a friend.

• Delores "Mom" Richeson: Thank you Mom for never once saying that my dreams weren't possible. You sacrificed much in your life, so I could try and achieve things in mine. I could never repay you for your love and belief that I could become anything I wanted to be. Thank you Mom and I love you.

• I would also like to thank God for everything that I am and everything that I have in my life.

There just has to be a better way to do business in the fitness industry

THE FITNESS INDUSTRY IS IN A state of change; I am a one-person missionary show, trying to institute this change. After years of business regression and retardation, the industry is finally showing signs of breaking away from its 30-year negative business image and practices — still the standard for doing business today for most owners.

Long-term contracts with high-pressure sales, gas station price war mentalities, and semi-naked models in our advertising that offend most of our women patrons were part of our past and are still part of business as it's done today. Couple this with the trend of building clubs with vast warehouse physical plants that have all the intimacy of standing in the middle of an Arkansas Wal-Mart during a two-for-one long underwear sale, and you have an industry that has stagnated and has been reduced to copying out-of-date and mostly unethical business practices from 30 years ago.

I became part of the fitness industry more than 20 years ago for two reasons. First of all, we offer a product that can make a difference in someone's life. If our product is delivered correctly, then our fitness businesses can initiate positive change in the people we serve. We can obviously change a person's physical shape with what we offer. But we can also subtly change their mental condition by allowing them to become part of something that

...we offer a product that can make a difference in someone's life.

becomes important in their lives — a place where they are always welcome, where they can make new friends, and a place that offers a social atmosphere linked to their physical conditioning.

Secondly, I realized that I could make a great deal of money doing something I loved, which was being in the fitness business. But sadly I realized that there were no real business principles being applied to this industry. It's almost as if the fitness business were a business backwater that modern concepts such as financial analysis, customer service, low-pressure/high-integrity sales and advanced marketing concepts had not yet reached.

Basically it was, and still is for most, an industry that is totally sales-driven. And this lopsided emphasis on sales prevents us from delivering our product, which again is to bring change through the delivery of our service.

Typical fitness facilities today are huge impersonal warehouses of equipment revolving around a sales team. The marketing is also a negative since it is entirely price-driven. This has proved to be totally ineffective in most markets for attracting deconditioned people, people who have had bad experiences at other gyms, or people who have never really been in a fitness facility.

Sales in these facilities are all based on closing the sale on the first visit, a system that is more than 30 years old, and one that most potential members find very repulsive. If this facility is so good, why is the person forced to make a decision during their first visit?

First-visit closes have been an unquestioned part of the industry since it started. But this system drives down the price we should be able to get for our memberships, because in only 30 minutes everything always comes down to price. There is simply nothing, other than the deal of the day, that can be intelligently discussed between a sales person and a prospective member in just 30 minutes.

As an industry, we haven't changed. Nor have we questioned the dogma that high-pressure/first-visit sales represent a behavior that is still propagated through the national conventions, by most industry magazines and by industry consultants who are failed owners who are now going to teach you their business systems.

Financially, most of these outdated business systems are self-defeating.

Financially, most of these outdated business systems are self-defeating. For example, the costs of running a fitness facility in the '90s is two to three times higher than it was in the early '80s. Yet many owners try to operate their facilities using the same price per member that clubs used 25 years ago. Simply, the volume that can be generated by traditional sales and marketing methods, with outdated pricing, is not enough to ensure clubs' survival.

Traditional fitness marketing is also a representation of the industry's past that leads to a business plan, that is doomed to fail before it can ever begin. Price-driven ads with big-haired, big-chested super models with 22-inch waists don't work anymore to attract enough potential members, because the ads' appeal is so limited.

Since the club's marketing is ineffective, the club then forces the salespeople to generate their own leads and to pressure prospective members to join on their first visit. Salespeople who are able to do this are expensive and, therefore, take up a disproportionate amount of the staffing budget. Because the salespeople are so overpaid, and the marketing is so expensive, there is no real money left for service people.

Without service people, the current members become frustrated and leave the system, which increases the demand for the salespeople to not only generate new sales, but to also replace the large number of people who drop out. More money has to go into marketing and more pressure is applied to the salespeople, who in turn apply it to the prospective members.

Many people who might be interested in working out in a fitness facility would never even set foot in a typical club, because they already know what is going to happen to them. They will be pressured into a decision, and then receive no help after the sale is closed.

The clubs will be crowded because of the volume approach that goes along with the low prices, and it will also be dirty and filled with broken equipment. Keep in mind that the standard way of doing business in this industry over the past 30 years or more has taught the average consumer this process.

All the large chains based on low pricing and volume marketing in the past 30 years have proved the weaknesses of traditional operating systems by bleeding red ink all over their investors. Even as this is written, the chain of the decade is gobbling up endless clubs by using venture capital, yet the owners are crying over lost revenues in financial magazines.

Their business systems simply don't work anymore. These systems are archaic and provide losses to the owners and investors, and worse yet, do immense damage to the members who bought into the clubs believing that they would get the help and service they rightfully expected. Huge chains with outside capital and lousy business systems, or any operator who follows these systems, also hurt the legitimate owners in the industry — by giving the consumer such a bad buying experience before we ever get a chance to meet them.

This book is about making money in the fitness industry, with the application of real business principles while maintaining your integrity. There is a better way to do business, breaking away from the traditional dogma our industry has been based on during its history, which has always reflected instant financial gratification for the owner at the expense of the consumer. Here are a few of the topics covered in this book that reflect changes from the old style of thinking:

• *Focusing*: You can't be everything to everybody in today's fitness market. Almost every major business or market has evolved from generalist to specialist. Retailing giants like Macy's and Sears have been replaced with retail specialists like Eddie Bauer and Victoria's Secret. Even lawyers and doctors have moved from being general practitioners to very narrowly focused specialists. The fitness industry must do the same to grow and thrive into the next century, yet many owners still practice the one-facility-fits-all theory.

• *Running the business by numbers*: There are formulas and numbers that can be applied to our businesses that can help an owner build a functional business plan. For example, an owner will make much better business decisions if he or she understands the true yield from a member payment, loss

This book is about making money in the fitness industry, with the application of real business principles while maintaining your integrity.

rates, and the expected net from each profit center. There are also important ratios that determine how much of the club's expenses need to be covered by the receivable check and what percentage of a club's income should come from its profit centers in order to decrease the dependency on new sales. By better understanding the financial side of the business, we can better understand how to break out of our old habits.

• *Staffing*: Staffing will be the most difficult issue to deal with in the coming decade. How you hire, train, motivate, and eventually let go of your employees will decide how successful you will be. At some point in time, most gyms will have much of the same equipment and programming. The difference between one club and another will be its focus and the staff that works in the gym. The club with the best staff will win.

• *Service*: We haven't even scratched the surface yet of how we define and deliver member service. Implementing true member service is expensive to maintain and difficult to create because of the entrepreneurial nature of our owners. "Entrepreneurial" is another word for control freak, and the very nature of a typical owner works against letting a member make a suggestion or point out a weakness in the club. To prosper, we need to redefine member service beyond the definition of vast rooms of equipment and free coffee to the members. Member service is not how much free stuff we include with a membership; it's the quality and image of the programs, services and amenities available to the member.

• *Marketing*: Traditional fitness marketing doesn't work because it has such a limited appeal. It's estimated that 92 percent of the people in this country have never set foot in a health club. Typical fitness marketing only appeals to the other 8 percent who have fitness experience, and it does nothing to develop the other 92 percent as a potential market for our clubs.

The fitness industry as a whole also works off many false assumptions that need to be questioned. This book works hard to uncover these fitness business myths. For example, most owners strongly believe that the typical prospective member only cares about price. Why do they believe that and base their business plan on this assumption, when it is so obviously false?

Some people are driven by price — this is the deciding factor as to what they buy and how they live. There are just as many other people who will pay extra for quality. There are Geo Metros and there are Mercedes. There is Nordstrom and there is Wal-Mart. The problem is that the false assumption most owners follow, is that everyone in the world is a Wal-Mart person seeking a discount.

The huge fitness chains demonstrate this assumption in their ads, and the rest of us follow. It's the traditional system of pricing, selling and marketing that forces the consumer to think price, not the price itself. Because of our belief in this false assumption, pricing in the industry for the majority of the fitness facility owners hasn't really changed in more than 20 years.

In my 20 years as an educator and consultant, I know that change is possible and that the false assumptions can be replaced with real business practices. I also know that change hurts. In this and any other industry, change means that you may be leading the charge and going against the rest

The fitness industry as a whole ... works off many false assumptions that need to be questioned.

of the pack. Someone has to do it, and hopefully, it will be the readers of this book who will help bring the fitness industry kicking and screaming into the next millennium.

Thomas Plummer
Frisco, Colorado

Conceptualizing the fitness business

Issues and concepts that affect today's fitness business

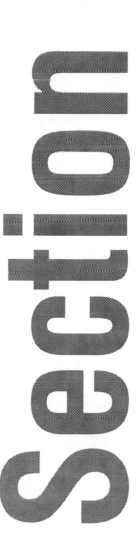

Chapter 1

If you're lost, it's because you're following the wrong path

Chapter 2

Many owners are so busy bobbing and weaving in reaction to their competitors that they don't have time to make money

Chapter 3

It's a business, not a baby

Chapter 4

What kind of business are you running anyway?

Chapter 5

There is no business plan that can overcome poor renewals

1

If you're lost, it's because you're following the wrong path

WHEN YOU CONCEPTUALIZE a new business, or re-evaluate an existing one, consider why you make the choices you do. Many times in the fitness industry, a business will fail because it's based on a business plan that never could have worked in the first place. This plan is usually based on someone else's patched-together concept or ideas copied from other existing businesses. When recreating a business or starting a new one, make sure you follow the right path.

Over the years, I've visited literally thousands of fitness facilities of all types. A good weekend on the road would always include visiting as many as 20 different gyms, Y's, recreation centers and any other fitness businesses that could be found in the city phone book. After a while, the facilities all started looking the same. Ugly front counters, blue and black Nautilus equipment 30 years out-of-date, poorly trained staff, gray carpets with some type of black specks, and a general sense that there were very few new and exciting ideas in our industry.

The problem is too much inbreeding. Everyone steals ideas from everyone else in the fitness business. I was doing the same, until it dawned on me that I had to be better than these businesses! Most fitness businesses haven't changed their base operating and design concepts in 35 years.

Cardio equipment, the most in-demand equipment in today's market and still growing, is almost always poorly displayed. Why? Because some brave soul built a mediocre cardio deck about 10 years ago and the next 2,000 people that opened a facility copied the idea and, in many cases, the

Most fitness businesses haven't changed their base operating and design concepts in 35 years.

3

actual design.

Don't think it works this way? Look back a few years to the introduction of teal and white equipment. One manufacturer brought some to a trade show, other manufacturers copied the colors, and then for several years you could walk into almost any gym in the country and find teal and white equipment — except for the hardcore guys, who all went with red and black.

By visiting hundreds of poorly designed and managed fitness businesses, you can get pulled down to their level. You visit a few weak gyms, say to yourself, "Wow, my place is better than that," and then fail to develop to higher levels because you settled for beating standards that are too low.

Many fitness businesses will fail because they follow the wrong business examples. For example, many owners still run ads featuring semi-naked models as artwork. The look of the models has changed somewhat over the years and, of course, the clothes have changed, but the ads are basically the same: models who are large-chested, have exceptionally small waists and are in full blown makeup. And, of course, don't forget the big hair. Today's version also always has a bare midriff featuring a flat, ripped stomach.

Owners justify these pictures as role models for our potential women members, even though the shape most of the models are in is attainable by a very small percentage of a club's members. The scary part is that when these ads are shown to women, more than 90 percent say using pictures of semi-naked models is somewhat offensive. A number of the women we talked to actually said that these pictures would prevent them from responding to an ad. This was because they felt they would have to be in good shape before they actually joined that facility.

These ads are a part of the history of this business. Almost every owner in the country has run this type of ad at some point in his or her career, including me. They are easy. Your ad person usually has a book of them, and they sort of fit the fitness theme. These ads are also a perfect example of following the wrong path.

To make money in the future, you need to question everything you know and do. Are you running your business based on principles copied from someone you think is making money? Are you making decisions based on habit because you've always done it that way? And are you using basic business principles that may be 35 years out-of-date and don't really work anymore in a competitive market?

It was easier to make money in the earlier days of our industry. Things that worked in the late '60s and '70s, such as discounted renewals, high-pressure sales and long-term contracts worked back then. In fact, everything worked back then. The consumer was less sophisticated and hadn't been exposed to nearly the number of sales pitches he or she is today. Potential members actually believed the old drop close — that if they didn't sign up today, they would lose money by having to pay more if they signed up tomorrow. Are there any consumers in today's market who haven't heard pitches for everything from stereos to in-line skates by the time they turn 21?

When conceptualizing a fitness business, either a new gym or recreating an existing facility, the hardest part is breaking away from the accepted norm.

You visit a few weak gyms, say to yourself, "Wow, my place is better than that," and then fail to develop to higher levels because you settled for beating standards that are too low.

Setting out on a new path is difficult because so many existing owners claim to be making so much money from copying the old methods of doing business.

You visit a national trade show or convention and everyone is rich, everything is working and the owner is always working on opening his or her next project. "Yeah, I hired this new guy who used to work for one of the big chains, and man this guy can sell. He even has an 80 percent closing rate. He's working with my staff and we're signing more contracts now than we have in years."

The first owner says high-pressure sales is the answer because he is writing a lot of contracts. The other guy thinks my sales are flat, so I need to copy this method and get myself a high-pressure sales guy if I want to make money too.

What the new guy and the owner with the new sales guy don't know is: Does what he is doing really work? What are the losses from such high-pressure sales? Do people sign up with this guy just to get out of the office and then don't pay later? What's happening to the gym's word-of-mouth reputation in the community? No one knows, but to an owner who has flat sales, this seems like a magical solution.

We know from research in this industry and from research done by the government's Small Business Administration that only about 15 percent of all small businesses can net 20 percent or better on a yearly basis. Despite this, the accepted norm would be to copy what everyone says at the shows, since they all claim they are making money with their ideas.

The real life business view, however, is that most of these people aren't really making the money they say they are, so copying their ideas will be counterproductive to your long-term business plan. Remember that you seldom hear or read about some owner who is getting their butt kicked. Everyone says they are making money whether they are or not. In a small industry such as ours, it's easy to get sucked down the wrong path

Another way to get on the wrong path is to pursue the illogical over the logical. In this business, we seem to follow the illogical. For example, why do most new gyms build sales offices? A sales office in a modern gym is not logical. Few of us are comfortable in an office environment sitting across the desk from someone. The only situation I can think of where you sit across a desk from someone and it's good news is when a lawyer tells you some distant relative died and left you a pile of money. And even then, someone had to die to make the good news happen. In the consumer's mind, most situations where they sit across from someone at a desk is a bad position to be in. Is sitting across a desk from a car salesperson a pleasant situation? Is sitting in front of a doctor good news? And anytime you're in front of a lawyer it has to be bad news. No matter what, it's going to cost you something.

Another illogical aspect of a sales office is that it takes consumers out of the environment that excited them in the first place. The colors, the music, the people: all excite people to buy memberships. The atmosphere in the facility is a strong part of the buying decision.

Why not sign the person up in a centrally located area, right in the mid-

The only situation I can think of where you sit across a desk from someone and it's good news is when a lawyer tells you some distant relative died and left you a pile of money. And even then, someone had to die to make the good news happen.

dle of the action — such as at the juice bar or at a high cafe table overlooking the action on the floor? We normally put in offices because everyone else has them in their facilities. None of us are comfortable in offices, but we'll make the illogical decision because it's the path everyone else took.

Another prime example of illogical paths is pricing. Most owners believe they have the best facilities in their communities, yet they are often priced lower than or the same as their competitors. Most of us associate the best with the most expensive. If one item is three dollars more than another item, it should be three dollars better.

Most of us go through life feeling "you get what you pay for." Yet when it comes to pricing a gym membership, most owners go for cheaper pricing. How can you be the best gym in town and also be the cheapest? It's not logical to price our product this way, yet we do it all the time because our competitors are making the same mistakes.

How can you be the best gym in town and also be the cheapest?

My last point is the application of good business principles. Why is it that good business principles often stop at the gym door? We see it often: A person who was successful in other businesses opens a gym and goes brain dead. Maybe it's the new baggy pants and fanny pack they're wearing that somehow makes the person go back to their pre-business days.

What works in other industries often can be applied to the fitness industry, especially when it comes from other service industries. Instead of studying other fitness businesses, we need to spend more time studying other good service businesses. Federal Express is an excellent model for many gyms to study. Fed Ex does not apologize for its prices, even though it's one of the most expensive overnight carriers. At any time, the company can tell you exactly where your package is and what's happening to it. If you had a very important document to send overnight, who would you trust, a low-priced alternative or would you go with the company that started it all? Keep in mind they can find any package at anytime, anywhere in the world. Most gyms can't even tell whether the person walking in the door is an active member or not.

I had a one-visit trial workout at a big-chain club near my house. The next day, I walked in and they didn't stop me at the desk. After three weeks, someone finally stopped me at the door and asked if I were a member. I said yes, and they let me in without proof. Because of the emphasis on new sales, no one ever stopped a person carrying a bag or in workout clothes. They must be already in the system, therefore they aren't new meat for the salespeople. I worked out free in that club for more than six months and no one ever stopped me or asked if I needed any help.

The path this club followed was based on years of high-pressure sales, service people that were expendable, a system geared totally toward writing new business instead of taking care of existing members, and an attitude of "If you don't bother them, they can't complain." This path is one that our industry has been following for three decades, and it is the wrong path for the coming competitive years.

If your business is flat, it may be because the path you chose to follow is not the right one for you or for your business. If you are opening a new club, spend less time looking at other gyms in your area and more time in businesses that excel in service, design and atmosphere. But above all, make sure what you do makes good business sense and is not something you do out of habit or because the guy down the street has a full parking lot.

... spend less time looking at other gyms in your area and more time in businesses that excel in service, design and atmosphere

Summary

Question everything you do and consider doing. Is it logical? Is it based on real numbers and not a story told to you at a convention or trade show? Does it make sense in today's marketplace with a more sophisticated and aware potential member?

Things you can do to use this material

1) Check your business plan to see how much is copied from other fitness businesses in your area. How do you know whether it really worked for your competitor?

2) Look at fewer gyms and, instead, look at other successful businesses in your area. What are they doing that makes them successful, and what can you learn from that?

3) Look at the design of you club. Most fitness businesses look too much alike. What design ideas can you steal from other businesses such as restaurants, nightclubs, banks or clothing stores? Gyms look alike because everyone steals from everyone else, and few people introduce new ideas.

4) Consider which parts of your business may be illogical. Can you be the best and the cheapest? Remember that price is part of your image. Does it make sense to have old-style habits such as sales offices? Can you be the best gym in the area and still go for cash or two-year memberships — two things that don't make sense to a more sophisticated potential member?

The stinky member

THERE IS NOT MUCH WORSE that can happen to a member in a gym than coming in for a workout, getting on a treadmill, and realizing that the person on the next treadmill is the club's resident stinky member.

This member, usually male, is characterized by a favorite, extremely disgusting tee shirt kept in the trunk of his car between workouts, unruly hair, mismatched shorts, and formerly white socks. The shoes, from the member's illustrious high school wrestling career, add to the general bouquet.

The staff knows that the member is a problem, but they choose to ignore him because there is no easy way to confront the issue without embarrassing the person.

Other members have repeatedly complained to the staff about the stinky member, forcing the owner to realize that if something isn't done soon, she may lose some of her hard-fought-for members.

The moral of the story

This is an example of a problem that should be handled immediately, meaning as soon as the staff gets wind of the problem (that had to be said), and most certainly after the first couple of member complaints. The key here is not the stinky member's feelings, which are going to get bruised no matter what action is taken, but rather the 13:1 rule.

The 13:1 rule states that if one

Other members have repeatedly complained to the staff about the stinky member

person says it (in this case other members are complaining to the staff), then at least 12 others think the same thing and have the same problem. These members, however, will be miserable in silence rather than say anything to anyone.

When managing a club business, we often ignore complaints, especially those that require an uncomfortable confrontation to solve. But if you apply the 13:1 rule, the problem takes on a more critical perspective.

For example, if five members complain about the stinky member, they in fact represent 5 x 13, or about 65 members, a significant portion of any club's membership. In this case, the longer we ignore the problem, the more members it affects, and the greater damage that can be done to the business. This occurs because we failed to deal with a problem in a timely manner and because the problem was larger than it seemed.

In the case of the stinky member, he needs to be politely taken to the office by a senior manager or owner, apprised of the situation in a straight-forward business manner, and worked through acceptable courses of action. Simple suggestions, such as wearing clean shirts, or perhaps showering before the workout, in the case of someone who might have a labor job of some sort, would be appropriate.

2

Many owners are so busy bobbing and weaving in reaction to their competitors, they don't have time to make money

OWNERS NEED TO LEARN to be proactive in their business, instead of reactive to their competition. To do this, they need to understand the importance of planning. Every owner should have a one-, three- and five-year business plan, as well as a 12-month marketing plan, staff training plan, development system and member service plan.

Most owners are totally reactionary by nature. If the guy down the street runs an ad, you run and ad; if the guy down the street lowers his price, you lower your price; if sales slow down for a day or two, you panic and run crazy specials.

The guy down the street is not any better. He is running ads under the same conditions — without a plan, and in reaction to current market conditions or to what competitors are doing.

There are many problems with being a reactionary manager, but perhaps the main one is that you *let* business happen, you don't *make* it happen. This means you're not creating or growing your business by a plan, but rather you're letting your business be dictated by the surrounding, short-term market conditions.

For example, let's say a club wants to generate 60 new memberships a month. Most clubs set a number, do some marketing and then hope for the best. Sales people may have a few quotas, the owner may increase marketing

If the guy down the street runs an ad, you run and ad; if the guy down the street lowers his price, you lower your price; if sales slow down for a day or two, you panic and run crazy specials.

for that month, but there is still no actual plan in place to generate that business.

There are several problems with this scenario that work against the owner's success. First of all, the sales goal is too short-term. Are the 60 sales part of a year-long sales goal based on last year's numbers, or is that number just what you happen to need this month to cover the operating expense? Most of the time, a goal such as the 60 sales is totally reactionary, meaning it's based on what you have to have this month to survive, and not based on any long-term growth formula for the business.

You also need to know how many potential members the club would need to generate to end up with 60 sales. If the club has a 40-percent closing rate for sales, then it has to have 150 potential members come through the door to end up with 60 sales.

You also need to know, in this example, exactly how much marketing to run. Before you can determine a marketing budget, however, you first need to know your average response rate for the last several months, as well as your cost per lead for potential members.

If the club has had a 1-percent response rate from its marketing, which is good in the real world these days, then it would have to run at least 15,000 pieces in the club's immediate 5-mile ring. Keep in mind that 80 percent of a club's membership comes from a 5-mile or 15-minute drive from the club.

If the club in this example is using direct mail, and is paying 25 cents for each piece, it would have to spend $3,750 for its marketing that month. This works out to $25 per lead if you divide the 15,000 needed pieces by the 1-percent response rate, and then divide that number (150) into the $3,750.

For these numbers to make sense, they need to be part of an annual plan and budgeting process for the club. When annual plans are used, another big problem of reactionary management is covered, which is lack of consistency.

In the example above, the club will probably not be successful in attracting its 150 potential members, because it has done nothing to create consistency in its marketing. Most marketing takes at least four months to become established, and then it has to be maintained every month. If you need 60 sales this month, but you don't start your marketing until this month, then your marketing doesn't have time to work, so you probably won't get the desired results.

If the club in the example was using a consistent 12-month marketing plan, it would have real numbers and percentages to work with. It could then increase its number of pieces and get some type of expected results, because that month's marketing would be related to all the marketing the club has done over the past 12 months.

Another problem with no long-term planning is that reactionary management simply wastes a tremendous amount of money. Using the above example again, if a club starts and stops its marketing, it would receive no cost savings from its printers, newspapers or even from its mailing costs if it doesn't run enough pieces to qualify for bulk mail rates.

You can't budget and negotiate long-term discounted rates if your mar-

Before you can determine a marketing budget, however, you first need to know your average response rate for the last several months, as well as your cost per lead for potential members.

keting plan is only by the month. For example, with typical newspaper inserts, an owner can save as much as 40 percent of the cost if they commit to a 12-month contract. Most owners won't, however, because they don't know what kind of marketing they will be running next month, let alone six months or a year from now.

Keep in mind that a reactionary management style is not limited just to marketing. Most reactionary managers are reactionary in all aspects of their business. A proactive manager would be watching the trends in the industry and making changes in their club before the market forces them to react.

An example here is the demise of aerobics in the late '90s. Class size shrank, total participation by the club's membership faded to less than 10 percent in most tested markets, and owners battled harder and harder to find consistent instructors. In the clubs that were surveyed around the country, the average program was losing as much as $2,500 per month and, in many cases, much more.

Reactionary managers kept trying to fix the same old problems, and kept the aerobics programs no matter how much money they were losing. In clubs run by proactive management, however, failing programs were replaced with new cardio presentations or with group cycling classes for which they could charge additional fees.

Problems are also encountered by a reactionary manager in staffing issues. Most major staffing issues start as little problems that could be handled early. For example, a club has a uniform policy backed up in writing in its employee manual. The club manager is reactionary, however. An employee shows up out of uniform and the manager grumbles a little, but basically ignores the problem. The employee has now been taught that small deviations from club policies are acceptable.

Most reactionary managers ignore things until they get so mad that they go from being quietly reactive to totally proactive, meaning somebody is going to pay and it's today. In the case of the employee and the uniform, by not being proactive and addressing the issue before it becomes a problem, the manager has left no out, except to overreact later when the employee's minor transgressions accumulate into something bigger.

The employee who was taught early that minor rule-breaking is acceptable, is the same one that drifts in 15 minutes late. This is the same employee who will always have problems with the uniform policy because there is no consistent, proactive stance from management. When the big day arrives that the manager is so upset that a confrontation takes place, the damage is already done. It would be very hard to retrain this employee to be any good, and in many cases it would be easier to replace the manager than it would be to replace all the employees.

The same holds true for member transgressions. The small things that members do, such as one guy always dropping the dumbbells, are usually ignored be a reactionary manager. These guys, however, cost the gym money in the long run, because they damage equipment, scare off the softer members who are intimidated by these types, and may eventually injure other members by having those dumbbells land on someone's feet.

A proactive manager would be watching the trends in the industry and making changes in their club before the market forces them to react.

11

If such members were corrected the first time, or simply removed from the club, all these problems would go away. Proactive managers live with more peace of mind. Reactionary managers are constantly in agony, because they only make decisions in a crisis mode.

For an owner to move into a proactive style, they should have a number of plans in place that help project the business into the future. Plans are really guides and goals that keep the business moving forward, instead of sideways away from the ultimate goal of profitability. Being proactive also means that sometimes you have to deviate from your plans. If a club fails down the street and you have a chance to pick up some used equipment at a good deal, or can take over their membership, being proactive means you should move on it.

Being proactive in this case means that there is an accrual fund for capital improvements and a set financial plan to understand the risks of taking in a large number of members at a price that doesn't jeopardize the business. Being reactive means taking the members and buying the equipment without understanding the ramifications for the rest of the business.

Business plans

In the fitness industry, it's easier to think of business plans as three distinct types. There is a *prospectus*, for raising money during the concept stage; a *development plan*, which is used to define a business before it is open; and *operating plans*, which are one-, three- and five-year projections/operational plans for existing businesses. Operating plans form the basis for proactive management.

THE PROSPECTUS

The prospectus is used to raise money for a new business. Most rookies make their major mistake here, by confusing a brief, but thorough prospectus with a lengthy development plan for the new business.

Investors and bankers are busy people normally. They don't usually have time to peruse 150 pages of wishful thinking, which is what most business plans resemble, to see if there is a business opportunity buried somewhere inside.

Investors normally want a brief, usually no more than 10 to 12 pages, that gives them an overview of the project, who is behind it, where the money is coming from, and how they, as the money people, will benefit if they invest.

A prospectus plan should include the following sections:

1) A one- to two-page overview describing what the project will entail. What it is, where it is, what it's for, who will run it, why that particular area and how long it will take to get the thing going are all basic questions that should be addressed.

2) The second section should be a one- to two-page projection describ-

Investors and bankers are busy people normally. They don't usually have time to peruse 150 pages of wishful thinking ...

ing the cost of the entire project. How much is the build-out for that location, how much equipment at what cost, how much reserve money is allotted, how much for fixtures, desks and programs, etc. Any other start-up costs that might exist for the project should also be discussed here.

3) The third section is usually only one page, and describes where the money for the project is coming from. Are the banks putting up the money? How much equity does the potential owner have invested? How much is expected to come from investors? And, where is the project financially at this moment?

4) The fourth section is the most important because it's a financial projection showing the ability to repay the banks and investors. How does money arrive in the business? Is there enough left over for investors? How does the business grow over a two-year period? What does it really take to run this business? And, what's left over after expenses? All this should be addressed in a formal two-year financial projection. This section should also include a breakdown of a typical month's expenses and a typical month's income stream.

5) This section shows what's in it for the investors. If they put money into this project, what kind of return on investment or equity is the owner offering? This section should detail what the owner is trying to raise and from what sources, as well as what is being offered in return — be it a fixed return, equity or both. Basically the investors want to know: If I put money into this project, what do I get back, besides the satisfaction of helping a young businessperson get started?

6) The next section should give a brief resumé of who is going to put the project together and who is going to run it on a day-to-day basis. Investors want to know if there is any special qualification, skill or experience the owner and key people possess that might guarantee this project has a chance.

7) The final section is a summary. Tell briefly what the project is, where it will be, how the money is going to be raised, when the project will open and who will run it. Keep it brief and simple here. If the investors want more information, they will ask.

In summary, keep this type of plan brief. Investors are busy people who won't sit and read a 150-page bound document. They might, however, sit and review a 10- to 12-page prospectus similar to what they get from other people who also want their money.

THE DEVELOPMENT PLAN

This is the masterwork plan that creates the business on paper before it exists in real life. Most people trying to start a fitness business for the first time spend way too much time writing and rewriting this plan. The best way to think of a development plan is that it helps to make sure that you have at least a working understanding of what the project will take before it is created.

Existing owners who are opening their next unit should always write one of these, because many times a project that looks good in your head

> **Basically the investors want to know: If I put money into this project, what do I get back, besides the satisfaction of helping a young businessperson get started?**

won't look so good when you take the time to write out a development plan.

For example, a common mistake owners make when they open a second unit, is that they don't put any systems in place. They've run their existing club by their personalities, rather than with systems that can be easily duplicated. A written development plan helps determine whether a system exists.

The development plan should have the following parts (length is irrelevant in a development plan; write what it takes for you to understand your project):

1) The overview should tightly define the scope of the project, the size, the location, why a club in the area is a good idea, what the target market is and an approximate target date for the completion of the project.

2) The second section is a description of the proposed fitness facility. How big, who for, what niche will it fill in the community, and how will it be different than your competitors should be addressed in this section.

3) The third section should be a complete demographic breakdown of the area. Pay special attention to the 15-minute drive time rule. How many people are there in a 3-mile and 5-mile ring from the proposed sight?

4) The fourth section is especially important because it should define your true target market. Most fitness projects are too broad in scope. Keep in mind that 80 percent of your potential members will probably come from a specific target market. For example, you might choose a high-energy rock-and-roll atmosphere for your gym, similar to most license-style facilities. The target market in this example would be people within three miles of the gym who are 24 to 40 years old. Remember: A common mistake with new gyms and by owners who want multiple facilities is to try to be everything to everybody.

5) This section should detail the needed capital for the project. Be sure to include a detailed equipment list not only for the workout equipment, but also for support of the profit centers, such as computer needs and license fees. Before you write your plan, be sure to get an idea of what the build-out costs are in your area. Also be sure to include a reserve of at least two months' operating expense. You will need it.

6) Section six should be the financial section. Include here two-year financial projections, a sample month's operating expense and a sample month's revenue projection.

7) If you have to use investors or the bank for the project, this section should detail how you will raise the money and what you will give to get it. Remember that investors are seeking either a return on their investment, equity or a combination of both.

8) Research and include a 12-month proposed marketing plan for the business. Be sure to cost this plan out, so it may be included as part of your projections. Start with a marketing budget for the first year of about 7 percent of your basic monthly operating expense. For example, if it will cost you about $50,000 a month to run your club, budget about $3,500 per month for marketing, which is about 7 percent.

9) The staffing section should be broken down into two parts. First, you

Most fitness projects are too broad in scope. Keep in mind that 80 percent of your potential members will probably come from a specific target market.

need to project your staffing needs for a typical month's worth of coverage. Break this coverage down to daily staffing costs, including salary and hourly costs. Include payroll tax projections, as well as proposed commissions and bonuses. Second, develop a staff training guide you can use for the first six months you're open, and for each job in the gym. What you want people to know, how and when you will train them, and how much training you will provide before an employee is allowed on the floor are all considerations that need to be addressed before you hire your first staff person.

10) A member service plan should also be included in your development plan. You should cover how to handle member complaints, surveys and information-gathering materials, things that can be added to the club the first year to increase member service, such as amenities in the locker rooms and staff training procedures that increase your member service response.

11) Multiple profit centers are a vital part of any club's business plan. An entire section should be devoted to the profit centers you will feature, especially to how these profit centers will be promoted. Include the start-up cost and expected return for each profit center. Be sure to include staff costs if they are separate from your staff projections.

12) Resumés from the owners and all key staff should also be included in the plan. What type of expertise do you really have to make money in the fitness business? What types of training, such as accounting classes or certifications, should you seek before you open? Any weaknesses should appear when you gather your resumés from the key players.

13) A summary sheet should be thrown in at the end. Since this is a development plan for your own use, the summary should be used to focus the entire project down to just a couple of pages. If you can't focus the entire project to two pages, you may not yet have a project clearly enough focused to work. Plus, if you have to show this plan to anyone, most people will start with the summary and only read selected sections anyway. Make this finish strong and concise.

OPERATING PLANS

One-year, three-year and five-year operating plans keep an owner who is already in business proactive. When people first write business plans, they almost always start from today forward, working toward a specific goal or idea. The best way to write plans, however, is start at the end and work your way backward. Start with the goal in mind, then work backward, breaking it down into the steps that it takes to get there.

Each plan has a slightly different feel to it. The one-year plan is considered a true operating plan. With this plan, you are addressing things that have to happen in a very short period of time. For example, what equipment do you need to add or replace in the next 12 months?

The three-year plan is a little more conceptual in nature. What programs may need to be replaced, what key staff will you most likely need to replace, or how can you refinance your business now that you've been around

The best way to write plans ... is start at the end and work your way backward.

15

a while to help reduce your debt structure? These are all questions that should be address in a three-year plan.

The five-year plan is primarily centered on long-range financial goals. Where will the club be financially in five years? What additional debt do you need to keep the facility competitive? Where will you be financially in your own life in five years? Should you move the business into your own building or continue to rent? All of these questions need to be addressed in this plan.

The one-year plan

The one-year plan should be broken down into these parts:

1) The physical plant

2) Equipment needs and changes

3) The projected financial growth of the business for the coming year

4) Individual plans such as member service and a 12-month marketing plan

5) Reductions or additions in your multiple profit centers

6) Sales goals and renewal projections

7) A staff development and training plan

Use these questions to trigger your writing:

• How much gross income can I project over the next year on an annual and monthly basis? How much money per month will the club receive? From what sources will this money come?

• How many sales does the club have to do on a monthly basis? What will the cost per sale be?

• What projected renewals should the club be doing on a month-to-month basis? How will that compare against last year's? What percentage increase is your goal?

• What's your target for total receivables growth? How much will you need to increase each month to reach that goal?

• What is your monthly marketing budget? What is your expected response rate from your marketing? What is your cost per lead and your club's monthly overall closing rate?

• What new profit centers will you add in the next 12 months? Where will the money come from for these additions? What profit centers need replacing?

• Where is your 12-month marketing plan?

• Where is your 12-month member service plan?

• What events do you have planned for the coming 12 months?

• How much should the club have in its regular savings account at the end of the next year? How much will be in the accrual account?

Who will be the manager for your next gym, and what are you doing to get that person ready?

• What type of further development does your lead staff need? Who on your staff can step up as a future leader, and what type of development do those people need?

• Who will be the manager for your next gym, and what are you doing to get that person ready?

• What will you do over the next 12 months to improve yourself and your business skills?

• What is your educational budget for staff development for the next 12 months?

• What equipment will be outdated in the next 12 months? What needs to be replaced?

• What physical plant changes do you need to make in the next year? Where will this money come from? How will it improve your business?

The three-year plan

The same basics apply to the three-year plan, except that they are extended further into the future. The difference, though, is that it looks at the overall financial structure of the business. How can you reduce the overall debt structure? Remember that you will always have some type of debt. But as the business matures, your goal is to reduce short-term debt, which is anything that is three years or less, with cheaper, long-term debt, which is usually five to seven years.

The five-year plan

The five-year plan should be the big picture plan designed to secure more equity in your business. Can you buy your building or build somewhere else in town? How many other units can you manage, or how many do you want to own? How can you protect your business as your main source of income? What major structural work does the club need to stay competitive, and how will you finance this change? Be sure to include a plan that puts you on the road to retirement, which includes funding some type of personal IRA account.

Summary

Most businesses are run by reactive management. This means decisions are usually made in a defensive mode, which is generally too late to do the business any good.

For example, you know that you are getting a lot of complaints about a lack of cardio pieces. You put off the decision to add, though, and just take the heat. Eventually, you cave in and add a few extra pieces after the complaints escalate. A proactive manager would analyze the initial complaints and act before the situation turns into a defensive standoff between management and members.

Proactive management can't happen without planning. A good owner will sit down once a year and write a one-year, three-year and five-year operational plan that projects the current business into the future. Future owners will create their new business on paper before it is created in the real world through the use of a prospectus which is used to raise money, and a development plan which is used to visualize the business on paper.

Future owners will create their new business on paper before it is created in the real world

Things you can do to use this material

If you haven't opened your first club yet:

1) Keep your business narrowly focused. Most new owners want to open the ultimate dream club their first time out. Keep your first project smaller, leaner and less risky.

2) Write the prospectus first before you write the development plan. It helps you keep the project focused and narrowly defined.

3) Learn the numbers. Start with projections, monthly expenses and the rent factor. These numbers drive the business and are the place to start for beginners.

4) Learn what you're really giving up to open the club. You have to give up something to get someone else's money, but learn what's acceptable and what isn't.

If you are currently operating a facility:

5) Start thinking proactive now. Weigh every decision, even the small ones, against what happens if you fail to act now, putting off the problem or decision until you're forced to react.

6) Take a weekend away and write your one-, three- and five-year plans. If you have senior staff, get them involved in the writing process. Update the plans on a yearly basis.

7) Use the plans to force yourself to look at the big picture. Most owners get so caught up in the day-to-day basis, that they fail to project decisions they make today out to the future of the business. Plans help you relate day-to-day decisions to a long-range look at your business.

Build a personal escape plan into the financial plan of your business.

8) Build your own future into the plans. Nothing lasts forever, including businesses. Someday, you might want to get out of your business. Build a personal escape plan into the financial plan of your business.

LESSONS FROM LIFE — #2

The weight dropper

EVERY GYM HAS A GUY like this as a member. Big arms, sort of fat, and always wears a tank top because he thinks he's the biggest guy in the gym.

He's also the guy that screams when he does incline dumbbell presses, while using the 50s and then drops them from five feet to the floor. Then he pops out of the chair and struts in front of the mirror looking at his chest. "Yeah, everyone look at me, I'm huge and I'm working the chest today!" The pros never do this, it's always the wannabes who raise the most hell in a club.

The salespeople are afraid to take women on tours when he is working out, and the rest of the staff thinks he is a nuisance but no one wants to deal with him. There is also the potential damage to the dumbbells, and the risk that he may injure someone by dropping those weights and having them bounce off someone else's foot.

The moral of the story

Guys like this represent an issue of control in the gym. He's a member, and he does pay, but he is somewhat out of control and if left unattended, he may damage the club's equipment or, worse, hurt another member. This type of person is a candidate for the Three Strikes and You're Out policy. This is a simple policy to follow, and helps management deal with problem children in a controlled

He's the guy that screams while using the 50s and then drops them from five feet to the floor

and professional manner.

The first time the member drops the dumbbells, gently warn him that this is not appropriate behavior for the gym and is against the rules. You do have to make sure, however, that this really is in your rules and that they are posted prominently somewhere in the club. All new members should also receive a copy of the club's rules when they get their first club information.

After warning the member, immediately go to the office and start a file with the member's name on it, and fill out an incident report. This is just a basic report that lists the member, the violation of policy, who warned him, the names of any witnesses that were around or staff who silently observed as you warned him, and the date the incident occurred.

If he does the same thing again, you warn him again and then write up a second incident report. You should have a witness with you the second time you warn him, since you are going to tell him that if it happens again, he's out of the club and his membership will be cancelled.

If there is a third time, cut him a check for any money that might be owed back to him. If he paid cash for example, take him into the office, and tell him he's out. Be sure and write up the third incident, and it always helps to have your assistant manager in the office as you let the guy go.

3

It's a business, not a baby

WHAT THE CONSUMER DEMANDS from a fitness facility changes from year to year. Yet many owners still hang on to past trends, trying to force their vision of fitness onto a resistant marketplace. Everything changes in time, but most owners are too emotionally tied to their clubs and programs to adapt to the current market conditions. What worked in the past won't necessarily work in the future, nor will it keep you competitive in a volatile consumer's market.

Have you ever been introduced to a friend's new baby, took one look at the kid, and thought to yourself: That just might be the ugliest baby I've ever seen. The kid is ugly, scrawny, has really strange, alien ears, yet the parents are telling you how beautiful the kid is. You can't believe you're both looking at the same kid. One side sees nothing but yuck, the other nothing but their precious newborn.

The fitness business is much the same way. Physical plants wear out, programs such as aerobics run their course, and hot trends such as racquetball, now played by a handful of old guys, have faded to the history stage of our business. In this, and virtually any business, nothing lasts forever.

In the club business, it's easy to get emotionally attached to a program or even to the gym itself. For many owners, it takes several years of planning and dreaming to get that first fitness business open. When it's finally done, a new owner may end up working about 100 hours a week for the first year or so in the business. It's easy to start losing sight of your gym as a business and to start thinking of it as your home.

The same is true for programming. Your first fitness experience may be in something such as aerobics. You start your first classes, get hooked and, over the years, it becomes part of your life. It's what got you started, helped you get into your first real fitness shape, and it's something that now as an

It's easy to start losing sight of your gym as a business and to start thinking of it as your home.

owner, you want to share with others.

The problem is that physical plants fade and need to be replaced. Programs hit a high in the market and then decline as the consumers move on to the next hot trend. Our emotional ties prevent us from realistically evaluating our business and being able to make the right business decisions.

For example, during a visit to a long-term client, I noticed that the physical plant was really starting to show its age. The gym was about five years old, the paint was worn, the equipment chipped and aged, and the design was not up to what was happening in the market.

The aerobics program, for instance, was a central feature in the gym with a beautiful glass room right in the middle of everything. The problem was that the usage in the program had declined over the years as the female members moved toward more weight training and the newer cardio equipment.

When I mentioned to the owners that their gym was looking sort of shabby, everyone became upset.

When I mentioned to the owners that their gym was looking sort of shabby, everyone became upset. "It's not worn-out, we get great comments on this gym all the time." "Everyone who comes in the door loves this gym. They say we're the prettiest gym in the area." These were several of the comments made by the staff and owners. It was as if I were looking at the baby and telling the truth, "Hey, I hate to tell you this, but your kid is really ugly."

They heard what they wanted to hear, and have become emotionally attached to a building and paint. After almost six months of getting a reality check, they finally agreed to a remodel. It wasn't cheap. They spent $250,000 to remodel a 12,000-square-foot license gym.

The owners moved and shrank the aerobics room into a back area, added a beautiful Cardio Theater area, increased the weights and machine footage, replaced some of the older, out-of-date equipment, and gave the place a fresh look with different colors and paint. Sales increased, but more importantly, renewals increased and stabilized for the next two years.

Even if the owners had not re-invested in their business, the club would not have failed. They were good business people and would have kept it going. But the business would not have enjoyed the financial success it eventually achieved, because they would have been trying to sell an out-of-date product to consumers in a competitive market.

Everything in the fitness industry seems to change on a pretty consistent basis. In fact, it changes roughly about every seven years. The following timeline is by no means complete, but it does illustrate some of the major changes in the industry:

The 1950s — There were gyms in the '50s, but they would seem somewhat strange to today's consumer. Much of the weight equipment was homemade, some of the clubs dressed their staff in white lab coats for that medical look, and a lot of the other equipment plugged into the wall, such as the old butt shakers and pony rollers. Working out was a fairly new concept for the average consumer and had not yet made its mainstream appearance.

Early 1960s — This was the spa era complete with pools, machines that you plugged in and moved for you, and everything chromed if possible. This is also the era in which long-term contracts originated, as well as high-pressure sales. The serious fitness lifestyle had started in California, but hadn't yet reached a broad appeal.

Late 1960s — This is where I think the modern fitness era began with the advent of Nautilus equipment. This was equipment that everyone could use on a regular basis in clean little centers in your neighborhood. Well, almost everyone could use it. It really helped if you were a 5-foot-10-inch male, but basically anyone could get a decent workout on the stuff.

The middle 1970s — Big was better and so came the racquet facilities. The era was also shared by the Nautilus Center; small, Nautilus-only facilities sprang up all over the country. Free weights were pretty rare in these days and through the early '80s. They were out there, but they were in specialized gyms that weren't really mainstream yet.

The early 1980s — This was the time of the mainstream fitness facility. The racquet guys were still firmly entrenched, but the neighborhood workout centers were making their play with Nautilus equipment and early aerobics programs.

The late 1980s — Here came the license guys, another major peak in the fitness business. Gyms with real equipment, real cardio with its first electronic pieces, and aerobic programs that were at their absolute peak.

The middle 1990s — This is the age of cardio equipment. Aerobics is on a decline, after a brief save from the step-style classes, free weights are back and beautiful, and group cycling classes are the current trend for that group exercise fix.

What can you learn from this very brief description of the fitness business? We can learn that nothing lasts forever. Even free weights, which everyone thinks has always been a vital part of the fitness business, was suspect in most of the 1970s. Pools were a major part of your business and sales plan in the spa era, yet almost no one would consider putting them into a new mid-size club in today's market.

And racquetball may be the best example of something most of the industry was very committed to in the 1970s, although it was very costly to build and implement. Yet, who in the mid-'90s would build a 16-court racquet facility?

Why don't people in the fitness business change to meet the demands of the market? Most people think that fitness owners, the license folks and the national chains drive change in the fitness industry, but in reality most change in our businesses comes from external forces. An example of owners being the last to know would be the advent of spinning™ classes and their spin-offs, which is a form of group exercise done on high-tech stationary bikes.

Why don't people in the fitness business change to meet the demands of the market?

Two years after the introduction of spin classes, more than 75 percent of seminar participants in the Thomas Plummer & Associates national seminar tour still hadn't taken a class. The members were talking about and requesting spin classes, but many of the owners couldn't respond because they didn't have any practical experience with something the members already were aware of and many had tried.

There are several sources that have major influences on the fitness in-

If we wanted to get basic, rocks would still get you in shape, provided you picked up enough of them often enough.

dustry and our offerings. First is the very low boredom threshold of our members. Many of our members in today's market love to work out and do so regularly, compared to the average participant in the '60s who tended to fade somewhat quicker.

But these new members also come at a high price. They get bored very easily and like to be entertained with newer and ever-changing equipment. Let's face it, the caveman who first picked up a rock and moved it from one side of the cave to the other was doing a type of resistance training. If we wanted to get basic, rocks would still get you in shape, provided you picked up enough of them often enough.

The members who work out on a regular basis, however, want their rocks changed frequently. An example is the stair climber. There was a time in the late '80s and early '90s that you could not get enough stair climbers into your gym. The members would wait in line for them, ignoring the electronic bikes that were the rage the previous years. But the member's love for the stair climbers soon faded, to be replaced by a new love for the treadmill.

As owners, we had rows of perfectly good stair climbers probably still not paid for, that we bought in response to members' demands. But they didn't want stairs anymore. They now wanted, in fact demanded, treadmills. Lines formed, sign-up sheets were hung, and the race was on to add treadmills to the club's cardio repertoire.

Simply put, the members were bored with the stairs and wanted to get on the next hot product. They had tried treadmills elsewhere or had seen pictures and articles in the national fitness magazines that touted the advantages of working out on treadmills, and cited the damage that might be done by doing too many stairs.

The national press does a lot to fuel change in the industry. But the press, being as it is, isn't really interested in writing about something that has been written about before in other publications or aired on other stations. The press is always looking for the next hot item or workout scheme.

When members see features about the treadmill craze, they feel they are missing something in their gyms, and there starts the demand for a new and expensive product you need to keep your fitness business competitive.

One form of change that owners do inadvertently create is change by default. This method of change was one of the prime reasons that aerobics faded from its once prominent role in the fitness industry. Owners simply stopped doing it and the programs faded. As long as owners participated in aerobics classes, they were willing to keep working toward keeping the classes fresh.

But as the owners stopped supporting the classes, support for the programs soon faded. This lack of owner commitment signalled the end for many aerobics programs in the country, because the owners, meaning the decision makers, had already moved on to something else in the gym, primarily cardio equipment and cardio entertainment areas.

Another example of change in the '90s, that caught many owners off guard, was the difficulty in hiring, training and keeping staff. Over a long period of time, from the mid-'80s to the present, staffing has risen to the No. 1

problem owners list in running their businesses. It's hard to find dedicated employees who will work for the wages the industry is used to paying. The fitness industry is also now competing for service employees against literally thousands of other industries who have the same employment needs and who are willing to pay more to attract a better class of worker.

Because owners didn't change to meet this shift in hiring and staffing, many have suffered in the business. The owners who prospered had to learn advanced hiring practices, be willing to pay higher wages and provide stronger benefit packages, and had to learn to motivate and develop a new type of employee.

How can owners deal with change effectively in the fitness business?

First of all, realize that change is an inevitable part of the business. Everything changes in life and the gym business is no exception. Imagine this scene from a mountaintop in Tibet.

The seeker of knowledge: Tell me wise master, what is the secret of life?

The wise man: The secret of life is change. Accept change, for everything in your life will change sooner or later.

The seeker: Does that mean everything wise one? My wife, my children, my business will change?

The wise man: Yes, everything changes. You will some day pass away, as will your family. Your business may go away. Everything changes. Except, of course, if you're in the gym business where most of you guys are five years or more out of date as to what's happening in the industry. There nothing changes, because everyone is so emotionally tied to programs, physical plants and equipment. There my son, if you don't want change, open a gym.

To be a successful owner, you must be open to change. In fact, you must learn to seek change. To be competitive in the fitness business is to respond to the changing needs of the members. Members are bored and fitness-aware in most markets, and they want to be the first to experience the new and different. Keep in mind that working out is somewhat boring to most people. To keep it interesting takes a challenge, and if you as an owner don't provide it, another club owner will.

What needs to change to keep members happy in the future?

The best thing about change is that it often can be managed and planned in advance. For most owners, change is simply trying to look ahead and anticipate the needs of your members and your business.

First of all, consider the physical plant. Physical plants wear out and usually do so at a much faster rate than is planned for by typical owners. A basic rule of thumb: To keep the club competitive, you usually have to spend

The best thing about change is that it often can be managed and planned in advance.

the same amount of money over every four-year period that you spent to build the club in the first place.

For example, if you initially spent $25 per square foot to build your club, and the club is 10,000 square feet, you'd have to spend the same $250,000 over every four year period after you open, to keep the club fresh and competitive. The initial build-out would not include equipment, but the re-investment would. Treadmills are a prime example. The industry went from having practically no treadmills to treadmills being must-have items in just a few years. If you opened your club with none or just a few, you would have had to add some during your first four years of operation.

Many owners also find that their existing physical plant no longer meets the business plan. You may have started out with limited cardio equipment and aerobics programs, and four years later find yourself with no aerobics and two to three times as much cardio. That type of change requires the ability to change the physical plant on a pretty regular basis.

Another type of collateral change that affects the physical plant is the member boredom factor. Fitness facilities are a lot like a good nightclub. They can be really hot for a while, and then everyone moves to the next hot spot down the street. People just get bored with the same look and feel every day.

It's sad, but some clubs never change. You can walk into a club one day and it looks exactly the same as it did several years ago. The same paint, same colors, same artwork and even the same staff uniforms. Owners will change their cars, their homes, their spouses, their hair and even their dogs before they realize they need to repaint the gym, give it a new look, move the equipment or simply add a few pieces of new equipment.

The three most important factors to change and manage in a gym are color, light and sound. These factors give the business depth and energy, and are also the ones that get worn out most quickly by the members.

Colors become dated in as little as two years. That color combination that was hot when you created the gym, often fades and becomes dated and boring in a short period of time.

A good habit to get into is to paint a different wall every month, and give the club an overall change in color scheme every two to three years. A wall that might have been white today and is some accent color tomorrow is noticed by the members and keeps the business fresh.

Light is the factor most often ignored by owners. They put the lights up and then that's the way they remain until the owner dies. By changing the placement and mixture of lights on a regular basis, you can control the energy and warmth in the club. For example, by adding bulb-type light fixtures over a juice bar that previously was only lit by the ceiling lights, you can add a center of warmth in the club that will draw the members to the area. For lighting to be effective in a gym, it has to be a mixture of your main lighting, usually some type of metal halogen fixture and incandescent light, which gives certain areas of the club warmth and atmosphere.

Equipment in the club is also a tough issue. The major problem is that most equipment becomes outdated before it wears out. You may have great cardio equipment, but it might be four years out of date and the kinds that

Owners will change their cars, their homes, their spouses, their hair and even their dogs before they realize they need to repaint the gym, give it a new look, move the equipment or simply add a few pieces of new equipment.

no one really wants to play on anymore. New equipment should be added and old equipment should be replaced on a very regular basis. If possible, a typical club should be adding a new piece of equipment as often as every other month. Major equipment replacement for the cardio area and select workout pieces should be looked at every three years or so.

A rule of thumb here is to budget a certain percentage of your monthly base operating expense each month for capital purchases. The recommended formula is $100 per every 1,000 square feet. For example, if your gym was 15,000 square feet, you would want to budget $1,500 per month for capital purchases. Even if you didn't spend the money that month, you would move it to a special savings account for future purchases.

A final point about change: Don't overlook the small changes. The small things add up over a period of time, and mean a lot to members. A painted wall, changes in the staff uniform shirts every quarter, or the addition of a new piece of plate-loaded equipment gives the members something new and interesting to talk about when they come in for their workouts.

A rule of thumb ... is to budget a certain percentage of your monthly base operating expense each month for capital purchases.

Summary

Everything changes. It's a simple fact of life. In the fitness business, it's vital that we learn to change to meet the changing demands and expectations of the members, and to meet the changing nature of the business itself.

Most change can be planned for and managed. Trends such as the advent of treadmills or the shift toward women moving in large numbers to the free-weight areas are easy to spot. These two trends could have been anticipated by simply responding to the requests of the members, looking around at trade shows and watching the types of articles the national consumer fitness magazines are running.

A final note: Don't be afraid of change. Change for the most part is good in our business. And some of our old business practices, such as high-pressure sales in offices, need to be changed and done away with anyway. One final point to keep in mind is that it's not what *you* want that will make you money, it's giving the members what *they* want. Without an openness to change, we usually make decisions based on internal factors and old habits.

Things you can do to use this material

1) Plan and budget for change. The money needed for change, such as ongoing improvements on the physical plant and capital purchases, should be budgeted for each month as part of your normal monthly operating expense.

2) Don't get emotionally involved with your business. It's a business, not a baby, and it will wear out and need fixing.

3) Don't get emotionally involved with your programs. Aerobics is a prime example of programming that ran its course, but was hard for most

owners to change because of the emotional attachment.

4) Survey your members often. What do they want? What doesn't the club have enough of? What have they tried at other clubs that they might want to see added to yours? What hot new products have they tried? Remember that it's not what you want that will make you money, it's what the members want.

5) Be willing to say you were wrong. We were wrong on childcare in the gyms for example. We always thought it would be a natural moneymaker with the types of members we had. It's not. It cost us a great deal of money to prove that we couldn't make money with it. The best solution was to cut the loss and concentrate on the things that do make money.

6) If it's not making money, drop it. Years ago, when the cost of starting a new club, as well as the cost of operation, was significantly lower, we could run programs such as childcare; we felt we had to offer it because the competition did. No longer. It costs far too much to start and operate the typical club these days. Our rule now is: If it doesn't net at least 20 percent on a monthly basis, and you can't fix it after a 90-day period, dump it and get on to the things that do make you money.

7) Get outside opinions. Remember the baby. Your club may be run down and hurting but you still see it in your mind as fresh as the day you opened. Get professional outside opinions on colors, light and sound at least once a year.

8) Remember that it's easier to get to be No. 1 than it is to stay No. 1. Ask any national league football team. Winning the Super Bowl one year doesn't guarantee the same will happen next year. Just because something worked in the past, such as pressure sales or going for cash memberships, doesn't mean it will work now. Technique and business strategies are also parts of the business that need to change and be reviewed on a regular basis.

If it doesn't net at least 20 percent on a monthly basis, and you can't fix it after a 90-day period, dump it and get on to the things that do make you money.

Old fat guys in running shorts

HE'S 40 YEARS OLD, worked in an office for 20 years, and is really out of shape, including the huge belly. After 15 years of marriage, the wife left him and he slowly became even worse as he ate and drank too much on his own.

Finally he met a woman and he has a date on Friday night. He's in the club on Monday and he's nervous because he's faced with the possibility of being naked with a stranger for the first time in 15 years — only five days from now. This guy is motivated to get in shape now, not tomorrow, and by Friday at the latest.

Our newly motivated member shows up for his first workout dressed in his black knee socks, headband, white T-shirt and those cheap discount store running shorts that have the high cuts up the side. He walks out of the locker room, takes one look around and says, "I'm the only geek in this place," and then never returns again.

The moral of the story

We should have never let this happen in the first place. As

He walks out of the locker room, takes one look around and says, "I'm the only geek in this place," and never returns

fitness professionals, most of us have forgotten what it's like to be a rookie again, and how embarrassed you can get doing something as simple as trying to workout.

Good member service means not embarrassing our members. When the member first signed with the club, someone should have gone through the club's starter kit, which has a separate section in this book, and made suggestions as to what to wear and where to buy it. Someone else should have suggested that maybe his outfit wasn't appropriate for the club and offered to get him a pair of baggy shorts and some white socks from the pro shop.

In this example the club probably lost a good member, because it assumed that everyone in the club understands all of those little rituals and quirks that are part of working out.

4

What kind of business are you running anyway?

ONE OF THE HARDEST challenges you'll face in the coming years is learning to focus or "niche" your business in relation to your community, your personal expectations of the business and your competition. In this era of maximum competition, learning to narrow and focus the scope of your business will give you a key competitive edge in the marketplace.

The current trend in the fitness business is a long, negative skid toward many of the bad habits of our past. Low, loss-leader pricing, large impersonal physical plants, no support systems, non-existent member service and a too-young, undertrained staff are all part of the large-chain approach to fitness in the latter part of the '90s. These old-style operating methods were also parts of our past — aspects of the business that have worked against clubs over the years because they were so negative in the consumer's mind.

This negative spiral or broad, unfocused business plan, based upon the "be everything to everybody concept" will have serious adverse effects on the entire industry for years to come. The average consumer has grown too sophisticated for these concepts, and is expecting more from today's fitness facility. Does any potential member really expect great service from a high-pressure sales factory? Do consumers really expect great help from a 19-year-old front counter kid who is in her first job? Probably not, yet many of today's businesses are still trying to sell these dated concepts.

This trend toward habits of our past highlights a major problem in the gym business, which is that we don't really understand what clients are buying when they make an investment in our business. Most owners think members buy the possibility of fitness — a place to workout. Or, they think members' final decisions are based on your facility having the ultimate line of equipment that can attack the outer part of your quads three inches above

Does any potential member really expect great service from a high-pressure sales factory?

31

your knee from 82 known, and three previously unknown, positions.

Yes, there was one bodybuilder in 1982 that was overly concerned about those three inches and who made his buying decision based on those choices. But if you base your business plan on this nonsense or once-in-a-million situation, you'll make the same mistake that many other club owners make in their business plans. You'll fill your facility with endless equipment stacked row after row, line up as much cardio equipment as you can get, make all the support services and amenities (such as locker rooms and service staff) minimal, and pressure people into buying because you have more stuff than the other guy.

Successful owners understand what they are really selling: the fitness experience.

Successful owners understand what they are really selling: the fitness experience. There have been major exceptions to this rule where sheer demand by the consumer has won out over the fitness experience, such as in high-density areas like Southern California and Manhattan. But even this is changing as competition fills these areas as well.

The fitness experience means that the consumer wants and demands more from the gym of their choice. They want equipment, but they also want a great deal of help learning to use it. They want to work out in a well-lit, exceptionally clean facility, surrounded by a slightly-older-than-expected communicative staff. If they need help with their diets, they expect it to be available. If they need training help and advice, they expect to get it. They may pay extra for some of these things, but they still expect the club to have them available.

It's not enough in a highly competitive industry to just have the best equipment, the most stuff or the biggest facility. Equipment is only part of the experience. And these large, impersonal and unfocused facilities work against the gyms, because a typical member doesn't associate biggest with best and most intimate service.

The key to the member's perception of the fitness experience is the atmosphere in which these elements are delivered. Think of a good restaurant. Great restaurants are not huge. They are not usually overcrowded, unless they have a planned 15- to 30-minute delay that keeps the customers in the bar working on drinks while they wait for a table.

The lighting in a good restaurant is warm and inviting, the guest can linger over wine or cocktails after the meal, and the service is supportive of an excellent dining experience. Even if the food is just average, an excellent dining experience can make it seem better than it is. The guest is buying a dining experience, not just food, which they could have bought at a drive-through window on the way home.

Both the restaurant and the fitness business are service businesses. If they are good, both try to sell an experience that surrounds the product they are delivering. If they are bad, they sell the product itself, much like an all-you-can-eat buffet that has no atmosphere or service, simply cheap food that, if eaten, may keep you alive.

This is why positioning, as it's called in the business books, is so important to owners who are trying to conceptualize their businesses to stay competitive into the future. Positioning has many definitions. It means how the business relates to other businesses in the area or to the rest of the industry. It also means how you define the business and the product it offers.

But for our use, we define positioning as the ability to focus the business from a "one-size-fits-all" concept to a narrowly defined, very specific business plan that specializes in one single aspect of the fitness business.

The one-size-fits-all model makes it very difficult to provide a salable fitness experience to the consumer, because the experience becomes so impersonal. There is no act, atmosphere or service to support the fitness experience the consumer was seeking, and no evidence that the business has any understanding of their specific needs.

Most club owners, however, believe they are already focused and that service is their niche. In fact, every human being that has ever owned a fitness business has claimed to have the best service in town. It's kind of like talking to 30 different parents at a school function. Every parent brags about their kid being above average and really special in school. Someone is lying. Who owns the average and below-average kids we read about in the papers? Which one of these parents owns the school idiot who blows up toilets, spits on the school nerd and is always in trouble?

Service as a whole in this industry sucks. It's so bad that "suck" is the only word to describe it. For example, you can't buy a cold non-workout drink in more than 50 percent of the gyms in this country. Only a small handfull of gyms in this country will actually let you try the facility for more than one workout before you have to make a buying decision. Very few offer amenities in the locker rooms. Most have no training advice available unless you pay. Guest policies are still left over from the '60s where the guest has to fill out 82 pages of worthless information and go on a two-hour tour before they can actually join their friend.

The sad thing is that most clubs believe they have covered the service niche, because they have a trainer or two on the floor and because they have more equipment than their competitor. Most of the clubs that fall into this trap of believing they have excellent service really don't, because they are comparing their service against other clubs in the industry.

In other words, they are comparing themselves against an already low standard. It's like being a kid and calling your friend names. "Hey, you're stupid," you yell, and she answers, "Well, I may be stupid but at least I'm not ugly." Who really won here, and is stupid really better than ugly?

Service in the fitness industry is sort of the same. As a whole, it is so bad that you can offer above-average service according to the industry standard and still stink. You are better than the other guy, but still not really much better off. You're stupid, but he is still ugly.

The standards we operate against haven't really changed in 20 years. For example, 20 years ago the salesperson would take the prospect into an office and high-pressure the person into a sale. Twenty years later, most of the large chains are still using sales offices, something the average consumer feels very negative about when they visit a gym.

Twenty years ago, the main way to advertise was to run price specials (sales) and then work to close the prospect during the first visit. This is still

The one-size-fits-all model makes it very difficult to provide a salable fitness experience to the consumer, because the experience becomes so impersonal.

the same operational procedure in most clubs today.

Twenty years ago, you had to bring your own lock, shower in questionable locker rooms and bring your own towel. Except in a limited number of clubs, you still have to bring your own lock, shower in death-defying conditions and bring your own towel.

One final comparison to note is that 20 years ago, a trainer would set you up on a program and then turn you loose after one to three workouts, whether you understood it or not. Twenty years later, most clubs still will set you up on a simple workout and then force you out on your own whether you are ready or not.

Nothing has changed much. The industry's perception of service is still about the same. A lot of the things we do out of habit today are based on things done at facilities that were mostly unfocused in their positioning, and that operated under the concept that their facilities met the service needs of every single type of consumer.

The problem with assuming you already have a service focus, based on your perception of service, is that you often aren't really giving consumers what they want.

The problem with assuming you already have a service focus, based on your perception of service, is that you often aren't really giving consumers what they want. Many business plans are based on assumptions that are no longer true or relevant in the gym business, meaning that the focus of the business is either too broad or too out of date.

For example, it's been extremely hard to make money with childcare, aerobics and racquet sports for most of the '90s. Childcare is based on too small of a population in the gym, yet by maintaining too broad of a focus with our business plans, we feel we have to have childcare to compete. Aerobics has faded away in many clubs as discussed in other chapters, yet owners are still developing new projects that include $75,000 aerobics rooms, something the majority of members would rather see replaced with extended cardio presentations.

Sure, some members still want childcare and aerobics. But do enough of these people really want it, and will enough pay for it to make it profitable for the club? Is the club offering these programs because they might make money, or because the owner's perception of service and quality includes these concepts, which might no longer be important to the majority of members?

Quality is also a focus that many clubs believe they already own. Advertising that you're the best club in the area is irrelevant to the average consumer. Everyone says they have the best gym. Have you ever heard an owner say, "Well, my gym really sucks compared to everyone else's, but we still manage to hang in there."

The problem for the owner who believes their club is already focused in the quality niche is that probably nine times out of 10, the average consumer can't tell the difference between a good gym and weak gym. This changes, of course, if the individual is involved in the club for some relevant period of time.

Another problem with the quality focus is that while most clubs seek quality, they tend to ignore the member's perception of real quality. In general, the club owner applies their own definition of quality to the club, regardless of what the member really wants.

For example, at one club, the owner set up a program where every new member had to go through a fitness analysis before they were allowed to work out. The analysis included a strength test and a body fat and basic diet analysis. The owner thought this was a wonderful competitive edge against the competitors who were not doing any initial work-ups.

The members, however, in response to a verbal survey, had no real interest in the analysis as a group. The majority preferred more intense and patient help with their initial programs, instead of being turned loose too soon. Many of the members were over 35, had limited gym experience and felt they needed more help understanding their programs, instead of getting analysis in areas they didn't feel were really relevant for novices.

The owner was providing a costly and labor-intensive service because he felt that it gave the club a quality edge in the marketplace. The members, however, felt that the club wasn't really meeting their needs as a group. While the owner's attempt to apply quality as the club's focus was a good idea, the applied definition was wrong.

The perception of quality is what people buy and, although your facility may be truly better than your competitors', a potential member may not perceive it as such. The sad truth is that most potential members feel that all gyms and fitness facilities are somewhat the same. And when you look at a typical grouping of clubs from almost any marketplace, they are basically the same.

Take the staff for example. Most gyms have the same configurations. The front counter people are typically young women who are constantly being replaced by other very young women, as the current position holder leaves for another job. Many of these women are too young and too inexperienced to have acquired the communication skills necessary to effectively deliver member service to a large range of members at the front counter.

The trainers and other support staff are also mostly very young folks who are willing to work for pretty low wages. The problem with a staff of mostly very young employees is that, due to the somewhat unstructured nature of the fitness business, it takes some maturity and intensive training to learn to give great member service.

We are not serving endless hamburgers. In the fitness business, an employee may be responsible for a variety of tasks throughout the day that aren't necessarily covered by a simple member service strategy.

The only real adult people working in most clubs are the sales people and managers, folks who seldom come into contact with as many members as the junior staff. These folks may know and be able to deliver member service, but it's the lower-level staff who are responsible for the daily image of the club.

The potential members who visit more than one club see this. All the staffs seem somewhat the same, all the equipment looks alike, and most of the club's programs and offerings are simply duplicates of a competitor's. The owners may say, "Hey, wait a minute, our spin program is twice as good as the guy's across the street. How can you compare us to them?" They can, be-

The perception of quality is what people buy and, although your facility may be truly better than your competitors', a potential member may not perceive it as such.

cause both programs look just alike to the consumer. The bikes are about the same, the room is about the same, and even the color of the schedule is like the competitors. In other words, there is no difference in the perception of quality between the two programs.

Quality and the perception of quality

Can you truly stand out in a competitive marketplace with better quality, or can you increase your quality and the perception of quality and really be different?

When you focus the business, you improve perception of quality. When you let the business become unfocused, the perception of quality in the member's mind goes down. Everything you do should increase the perception of quality and narrow the focus of the business.

For example, consider the two following scenarios and try to evaluate the focus and perception of quality from the member's viewpoint:

In the first example, we have a 40,000-square-foot facility that offers everything. The club has weight equipment, aerobics, spin programs, cardio equipment, children's programming, senior programming, basketball on a half court, weight loss, personal trainers and a small pro-shop and juice counter. Let's look at some typical questions a potential member might ask about the club, and the problems these questions could raise for the owner.

WHO IS THIS CLUB FOR?

It's a multipurpose club that's for everyone. Without a specific focus, such as a family recreation center for example, this club would have a hard time even putting together a marketing piece. Who would the piece target? How could you put together a piece that goes after absolutely everyone in the community?

WHAT KIND OF PERSONAL ATTENTION CAN A CLUB OF THIS SIZE OFFER ME?

The club may claim a lot of personal attention but, in reality, how much real attention can a club of this size give the individual member in most markets. The exception might be rural markets where the cost of doing business is cheaper. But in most markets, this club would need to do a lot of sales, probably between 75 to 150 per month depending on the market, to stay in business. That situation usually doesn't lend itself to the deliverance of great member service. The club could indeed give decent service if the circumstances were right, but the feel of such a large facility works against the owner. It just doesn't feel that such a large business could give great personal service.

Without a specific focus, such as a family recreation center for example, this club would have a hard time even putting together a marketing piece.

36

HOW WOULD THE MEMBER MIX WORK?

A club with such a broad focus would have trouble mixing such a wide range of members. Do small children and serious lifters work together? Do high-energy folks in their late 20s work well with a daytime senior population? Most clubs that operate unfocused try to segregate the different populations by either time or into separate areas in the club, neither of which works well.

For example, a serious cardio person that stops by the facility during their lunch hour will be frustrated when faced with a herd of little old ladies on the treadmills walking at one mile an hour and watching soaps. The mix is bad because the focus is bad.

Keep in mind that it's not the club's size that doesn't work, it's the lack of focus and the member's perception of quality. Clubs this size that are narrowly focused can and do work, but the owners face problems that smaller, more intimate facilities don't. Common sense tells you, however, that the bigger club should make more money because it's bigger and can hold more members. Be everything to everyone seems logical, but a club like this could probably make more money by going after a narrower niche, such as becoming a family recreation center or corporate club.

From the member's perspective, how can a club so big give any kind of personal service? If you want service, don't you usually go to the small, personalized specialty stores? And how can a club this size really specialize and service so many different groups of people? The club may have a little bit of everything, but nothing is complete. A good example of this is the new breed of recreation centers going up around the country. They're big, well-capitalized and are built to serve the entire community.

But these types of facilities seldom work financially, or meet the member's expectations of quality. For example, two facilities were built a short distance apart near the ski areas in central Colorado. They were built as community recreation centers, and both enjoy a great tax base for support. The clubs have some of everything, but nothing is really done right.

For example, each facility has weight equipment, but since the facilities are trying to offer so many different programs to so many different people, neither is really a complete weight room. Both facilities have rooms that are small, cramped, dangerous to the user and have low-end equipment furnished by the lowest bidder. There is enough equipment for basic workouts, but not enough for quality workouts. The average person or novice could enjoy the rooms, but anyone with any higher expectations wouldn't be happy.

Both facilities also have running tracks that are used by a small percentage of the members. But both facilities have lousy cardio presentations — the equipment most desired and expected by members all around the country — probably in part due to the commitment to the track. They have cardio, but just a representation and not enough to satisfy the needs of most of the facilities' clients.

If your business has too broad a focus, you end up like these recreation

Be everything to everyone seems logical, but a club like this could probably make more money by going after a narrower niche, such as becoming a family recreation center or corporate club.

... saying, "we'll put a little of everything in this place and try to make as many people as possible happy" ... just doesn't work, because the offerings never really satisfy any specific group.

facilities. You have a representation of everything, but nothing is complete or focused toward any specific group. This leaves the users of those areas frustrated, because those areas or that equipment really doesn't satisfy the need.

If you have to wait for a treadmill because there are only three or four, it's very frustrating if that's the reason you joined in the first place. It's like saying, "we'll put a little of everything in this place and try to make as many people as possible happy." It just doesn't work, because the offerings never really satisfy any specific group.

How can an owner focus a business? He or she needs to start by understanding the word "category." Category to us means that you are picking one specific niche to make your own from the broader category of fitness facility. Your goal is to choose, develop and then own the specific niche in that category for your market.

Keep in mind that the goal is to focus the category down to one very specific point. For example, a large category may be full retail, such as a Wal-Mart store that carries one of just about everything on the planet. It would be hard to open a Wal-Mart style store across the street because they own that category.

A business person, could, however, open a specialty bookstore right next door and still do well. Wal-Mart sells books, but the offerings are usually somewhat limited. If you wanted a popular book, you may go to Wal-Mart. But if you wanted a specific business book, sports book or book that was printed a few years ago, you need to seek a specialist.

Also keep in mind that in the fitness business, you can't be everything to everyone. In fact, trying to appeal to every single person in the market is impossible. Take price for example. There is no one price that appeals to every consumer. If the price is too high, it may limit folks looking just for cheap rates. If the price is too low, the perception of quality won't be there, and folks looking for a full-service, top-end club won't respond.

Another example is the karate school business. It makes sense to have a karate school open to all students of all ages. But this is not the way to maximize the business in most markets.

Several martial arts organizations have, for example, experimented with children's-only facilities and have experienced great success. By being open to just children, you are sending the message that you specialize in children, that your children will be safe here since they don't have to interact with adults, and that the entire staff and facility is geared toward the needs of kids.

Most fitness businesses that wish to get focused need to follow this example and learn to subtract. Many facilities simply offer too many different types of programs that try to appeal to too many different types of people.

Keep in mind that common sense tells you to offer as many things as possible so your business will appeal to as many different types of people as possible. But common sense doesn't always work in the real business world. In the karate school example, for instance, the business that specialized in kids prospered because parents who would not have considered the regular schools would take a chance on a kids-only school. The generalist didn't appeal, whereas the specialist did.

Looking again at the recreation facilities in Colorado, a fitness facility that specializes in adults between 24 and 45 years old could successfully compete against the unfocused recreation centers. This type of adult center could specialize in adult training needs, nutritional guidance, music that is more specific for this age group, and could plan and decorate the facility for an adult population. Locker rooms, for example, could be several levels better than those offered by a recreation center that services large groups of kids.

Niches, or areas of focus, that are possible in the fitness business include, but are not necessarily limited to, the following:

- quality niche or elite club
- price niche
- women's-only niche
- high-energy rock-and-roll niche, such as a licensed gym
- very serious or hardcore niche
- corporate niche
- neighborhood or community niche, appropriate in more rural areas
- family center niche

These are all niches that work in a variety of areas around the country. Factors such as population density, competition, personal desires and expectations of the business, and capital will all affect the choice the owner will make in selecting a specific niche. Also, notice the narrow scope of each niche. If you own a high-energy rock-and-roll license gym that appeals to folks in their mid-20s to about 40 years old, you probably won't do well in the family niche since the two don't mix well.

A final point to note is that when you are selling a service, as we do in the fitness industry, we are ultimately selling a relationship. By focusing your business, you will be able to build stronger and more long-term relationships with the customers who eventually choose your business.

This will happen, because your gym will be filled with folks who chose your business because it matched them and their perceptions of the fitness business, as opposed to your building a business around whoever happens to join. We, in fact, are learning to seek a very specific member group, instead of trying to match our business concept to whomever shows up at the door.

This selection process allows you as an owner to be more proactive in the running and decision-making process of your business. By planning a business that targets a specific clientele, we can better serve our customers, better prepare for their needs, and build better relationships, because we specialize in their individual needs.

By focusing your business, you will be able to build stronger and more long-term relationships with the customers who eventually choose your business.

Summary

The trend in the industry is toward unfocused, impersonal facilities that attempt to appeal to an exceptionally wide range of clients. This type of facility and owner doesn't really seem to understand what the consumer is buying. Members don't buy endless rows of equipment and workouts. They do and will buy the fitness experience.

Your gym may really be better than everyone else's in town, but the member may not perceive the difference in quality.

Part of the fitness experience is developing a perception of quality in the business. Your gym may really be better than everyone else's in town, but the member may not perceive the difference in quality. All of your marketing and business planning should be centered on developing this perception in the member's mind.

Many clubs can't develop or improve this perception of quality because of the fuzziness of their focus. Trying to be everything to everybody does not increase your potential business, but rather limits it because there is no specific appeal for any one group.

To be successful in the coming years, you need to learn to focus by limiting or narrowing your concept. A family center or women's-only center are excellent examples of businesses that have a narrow and specific focus under the general category of a fitness facility.

Things you can do to use this material

1) Pick a niche or focus, and specialize your entire operation in that area.

2) Look at your existing business, and decide what areas or programming you could eliminate to more narrowly define your focus. Start with the areas that are the least profitable or that appeal to the smallest percentage of your members. For example, if you have 1,500 members and only 4 percent use your childcare facilities, you might consider losing this program and replacing it with something that has more appeal for the other 96 percent of your members. A good reference number is the 10-percent participation rate. If fewer than 10 percent of your members are supporting a specific program or profit center, you should consider replacing it with something that might have a wider appeal or that is more current.

3) Be different. Remember that it's hard for the individual member to really understand that your club is better than a competitor's. Instead of having the same programs that everyone else has and then trying to simply make them better, why not try to offer something different.

For example, a potential member may check into a large, multipurpose facility, but then decide to choose yours. Why? Because he's an executive who wants to work out with other adults, and yours is a club that caters to adults in the 25- to 45-year-old range with matching facilities and services. The multipurpose facility may have the same equipment, but not the same perception of specialization and fulfillment of the client's specific needs.

The world's strongest man

THIS IS A TRUE STORY from Vinny Consalvo, a club owner in the New York area. A young male came into the club and said he was training for the World's Strongest Man contest. Part of the contest was that he had to walk 20 yards with 800 pounds on his shoulders.

The guy figured he could train in Vinny's gym by putting 800 pounds on a bar and walking out of the squat rack 10 yards and then turn around and come back to the rack.

On his first attempt, he fell backwards getting out of the rack and ripped the rack out of the bolts that had it secured to the floor. "I got it, I got it now," he said.

On the second attempt, he made it out the ten yards and started to turn. His two spotters were slowly following him around in case he had trouble. As he started to turn, momentum took over and he started a spin he couldn't stop. The spotters panicked and ran. As the guy spun around he was yelling, "Help me, help me."

Vinny ran onto the floor, got the guy stabilized, and helped him back into the rack. After he racked the guy said, "Next time maybe I shouldn't turn so fast."

As the guy spun around he was yelling, "Help me, help me."

The moral of the story

Sometimes it's not worth taking their money.

Vinny went into his office, cut the guy a check for the balance of his cash membership, and then threw him out. Sometimes it's not worth the money they want to pay for the grief you have to endure to have them as members.

Gyms are a happy balance of people getting along and co-existing, while they pursue a common goal. In our short-term greed, we sometimes take people into the club who can upset this harmony because they are willing to pay the price we demand. In the long run, we're better off protecting the mix than we are taking the money.

5

There is no business plan in the world that can overcome poor renewals

RENEWALS, OR KEEPING the business you've already purchased, is one of the two most important issues, along with staffing, that owners will face in the coming years. As more clubs open, and more members continue to work out year after year, it becomes more important to learn how to keep the members you've already obtained, thereby reducing operating costs in the form of lower advertising cost, lower sales expense and less wear and tear on the club.

For years, the large majority of the fitness business has been geared toward creating business plans strictly focusing on bringing in new members. For example, it's not unusual to see a rookie owner with a 150-page business plan containing 50 pages of marketing and sales training, and only a paragraph or two on keeping those members once they are signed up.

It's even more sad to have a future owner point to a specific month in the future in this same plan and show the break-even point, based on having a certain number of members (especially since the owner never shows any members dropping out or going away). Sign up 1,500, keep 1,500 and at this point the club will break even. It's hard to look at their faces when you show them that a typical club loses about 80 percent of its members on a year-to-year basis.

Besides business plans, almost all of the industry's literature about how to do business, most of our staff training and most of the owner's thinking is devoted to sales, marketing, and doing whatever it takes to keep up the constant flow of new members.

For years, the large majority of the fitness business has been geared toward creating business plans strictly focusing on bringing in new members.

As owners, we've never really maximized the potential of our businesses because we've never really maximized the vast, untapped income available through renewals. And this significant source of potential revenue will become more important in the future for two important reasons: increased competition and the increasing cost of capitalization.

In theory, we all know that renewals gain importance as competition increases. Everyone sits around the bars at the trade shows talking about how little worried they are that this month's going-public, mega-chain, discount fitness show is coming to their town. Why don't these owners act worried? Because they know all the right things to say to cover their fear. "Our members love us because we have the best member service anywhere. These new guys may be successful in California but their stuff won't work here. No one is going to leave my club." When all else fails, denial works.

These owners say the right things, but then they turn around and do the opposite. This means that as competition increases, they spend more money on new sales forcing them to decrease the money they spend on keeping the members they already own. Why? Because they secretly know their members don't really love them. Because they secretly know they haven't spent money to renew their physical plants in years. And because they never really thought competition would come to their town, so they never really had to learn to be good operators.

The owners in this example really have only one option and that's to start buying new sales, because it's too late now to change the other factors in a short period of time.

The owners in this example really have only one option and that's to start buying new sales, because it's too late now to change the other factors in a short period of time. Renewals have to be part of your one-year, three-year and five-year business plans because when a competitor opens next month, it's too late to make the changes necessary to protect your membership.

The second reason renewals are gaining importance beyond talking a good game is the increased cost of capitalization. Increased capitalization, or the money it takes to start up and maintain a good gym in the '90s and beyond, and the increased cost of running a fitness business on a month-to-month basis, forces up the cost of buying new sales. Simply put, as gyms cost more to build, which adds to the ever increasing cost of running a business on a monthly basis, capitalization forces the clubs to spend more to buy new sales.

For example, a club might spend the following to buy a new sale:

•Cost per marketing lead (means what it costs in marketing dollars to bring someone through the door/the club spends $3,000 per month for marketing and averages 60 new sales): $50

•Cost of commission (what the club pays a salesperson to write the sale; keep in mind the more complicated the system the higher cost per sale): $40

•Hard costs to start the member including paperwork and staff needs (there is a hard cost to start every new member that includes labor for the first few workouts, paperwork and administrative costs, and any other auxiliary costs such as first-visit incentives): $35

In this example, the club would spend about $125 to buy a new sale. The formula gets more complicated when the cost of doing business for the gym increases. A higher cost of doing business, coupled with a low renewal rate for the club, means a greater demand for new sales to feed the business.

This dependency on new sales, called front-loading, or running the business by the front door, has a history in the industry that's at least 30 years old. High-pressure sales, tied to extremely low priced renewals, such as $89 a year, created a system where no one really cared if expired members came back or not. In a business sense, it was actually better for the club if the expired members didn't come back, because the return-per-member from the discounted renewals was so low. At $89 per year, if the person takes a shower each time they're in the club you would lose money. And it's a total loss if they use any toilet paper. They should bring their own for $89 a year.

What's actually good for a renewal rate? Keep in mind a renewal rate means how many members stay with the club year after year. For example, if a club signed up 100 members in January of 1997, lost 10 percent, or 10 members because of the loss rate, meaning they didn't pay to term for whatever reason, then the club has a chance of resigning some portion of the remaining 90 members.

There are a lot of owners out there who would consider selling their spouses, and throw in the children for free, if they could hit and maintain a renewal rate of 40 percent, especially since the national average according to our data hovers around 20 percent.

In the example above where the club has 90 members to possibly renew at the end of one year, a 20-percent renewal rate would give the club 18 members going into the second year. Thirty-six members renewing, or 40 percent, would be well above the industry average. In harsh terms, this means that if the club has 1,000 members today, 12 months from now it'll have 400 left.

The question, then, is not whether the club is doing well with 36 renewals. The real question is what happened to the other 60 percent that didn't renew? What are we doing wrong in the industry that drives more than 60 percent of our existing members away on a yearly basis, and why are we so ready to continue to pay such a high cost to buy new sales? All most clubs really do is replace the members they lose each month, instead of being able to take the business to the next level.

Most owners start at a disadvantage in the first place. They assume, as have many of their predecessors, that the member will not renew anyway no matter what they do as owners. But is this really a self-fulfilling prophecy?

For example, it's common for an owner to sell 24-month contracts to the members, rather than the more efficient 12-month contract, so he or she won't have to make a second buying decision at the end of the first year. But 24-month contracts are harder to sell and require more pressure at point-of-sale. This requires a better salesperson, who requires more money, which decreases the money in the gym available for customer service and re-investment in equipment, which ultimately leads to the member not renewing because he or she didn't get the help and service they wanted.

The assumption, and the supporting management style, was that the

They assume, as have many of their predecessors, that the member will not renew anyway no matter what they do as owners. But is this really a self-fulfilling prophecy?

member would never renew if given a chance. In this example, the owner was correct because the member really never had a chance to renew. All the resources of the gym were dedicated to generating new members leaving very little to service the members who have already bought.

There was one chain of clubs in the southern part of the country that refused to believe that the member would ever stay in the club past their initial membership. And the club did everything possible to make this come true. The sales team was most of the staff, received most of the training, and by far took the largest percentage of the payroll, which was high anyway because of the emphasis on driving new sales.

Marketing expenses in this six-club chain were high, because the clubs were so dependent on new sales that they had to spend a great deal of money every month to buy new leads. The staff also turned over often, because of the pressure of generating these new sales.

The front counter and other support people in these clubs were the youngest and cheapest employees the club could hire, because all the money went to the salespeople. This meant that service in the club was very poor because the staff was undertrained and inexperienced in the positions they held. The only trainers in the club were outside trainers who were not interested in servicing people except for money.

The physical plants were also very run-down, including your basic white walls, no juice counters and out-of-date or insufficient equipment. And the locker rooms would make your mother cry.

Would this type of club have very good renewals? Of course not. It's pretty easy to see that the club and salespeople were only interested in the member before the sale. There was absolutely no interest in the member after the sale.

These clubs were eventually sold because this type of high-pressure front-loading system will only work for so long, especially outside of very heavily populated markets.

These clubs were eventually sold because this type of high-pressure front-loading system will only work for so long, especially outside of very heavily populated markets. After a while, you burn up the market because you can only feed so many members through this system before running out of potential people. Remember, more than 80 percent of our members come from within a 15-minute driving time from the club. Unless you change your marketing and attract a different type of member that is even more service-driven, such as the deconditioned folks, you'll run out of sufficient new sales.

Without a strong renewal base, most clubs go this same route. The club may be hot for a year or two, but eventually you run out of potential members because you burn up your marketplace. The renewals would eventually compound over the years, adding up to a steady and continually increasing source of revenue for the club that would eventually start to decrease the dependency on new sales.

The next logical step is to learn why people who have paid us for 12 months decide they no longer wish to be part of the club. When people join a club, they initiate a trust relationship. If they don't renew, that trust relationship was somehow broken along the way.

Most people who join a club make a commitment to that club. They say, "Okay, I'm here, now let's get this relationship started." As gym people, however, we usually say, "Yes, I know you're a new member, but could you please get the hell out of the way because I'm busy trying to sign up new people to replace you, because I'm planning on giving you such bad service."

Six basic renewal mistakes

There are six core mistakes most owners make when it comes to re-newals. These are the basic mistakes that experienced owners can move be-yond with time and a good business plan. If your renewals are mediocre, or you're new in the business, start here and build.

1) THE FAILURE TO UNDERSTAND THE IMPORTANCE OF THE MEMBER'S FIRST 30 DAYS AS A NEW MEMBER

When do members make the decision to renew? Most clubs weight the decision toward the end of the member's time. For example, a club may send out a 60-day notice of renewal, a 30-day notice and then call the member during the last two weeks.

This is OK for a small percentage of members, but it's way too late for most — about 11 months too late for most. Many members make a decision to renew during their first 30 days, not their last. It's a lot like golf. If you are well-grounded in the basics early in your career, the game is more enjoyable and you might stick with it longer.

It's the same in a gym. If you get started right, are accepted into the club by the staff and other members, and start your fitness program with a good grounding in the basics, you will most likely stay longer and pay longer than a member who did not have a good start to their membership.

Another analogy might be a meal in a restaurant. The meal is mediocre, the service fair, the atmosphere nothing special but the waiter comes up and asks if everything is all right. You say yes, but in your mind you know that you'll never come back again. You just want to finish your meal and be gone.

It's somewhat the same in the gym. The service is at best average, the at-mosphere is nothing outstanding, and the equipment is adequate but maybe a little out-of-date. But when anyone asks if you're happy, a special feat in it-self, you say yes knowing that you made the wrong choice but you'll live with it for the year and be gone.

Many clubs actually create barriers to their member's happiness during the first 30 days. Limited number of start-up workouts, not enough support material as to the systems and happenings in the gym, limited opportunities to meet other members, and an uncaring and service-limited staff are all problems a member would have to overcome to remain a happy member for any length of time in that gym.

For example, let's take a new member who's deconditioned, in her late 30s, and hasn't been in a gym environment for a number of years. The club has a policy that it will work a member out three times and then they're on their own. Three times is probably not enough for this person. She comes in

Many clubs actually create barriers to their member's happiness during the first 30 days.

after she is turned loose, tries to figure it out on her own, gets frustrated and leaves. The club writes her off as someone who wasn't really serious about fitness and would have quit anyway. The member writes the club off because of its lack of service. What's the chance she'll renew at the end of her year?

A second example would be a new member who survives the training process and starts to attend the gym on a regular basis. Toward the end of his first 30 days he tries to write a check for $18 for a ball cap from the pro shop as a gift for his brother. The new person at the front counter, who is just following the gym policy, IDs the member to write a check.

She doesn't know his name, IDs someone who has a $40 a month contract with the facility and creates a situation of non-trust with a new member. The policy itself is nonsense. We already have enough information to go after the person if they write a bad check from the info on the contract. The policy should be for non-members only.

And because this club doesn't understand the importance of member service in relationship to long-term renewals, it doesn't understand the value of having a competent person at the front counter. This is usually the lowest paying and most undertrained job in the system, yet this person has direct access to every member of the club.

This person, especially during prime time, should be one of the strongest employees on the staff, not one of the weakest. By not learning a member's name and by not knowing when to stray or question a club policy, he or she just cost this club a member. He may not quit yet, but can he expect the service to improve over the rest of his membership?

2) LACK OF MEMBER SERVICE

Paying for a membership every month at a place that doesn't even know your name, never knowing when you come in if you'll have a 10-minute or 30-minute wait for equipment, and not even being able to buy a cold drink (besides some strange bodybuilding brew) will wear on a member after a while.

In this industry, you can provide better service than your competitors and still be lousy. As an industry, our standards are just too low.

Most members don't leave us at the end of their year, they're driven away by horrible service. In this industry, you can provide better service than your competitors and still be lousy. As an industry, our standards are just too low.

Every owner talks about the quality of their member service in the gym but they usually define it as to how clean their clubs are, how often the front counter people smile or how many trainers they have on the floor. But a clean club and a courteous staff are expected by the member as part of the core package that you have to offer just to be competitive.

These items are not bonuses to the members, they are base expectations, something the member expects as part of the package but not anything they are wildly excited about either.

When it comes to renewals, the club has to move beyond base expectations. For example, I expect you to know my name since I'm paying you. I didn't expect you to invite me to a member Christmas party. I expect enough help to keep my routine fresh and challenging. I didn't expect a weekly group two-hour seminar with a trainer on learning more about the body parts and how to train them effectively. I expect enough cardio to get my workout done in a realistic amount of time. I didn't expect a new piece of cardio added every two months and I certainly didn't expect a Cardio Theater type of system.

Strong examples of the lack of member support and member service are nutrition programs. Everyone in the fitness business understands that working out is only a small part of the formula, when it comes to lifetime fitness.

Without an understanding of nutrition and its relationship to training, most members could work out for years and never get any great results. Without results, they lose interest and quit. They don't quit today, but at the end of the membership. It's like we only give them part of the formula for success, and the smallest part at that. "Yep, I've worked out in this gym for two years now and not a damn thing on my body has changed except for a thinner billfold. Let me at that renewal."

How could an owner operate a gym without a nutrition program? The members are looking for a total support system and we're saying that all we offer is the workout part. But a nutrition program is not writing out a program on the back of a workout card on a clipboard. The members expect more and will leave us without a solution. Without results there is no renewal.

3) FAILURE TO REINVEST IN THEIR BUSINESSES

It's common to visit someone's super club that everyone in the industry raved about several years ago and find it already starting to run down and only surviving off of its old glory. Clubs are high-maintenance items that need attention daily, not yearly. Equipment changes, paint fades, good design ideas become stale, and even the most creative physical plants become out-of-date in a very short period of time.

Clubs go through three levels of maturation. Each level is driven by renewals. If an owner misses one level, it's hard to move to the next. The rule of thumb is that it takes the same amount of money every four years to keep the club competitive that it did to start the club, minus equipment and operational losses during the first year.

For example, if a club that was 10,000 square feet costs $25 per foot to build out when it was opened, or $250,000, that same amount of money would have to be spent over every four-year period to keep that club competitive in the marketplace. Where does this money come from? It should come from renewals.

> **Equipment changes, paint fades, good design ideas become stale, and even the most creative physical plants become out-of-date in a very short period of time.**

Stage one level of maturation
The first stage of maturation comes at the thirteenth month, or when the first round of renewals should kick in. If the club averages 60 new sales a month during the first year, then during the thirteenth month it should do its 60 sales and realize additional income from its first wave of renewals. If the

club renews 40 percent, and has a loss rate of 10 percent, the rate to be expected from 12-month contracts collected by a strong third-party collector, then the club should renew about 22 members.

To further explain, the club could have had 60 members up for renewal during the thirteenth month, but lost 10 percent, or 6 members, during the year. That leaves 56 possibilities for renewal. If the club renews 40 percent, it would end up with 22 members after rounding up. This surge of renewals added to the new sales should have increased the club's monthly revenue from membership income, at no additional expense to the club.

Stage two level of maturation

The same thing should happen again at the twenty-fifth month as the second wave of renewals kicks in, and members from the first year start their second round of renewals. This second wave of renewals should again affect the club's income without expense.

Stage three level of maturation

The third stage of maturation is when the club would be fully mature with its membership. It is also the stage where the club continues to prosper or it starts to decline. This stage occurs at about 48 months and is the point where the equipment and physical plant start to decay. The owner should have been reinvesting in the club all along, but if he or she doesn't re-invest at this crucial stage the business starts to fade.

For example, a four-year-old club may have a lot of well-maintained cardio equipment that was in style when the club opened. Four years later, those upright bikes and all those stair climbers still work and look great but they're not what the members want anymore. The club would need to replace a sizable chunk of its equipment with whatever is in the industry at the time. In this example, the owner probably missed the treadmill, recumbent bike and elliptical drive boom.

Where would the money have come from to replace the old equipment and to update the physical plant? This money would have come from the stages of maturation driven by the renewals in the club. Without the renewals there would be no surge in the income. Without the maturation effect in the club's revenues from the combination of new sales and renewals, there would never be enough money to continually re-invest in the club.

How renewals affect a maturing club

This chart is an illustration of how renewals compound over the years to affect a maturing club. The sales numbers are not corrected for loss rates, but serve mainly as example as to how important renewals are to a club in today's market.

1) During the first year, the club signs up an average of 75 new members a month.

75 x 12 months = 900 new members during the first year
At the end of year one, the club has 900 new members.

Where would the money have come from to replace the old equipment and to update the physical plant? This money would have come from the stages of maturation driven by the renewals in the club.

2) During the second year, it continues to average 75 new members a month for the year. The club also renews 40 percent of the members it signed up during the first year.

> Year two/75 new members per month x 12 months = 900 new members
> 360 renewals from year one/900 year one members x .40 = 360 renewals
> At the end of the second year, the club would have 1260 active members.

3) During the third year, the club signs up 75 new members a month, or 900 for this particular year. The club also renews 40 percent of the members it signed up during year two. Members from year one also continue by renewing for another year. These members are in their third year and will renew at about a 60 percent renewal rate.

> Year three/75 new members a month for 12 months = 900 new members
> 360 renewals from year two, or 900 x .40 = 360 renewals
> 216 renewals from members from year one, or 360 x .60 = 216
> At the end of year three, the club would have 1470 active members.

At the end of year three, 39 percent of all the members in the club are renewals.

4) Year four is where the club starts to really benefit from the compounding effect of the renewals. Note that, as members stay longer in the system, they renew at a higher rate.

> Year four/75 new members a month for 12 months = 900 new members
> 360 renewals from year three, or 900 x .40 = 360
> 216 renewals from year two, or 360 x .40 = 216
> 173 renewals from year one, or 216 x .80 = 173
> At the end of year four, the club would have 1649 active members.

At the end of year four, 45 percent of all the members in the club are renewals.

5) Year five shows the transition where half the members in the club are renewals.

> Year five/75 new members a month for 12 months = 900 new members
> 360 renewals from year four, or 900 x .40 = 360
> 216 renewals from year three, or 360 x .60 = 216
> 173 renewals from year two, or 216 x .80 = 173
> 138 renewals from year one, or 173 x .80 = 138

At the end of year five, approximately 50 percent of all members in the club are renewals.

At the end of year five, approximately 50 percent of all members in the club are renewals.

4) NO TRIAL PERIOD

This does not obviously appear as something that would help your renewals 12 months into the future, but a solid initial trial period where the member can actually try before they buy cuts your losses and increases your renewals. The only people you are signing up are people who truly want a membership, and are fully aware of what they are buying. These members weren't drop closed or beaten into submission in an office.

They had a chance to try before they made a buying decision. When they do decide to buy, they are real members committed to the club and will only leave because of poor member service or because one of the other mistakes listed in this section drives them out.

But the trial period has to be a real one. One workout or even one week isn't enough to base a buying decision on. Before a member will invest, which is how most see joining a club, and before they reinvest as renewals, they need to understand and feel comfortable about the product. Once they make the decision, instead of a drop-closing ex-used car salesperson talking them into it, they are reluctant to walk away because the responsibility belongs to them instead of blaming someone else for forcing their decision.

5) FAILURE TO KEEP THE CLUB COMPETITIVE

This is different from re-investing in the club in that a club can be clean, freshly painted and improved, have new carpet and even some new equipment, and still not even be close to being competitive.

To understand the theory of keeping clubs competitive, you need to understand how the nightclub business works. A club may be extremely popular, packed for six months straight with a line and a mega-monster doorman guarding the entry. One month later, no one visits anymore because the patrons have all moved on to the next club of the moment.

The fitness business should try harder to emulate part of this theory. Most clubs stay static too long. The equipment never changes, either by additions or replacements, or by simply moving it around once in a while. The walls may be repainted but always in the same colors. The owners invest in some artwork but since they paid a lot to have it done, it stays on the walls year after year. Even the staff wears the same uniforms for a year at a time.

What does all this mean to the members? You have members not renewing simply because they are absolutely, positively, incredibly bored beyond the human capacity for tears. The members wanted to stay, they really did, but they need to be challenged, entertained and fussed over much more frequently than most owners are willing to do.

Cardio equipment may be the best example of what it takes to stay competitive in the fitness industry. When cardio first started to gain acceptance, all anyone had were old style mechanical bikes. Then came the upright electronic bikes and every person in the gym was fighting over whose turn it was. The bikes shocked a complacent industry, because for the first time owners had to part with the real bucks for cardio equipment.

Before a member will invest, which is how most see joining a club, and before they re-invest as renewals, they need to understand and feel comfortable about the product.

The bikes were the members' rage until the stair machines entered the stage. They were new, fresh and the members could cheat beyond belief. The first StairMaster brand machines stormed the industry not only because the machines provided a great way to do cardio, but for the lazier members they were also great triceps machines.

Extend those arms, lock those elbows, and wiggle the ankles. The members not only looked good but they could actually stay on for an hour at a time. This gave those members great status in the gym. And some were even reportedly seen sweating, but that was only in the southern states.

The members need change. They are aware, through magazines and by visiting other gyms, of what's hot and what's coming next. Change makes it more fun and who knows, maybe that next machine will be the one that gets that particular member in shape. At least he thinks so.

6) FAILURE TO TARGET RENEWALS

Eighty percent of your business is derived from 20 percent of the customers. In any club there is a core of members who provide an over-proportional share of the club's revenue.

This core of members brings in the most referrals, supports the profit centers in the gym, and usually spends the most money overall throughout the year. In relationship to renewals, this means we need to learn to target the renewals we really want and not necessarily all of them.

Yes, we need to concentrate on the member's first 30 days because many of the members set their perceptions of what the club is about during that time. But we also need to be aware of the period at the end of the memberships too, and then spend our time and energy on the members we really want to keep and who we depend on for the money they spend with us.

For example, a member who participates in the club's nutrition program, trains regularly, makes a few pro shop purchases on a frequent basis, and who participates in the club's social events is more important to the club's revenue stream. This member becomes even more important when compared to one who trains infrequently and who doesn't support the club beyond the membership.

Some clubs develop special teams to chase renewals. This could be a small group of the best employees, or just one key employee in the smaller clubs who dedicates special time to contacting and surveying targeted members up for renewal.

The focus of the group is to learn how to identify and fix the problems the potential renewals present when they are contacted. Many members who do decide to leave could be saved if someone contacted them for a different reason than to just get the person to renew. These members may have small problems that they have never had a chance to express to anyone in any authority on the staff, usually problems that could be solved simply.

When chasing lost renewals, try to talk to as many as possible about why they didn't renew. What went wrong? How could the staff have gotten involved earlier to save the person? Talking to lost customers can help you

Many members who do decide to leave could be saved if someone contacted them for a different reason than to just get the person to renew.

figure out where your business has failed in the past, where it is today and where it should go tomorrow.

Summary

If we lost a member, it's because we didn't make them a friend.

Remember, if given the choice, people always prefer to do business with a friend, even if they sometimes can make a better deal elsewhere. If we lost a member, it's because we didn't make them a friend. This sounds simplistic but you see it all the time at the best restaurants. People like to be known and they like to feel that they belong to something bigger than themselves.

Even that one really fat guy who has been in the club for years, and who never gets any results at all, likes to hang around if he feels welcome and accepted. If a member doesn't renew with us — and remember the financial implications of that situation — we have to assume it's our fault and we will do whatever it takes to get them back.

Things you can do to use this material

1) Renewals will be one of the two most important issues you have to deal with in the fitness industry in the coming years, meaning that part of your ongoing business plan includes sections on how to exceed the national average in your business.

2) Track and be aware of the renewal average in your business. This is one of the most important numbers you need to know because it reflects how your business plan and member service plan is working.

3) Remember that the members are a lot like you. They get bored easily, need to be challenged, seek new and exciting things, and don't like to be taken for granted. For more information on being taken for granted, see your spouse.

4) Renewals will take the pressure off of new sales in a fitness business. Eventually, in most market places, you will run out of new sales.

5) Put together a system that increases a member's chance for success during his or her first 30 days. Keep the rules flexible, and do whatever it takes to get the member started correctly and confidently. Remember that no one rule will work for every new member.

6) Member service starts at the front counter. Hire older, more mature front counter people that have good communication skills. These folks set the tone for member service in the club and directly affect the club's renewals.

7) Clubs are extremely high maintenance. To stay competitive and to keep renewals, the owners need to continually reinvest in their businesses. Two rule of thumbs are to budget $100 per thousand square feet per month for repair and maintenance, with a minimum of $1,000, and another $100 per thousand square feet for capital improvement, with the same minimum. If the money is not spent that particular month, it should be moved to an ac-

crual savings account for the club since it will be needed eventually.

8) Everything changes, including what members want and expect from a club. Great equipment that works means nothing if it's out of date or out of style. The members seek change and know what's coming next in the industry. To stay competitive, and again to keep those renewals, the clubs have to change to reflect the current trends in the marketplace.

9) Move away from the emphasis on first-visit closing. You still have to sell memberships in this business, but *when* you sell can change. Move toward a trial membership system that truly allows a potential member to try before they buy.

10) All renewals are not equal. Track and document how members support the club. Target renewals that are the best members, meaning those that come regularly, come to the social events, bring guests and spend money in the club's multiple profit centers.

Move away from the emphasis on first-visit closing. You still have to sell memberships in this business, but *when* you sell can change.

55

The club business starts with the financial foundation

Building the right financial foundation is the most important decision you'll make in the club business

Chapter 6

Don't repeat the biggest mistake ever made in the fitness industry

Chapter 7

If your financial foundation is right, you can make a lot of mistakes and still stay in business

Chapter 8

But getting cash from the members seems like so much fun!

Chapter 9

Short-term debt has killed more fitness businesses than bad breath in salespeople

Section Two

LESSONS FROM LIFE — #5

Hiring relatives

IN THE CASE OF ONE licensed gym, the owners, a couple in their early forties, brought their son into the business as the manager. Their goal was to teach him the business and then let him take it over and eventually buy them out. This gave him a great start and ensured that they would have a buyer for their business down the road.

The problem was that the son was totally unfit for the business. He was quiet, didn't really like to work out, and believed that the women members of the staff were there as sort of a dating stable.

In a very short period of time, the owners realized that they made a mistake. But by this time it was even more complicated since they now had their daughter in the business doing the books, an area that she too wasn't qualified to handle.

The moral of the story

Don't hire relatives unless you're willing to discipline and get rid of them if necessary, just like you would with any other employees.

He was quiet, didn't really like to work out, and believed that the women members of the staff were there as sort of a dating stable

The owners in this story agonized and tried to salvage their family members for so long that it eventually wiped out much of the club's profitability for that year. Because the employees were relatives, the owners weren't able to mentally apply the same standards to them as they would to anyone else. The son would come in late, leave early, and let important work pile up. The daughter would do the same (except she hid things, like stacks of contracts that needed entering), hoping that she could catch up later. She never did.

Relatives in the business should undergo the same disciplinary procedures as the other employees. If the rest of the team sees relatives getting away with things, then they feel cheated or abused and then they are unwilling to work. Don't hire relatives unless you're willing to correct their mistakes.

6

Don't repeat the biggest mistake ever made in the fitness industry

YEAR AFTER YEAR, decade after decade, the incoming generation of new owners following those who have gone before them will make the same mistake the industry has made over and over again. What's this catastrophic mistake each generation in the club business seems doomed to repeat? We set our prices too low. It seems like the biggest and most oft-repeated mistake would be something more dynamic to talk about. It's not about opening with the wrong partners. It's not about being totally undercapitalized. It's not about dumping your spouse and running away with one of your good-looking personal training clients. It's simply that we price the gym too low for the market.

It's simply that we price the gym too low for the market.

Historically, the industry has always kept the price low by waging price wars against our competitors. In the '70s, a member paid around $20 per month for a membership to a typical mainstream health club. In the '90s, in markets such as Denver, Colorado, a person can still join a fitness center for about $20 per month. There is even a national chain that advertises $19 a month in all of its markets. Is this a loss leader, something we offer cheap but then try and up-sell when the client is in the office, or is this price a play to gobble up the market, which is also dumb because it assumes every person in the country is only concerned about price?

The cost of opening a gym has increased by 1,000 to 4,000 percent in most markets around the country compared to the '70s, but the owners are still trying to charge the same. They still believe that price drives the memberships, even though today's sophisticated members have proved that this is no longer true.

The problem with the price being too low is that it affects virtually every other part of the business. If the price is too low, the club is forced to produce an unrealistic number of sales. If the price is too low, the collectibility of the memberships may decrease.

And most importantly, if the price is too low, the multiple profit centers in the club may not work because the club is filled with price-driven members — the cheapest human beings on the planet. Keep in mind that it's hard to sell multiple profit centers to guys who bring empty milk jugs full of sports drinks. And senior citizens who are in on the lowest membership possible aren't likely to kick in for that expensive nutrition program.

Pricing has grown to be the biggest mistake because it's so misunderstood. It's often left to last when it comes to developing a business plan because it seems so simple: Look at what the competitor charges, set our prices a few dollars lower, and then claim that our club is better that anyone else's. Therefore, the member is getting a better buy from us. Again, does the member really logically believe that your business can be the best and the cheapest at the same time? Or does it seem logical to the consumer that he or she will really have a good experience and get enough help and service in a business that prices itself at $19 per month?

Setting a price has almost taken on magical proportions to some owners in the industry. "Find that one magic price and every potential member will buy." The myths associated with pricing have evolved to become some of the biggest sacred cows in the business. "Sacred cows" are beliefs that are repeated so often they become the unquestionable truth.

For example, one very entrenched cow in the industry might be, "You have to have a childcare room in the club. Most members won't use it, but they want to see it when they join." Another cow might be, "Without aerobics, you'll never get any women in the club." And don't forget an all-time favorite, "Cash is king. You have to go for all the cash you can get when you open your club."

All of these premises were thought to be the absolute law at one time or another in the industry. And all eventually were proven to be untrue. Clubs don't have to have childcare to be profitable, and cardio and other styles of group workouts such as spin replaced aerobics eons ago. Cash lowers the return-per-member so substantially that most owners, especially those who run multiple units, are much better off without the cash.

But the preeminent sacred cow of all time in the fitness industry is setting the price low so the club will attract more members. The rule was that the lower the price was set, the more members, or higher volume, the club would attract. For example, why set your monthly price at $40 and limit your membership? Why not set it at $20 and attract a lot more members?

Hey, why not set it at $2 per month per member and hope every living human being, and maybe a few dogs too, who live in a 15-mile radius around the club joins. These are also the same theoreticians who suggest building endlessly bigger clubs without regard to the market or club's focus. "Hey,

And most importantly, if the price is too low, the multiple profit centers in the club may not work because the club is filled with price-driven members — the cheapest human beings on the planet.

John opened a 20,000 square foot club and has 2,000 members already. I'll open a 30,000 square foot facility and kick his butt because I'll have 3,000 members."

The assumption is that the bigger your facility, the more members you will attract. This follows the previous assumption that the lower the price you set, the more members you will attract. If this flawed logic were true, all you would have to do to be successful in the club business would be to build a 50,000-square-foot facility and offer $10-a-month memberships.

Lowering the price can increase the number of new members to a certain degree, but only in very specific markets around the country and only for a limited time. Setting a club's price low still works somewhat in very high volume markets, for example, such as parts of California or New York City.

These are both extremely densely populated markets with an all most endless supply of new members. This system does attract more members over a short period of time compared to a club that sets its prices higher.

The definition of what's considered a low price is very regional in nature and may be $24 a month per member in California or $40 per month in New York, both low prices for those areas.

For the sake of a consistent example, define low pricing as anything under $30 per month per member, intermediate pricing as $30 to 40, and higher pricing as over $40. This would be an example of a typical mainstream fitness facility.

Large tennis facilities would probably not fall into these categories unless they are offering separate pricing for their fitness areas. These prices are also not adjusted for areas such as New York City, where $40 per month is unusually low. And in three to five years after this book is published, you could probably add $10 to each example to keep it current.

The major problem with low pricing for most owners is that it predetermines the club's operational philosophy. Low prices usually force a club into a sales-driven style of operation. In other words, low pricing determines how you have to run your club.

Sales-driven means the club has to focus on sheer sales numbers. The lower the price, the more members the club is forced to sign up. Once the club becomes sales-driven, it can no longer be service-driven. The two types are mutually exclusive. You can't run a sales-driven club seeking high volume and also offer great service. They just can't exist at the same time in the same gym.

When a club is sales-driven, all of the club's resources have to be spent in the generation of new sales. For example, it's usually pretty easy to spot a sales-driven club. Once you're in the club, you notice the five or six sales offices by the front door. All of the senior or high level staff are salespeople who hover around the front waiting for the next "up," or are in their offices working draw boxes or making cold calls to people's homes.

In this type of club, it's pretty unusual to find anyone out on the floor helping members or providing any type of service, since all the club's payroll dollars are spent on the sales force and the commissions it takes to keep the volume running. The counter people in this type of club are also an indica-

Once the club becomes sales-driven, it can no longer be service-driven. The two types are mutually exclusive.

tion of the type of operational philosophy the owners are following. Instead of a mature, service-oriented front counter force, you'll find a very young, undertrained and underpaid counter person who probably hasn't been on the job very long.

The club simply can't provide service because the owners don't have the additional revenue and probably don't believe in it anyhow. Each day the club is judged successful or not by the number of sales generated that day. Note here that there is no other revenue in these clubs from multiple profit centers because this style of club can't control them. Why? Because all the real people are in sales, and the rest are warm bodies who are passing through on their way to other jobs.

The owners and management would have a hard time controlling the profit centers, because they don't have the more experienced and mature person to supervise them. Again, the club doesn't have these people because all of the best people are in sales, and because of their quotas, these people can't do anything but sell. Once you lower the price, you set all of these other factors into motion that force you into this type of operational method.

The reason this method is so destructive for most owners is that continued high sales can't be projected into the future. Except in very densely populated markets, the club eventually runs out of enough prospects, which is attributed to two reasons:

First of all, 80 percent of a club's members usually come from a 15-minute drive time from the club. Yes, there is that one crazy member who drives from upstate Iowa to Texas once a week — because you own a super hip quad thruster handmade in Bolivia by a former Mr. Universe. Most of your members, however, come from a 15-minute drive time, or usually a three- to five-mile ring around the club.

Low pricing and high volume generally means that the club runs price-driven ads, meaning some type of sale of the week, as its primary marketing tool. Price ads eventually ruin your market, or in other words, the longer you run price-driven ads, the smaller the market gets because you've burned up everyone in your ring that is motivated by a cheap price.

Clubs that continually run low price do nothing to develop the rest of the market as potential members. For example, in surveys run by a major news group, it's estimated that 92 percent of all the people in this country have never set foot in a health club. When we discuss marketing later in this book, we'll discuss how to go after these people and why they don't respond to price ads. For now, though, we need to understand that most price-driven marketing only appeals to the other 8 percent, or those who already have experience with fitness facilities.

Ads based on low price assume that the potential member already has some type of experience with a fitness facility, knows what he or she is looking for in a club, and price is the deciding factor.

Ads based on low price assume that the potential member already has some type of experience with a fitness facility, knows what he or she is looking for in a club, and price is the deciding factor. These ads do nothing to attract someone who has no experience with a fitness club, because they don't understand if the price is a good value or not since they have never really been in a club.

Low price featured in ads also does nothing to attract those people who

62

want to buy quality and are willing to pay for it. There are certain folks who want cheap and will take everything that goes along with a cheaply priced membership, such as lines, no help and a worn or outdated physical plant.

There are also folks who appreciate quality and who will pay more for more personal attention, the privilege of not having to stand in line, and for more services and amenities than the typical club can provide.

Another problem with the seemingly endless list of issues associated with low pricing, especially as it relates to the consumer, is that the owner most of the time doesn't really understand what he or she is selling. They confuse what we're selling in this industry, an intangible, with what retail stores sell, which are commodities. Many owners, for example, want to price like WalMart does, meaning price low and go for shear numbers. But we're not selling a commodity, we're selling a service.

For example, if a giant retailer puts toothpaste on sale for $1, the consumer may drive there and shop because the product is cheaper than they can get it at the store they normally shop at, which sells the same toothpaste for $1.50. The commodity is exactly the same in each case but one is selling it cheaper. In this case, the cheaper product is the best buy.

Again, we aren't selling a commodity, we're selling a service. And in most services, the consumer thinks that the highest priced service is the best. For example, if you're suffering from some terrible illness, do you want the cheapest doctor you can find treating you? If you are in serious legal trouble, do you want the cheapest lawyer you can find defending you?

Did O.J. have his nephew right out of law school defending him, or did he have the best and most expensive lawyer he could find? With services, the cheapest is usually the worst.

Most of the time, the consumer equates price with quality. The higher the price the club charges, the higher the quality of service the member will receive. The cheaper the price, the lower the quality of service the person will receive. Price is part of the club's image.

Most owners believe they have the best club around, but if the price is the same as the competitor's price, then the club is exactly the same in the consumer's mind. Price is part of our image and many sales are lost or won before the potential member ever gets into the club.

The alternative to the sales-driven operational plan, especially in competitive markets, is the return per member philosophy. The return-per-member system strives for a higher return-per-member, or learning to make more money from fewer members.

In this operational method, which will be the next level of owner growth in the industry, the emphasis shifts away from sales-driven, toward a more service-driven environment that works off of a low-pressure sales system, multiple profit centers and an increased emphasis on renewals.

The owner learns to work off of a lower number of new sales, make more money from the ones already in the system, and keeps those members longer, driving down the continued need for high volume and driving down the cost of doing business.

For example, if there were only 100 potential members in a market, the

> ... we aren't selling a commodity, we're selling a service. And in most services, the consumer thinks that the highest priced service is the best.

club would be better off with 60 of them paying $40 per month than having all 100 paying $25 per month. The club would make $100 less each month in this example, but the cost of the sales would be cheaper in lower commissions, ad costs would probably be lower, wear and tear on the club would be less with fewer members, and staffing costs would be lower with fewer members to take care of over the same period of time.

The club in this example with the higher price would also most likely make more money in the long run from its profit centers. Its members are already used to paying a higher price and were probably not attracted just by price. They would be much more likely to spend money on a club's profit centers since they didn't join because of a cheap price. They are used to spending money and will continue doing so.

These members will also be stronger candidates for renewal. Since the club has fewer members, and is charging a higher rate for the members it does have, it should be able to provide more personal attention and member service, something the other club can't because of its lower return per member.

Another key point to consider in the volume versus return-per-member debate is the degree of vulnerability a business has. No business is ever 100 percent risk-free. As an owner, you have to come up with a business plan that decreases your vulnerability, yet gives you the best chance to make money.

The problem with a low-price/sales-driven business plan is that it's almost impossible to defend. A business based on selling the lowest price to the greatest number of members has nowhere to retreat in time of war, meaning competitors are trying to put you out of business.

A business based on selling the lowest price to the greatest number of members has nowhere to retreat in time of war, meaning competitors are trying to put you out of business.

Since a low-price/sales-driven club is based on volume, any decrease in the new member stream can drastically affect the club's bottom line in a very short period of time, especially if the club has no other source of income except new sales.

If a competitor came in and offered a higher price membership, it wouldn't take away a huge number of members from the low-price operator. It doesn't have to. It only has to take away the best, meaning those who will pay more for a club that doesn't have the implied problems the low-price operator does. A good competitor only has to take a small percentage of members (which is probably the low-priced guy's best members since they are willing to leave for a higher-priced but better quality gym) to hurt a volume-driven business plan.

For most low-priced operators, a 10-percent reduction in monthly business would severely hurt them since their profit margins are usually pretty tight. There are, of course, exceptions to every rule, but defending a high-volume, low-priced facility against aggressive competitors is not something most owners would wish to attempt.

Another point of vulnerability is that the club is totally dependent on just one source of income. In competitive markets, it's wise to spread the risk among several different areas. If a high-volume club is totally dependent on sales and has no other source of income such as multiple profit centers, the club is at risk. For example, if just one or two people generate the majority of those sales, and those people leave, the club's business will immediately suffer.

In a return-per-member business plan, revenue should be spread over several different areas. In this case, if the club loses a key sales person, it still has time to react and probably won't suffer too much because there is still revenue from the multiple profit centers.

Summary

The emphasis in the coming years will be away from sales-driven operational methods and toward trying to drive up the return per member. Sales-driven/low-price operations have been part of the industry since it began, but with the increased cost of doing business, increased competition, a more sophisticated member base and more business-aware owners, this system is no longer the way to operate.

Owners also have more to risk now than ever before, because the cost of starting up fitness facilities has dramatically increased over the years. With this increased risk comes the need to decrease the business's vulnerability. Running a business plan that's not defensible is not a method of decreasing risk.

Decreasing risk and vulnerability only comes from seeking a higher return per member or, in other words, learning to make more money from the members we already have. Most clubs in the industry, because of their low-price/sales-driven system, simply spend all their time and money replacing the members they once had. To be successful in the future, we need to keep the members longer, and make more money from those members already in the club.

The mistake that underlies the sales-driven operational style is setting the club's membership price too low. Once the club establishes a low price, the owner is forced to run the club in a specific method, meaning everything has to be geared toward developing volume.

We have to keep in mind that price is part of the club's image. To be the best, the club has to price itself accordingly. The consumer associates price with quality. If the price is too good to be true, then it probably is. Finally, keep in mind that we are selling a service, not a commodity. The better the service, the more the member would have to pay for it in the real world, and the more the member should be paying for it in the fitness world.

> **The emphasis in the coming years will be away from sales-driven operational methods and toward trying to drive up the return per member.**

Things you can do to use this material

1) Setting the price too low is the biggest mistake we make in the club industry.

2) When in competition with like businesses, or businesses in the same category, consider setting your price a few dollars higher.

3) Price determines how you run your business. If all your time and energy is spent on just sales and replacing members you have had and then lost, switch slowly to a return-per-member system.

4) To switch to a return-per-member system, do it over a year's period of time. Raise the monthly price slowly and if you're discounting for cash, also raise that price slowly over the next year. If your business is dependent on cash, you don't want to hurt yourself by cutting the cash off too quickly. It's better to slowly wean yourself away from your current system.

5) Add a little older and more mature counter people, and then introduce one profit center at a time. As the profit centers start to work, your need for a high number of new sales should start to decrease.

Keep in mind that it's OK to lose a few people each month because your price is too high.

6) Keep in mind that it's OK to lose a few people each month because your price is too high. Almost all of your staff, and most owners too, panic if someone walks out because of price. A good rule of thumb is that if 20 percent of your potential members left because of a price objection, you are probably priced right for the market.

7) The most objections on pricing you get will come from your young staff. To them, $40 or more a month is high and they judge all potential members according to their personal situation. Train hard and heavy on the true worth of your business and why you price accordingly.

8) Change your marketing away from price-driven ads and replace it with an exposure type of ad. Exposure means try before you buy. This type of ad attracts people price ads never will, and brings in people more interested in service instead of price.

Being absentee too soon

A CLASSIC TALE OF WOE in the fitness business is when the owner who just starts to taste a little success decides to turn the club over to a manager and plays golf every day.

One owner in particular worked very hard for three years and finally had the club doing some serious numbers. Once he experienced a little success, he walked away from the daily management of the club to pursue a lifetime dream, to someday try and make it on the Senior's Golf Tour.

He hired a manager, left her in complete control, and then just started dropping by the club as he felt like it, usually just to pick up money. His new lifestyle put a financial drain on the club, because he would take everything beyond the basic bill paying money as his salary.

Eventually the club started to run down because of the lack of money to replace and upgrade equipment and the club's physical plant. The club also started to lose some of its production because no one was really supervising or watching the manager. She was doing a good job, but she didn't have the experience to go totally solo so shortly after getting the job.

The moral of the story

It's your business and your responsibility to make it work. Most small businesses need

He walked away from the daily management of the club to pursue a lifetime dream, to someday try and make it on the Senior's Golf Tour

constant guidance and supervision and no matter how well you hire, you seldom get someone who will respect the business as much as the person who began it.

I once had a school project to analyze a business that I didn't really have any experience with at the time. I chose to do a restaurant and ended up studying a Chinese restaurant owned by a Chinese family who had been in the states for 10 years, during five of which they owned their own business.

Everyone working in the restaurant was family but only the father was the boss. All family members were treated just like employees but were expected to do their jobs as a family member would do.

After five years, the owner still put in his 50 hours per week. The restaurant was very financially successful, and the owner planned to work it hard and then sell it to one of the other family members. But while he was there, he worked just as hard after five years as he did to get it started.

The gym owner could have hired a strong second-in-command and turned over much of the responsibility of running the club to her. But he still should have spent enough time in the business each week to guide it, and to train the manager to higher levels.

7

If your financial foundation is right, you can make a lot of mistakes and still stay in business

How you charge your members and collect their dues is the most important decision you make as an owner. If the financial foundation is right, you can make a lot of mistakes and still stay in business. If you're wrong, there is nothing you can do to save your business. In other words, all the sales in the fitness universe won't overcome a bad financial foundation.

Everyone agrees. The goal of any business is to be profitable. We all talk about it, everyone seeks it, but just what is "profitable" in the fitness business? In other words, how does an owner know if their profit is enough or if it's on track for future growth?

If you're losing money, that's pretty much bad form in the industry, and it also answers the question about profitability. One seldom hears, "Yeah, I could have made money last month, but I decided to take a $10,000 loss instead." Losses, or brackets on the old financial statements, are not considered desirable. But when your business does break through on the plus side, how much is enough?

We've been looking at the profitability of fitness businesses for more than 20 years, which has enabled us to group fitness businesses by their net monthly income. In the fitness industry, almost all numbers and ratios are easier to comprehend and relate if they are looked at on a monthly basis instead of an annual.

From our research, we find that only 10 to 15 percent of the clubs in the country net 20 percent on a monthly basis. This is, of course, on a pre-tax

One seldom hears, "Yeah, I could have made money last month, but I decided to take a $10,000 loss instead."

basis and only includes the owner's salary if they are working on-site fulfilling the job of manager. The fluctuation from 10 to 15 percent is somewhat regional, meaning the more profitable clubs are usually in the Northeast where the per-member monthly dues are higher. The other exception is in the South or parts of the Midwest where the cost of operation is so much lower.

For example, a profitable 15,000-square-foot club in the Northwest might have an overhead of $60,000 per month and deposit on the average $72,000 to $75,000 per month. To live and operate in the more expensive markets, such as Connecticut, a profitable 15,000-square-foot club might cost $90,000 to $100,000 to operate on a monthly basis with a deposit of $120,000 to $130,000. Both of these examples show profitability at 20 percent on a monthly basis. There are more clubs in this profit range in this part of the country than in other parts.

Parts of the South and the Midwest also show steady profitability, but that's often because of lower rent factors. A facility in Alabama or Iowa that is the same size as one in the Northwest might have $20,000 less operating expense than a Northeast or west coast club. This decrease in expense is due to lower rents and much lower payroll expense.

For example, a 15,000-square-foot club in certain parts of the Midwest might only cost $35,000 to $40,000 to operate and might deposit $50,000 a month. The operating costs are lower and the club deposits less, but the 20 percent net is still intact.

The other 85 percent of club owners in the country *don't* net 20 percent on a monthly basis.

The other 85 percent of club owners in the country *don't* net 20 percent on a monthly basis. Many of them are at best month-to-month operations with little or no profits. But this is starting to change in the industry as real business people own or start to invest in clubs. "Real" is defined as people who understand business and who run their facilities with the idea of making a profit — something a lot of owners don't forecast in their business plans.

The percentage of owners in the 20-percent range should not be discouraging. It's not just our industry, but most small business in general. Most small businesses in the country, such as mom and pop dry cleaners, flower shops, gift shops or independently owned restaurants, are really just month-to-month businesses. The difference is that you can start a flower shop or card shop for a lot less than a full-blown fitness facility.

In the past, this has not been true for many of our owners who have grown up in the fitness industry as sales people. They start as trainers, become salespeople and eventually manage and then own their own facilities. The problem with these owners is that their only business plan or solution is sales. They believe that if there are enough sales that all business problems will go away.

The difference between the 10 to 15 percent and the rest, or the real people and the sales people, is often how they develop and handle their most important asset: their receivables base.

While there are a few small exceptions, most of the profitable clubs' business basics are the same. For example, most clubs that make money —

those that net 20 percent or better — put more emphasis on member service, hire an older and more mature staff, and have four or more thriving multiple profit centers. These clubs also use 12-month contracts, price their monthly memberships in the $35 to $55 range, and have a strong receivables base that allows them to project their business into the future.

The key to the business is receivables. The strength of the receivables base drives the business. Without strong receivables, the business might be healthy in the short run, but it will most likely never be profitable in the long run.

Before going further, let's define what a receivables base really is. Simply put, it means people owe you money that you hope to collect some time in the future. A more specific definition that fits our industry is this: If you never sold another new membership at your facility, how much money could you count on collecting in the next 12 months?

Another simple way to look at it: Let's say you have a very, very small club with only four members. We're talking really elite here. The club has payments of $40 per month and uses the preferable tool for club memberships, the 12-month contract.

For example:

Bill is a new member and owes 12 payments.
$$12 \times \$40 = \$480$$
Ann has been at the club for six months and still owes six more payments.
$$6 \times \$40 = \$240$$
Joe has only three payments left on his membership.
$$3 \times \$40 = \$120$$
Joan has been around for a full membership and owes only one payment.
$$1 \times \$40 = \$40$$
The total outstanding payments = $880

This club's total receivables base, meaning all the money it could hope to collect during the next year if it never sold another membership would be $880, the total of all outstanding member payments yet to be paid.

Why are receivables so important to a fitness business? Because each month, the business receives a check from the member payments that affects the stability and the profitability of the business. Once this check gets strong enough, the business is less vulnerable and becomes able to grow to the next level. The next level is reinvestment in the physical plant and stronger growth in the future through the maintenance of the membership base, which translates to increased renewals of existing members.

For a business to be healthy and stable, a certain percentage of the club's base operating expense (BOE) should be covered by the monthly receivables. The BOE is defined as what it takes the business to pay its monthly expenses minus the owner's salary. Rent or mortgage, payroll and general operating expenses are all included in BOE.

The goal for a healthy business is to get 70 percent coverage of the BOE by the monthly receivables income. For example, a club's BOE is $50,000 per

If you never sold another new membership at your facility, how much money could you count on collecting in the next 12 months?

month and the monthly check from the member payments from the receivables is $35,000.

$35,000 receivables income
$50,000 BOE

In this example, the receivables cover 70 percent of the monthly BOE. This coverage is one of the first and most important an owner should analyze in their business. A new business just starting out can hit this ratio at about the thirteenth month of operation, which is the first level of maturity a club business goes through, due to the first influx of renewals.

It's possible to do better than 70 percent coverage of the BOE. In fact, about 5 percent of the businesses in the industry achieve 100 percent coverage, which can happen beginning around the twenty-fifth month of operation — the second level of maturity a club passes through as the second round of member renewals occurs.

How important is this ratio? It's the most important number to watch in your business. If your club's receivables ever achieve this percentage of the BOE, you can make a lot of mistakes and still survive. You could also last in a fight against a new or existing competitor, because at this point you have income that can be counted on for at least five months before it starts to deteriorate, even if new sales slow down. This should give you plenty of time to react and revise your business plan, without having to make major mistakes because you're rushed.

A second ratio to look at is the relationship between your total outstanding receivables and your monthly BOE. The desirable ratio is 5 to 1, meaning your outstanding receivables are five times greater than your monthly operating expenses. For example, Club A has a $50,000-a-month BOE and a $300,000 outstanding receivables base or:

$300,000 receivables base
$50,000 BOE

In this example, Club A has a 6-to-1 ratio of outstanding receivables to its BOE.

In a second example, Club B has a $48,000-a-month BOE and a $210,000 outstanding receivables base or:

$210,000 receivables base
$48,000 BOE

In the second example, Club B has a 4.3-to-1 ratio of outstanding receivables to its monthly BOE.

The 5-to-1 ratio, if achieved, greatly decreases a club's vulnerability in the marketplace. If the owner had to step away from the business due to illness or family matters (and remember that most owners are the key person in their organization), the business' income could dramatically decline. Or if a

You could also last in a fight against a new or existing competitor, because at this point you have income that can be counted on for at least five months before it starts to deteriorate, even if new sales slow down.

tough competitor opened and you needed time to rebuild, or if there was simply a downturn in the local economy, the club could count on a reasonable amount of income projected into the future.

Without a 5-to-1 ratio, Club B would not have sufficient reserves if any of these things happened. The owners would have to scramble to survive, which leads to mistakes, such as discounting new memberships which makes existing members who paid more furious. Other scrambling-style mistakes are offering cash specials, which immediately decreases the return per member and will destroy a club in the long run, or other short-term solutions that eventually weaken and then destroy a business plan.

Note that both the Club A and Club B examples are based on 12-month contracts. Long-term contracts, meaning two years or longer, have extremely high loss rates, which will be discussed later in this section. If you are currently using 24-month contracts, simply divide by two and then apply the formula.

If you use strictly open-end memberships, which are also called month-to-month memberships, you have no ratio and no real long-term stability in the business. Open-end memberships will also be discussed later in this section, but for discussion here, you need to understand that if you use open-end memberships, you have cash flow, but no long-term receivables base. The cash flow has value but it can very easily be disrupted since there is no established obligation on the member's part.

Obligation and method of payment

When working to establish a receivables base, you have to learn to recognize the difference between obligation and method of payment, which are often confused by even experienced fitness business owners.

Obligation is the time commitment the member agrees to when they join the club. This commitment may be one week, one month, six months or even three years if the member is crazy enough to join a club that has its business plan rooted in the '60s.

Members in today's market have been known to become a little distrustful when their memberships last longer than their car leases or marriages. These clubs need to wake up and realize that Elvis is dead (maybe), televisions now have color and the members are much more sophisticated than we give them credit for when it comes to making business decisions.

Method of payment is how the member elects to make their payment each month, meaning they have a choice instead of being forced into a specific payment method. We're still talking about making payments each month at this point and not about cash or paid-in-full memberships. Paid-in-full memberships will be briefly discussed here and covered in depth later in this section.

Method of payment is also where the confusion arises for many owners and their staffs, because of the advent of electronic funds transfer (EFT) that has been a steadily growing part of the industry since the mid-'80s.

Members in today's market have been known to become a little distrustful when their memberships last longer than their car leases or marriages.

EFT means that the member authorizes the club to make a monthly deduction from a checking account, savings account or credit card. Because of some of the ad campaigns run over the years by some of the EFT companies, many owners confuse obligations, or the contractual time a member commits to, with EFT, or the automatic deduction of funds.

Setting a member up on EFT does not mean the member guarantees to pay; it just means they are allowing the club to deduct the monthly payment until the member says stop. EFT does not imply obligation. Obligation has to be established first, and method of payment later.

Some of the EFT companies make claims such as, "Collect all the money from all the members every month automatically." The implied claim is that the member no longer has to make a decision each month to write a check, and that the money would be drafted from the member's account or credit card automatically without any interference from the member.

This is not only not true, but actually misleading to club owners, because they are expecting the system to be somewhat bonehead proof. They are not usually ready to handle common EFT problems that arise in every club's account, such as closed accounts, nonsufficient funds or bank routing problems.

The club owner should first focus on establishing an obligation with the member, and then allow the member to choose the method of payment.

The club owner should first focus on establishing an obligation with the member, and then allow the member to choose the method of payment. Keep in mind that the development of an outstanding receivables base, which should be every owner's goal, is based on a time obligation from the member. Twelve-month memberships are the tool of choice for obligation because of their low loss rate which, again, will be discussed later in this chapter.

Although EFT does perform slightly better than allowing members to write checks each month, usually about 5 to 7 percent better on the average, there are still some major problems when using it exclusively or, worse, forcing it upon the members as their only method of payment.

For example, let's look at the following chart, which is a simple, and somewhat stereotypical, representation of a club's membership.

10. Wealthy person, great watch, real car, spends money in the club, probably in their late 40s.
9. Not quite as wealthy but is still in the game.
8. This person is a solid citizen, a family person, has a good job, good income and is a regular member.

---

7. This person is on a career track, has a new family, real house payment and is just now getting to the point that there is a little discretionary income.
6. This person is acquiring their first assets, maybe their first nice home and corresponding payment, has a lot of credit card debt, but is on the right track.
5. This person is a young executive or manager, maybe is renting or owns a small condo, in credit card debt, but having a great time.

4. The person here is on their second or third step in a new career, has a new car, a bigger apartment, and is leveraged to just above the eyes in credit and consumer debt, but doesn't care because he or she is having a great time in life and they'll deal with it later.

_____

3. This is your basic solid blue-collar type, living check to check, but pays his or her bills on time and still lives in their means.

2. First real job, first steady income and always spends just a little more than they make.

1. This person has their hat on backwards; no checking account or savings account, and couldn't get a credit card if their life depended on it. Don't forget their cut-off shorts and combat boots. Tattoos are optional.

Again, this is an illustration of a range of members that might belong to a typical club. Each member is different and those differences mean that not every member would accept the same system or method of payment. There is no one-size-fits-all.

Despite the hype about its ease of use, EFT is still not totally accepted by all consumers. This is changing and in the coming years it will grow, especially as those folks who are now in their 20s and 30s grow into middle age.

The people in the 8, 9 and 10 slots are those who seldom bounce checks, may be more sophisticated when it comes to money, and may choose to use EFT as a method of payment because they understand it and are comfortable with it.

On the other hand, these folks might also be your slightly older folks in the club who did not grow up with EFT and who prefer to pay with a method of payment that they are more used to, such as writing a check for their membership each month. In other words, the people in these slots would probably agree to a 12-month membership but may, or may not, allow an EFT draft depending on their age and personal experience with the method.

Slots 4, 5, 6 and 7 are usually people who are a little older than the lower slots, meaning mid 20s to early 40s, involved in a career, but are often check-to-check folks. They may agree to EFT but often prefer to write a check because of float in their accounts. Clubs that force EFT may get some of these folks in this group, but these are often where the account problems occur.

Many of these people would also not join a club that forces EFT because of the lack of control on when the money is taken from their accounts. The obligation is not the problem; it's how they get to pay that matters to them. Some clubs claim they have no problem forcing EFT on the people who come into the club. It's the people who don't come in because the club only has EFT that are the problem, because the system is limiting the business potential of the club.

The bottom echelon, slots 1, 2 and 3, and even stretching into 4 a little, are the people who don't even get to play in most club's memberships systems. Clubs that force EFT eliminate these folks altogether, which is bad business because of two reasons. First of all, clubs are still the best social outlets in

Many of these people would also not join a club that forces EFT because of the lack of control on when the money is taken from their accounts.

a community. For $30 to $40 per month in most markets, a member can come every day, stay as long as they like, take a shower, meet their friends and generally hang out and work out. Clubs are still the best entertainment buy around.

For many people in the lower slots on the chart, the club becomes one of the most important aspects of their life. A lot of sacrifices will be made when it comes to paying other bills just so the person can keep that membership going.

The second reason it's bad business to eliminate these folks is actually the other side of the same reason most clubs force EFT — to keep these folks out in the first place. Some of these people are horrible bill-payers. They don't have checking accounts and the concept of credit cards is only something they dream about at night. But these people may actually pay for a while, which is money the club wouldn't have had if it hadn't allowed these people to try.

No owner should ever expect to collect all the money from all the members. It's just a dream to expect to come up with a 100-percent perfect collection system. But losing money is frustrating, and when a member stiffs you as an owner, you vow to never let it happen again. A lot of financial vendors in the industry, such as the EFT companies, capitalize well on this emotion; the owners become so frustrated when it comes to collecting payments from the members. Often, it's not the members but the system the club is using for charging and collecting memberships that's the problem.

You can't expect to collect all the money. It's not reality. The reality is, however, that whoever collects the most money from the most members wins. Every decision you make when it comes to building a financial foundation should be based on collecting the most money from the most members.

That's why 24-month contracts are no good. The losses are too high and you don't collect as much money as you should per member. That's why discounting for cash is no good either. It lowers the return per member too much. And that's why forcing EFT as a method of payment and confusing it with an obligation is not workable either. It eliminates potential members, creates losses the club can't handle, such as closed accounts, and forces a system that much of the population still hasn't totally accepted as part of their personal financial life.

The final point when it comes to obligation and method of payment is that the club establishes the desired obligation it seeks from its members. As we'll discuss later, 12-month contracts, with variations as needed, are the heart of your membership system because it allows the club to build up a strong receivables base with minimum losses.

Once the member agrees to the obligation, they should have the choice of method of payment. Some people will seek EFT, some will pay by check each month as they do their other bills. EFT is cheaper to have serviced by a club and checks are usually a little more expensive to process, especially if you are using a third-party financial service company.

Some clubs, therefore, do charge members who want to write checks

No owner should ever expect to collect all the money from all the members. It's just a dream to expect to come up with a 100-percent perfect collection system.

up to $5 more a month over their EFT rate. For example, a club's monthly EFT rate might be $34 and it might charge $39 for these same folks who want to write a check instead of agreeing to a draft.

Other clubs simply charge the same and let the members decide what's best for them. Either way is acceptable as long as the member gets to make the final decision instead of being forced into something they are not comfortable with. Keep in mind that what seems best for the owners is not necessarily what's best for the members when it comes to member service.

Increased yield

By choosing a financial system that increases return per member, and by making choices dependent on loss rates and membership collectables, we are ultimately trying to drive up the yield. Simply defined, the yield is what's really left over from the member's monthly payment after certain adjustments are made. The higher the yield, the stronger the receivables base and the more money the club actually has to work with each month.

For example, many novice owners build business projections based on a certain payment amount, such as $40 per month per member, but never adjust for loss rates, cancellation rates, cost of collection or the impact of "free" services — all of which affect the final yield from that payment.

Freebies, such as free childcare, free coffee, free towel service and other giveaways in the name of member service or beating the competition all work to lower the yield. It's true that the cost of these services is shown on the expense side of the financial statements as part of doing business, but there is no quantifiable co-entry on the revenue side. In other words, these free services decrease the yield without demonstrating any corresponding increase on the revenue side.

To better understand yield, let's start with a payment amount of $40 and work through each factor that affects the ultimate yield from this payment. Again, the major factors are loss rates, cancellation rates, cost of collection and the impact of free services.

> **By choosing a financial system that increases return per member, and by making choices dependent on loss rates and membership collectables, we are ultimately trying to drive up the yield.**

Loss rates

It is impossible to collect all the money from all the members, a point we've already established. Your goal, then, is to collect the most money from the most members.

Simply defined, money is lost when someone who contracted to pay you doesn't pay, for whatever reason. A member who dies is a loss, because the contract doesn't get paid. We track loss by figuring out how much we can expect to collect from the contracts made with the members who take a chance on our clubs.

Each tool we use to obligate members has its own verifiable loss rate that can be tracked on a monthly basis. The largest and most credible financial service companies in the industry, as well as my own company, have been tracking loss rates since the early '70s.

Many owners hurt their receivables base and, therefore, their businesses by choosing the wrong tool as their primary membership agreement to establish obligation. An analysis of each tool currently in use in the industry and its loss rate shows how the receivables base is affected and, ultimately, the final yield.

OPEN-END, MONTH-TO-MONTH, PAY-AS-YOU-GO MEMBERSHIPS

Open-end, month-to-month and pay-as-you-go memberships are all different names for the same tool. Each means that the member has a very short obligation to the club. They commit to the end of the current month and can quit at any time with some type of formal notice to the club. If the member is being drafted on EFT, by law they can notify their bank and have the draft immediately cancelled.

Loss rates for this tool are about 3 to 4 percent monthly or about 36 to 48 percent annually. Losing 3 to 4 percent of your members each month is not too scary for most owners, but compounded over 12 months, it can add up to losing 36 to 48 out of every 100 members the club has.

For example, if you use open-end contracts and sign-up 100 people in January, by the January of the next year, you will only have between 52 to 64 people still left as members.

The big picture here is that the club incurred the cost of advertising to get the members, paid commissions to sign them up, paid staffing costs (we hope) to get them started on their programs, and suffered the wear and tear on the club from members who didn't stick around.

It's not a good business plan if you only keep half the members you sign up over a year's time. If the club can't keep the members it enrolls because of no-obligation memberships, all of the club's resources — key staff and payroll dollars — have to be dedicated to replacing those members.

Open-end memberships can be part of a club's financial system if they are used as a more expensive alternative to a 12-month contract.

Open-end memberships can be part of a club's financial system if they are used as a more expensive alternative to a 12-month contract. For example, if a club has a monthly price of $39 per month per member, it could offer an open-end membership at $46 to $48 per month. If the club is located in a heavily competitive market, it could still offer an open-end membership, but the majority of members would most likely choose the 12-month plan because of the price advantage. This, then, strengthens the receivables base.

As for yield: If a club lost 40 percent on every dollar of the membership dues, a $40 payment would already be reduced to $24 ($40 x 60 percent = $24). Therefore, an open-end membership, because of its extreme loss rate and effect on the yield, is not a good tool for most clubs.

24-month contracts

Two-year, or 24-month contracts have been an ugly habit in the industry for most of its history. The use of long-term contracts, those 24 months or longer, have been traced back, depending on who you believe, to the early life insurance guys in the '50s or to the Arthur Murray Dance Studios from the same era. Learn to dance, but sign up for the next five years and receive a great discount.

While 24-month contracts have been a standard for years, they are hard to sell to a more sophisticated clientele, and they are much more difficult to collect. It's interesting to note that every major failure in the history of the fitness industry, as well as some large chains that are still in business posting losses year after year, all used or use a 24-month contract as their base membership tool.

The loss rate for 24-month contracts is about 3 percent a month or 36 percent on a national average. There are exceptions to every rule, and there have been a very small handful of clubs which have used 24-month contracts and survived for any length of time. Most have not. Loss rates are also the most important number that affects yield and the receivables base, yet most owners don't track this vital statistic and the drastic effect it can have on their business.

If you have 100 members and you lose two each month for nonpayment, you have a loss rate of 2 percent or a 24-percent annual loss rate. Don't count members that move or cancellations as part of your loss rate formula. Those numbers are tracked separately under the cancellation rate.

Let's look at a typical membership that's being sold in the Denver, Colo., market in 1998 and see the results of using a 24-month contract. This is also a representation of a membership that has been sold in the industry for more than 30 years.

The club offers a floating membership fee, meaning the salesperson has the discretion to give a potential member virtually anything they want as long as the salesperson can get some type of membership sale. The club actually lists a membership fee of $150, but only the dumbest human beings on the planet ever really paid that much.

The monthly dues for the club, which is how much each member pays each month, are $20 (actually 19.95, but rounded off here for ease of calculation) for a two-year contractual membership.

Some form of a two-year, $20-a-month membership has been used for years in the industry. Salespeople love this membership because it's harder to sell than a simpler, one-year membership. The contract amount is also bigger at $20 per month x 24 months = $480, and leads to bigger commissions for the salesperson.

The reality, however, is that the more salesmanship and pressure it takes to get a member to sign up, the bigger the losses will be. Salespeople usually don't care or understand about losses. All they know is their job, which is that they are supposed to write a lot of "gross," which results from the sale of two-year contracts. The salespeople don't have to look at the end result,

> It's interesting to note that every major failure in the history of the fitness industry, as well as some large chains that are still in business posting losses year after year, all used or use a 24-month contract as their base membership tool.

which is that the product they sell may not be very collectable.

In a sales-driven system, 24-month contracts rule the world, because most old-style owners only understand putting gross on the board. But then the vicious cycle of selling to replace lost members starts again.

Since two-year memberships really don't make sense to a potential member anymore, it's a harder product to sell. Since it's harder to sell, you need a much more sophisticated sales system, which means a more expensive sale and a more expensive salesperson.

Since a lot of the club's staffing budget has to be dedicated to sales, service suffers. And lousy service, coupled with a tool that has at least a 36-percent loss rate, leads to a lot of missing members who either left because of no help or balked at the long-term, 24-month contract. At this point, the club's income drops on the backend as members disappear, there is no multiple profit center income, and the owners do the only thing they usually know how to do: pressure the sales staff to write more gross.

Salespeople working in an old-style system selling two-year contracts have a stinky job. Cold calling people who are eating dinner at their homes and trying to set appointments out of lead boxes always make for a good time at the gym job. And don't forget harassing members for the names of their buddies or slamming people foolish enough to actually walk in because the salesperson has to make quota or lose their job.

These are all part of a typical day in a high-pressure sales-driven system that leads, in the short run, to very highly paid employees. Those who do manage to temporarily survive in this pressure earn pretty big money for this industry, often $4,000 to $5,000 or more a month. This is good for them, but bad for the club, since a simpler system could have led to lower-cost employees and a lower cost per sale.

You still need to sell, but you also need to create a system that only needs one strong sales trainer and that functions on a much simpler basis with fewer old salesdog-types of people.

Your first hint that you have old salesdogs on your staff is when your top three salespeople used to sell used cars, door-to-door life insurance and worked as cold callers for long distance phone services.

What causes so much pressure in this type of system? No one has ever really stepped back and looked at the system itself. The owners provide more sales training, more marketing, more lead boxes and more pressure on the salespeople, but no one looks at the 24-month contract as the culprit.

The 24-month contract simply can't be collected, which causes all of the other problems that then follow. Look at the actual yield after losses and you can see where the problem begins. For example:

$20 x 24 months = $480 in gross contract sales
to be collected over two years
$480 x .64 percent (36 percent annual loss rate) = $307.20

The club can expect a yield of about $307 from a $480 contract. This is before club cancellations, cost of collection or the effect of free services.

> **And lousy service, coupled with a tool that has at least a 36-percent loss rate, leads to a lot of missing members who either left because of no help or balked at the long-term, 24-month contract.**

The insurmountable problem with this amount is that the money arrives over two years, or another way to look at it is that the $20 payment becomes $12.80.

Another side problem with 24-month contracts is the time the losses occur. The losses are not spread out over the full two-year period but happen disproportionately during the first month, third month and again around the sixth month.

Buyer's regret, where the consumer has severe second thoughts about the purchase they just made, happens frequently at the one-month point. The person just starts working out, is not yet in a routine, and then misses a few workouts. The person also realizes that they are not going to get any real service from a sales-driven club. In fact, they've been there a month and no one even knows their name.

Then, while they are reading their bank statement and notice the payment was taken out, they realize there are still 23 more payments to be made on that impulse contract they felt forced into from a high-pressure salesperson. This is the type of person that defaults on that contract early and may not even make that first payment at all.

At the third month, a person that defaults might be one who comes into the club expecting to change themselves in a short period of time. Around the third month, reality hits. Working out is not an overnight commitment, and getting in shape will take a long time. A sales-driven club focusing on 24-month contracts adds to the member's frustration because some service and direction, that might have led to some results, would have kept the person motivated and in the system.

In the person's mind, they still have two years left on that membership, which can be overwhelming, and they walk away from the membership. The same people, coming to the same realization, will often pay a 12-month contract to term because there are only eight to nine payments left instead of 20 to 21. Without service, the person may not train, but they are more likely to finish the 12-month commitment instead of the 24-month commitment.

Six months is when the lack of service and the physical plant start to strangle the member. The person may be working out faithfully on their own, but not getting any results because they are just winging it doing an old high school workout or trying to learn from books and magazines. This, coupled with the fact that many sales-driven clubs fail to reinvest in their physical plants because of the ongoing cost of the sales effort, costs clubs members.

Coming in to do your workout and finding four treadmills out of order and the rest in use can wear a member down over a six-month period, and they take it out on the club by defaulting on the contract.

Keep in mind that it's a lot easier for most consumers to walk away from a fitness facility membership than it used to be. Many credit agencies and other credit providers don't recognize a health club contract as a real obligation because of the reputation the high-pressure, sales-driven fitness clubs have given the industry.

Because of the high loss rates and low yields, and because of the actual yield arriving over a two-year period, the 24-month contract is an extremely

Then, while they are reading their bank statement and notice the payment was taken out, they realize there are still 23 more payments to be made on that impulse contract they felt forced into from a high-pressure salesperson.

hard tool to make money with. In the end, it doesn't matter how good your sales force is if your basic membership tool doesn't allow you to collect enough money from enough members.

12-MONTH CONTRACTS

A 12-month contract, with its low loss rates, high rate of collection and appeal to members, is the ideal foundational tool for clubs to use to establish obligation.

As mentioned earlier, a sample club in the Denver, Colo., market was offering a membership at $20 for 24 months, or $480. This membership only yielded the club $307.

Loss rates for 12-month memberships are only about 8 to 12 percent on a national average, again depending on region and how they are sold. Remember, the higher the pressure at the point of sale, the higher the loss rate.

The same club in Denver was offering a $30-per-month 12-month membership, equaling $360, for those potential members who balked at the 24-month commitment. The club and its sales force, though, worked hard to force the 24-month contract onto its potential members, mainly because of the larger gross sale at $480.

But what is the real net result to the club from a 12-month membership? First of all, the gross is obviously smaller at $360 compared to $480. But the final yield is surprisingly strong. For example, let's figure the loss rate at the mid range, or 10 percent, and apply it to the 12-month membership.

$360 x .90 (10 percent loss rate) = $324

The club can expect a return of about $324 from every $360 membership it sells. Again, this is before club cancellations, cost of collection or the effect of the free services.

The key here, however, is when the money arrives. In the 24-month example, $307 arrives over a two-year period. In the 12-month membership illustration, $324 arrives over only a 12-month period. Which tool would be more effective to maintain cash flow in a fitness facility? A membership that supplies $307 of income over 24 months or one that supplies $324 over 12 months?

This should be an easy choice but it goes against all human, and salespeople's, nature to believe that the smaller gross gives a higher yield for the business.

A WORKING MEMBERSHIP CONCEPT

If the 12-month contract is the ideal tool, it should be the foundation of your membership system. But first, let's consider a major mistake most owners make when it comes to creating a membership structure: too many choices.

A typical club might have a one-week, one-month, three-month, six-

Which tool would be more effective to maintain cash flow in a fitness facility? A membership that supplies $307 of income over 24 months or one that supplies $324 over 12 months?

month and 12-month membership. Of course, these are the monthly payment memberships. If you want to pay cash, add one month to the one-month membership, three months to the three-month, six to the six-month and so on.

Oh, we forget to mention that if you're a policeman or a fireman you get 20 percent off any membership. If you're a teacher take off 10 percent. If you work for Company A, we have a special membership set up where you only pay every other Wednesday on off months only! And don't forget....

Get the idea? Most clubs have way too many membership choices. Research over the years by ad folks and others who study consumer-buying habits shows that the consumer only needs and wants two choices or their little heads shut down. Compare this information to clubs that have multiple-page membership options.

Keeping two choices as a key parameter, a suggested membership structure might look like this:

A $65 one-time membership — $39 a month x 12 months

This is the monthly if the member elects to take EFT. If the member wishes to write a check, the club would simply add $5 to the monthly payment, or it would go from $39 to $44 for those not opting for EFT. The member has to have, however, the final choice when it comes to choosing for how they pay for their membership.

Before we discuss the one-time membership fee and its importance, consider the following chart and the relationships of the monthly prices to the other clubs in the area. If you're the only club in your market, don't tell anyone where you're at, but the rules still apply:

Our club	Price strategy	The competition
$29	Beat price	
$35	Meet price	$35
$39	Beat quality	

In the consumer's head, the relationship between your price and the competitor's price is important. Pricing is part of your marketing and part of your club's image in the marketplace.

In the above chart, most clubs would price their membership below the competitors by a few dollars a month hoping they would look like a better deal. But again, we are selling a service and the consumer knows that the best service is not the cheapest service. In fact, it usually works just the opposite. How much service can a club provide if it's the cheapest in the market?

Price is the deciding factor for a certain segment. But there is an equal or greater number that is more concerned about service and perceived value, something the low-price guys can never demonstrate.

Pricing the facility the same as the competitor prices theirs sends a message to the consumer that the businesses are the same. Your club may be

Price is the deciding factor for a certain segment. But there is an equal or greater number that is more concerned about service and perceived value, something the low-price guys can never demonstrate.

cleaner, have better service and be better equipped, but that's hard to prove in a typical 30-minute sales presentation. Price is not the deciding factor for many people, but when memberships are sold based on price, members are forced into that niche.

Pricing memberships higher than a competitor, by at least $4 per month and by as much as $20 or more for a mature club, makes a statement to the consumer that this club is different in quality and service. The consumer says, "This club is $10 more per month than the other clubs I've looked at. It must therefore be better because it costs more." Very few consumers really believe that cheaper is better for almost any product or service. It makes sense, then, to price the facility slightly higher than a comparable competitor because of the quality image.

THE ONE-TIME MEMBERSHIP FEE

The one-time membership fee is money the club gets in addition to the monthly membership payments. In the membership example above, the club was asking for $65 in addition to 12 payments of $39. That makes the entire gross membership worth $533 to the club before losses and other adjustments.

The membership fee can change throughout the year depending upon seasonal or current market conditions, but the monthly dues have to stay the same or go up. No new member can ever pay less than a member who has joined before they did.

The club does, however, always have to offer at least one membership with a one-time fee of less than $90. Again, studies conducted over the years by people who study consumer buying habits show that any money outlay over $90 becomes a family decision that has to be discussed with significant others. If a person is a non-family person, laying out over $90 often forces the person to stop, go home and think about the decision before the money is spent. Even clubs that cater to an elite clientele should have one of their two choices below $90 as a getting started amount for the member.

Even clubs that cater to an elite clientele should have one of their two choices below $90 as a getting started amount for the member.

The membership fee is important to the club because most of the labor and administrative costs a club incurs for a new member happen during the first 30 days of membership. Sales commissions and marketing costs should also be somewhat defrayed by the membership fee.

Another important consideration we've discovered over the years is that a great majority of members make the decision to pay their memberships to term and eventually renew during their first 30 days as a member. Therefore, the member has to experience the best service possible, with the best staff and training support, during the first 30 days. This costs money — money that should be delivered in the form of a membership fee.

Another factor connected to the membership fee is that members are more likely to continue paying for their membership if they have to make an initial investment. In the case of a 12-month membership at $40 per month, or $480, the member should put down a minimum of 10 percent or $48 as a membership fee. This lowers the loss rate and increases how collectable the contract will be.

A SAMPLE MEMBERSHIP STRUCTURE BASED ON A 12-MONTH CONTRACT

A sample membership structure would look something like this:

A $65 membership fee----$39 a month EFT x 12 months
Or a $65 membership fee----$44 a month for a
check/coupon system x 12 months

These represent the options the member would receive when the prices are given during the tour. Remember, the simpler the system, the less sophisticated the sales staff has to be and the less expensive the cost per sale.

The following short-term membership option could also be used for potential members passing through the area, or for people who just want a short-term membership. This is usually presented and sold only by permission of the manager on duty or by the owner. The short-term option is not presented as part of the normal sales presentation unless the member requests it or says they are not a local resident but someone just in the area for a short period of time.

A three-month membership presented at $179

There is no financing available for this option. The $179 is also in relation to the example above that has a monthly payment of $39. When the short-term membership is taken times four, or $179 x 4, it should be substantially more than paying the regular membership.

THE DAILY OPTION

Every club should offer a daily drop-in option, but many clubs make a mistake by pricing the daily fee too low. A drop-in single workout should be in the $8 to $20 range depending on the region, whether the club is in a resort area with high peaks of usage through the year, or whether it is in a highly transient area such as a club near hotels.

One option for resort clubs is to offer a punch pass rather than a one-week or one-month membership. A punch pass usually generates much more revenue for the club than a short-term membership.

For example, a club with a $10 drop-in fee might sell a 10-workout punch pass for $80. The club still gets $8 per workout, the member thinks they are getting a deal because they saved $20 off of the regular drop-in fee, and the club is not giving up unlimited usage for a fixed fee.

Everything in the sample structure is designed to minimize the loss rate and to increase the yield. Other options, such as family and corporate memberships, will be discussed later in this section.

Every club should offer a daily drop-in option, but many clubs make a mistake by pricing the daily fee too low.

Club cancellations and the effect on yield

Loss rates can cost a club about 1 to 4 percent of its membership each month depending on the tool used. A scary concept is that many clubs give away another 1 to 4 percent on top of the loss rates because they don't have a strong, consistent policy in place to handle cancellations.

Cancellations affect your total outstanding receivables base, like loss rates, but are categorized differently. Loss rates are usually the member's decision not to pay. There is an obligation but the member breaks it by ignoring the contract. Cancellations are decisions made by the club to let a member out of a contract.

Some are valid, such as moving more than 25 miles away from the club. Most are not valid and could be saved, except that the club chooses to let the member out of the valid contract anyway. For example, a member tells the manager that she is losing her job and doesn't want to pay anymore. The manager believes her story and cancels the contracts. Legally, the club has no obligation to cancel this agreement. This is lost money that the club should have collected but didn't because of no set policy to handle these situations.

Most states have specific laws that dictate how clubs are supposed to deal with members who sign contracts and then try to get out of them. How clubs choose to vary from these laws in favor of the members is where the problem occurs. For example, the law that states the club has to cancel a member that moves more than 25 miles from the club is pretty standard around the country. This is a fair law for both the member and the club. But how this law is enforced is the issue.

If a member walks in and says she has accepted a job in the next town, and wants to cancel, the manager who knows the member and likes her as a friend simply believes the story. The contract, which the club acquired through a marketing, sales and administrative expense, is cancelled and becomes a loss for the club. Should the manager cancel in this case? Yes, if the member verifies the move. The mistake the manager made is not having a strict, and verifiable, policy in place. The manager should have said, "Yes, we'll cancel, but please send us a copy of a utility bill with your name and new address on it first. When we receive that we'll be happy to cancel you immediately."

Cancellation losses usually mean that the club simply lets business it paid for disappear either because the manager is too nice, there is no formal club policy or the management doesn't want to be the bad guys because they unreasonably fear bad word-of-mouth in their community. No matter the reason, the club is losing money that it should have collected.

To prevent unnecessary losses, set up a strict policy, follow the rules dictated by the state you do business in, and be reluctant to give up business you already paid for.

A good goal for club cancellations, which reflects the normal moving and medical action most clubs encounter, is to try to keep cancellation rates the same as the loss rates for 12-month contracts. Again, this rate is about 8

Loss rates are usually the member's decision not to pay. ... Cancellations are decisions made by the club to let a member out of a contract.

to 12 percent annually, or about 1 percent a month.

This additional loss drives the yield down even further. A 12-percent loss rate, coupled with a 12-percent cancellation rate, means that the club loses 24 percent on every membership dollar it generates, and these numbers are at the end of the scales compared with the large majority of clubs around the country. The wrong tool and a manager who can't say no can easily get the club to the 50-cents-on-the-dollar loss mark.

Remember that the owner has the discretion to break the rules. An owner can believe a hard-luck story if they desire, because the loss ultimately is their money. But the rest of the team should have a formalized policy to follow and the exceptions should be handled by the owners or senior manager.

Cost of collection

There is always going to be a cost of collection. It doesn't matter if you're a control freak and try to collect your own memberships, or if you use a third-party service company. There is going to be some amount of collection cost for every dollar of membership revenue.

The real issue is how much you get in return for that dollar. This is where many owners get confused. They only look at what collecting the memberships costs and not what is generated in return for that cost. Your club can write all the memberships in the world, but if you use the wrong tool and have an inefficient collection system, you will eventually fail.

A FEW BASIC COLLECTION RULES

You can't be the good person and the bad person at the same time. In the fitness business, we are in the business of relationships; the members begin to trust us and feel that the club is a mix of their home and their favorite bar or other social hangout.

Once they become regulars, and often friends, they become hard to collect from each month. Some of the members have real financial difficulties we shouldn't become involved in, because it ends up costing us money. Other members try to work us over because they don't want to pay that month. We really don't want to hear that story either because that one also ends up costing us money.

Members associate attendance with payment. Where you collect member payments is almost as important as how you collect. When members pay at the club each month, they start to associate attendance with payment. Associating attendance with payment means that if the member works out that month they feel an obligation to pay. If they stayed away from the club, however, they don't feel they have to pay, even if they have a contract.

More money will be collected in the long run if the member's regular payments are handled outside the club. The only payments that should be

> **Your club can write all the memberships in the world, but if you use the wrong tool and have an inefficient collection system, you will eventually fail.**

collected in the club are the ones from problem members. Most clubs would collect more money if they would stay out of the collection process and let their third-party company handle the regular payment. The club should only be involved in the collection process if the member is severely past due, usually in the 75- to 90-day range.

THREE METHODS OF COLLECTING MEMBERSHIP MONEY

Doing it yourself. Most owners try collecting membership money themselves at one time or another, but this method of collection has many problems that make it a poor option for most clubs.

First of all, you can manage more than you can do yourself. Control freaks love to collect their own memberships because they have a stronger illusion of control. But one person can only do and control so much. As with accounting and legal issues, you're better off to farm out these processes and then manage them, instead of trying to create all of these systems in-house.

Collecting your own memberships also eliminates the power of a third party, and members do associate attendance with payment. Even if you set up your own image of third-party collection, you're still collecting your own paper and the members do figure out that it's still you.

There is also no cost effectiveness when it comes to collecting your own memberships. The club incurs costs whether the membership is collected or not. You can pay a lot to set up your own collection system and still not really collect that large a percentage of the outstanding receivables base.

This system is also very vulnerable to employee instability. If your entire receivables base is entrusted to one or two employees and something happens to those employees, the club is at risk because the receivables base is the most valuable asset the club owns.

For example, in the last four years we have tried to salvage five clubs that have been hit by embezzlement or by the death of the primary person running the collection effort. The clubs were simply trusting too big of an asset to too few people.

Using an outside processor. Processors are companies that specialize in the simple processing of EFT accounts. If the accounts are clean, meaning everyone pays and no one moves or closes an account, then these companies can do a fair job. If the member accounts have any problems, they are sent back to the clubs to be handled. Processors mean just that: they process accounts but provide no collection effort whatsoever.

There are several problems with this that affect the receivables base and, ultimately, the yield. First of all, losses are too big too soon. This means that many of these accounts that are kicked out of a processor's system and returned to the club could have been saved, but these clubs are usually not set up to handle member account problems. The club tries a few simple phone calls, saves an account or two, and then sends the rest to a full-blown collection company that charges 33 to 50 percent of what it collects.

If there had been a real collection effort earlier in the process, many of

If your entire receivables base is entrusted to one or two employees and something happens to those employees, the club is at risk because the receivables base is the most valuable asset the club owns.

these accounts could have been saved at a more reasonable cost. Keep in mind that we are selling future service paper and not tangible assets. It takes a more sophisticated and strategic collection effort to handle future service contracts. Processors provide no collection effort at all, and the club usually does not have anyone trained in the consistent collection of memberships on their staff.

Another problem with using processors is that collection problems are not handled quickly enough by either the processor when the problems first occur, or by the club when the contract is returned. Speed is of the essence when it comes to solving collection problems, and this system doesn't allow this.

There are also many false and unnecessary costs when it comes to using a processor. The processing companies charge when they collect, as they should, and also when they don't collect, which they shouldn't. They get paid whether they get your money or not, which reduces the overall yield from the receivables base.

Third-party financial service companies. While there are only a few really legitimate third-party financial service companies in the industry, this is the best option for the majority of the clubs to use.

Using a third-party company means that you pay someone else to service and collect your membership contracts. It also means that you don't incur any cost unless the member's money is collected.

Many of our members in the fitness business are in their 20s and 30s. It's not unusual for these folks to spend just as much as they make each month, if not more, by using credit cards and short-term debt. A strong third-party financial company brings the illusion of power to the game and trains many of our younger and more leveraged clients to become good, regular payers.

Using a third-party company also separates the good guys, which are us, from the "bad guys," which are those people who actually collect bills in our name. This allows the club to maintain its relationship with its members who were so hard to build in the first place.

This doesn't mean that the club has to abuse and ignore members who don't pay. A combined effort by the third-party company and by the club, which only happens when chasing those severely past due members, should produce a higher return per member when it comes to the yield.

A final point about the use of third-party financial service companies is that it allows for verification of a club's receivables base. If an owner wants to borrow money from a bank, or sell or buy a club, the most important asset to be considered is the existing receivables base. Used equipment is only worth so much, and claiming to have a certain number of members means nothing unless they are individually represented by a part of the receivables base.

If the club is collecting its own paper, it's almost impossible to verify the authenticity of the numbers. The obvious method would be to tie the receivables base to bank deposits, but a few unethical owners in the past have been known to pad deposits prior to the sale to drive up the price. Without

A strong third-party financial company brings the illusion of power to the game and trains many of our younger and more leveraged clients to become good, regular payers.

complete member-by-member audit, you could never completely verify a receivables base collected at the club: there are simply too many ways to fake the numbers. If a legitimate third-party company holds the receivables, the verification of the asset is much easier and much more reliable.

A working average for collection cost should be about 7 percent of what's collected. Keep in mind that you can find a way to do collections for less, but what do you get for that cost? Again, it's not the cost but what you can get in return.

Where is the yield at this point?

So far in our examples, the yield from a member payment has been reduced by loss rate, a cancellation rate and by the cost of collection. For example:

The member payment	$40.00
10 percent loss rate	–$4.00
	$36.00
–10 percent cancellation rate	–$3.60
	$32.40
–7 percent cost of collection	–$2.26
A final yield of	$30.14

The final factor — giving away everything in the name of member service.

Member service is not usually defined as giving away a lot of stuff for free.

Member service is not usually defined as giving away a lot of stuff for free. But many owners confuse the giving away of services with providing member service. Coffee is a good example. Many clubs have gotten into the habit over the years of giving away free coffee to the morning members.

Is member service giving away free coffee? Or is having two kinds of a high-quality, fresh coffee for sale in oversized cups with sippy lids member service? Is it the cheap, free coffee, or the availability of a high-quality fresh product that sets the club apart from the competition and provides what the members really want. Yes, there is that one member moron who'll leave because they didn't get that free cup of cheap, tasteless coffee. So send them to the competition, and let them drink their free swill and reduce their yield.

Another example is childcare. The average 15,000-square-foot fitness facility with 2,000 members will lose about $1,200 to $1,500 a month on childcare. Why? Because the common belief in the industry is that you have to have childcare and it has to be cheap. And because the club down the street gives it away for free, we think we have to do the same. They lose money because they have a bad business plan; therefore, we lose money because we copy the same bad plan.

Is member service childcare in a small cramped room for free? Or is it a larger, better decorated room with a better-trained childcare provider that's offered at a reasonable price? Would parents prefer free, but low-quality childcare, or good, high-quality at a reasonable price?

Member service doesn't have to always be free or cheap, and we definitely don't have to lose money just because the competition is stupid enough to lose money.

The problem with the coffee, childcare and other free services, such as towel service, is that it lowers the yield. For example, if your free childcare program costs $2,000 per month to run, and if your club has 2,000 members making payments each month, you've lowered the yield by a dollar per member. Throw in two or three other free services and the yield drops even more substantially.

Starting with the yield example we illustrated above, we're working with $30.14 out of a payment of $40 before subtracting free stuff. The adjusted example is:

> After loss rate, cancellation rate and cost of collection the yield is $30.14
> −$2 per member for a club offering childcare,
> towel service and free coffee   −$2.00
> The adjusted yield is $28.14

The yield, or the money the club really has to work with out of the member's $40 payment, is only $28.14 per member each month.

In other words, owners need to learn to charge for or eliminate these services and amenities. With the increased cost of doing business in today's market, we can't afford to give these things away free. Even free coffee, which used to be so cheap, now can cost a club with 1,500 members $700 to $800 per month. Another way to look at this is $800 equals 20 $40 member payments before yield adjustments, and 28 member payments after the yield adjustments are applied. This also doesn't count the sales and ad costs to sell these memberships.

Other factors that affect the yield

Corporate rates, family discounts, student rates and other specials that lower the membership payment, and therefore the yield, are beginning to fade from the industry.

Where in the real world do you get half off for a second member of the family? "Hello, dinner for two please and can I get my significant other half off please?" Most restaurants worth eating at would laugh in your face and then toss you on the street just for asking.

Corporate memberships are also starting to lose popularity. Except for a few notable exceptions, most clubs don't do well selling corporate memberships. The clubs have to dedicate too much money and too many of its resources to reach companies that want discounts that are far too great. Some clubs still do well with corporate memberships, but would they get the same members anyway at full price if the club was the convenient option in the neighborhood?

So what's the trend? It's away from offering so many discounts and specialized memberships that lower the return per member. A few pioneering clubs are actually giving no discounts to second members of the family and

"Hello, dinner for two please and can I get my significant other half off please?"

no corporate rates. Everyone pays full price for their membership, the same that the other members in the club paid. These club owners are feeling that it's better to make more money from fewer members than it is to discount everything for the sake of having a larger membership number.

There is a compromise position, however, for those owners who can't break away from the discounting tradition. For example:

The club has a $65 membership fee and $39-per-month payments for 12 months.

Subtract $5 per month from the monthly payment if the member pays EFT as in the example, for the second member of the family, corporate memberships, senior memberships, full-time student memberships and any others you feel qualify for a discount. It would also not hurt the cash flow too much to offer a small discount on the membership fee in this example too, say in the 20-percent range. If the member didn't elect to use EFT and is paying $44 each month by check, subtract the $5 from that rate.

Some clubs in rural markets, however, may be forced to offer a flat family membership. A family membership should have a membership fee of no more than $90, and the monthly payment, no matter how many kids in the family, should stay under $100. If a family had four kids, they've probably already suffered enough. Don't add to their financial misery by charging more than $100 per month in payments.

A family membership should have a membership fee of no more than $90, and the monthly payment, no matter how many kids in the family, should stay under $100.

Summary

Profitability is the desired goal in business. In the fitness business, the ability to make a profit is often determined by the choices that the owner makes when it comes to putting together the club's financial foundation.

The profit goal for most fitness businesses is to net 20 percent. Most clubs can never achieve this, because the tools the owner chooses for charging and collecting from the members, prevent this net from happening. If the owner picks the wrong tool, 24-month contracts for example, then the receivables base is weakened, which affects the final yield the club can expect from a member payment.

The yield is what the club has left over from a member payment. The club may sign members up for a $40 payment, but that doesn't mean the club has $40 to work with when the member pays. The actual yield may be less than $30 in many cases.

The yield from a payment is affected by loss rates, cancellation rates, cost of collection and the club's adherence to 30-year-old out-of-date practices, such as offering losing programs because the competition does. All these lower the yield in some manner.

The owner's goal, therefore, should be to make choices in the business that strengthen the receivables base and increase the yield. A simple choice such as using a strong third-party collector, rather than collecting your own memberships, can affect the yield from a payment by as much as $5 or more, or $60 or more per member on an annual basis.

The choices an owner makes when it comes to charging the members also affects the entire way the club will be operated. For example, an owner who uses a complicated, low-yield system will normally end up with a sales-driven club that spends most of its time and resources chasing endless new sales. Clubs that use efficient and simple systems can have a lower cost per sale and put more money into the service end of the business. This allows the owner to concentrate on renewals, which decreases the dependence on new sales.

Things you can do to use this material:

1) Always start with the financial foundation when you start a new business, or try to restructure an existing one. How you charge and how you collect from your members is a major factor in determining how profitable your business will ultimately be.

2) If you're in an existing club, analyze the receivables base and determine the relationship between the BOE (base operating expense) and the monthly receivables check. Your goal is to achieve 70-percent coverage of the BOE from the monthly payments you receive from members.

3) Base your membership structure on the 12-month membership commitment. These memberships have the lowest loss rate, highest yield and lowest cost per membership in sales cost.

4) Design your membership structure to be simple. In a mature club, the number of memberships grows as the club gets older. Every year, sit down and look at the offerings and try to get the structure down to its simplest form. Two choices are optimum for most clubs.

5) Be sure to offer at least one of your memberships with a $90 or less membership fee. Even a $99 one-time membership fee limits membership compared to $90.

6) Design your club to give the maximum service you can afford during the member's first 30 days. Your loss rates will be lower and your renewal rates higher if the member starts off their membership understanding how the club works, being comfortable with their workout, and knowing the staff and some of the other members.

7) Learn to manage rather than trying to do everything yourself. Most fitness owners are entrepreneurs, which is another word for doing everything yourself. You can manage more than you can do, and your business will never reach its true potential unless you learn this rule. The decision here is whether you should collect your own memberships. You could create a system to do this, but why not farm this service out so you can concentrate your efforts on managing and growing your business?

8) Figure the yield on your member payments on a quarterly basis. The goal is to increase the yield, which also strengthens the receivables base. A low yield is the sign of a weak and deteriorating receivables base.

Clubs that use efficient and simple systems can have a lower cost per sale and put more money into the service end of the business.

We do a lot of things out of habit in this business that don't really make the club any money.

9) If you can't net at least 20 percent on each program in your business, then eliminate them. We do a lot of things out of habit in this business that don't really make the club any money. Analyze all of your club offerings, such as childcare, towel service, juice bar and any other component that is an expense to the business. Do this on a monthly basis by simply looking at the cost of the program and the revenue it generates. If you want to net 20 percent overall in your business, then every part of the business has to do at least 20 percent. Eliminate the losers, and don't worry about the competition offering that program for free. Just because they're losing money doesn't mean we have to do the same thing.

LESSONS FROM LIFE — #7

You can't teach an old dog new tricks

THERE WAS A FITNESS DIRECTOR in a club in Colorado who was about 40 years old. She had been teaching aerobics for 15 years and was also a certified trainer. Somewhere, at some stage in her life, time stopped for her. She got to a certain point and then just failed to learn anymore about the fitness business.

Her aerobic classes dropped to just two or three people each but she refused to change her classes or even consider eliminating the program. She felt that what she offered was what the members needed. It didn't matter to her that what was being offered was not what they wanted, so they just didn't participate.

She was also faced with personal training clients who wanted advice on supplements. This fitness director had been taught years ago that you didn't need supplements if you ate a balanced meal. Most trainers today believe that even if you train hard, you might need some supplements. Her clients wanted supplements and ended up taking them, based on the advice they received from a trainer at another club where they later became members.

Her personal biases, that were based on information 15 years

Her aerobic classes dropped to just two or three people each but she refused to change her classes or even consider eliminating the program

old, hurt the club's business because she gave the members what she thought they needed instead of trying to change and give them what they wanted.

The moral of the story

It's not what *you* want that makes the club money; it's learning to give the members what *they* want.

The fitness industry is in a constant state of change with its offerings and knowledge base. For example, it wasn't too many years ago that the accepted training system was set until you failed and then moved on to the next machine. And don't forget the bodybuilders who used to train by eating nothing but massive chunks of beef and who were terrified at the thought of eating carbs.

Member service is learning to give the members current offerings and knowing when to drop the old programs that lose money. Member service is also having an educated and up-to-date staff that can adapt to changes in industry philosophy and information.

8

But getting cash from the members seems like so much fun!

GOING FOR CASH, meaning having members pay for their membership in full up front, is not only an old tradition in the fitness industry, but also part of the lore from the early days when everything was freestyle and easy.

In the '60s and '70s, it wasn't unusual for the club to receive the large majority of its membership money in cash. Remember this was when cash was cash, not checks or credit cards.

A gathering of gym managers and owners was a very odd sight in those early days. Most of the public still wasn't used to people in workout clothes, tight-fitting golf shirts or any other clothing that accented bodies out of the norm in that time period. Big arms, big chests, narrow waists and bulging necks were out of most folks understanding, and to see eight or nine guys at one table in shape and dressed in odd clothes was often startling to the public.

The oddest part of the gatherings, though, was the gym bags. You might see a big group of owners, regional people and the local managers all together for lunch and everyone who was anyone had a gym bag placed between their feet under the table. Imagine a group of the first professionals in the fitness business, decked out in golf shirts and short-sleeved shirts and ties, all eating monster lunches. This group could always gather attention because they were young, buff and usually extremely outgoing. Everyone thought these guys were fitness fanatics, because no matter where they went, they all carried gym bags.

These silly, naive people were wrong. The gym bags contained the cash they skimmed from the business. There was a lot of money in the industry in

These silly, naive people were wrong. The gym bags contained the cash they skimmed from the business.

those days and most owners lived large in life. Showy cars, trips to Las Vegas, flashy female companions and a whole lot of gold: all part of doing business for many of the predominantly male owners in that era.

But maintaining this lifestyle required a lot of cash. Not credit cards. Not checks. Just plain, simple cash. Amazingly enough, this cash was always handy in the gym bags just under the table, locked in the trunk or behind the seat.

A classic story from those early days involved a group of regional managers, local managers and the owner from a large chain in the northeast. This group had put together a great quarter of business and everyone celebrated with a trip to Las Vegas. The group checked into Caesar's Palace, got drunk and started a fireworks fight in their grand suite. Security came, assessed the damages and started to throw everyone out of the hotel. The damages were allegedly $35,000, a lot of money in the early '70s. The group pulled out the gym bags, gave the hotel cash for the destruction and finished the weekend as planned.

Amazingly enough, this cash was always handy in the gym bags just under the table, locked in the trunk or behind the seat.

Cash was the logical choice for owners in the early days

Cash made sense in those days for the owners. Collection systems were still in their infancy which made collecting from the members somewhat difficult. You could write a lot of contracts, but getting paid was another story altogether. Getting cash up front solved this problem, and collections from the members were nothing to worry about.

Cash was also worth more to the owner in the early days of the industry. Many spas and early fitness facilities in the late '60s charged the exact same monthly membership price, about $24 a month, as a lot of clubs do today. But it costs the average club today 800 to 1,200 percent more a month to operate than it did in the late '60s and early '70s. It's like having your current memberships and a facility that cost $12,000 a month to run, instead of the $50,000 you really are paying. If you had cash in those early days, you had a lot of buying power at your disposal.

The best reason of all to get a bunch of cash in those days, however, was that you could steal it from your own business. Another word for this was "skim." Cash comes into the business, but disappears before it can ever be deposited.

Because of the buying power and the attitude of the IRS in those days, taking the cash made perfect business sense, if not to the IRS, at least to the owners. There weren't really enough valid deductions available to the owners at tax time to overcome the extreme profits that were possible. Money came so quick and easy to so many guys who weren't real business people, that going legitimate just wasn't an option to most owners. Couple this with the fact that most of these owners learned the business from another non-business person who had the job before them, and ended up with no choice but to skim. It was in your blood by the time you became an owner.

Once you had the cash, you could spend it somewhat freely without the fear of being caught by the IRS. Skimming cash meant avoiding taxes and not worrying about getting caught.

In today's business climate, skimming doesn't make sense, although there are many owners still in business from the old days who can't break the cash habit. An aggressive accountant can keep your tax burden down, and investing clean money will yield a far better return than cash buried in a lock box in your garage floor. It's not as much fun as cash in a box, but it does make more business sense.

It's also hard to spend cash today, except on minor purchases or as walking-around money. Any large deposits or purchases, usually in the $5,000 range, can be reported to the IRS. The days of whipping $10,000 out of a workout bag for a car are long, long gone.

Another factor that changes how an owner should view cash is that there is very little actual cash anymore. Cash has been replaced by credit cards, checks and debits. If a member pays in full for a membership today, you will get only about one in 10 members who actually give you cash.

The exception to this rule is when the cash price of a membership falls below $300. You receive more cash when the price is below $300, but the return per member drops so low it isn't worth it, although many of the less sophisticated owners coming into the business still keep trying.

Keep in mind that a good base rule to work with is that most clubs have to get between $39 to 59 per month per member to net 20 percent. This isn't an absolute rule, but it's a good guideline for most club owners to start with — when it comes to putting together their financial plan.

The who that charge $149 a year get almost all cash. It's important for these guys to get cash because $149 a year is a going-out-of-business sale. The cash they take in is what they use to pay for the U-Haul they use to get out of town before the members they sold yesterday find out they're leaving.

It's important for these guys to get cash because $149 a year is a going-out-of-business sale.

Cash discounting lowers the return per member and the yield

The big issue problem with getting paid in full up front for a membership is that the owner usually gave the member a discount to get the sale. Discounting for cash lowers the return per member, which ultimately drives down the yield because of the reduction in the average payment.

For example, if your monthly payment is $40 and you use 12-month memberships, your annual membership is $480. Your average monthly payment is also $40 if you're not offering any other discounts, i.e. a second member of the family at $30 would lower the average.

If you discount for cash and sell a prepaid annual membership for $360, your average payment is now $30 a month. If you sold half your memberships at $40 a month and half in prepaid memberships, your average monthly would drop to $35, which substantially drops the yield. For more information on yield, please refer to the preceding chapter.

But a business can still benefit from a certain amount of cash flow. How much cash is enough and at what price? The goal is to get enough cash to positively affect the business, without lowering the return per member by discounting. The trend of today's more sophisticated business owners is to move away from discounting for cash. You still go for a certain percentage of cash flow from your memberships, but without discounting a paid-in-full.

Discounting is a negative to the consumer, especially if used to pressure a member into making an immediate buying decision. The member may be happy that they negotiated a discount but, when they leave, the doubts begin. "Could I have held out for more?" "Does everyone get this much of a break?" "What would have happened if I wouldn't have asked? Would I have been a sucker and paid full price?" These are all questions raised in the member's mind, undermining the long-term integrity of the club and eventually negatively affecting the club's business performance.

Memberships were originally discounted by the cost of collection a club would incur to collect an annual membership and by an amount adjusted for expected losses. For example, a $480 membership might be discounted 20 percent to compensate for collection costs and losses. The 20-percent discount, which is $76, would leave $404, or the amount the owner would hope to yield from that membership anyway.

The preferred method is to not discount the membership, but still go for a few paid-in-full memberships at point-of-sale. To do this, clubs offer the annual membership and the cash membership at the same price. If the member pays cash, however, they get additional time added to the membership along with other small incentives.

For example, a club might offer a $40-a-month membership for 12 months, with a $65 membership fee. This equals $480 plus $65, or $545. The member can elect to pay $65 to get started, and then $40 a month for 12 months. If the member wants to pay cash, or the $545, they get an additional month added to the 12 and a gift certificate worth $25 for the club's pro shop.

This also solves the integrity problem for the club. Each member pays the same $545 for their membership. The ones who pay cash get a little more for their money, but the total amount of money is the same as the other guy is paying.

When you discount, you have two members paying different prices for the same membership. It makes sense to the club to discount to save the costs, but it's very hard to explain the difference in price to a member who paid more today than someone who paid cash yesterday.

Positive incentives for cash also keep the return per member and the yield higher, which is better for the overall strength of the business. You're still getting a certain percentage of cash, but you're getting it at a higher rate.

The rule of thumb for cash is 90:10

So how much cash is enough? Follow the 90:10 rule for cash. If a club

It makes sense to the club to discount to save the costs, but it's very hard to explain the difference in price to a member who paid more today than someone who paid cash yesterday.

signs up 100 new members, 90 should choose paying monthly which adds to the receivable base, and 10 should choose cash. Again, this is full price cash and not discounted.

This rule is also a good indicator of how your pricing is set in relationship to the marketplace. If too many people pay for their memberships in full up front, either your discount is too big or your prices are too cheap for your market. In other words, it's too easy to pay it all at once, therefore it must be too cheap. Check the 90:10 rule monthly to keep your cash stream intact and yet still build your receivables base.

The 90:10 rule is also good for building a business plan for either a new or existing fitness business. To project cash for the business, figure about one out of 10 members paying in full for their annual membership and keep the cash price the same as the annual.

Many clubs get stuck on being too dependent on cash, which is hard to break away from when you're ready to make a change to increase the stability of the business. If you're discounting big to get cash, and then use the cash each month to pay the bills, it's hard to switch to a membership system that builds a long-term receivables base.

It will take most clubs at least a year to switch from a cash dependency to a 90:10 mix of receivable memberships and cash. The key is to make the transition slowly, so the club doesn't suffer financially from an immediate loss of cash flow.

For example, look at the following club and its current cash flow position:

> Club A is a basic workout club, has no amenities, no service except a counter person and is two years old. The club is 10,000 square feet. The basic monthly operating expense for the club is $35,000, considerably lower than comparable clubs in this size group, but it has fewer employees and very basic equipment consisting of mostly free weights. The main membership the club sells is a $299 annual prepaid. The club also sells a six-month membership for $180, a three-month for $99, and a monthly membership for $50. There is a small pro shop in the club and it also sells workout drinks. The club has developed a small receivables base over the two years and currently has 200 members paying $20 per month on an annual membership.

The club's income (monthly)

New annual paid-in-full	30 x $299	= $8,970
Receivables income	200 x $20	= $4,000
New six-month members	10 x $180	= $1,800
New three-month members	20 x $99	= $1,980
One-month members (ongoing basis)	150 x $50	= $7,500
Renewal income (monthly income from ongoing members except for monthly members) 75 members paying a combined total of		$10,000
Profit center income		= $3,000
Club's total income		= $37,250

> If too many people pay for their memberships in full up front, either your discount is too big or your prices are too cheap for your market.

The club claims 900 to 1,000 members, but realistically only has about 600 to 700 paying at any one time. The club also averages about 70 new members a month in some combination of one-month, three-month, six-month, and annual memberships.

This would be a typical average for a cash-dependent club. In the heavy selling months the club could do better; in the slower months it might do a lot worse. The average would be to break even.

Also note that the monthly operating expense has probably been stripped down to match the cash flow. Service staff and even the sales force would be cut to keep the club afloat. These types of clubs ultimately fail, because there is never enough income in the third and fourth years to reinvest and keep the club competitive in the market.

These [cash-dependent] clubs ultimately fail, because there is never enough income in the third and fourth years to reinvest and keep the club competitive in the market.

A transition strategy

First of all, don't punish the existing members. A workout strategy to get away from the cash dependency should be directed at the new members. The existing members should be given some gentle options to guide them to a more optimal payment position, but the brunt of the change should be aimed at the new members.

THE PRICING STRATEGY FOR NEW MEMBERS

Paid-in-full annual memberships	=	$329
Receivable memberships would be offered with a $45		
membership fee and $29 per month for 12 months	=	$393
A three-month cash membership would be offered	=	$129

The one-month and six-month memberships would be dropped.

THE PRICING STRATEGY FOR EXISTING MEMBERS

The goal is to steer as many members as possible toward 12-month contracts. The strategy is to give them an option to keep paying by their current method, or they would have 60 days to switch to a 12-month membership. The 12-month membership would offer a savings for the member and an advantage for the club, because it helps to start developing a stronger receivables base.

All existing annual members may lock into a 12-month contract, pay no membership fee, and be guaranteed the monthly rate forever, as long as they renew within 30 days of expiration. This would have a membership of $0 and monthly payments of $26 for 12 months = $312.

THE CLUB'S REVISED INCOME DURING THE FIRST MONTH OF TRANSITION

New annual paid-in-full memberships	25 x $329 =	$8,225
Existing receivable income	200 x $20 =	$4,000
New three-month members	40 x $129 =	$5,160
One-month members	140 x $50 =	$7,000
Renewal income from existing members		
(40 percent convert to annual memberships)	=	$6,000
New receivable income from existing members paying their first month		
dues. This is a combination of previous one-month members and other		
assorted members from the other memberships	80 x $26 =	$2,080
New income from membership fees of new members	30 x $45 =	$1,350
Profit center income	=	$3,000
Club's total income	=	$36,815

The club should be able to sell more three-month memberships since the one-month is gone. Not everyone who would have bought a one-month will now buy a three-month but a certain percentage will. And although the existing one-month members started to fall off and the renewal income was shifted to the new annual memberships at $26 per month, the club is still generating more income than it did on a strictly cash basis.

The club should continue to grow from this point, due to the steadily rising receivables base that grows each month as member payments start to accumulate and as new sales are added. The revenue from existing monthly members will continue to deteriorate slightly each month as they move or shift to other memberships and since no new monthly people are being added.

The club should run like this for about three months and then raise the price again. The goal is to slowly steer new members away from cash and toward receivable memberships.

The goal is to slowly steer new members away from cash and toward receivable memberships.

The three-month hike

Paid-in-full memberships would increase to $349. The annual receivable membership would increase to a $55 membership fee and the monthly payments would increase to $34 a month for the 12-month period.

The club should then continue to raise the cash price by $10 about every six weeks. As the cash increases each month, a few more new members will elect monthly payments. The club slowly breaks the dependency on money up front by developing the receivables base over a year's time.

At the end of one year, the club could have increased its annual membership to:

A membership fee of $65 and monthly payments
of $39 for 12 months = $533
The prepaid cash price could be raised = $469

Sometime in the next six months, the club should raise the cash price to match the annual monthly membership, thus eliminating the discounting altogether.

Summary

Cash used to be the foundational tool for many of the early owners in the industry. In fact, the old saying used to be, "Cash is king." Cash is no longer king in the industry for many reasons. Cash (memberships that are paid in full up front), is obtained by discounting the membership. This lowers the return per member and the yield the owner receives from that membership.

The ownership in the industry has also changed in the last few years. More and more owners are sophisticated business people who understand that building a strong and dependable receivables base is a far superior business plan to becoming endlessly dependent on cash from the sale of paid-in-full memberships.

The rule of thumb for most owners to follow is the 90:10 rule. This means that 90 out of every 100 members choose to pay their memberships monthly as part of a 12-month membership. The other 10 choose to pay for their membership in full up front by either cash, credit card or check.

While it's not as common in today's market to find clubs totally dependent on cash, it's still a problem that affects the rest of the industry. When these clubs fail, and most do, they're the ones that do the most damage to the image of the industry since they were most likely still selling full paid memberships the day before they closed.

It takes about a year's time for a club totally dependent on cash flow from prepaid memberships to work its way out. This should be done slowly with a set plan. Again, the ultimate goal is to work toward the 90:10 ratio.

Cash flow from the sale of prepaid memberships is still good for the club, if it is obtained without discounting and if the amount is kept within reason. If the club gets too much cash, it's usually a sign that the prices the club has chosen are too cheap for the marketplace.

> **More and more owners are sophisticated business people who understand that building a strong and dependable receivables base is a far superior business plan to becoming endlessly dependent on cash from the sale of paid-in-full memberships.**

Things you can do to use this material

1) Analyze the amount of cash (again meaning prepaid memberships) the club is currently receiving each month. If the percentage of prepaid memberships is higher than the 90:10 rule, see if the discount is too large, compared to the regular receivable membership, or if the overall price is too low and it's too easy for the consumer to pay for the whole thing.

2) If your club is not yet open, estimate the amount of receivable memberships you will sell, compared to the amount of prepaid ones. If your plan is too dependent on the cash flow from too many prepaid memberships, you have a problem that will eventually hurt the long-term future of your club.

3) If you're currently discounting for cash, or are too dependent on paid-in-full memberships, set a one-year plan to decrease this vulnerability.

4) Are your prices too low for the market? Most clubs can raise their prices and not hurt the overall volume of sales.

LESSONS FROM LIFE — #8

When the members run the club

WE ONCE HAD TO FIRE an aerobics director who had been with the club since the current partners took it over several years earlier. The guy who was fired had saved the old program and built it up to be the most successful program in town, attracting members from other clubs. and instructors from all over the area since this program offered the highest pay.

He was fired because he was also one of the most disorganized and unreliable people you could have as an employee. He attracted great instructors and then he would lose all of their paperwork. Once he even scheduled a Saturday training session for the entire aerobics staff, and then forgot about it and left town for the weekend.

Once word spread that he was fired, rumors spread at an outrageous pace throughout the club. The next evening, there were 105 members standing at the desk signing a petition to demand that the club rehire the director or they would all cancel their memberships.

The moral of the story

You can't let the members take over control of the club.

The members were demanding service, but member service ends where bad business begins. In this case, the members wanted to continue a situation that was costing the club its

The next evening, there were 105 members standing at the desk signing a petition to demand that the club rehire the director

image and reputation because the guy who built the program was also starting to kill it.

The owner of the club stood up on a chair, briefly stated why he had made the decision to let the director go without violating the employee's privacy, and then

let the members vent for 30 minutes.

At the end of the 30 minutes, he told the group that he was sorry they weren't happy, but for the sake of the business he had to stick with his decision. If anyone was so unhappy that they wanted to cancel their memberships, he would be in the office and cancel each member personally if they desired.

The club lost three members, but more importantly, the owner hadn't given up control of his club to the members. If he had been a more inexperienced owner, he might have given in and believed such a large number of people would cancel their memberships.

Most members join a club because it's convenient to them. Very few staff people, such as aerobics instructors or personal trainers, have the power to disrupt your club because they are unhappy and then threaten to take a large chunk of your members with them.

9

Short-term debt has killed more fitness businesses than bad breath in salespeople

A FITNESS BUSINESS can only handle a certain amount of short-term debt at any time during the business' development. When short-term debt rises above a defined percentage of a club's monthly base operation expense, the club is in trouble, although it may not realize it.

In the old days, everyone thought the absolute kiss of death was a salesperson with really bad breath. There was just no other way you could hurt a fitness business worse than by having your lead salesperson slam down three slices of garlic pizza and then tour prospective members. The prospect's reaction was always the same: disbelief, shock and then maximum distancing.

As the fitness industry has matured, the newer generation of owners with better business skills has identified and is dealing with a new killer. This killer is not just in the fitness industry; it is common to almost all small business in general. This hideous beast is too much short-term debt — a killer that slowly chokes a small business to death.

A simple definition of short-term debt is garbage debt. This is high-interest, short-term obligation that is easily obtainable by most owners. And, since it is seldom acquired all at one time, it sneaks up on owners over a year or two of normal business.

Equipment leases are a good example of short-term debt. Most equipment leases in the industry are for a three-year period. This is a very aggressive payback at a very high interest rate. Other examples are car leases, credit card debt, short-term bank notes and other borrowed money that has a high interest rate attached with a three-year or less payback.

This hideous beast is too much short-term debt — a killer that slowly chokes a small business to death.

107

High interest and short-term debt hurt the business

The two negatives that most affect an owner are the interest and the payback period. In almost any state of the economy, interest can be defined as high if it is 12 percent or more. It's not unusual for an owner to have two to three leases at 18 percent and higher plus a credit card or two at 18 to 21 percent. Short-term debt is defined as any debt with a payback period of three years or less. Car leases that are run through the business are perfect examples of a three-year, high-interest obligation.

The reason so many owners get buried by so much short-term debt is that the loans and leases are so easy to get and so logical to the owners.

The reason so many owners get buried by so much short-term debt is that the loans and leases are so easy to get and so logical to the owners. Almost any vendor at any trade show can get an owner a quick three-year lease on a pile of equipment. A few papers and a quick pulse check and there you go, new equipment for the gym.

From an owner's viewpoint, these leases make so much sense. Pay them off in just three years and own the equipment free and clear. Suffer a little now and make money on the back end after the equipment payments are over.

The problem with this thinking is that it breaks a basic tenet of owning a small business. There will always be debt. If you want to continue to grow the business, eventually take money out of the business for yourself and stay competitive in the marketplace, you will always have some amount of debt. The key is not the debt itself, but how the debt is managed so that it fits your operational plan yet still allows the business to become stable.

For example, there is a family-owned licensed gym in Florida that is virtually debt free. The owners have an 8,000-square-foot gym with about 1,200 members. The gym's base operating expense is about $40,000 per month, and they deposit around $43,000 to $45,000 on a typical month, and up to $50,000 during a few of the happening business months of the year.

The club is a little over five years old and is a very clean and organized business. It also has 30 pieces of cardio equipment that are completely paid off.

This club will start encountering some severe financial problems during the next few years, especially with the addition of new and brighter competitors, unless the owners rethink their debt-free plan.

The colors are outdated and the physical plant needs quite a bit of upgrading. The cardio works, but it's not cardio anyone wants to use anymore. The members want what's next and what's hot, not eight upright bikes that are at least five years out of style.

The club needs to reinvest, but the owners are living off of the net each month. They've saved about $50,000 over the last three years, but they could reinvest the entire amount and still not bring the club back to a competitive position. Besides, a typical club should have at least one month's BOE in reserve and preferably two months.

The only solution is to get in debt: controlled, managed debt

A rule to follow for planning is that every four years, you have to spend what you spent to build-out the club when you opened. For example, if you spent $25 a foot to build-out an 8,000-square-foot club, or a total of $200,000, you would have to spend another $200,000 during every four-year period to keep the club competitive. The original $25-per-foot build-out didn't include equipment, but the reinvestment money that needs to be spent every four years includes equipment purchases and upgrades.

The fitness business is a lot like the nightclub business. A nightclub may be wildly successful for two years and then fade out as some other place becomes that month's hot spot. When this happens, the owners rip out the old look, give it a new theme and go again. One year it's a heavy metal dance club, and the next year it's a sports bar. The owners simply changed the décor to match the changing needs and wants of the market.

Most fitness owners don't understand this concept. Once the gym is built, it becomes part of the family and there isn't much you can do to get them to make major changes on a regular basis. That's why you see so many pathetically old physical plants and equipment in the industry. It's theirs, it's paid for and they're going to keep it like that forever.

Besides, just last week a prospective member said it's the best club he's ever been in. It may have been the only club or he may have been working out in even a worse dump, but the comment is enough to keep the owners going for another year or two without having to fix up the club. These owners refuse to meet the changing demands and wants of the consumer and eventually the business will suffer because of this attitude.

The vehicle for this change is controlled debt. Controlled debt means there is a balance between short-term and long-term debt and between short-term debt and the monthly base operating expense. The pivotal point in a club's development is the five-year mark. All the original short-term debt should be paid off and the club's first bank loan or investor note should be gone at the end of the fifth year.

> **These owners refuse to meet the changing demands and wants of the consumer and eventually the business will suffer because of this attitude.**

A club can only handle 10 percent of BOE in short-term debt during the first three years

As for short-term debt, the club can handle up to 10 percent of monthly base operating expense during the first three years of operation. For example, if a club has a BOE of $50,000, it can handle up to 10 percent, or $5,000 in monthly principal and interest payments. Remember, short-term debt is defined as equipment leases, credit cards, short-term bank loans, car leases and any other debt that has to be paid off in three years or less.

Anything over 10 percent starts to choke the club due to the high interest, especially from the credit cards, personal bank notes and accelerated payments. Because too much money goes toward interest and accelerated debt reduction, the business is unable to get healthy with money spent on profit center development, keeping the club competitive with equipment, and developing a two-month operating reserve.

After the third year of business, the 10-percent short-term debt ratio should start to decrease. For example, during the first year, the owner buys five treadmills and puts 10 percent down on the lease. At the end of three years, the owner now wants to add four elliptical machines. But this time, the owner puts 30 percent down and has a much smaller monthly payment than the old treadmill payment. Therefore, the owner has reduced the short-term debt ratio.

By the fifth year, the short-term debt ratio should drop to a maximum of 5 percent of the BOE. By this time, the owner should have a stronger equity position in the equipment, for example, or should have refinanced all the short-term debt into a long-term obligation.

The club also probably has a long-term note as part of the debt structure for the first five years. In the family owned club in Florida, it had a five-year note for $250,000 as startup and build-out capital. The owners also had about $150,000 cash to put into the project.

A five-year note for $250,000 would have a monthly payment of about $5,000, which would be another 10 percent of the BOE. Depending on the short-term debt, this club might have a total debt percentage of 15 to 20 percent of BOE for the first three years of operation.

The goal is to lower the overall debt percentage to 10 percent of BOE, meaning 3 to 5 percent short-term and the rest long-term, which is the percentage the club will probably carry forever as it remodels, upgrades and trades equipment over the coming years.

The goal is to lower the overall debt percentage to 10 percent of BOE, meaning 3 to 5 percent short-term and the rest long-term, which is the percentage the club will probably carry forever as it remodels, upgrades and trades equipment over the coming years.

One primary tool to reduce the total debt ratio is to refinance with long-term debt every three to five years. Optimum long-term debt is five to seven years. Although 10 years makes business sense if the interest rate is 8 percent or less.

For example, if a club has a five-year $100,000 note at 10 percent, the payment is about $2,100 per month. If the long-term debt ratio drops to 5 percent of BOE during the fifth year, the club could simply borrow another $100,000 and maintain the same payment, which is built in as part of the club's BOE. If the club needed money earlier, it could refinance sometime during years three to five, allowing the club to take out and reinvest whatever it has previously paid down on the note.

Summary

Short-term debt probably kills more small businesses than almost anything else. Start-up clubs are notoriously undercapitalized so most owners fill the gap by taking on too many high-interest, short-term obligations. The most a club should have in short-term debt during the first three years of operation is 10 percent of BOE, which is the club's base monthly operating expense, and it should reduce this percentage to 5 percent by year five.

Year five is pivotal for a club business. The club's total debt structure should be refinanced or restructured during year five so that the combination of short-term and long-term debt is no more than 10 percent of BOE. Preferably, this ratio should be in the 5 to 8 percent range of BOE, but again, it should cap at no more than 10 percent of the club's base monthly operating expense.

Every club will always have debt it wants to keep growing and stay competitive. Controlling and understanding this debt and how it affects the business is what sets successful clubs apart from non-producing businesses.

Things you can do to use this material

1) When you open a new business, analyze how you are going to capitalize the business. If you are dependent on too many short-term leases and loans to get started, you will eventually encounter some tough spots in years three to five of your new business.

2) Put together an aggressive plan in years three to five to refinance and restructure your business to bring down the total debt ratio. Don't forget traditional bank financing and Small Business Administration loans as sources of revenue.

3) Build a set amount of money into your BOE that's used for retirement funds. Don't put all the cash back into the business forever. Everything eventually ends, and when it's time to walk away from your business you should have money you've put away outside of what the business is worth.

4) Set up a capital purchase accrual account for the business, and budget about $100 per 1,000 square feet per month for future capital purchases. For example, if you have a 10,000-square-foot gym, you should be saving $1,000 per month for future equipment purchases, which will eventually drive down the debt ratio as you start to pay cash for your equipment additions. Get into the habit of moving this money into the account each month, even if you don't have any immediate equipment needs. The money will then be there when you need it.

5) Don't become a fanatic about reducing your debt. Some owners are so aggressive about paying off loans that they hurt the business. If you have a little extra money each month, pay a payment and a half toward your notes. Much more than this starts to work against you, because it's usually at the expense of building a reserve fund, taking money out of the business for the owners, or building up an accrual account for future purchases. Also note that the extra money you pay on notes may be considered as phantom income, or profits you have to pay taxes on at the end of the year.

Some owners are so aggressive about paying off loans that they hurt the business.

Real member service is the next big step for the fitness industry

Member service equals renewals, and repeat business is the future of any fitness business

Chapter 10

Hiding from your members isn't usually considered a good form of member service

Chapter 11

Beware: The members have this secret urge to get even

LESSONS FROM LIFE — #9

The prima donna employee

THIS STORY COMES FROM the owners of a licensed gym in New Jersey.

They had an employee who was their lead salesperson and had worked in the gym for about six years. He was a tall bodybuilder and somewhat domineering person who completely dominated the rest of the staff. He produced a reasonable amount of sales each month and had the owners convinced that if they lost him, sales would come to a screeching halt.

There were also side issues involved that made working with him even that much more difficult. His wife was one of the owner's best friends and they felt somewhat obligated to keep him around even when he started to cause more discord with the rest of the employees.

The situation eventually came to a head when he was involved in a screaming argument at the front counter with another employee as to who was going to take the next tour. The problem was that the next tour was standing about three feet away waiting for the argument to be settled.

The owners wanted to let him go earlier but they were afraid production would slow down and that he would be hard to replace. And there was the personal issue between the employee's wife and one of the owners.

The problem was that the next tour was standing about three feet away waiting for the argument to be settled

The moral of the story

No one employee is important enough to hold you hostage. If they are, then your business is too dependent on personalities and not enough on systems.

Everyone can be replaced. The problem is that you may be actually losing money while you get up the courage to make the decision to let the star employee

go from your business. In this case, it would be hard to measure the damage this employee did to the other staff members, the members themselves, and to the overall production of the business.

Once the owners decided to let him go, business decreased for about a month and then increased beyond prior levels because the entire staff got involved in the sales effort instead of being dependent on the output of just one person.

Prima donna employees tend to hold everyone hostage by always threatening to leave if they don't get what they want. Often, it's better to let them go and get on with your life and your business. In many cases, the business will improve due to a better atmosphere and a redeployment of the tasks one person was doing now divided among several other staff people.

10

Hiding from your members isn't usually considered a good form of member service

SOMEWHERE, AT SOMETIME, SOMEONE is going to figure out that the most important part of getting enough customers is keeping the ones we already have. In other words, we're in the business of repeat business.

Eventually, in almost every market, the new sale cycle will start to deteriorate. The club may run hot for a year or two, but then it settles into a level of new sales that becomes pretty steady from that point forward. There are always a few months that are records or over the norm, but the year-to-year average usually doesn't change beyond a few points either way.

This proves the point that renewals become so important to the future growth of the business. The following chart illustrates how member service and renewals are related in the business:

Member service = renewals
Renewals = lower operating costs for the business and an
increased gross in membership at a lower cost, which means
more overall efficiency in the operation
More efficiency = less vulnerability

The opposite side of this formula is what happens to clubs that ignore the internal and just focus on the external aspect of the business, which is called frontloading, or the total focus on nothing but new sales. The following formula illustrates how this could also affect your business:

> The club may run hot for a year or two, but then it settles into a level of new sales that becomes pretty steady from that point forward.

Low member service = low renewals
Low renewals = demand for new sales to replace lost members
Demand for new sales = increased sales and operating costs in the
form of more advertising, increased commissions and
higher employee-related costs
Dependency on high volume of new sales = high vulnerability to
competition and other fluctuating market conditions

**Member service is
key, but it is also
one of those subjects
that is so subjective
in nature (full of
B.S.) that everyone
who talks about
member service is an
expert because no
one else knows what
the hell they are
talking about either.**

Member service is key, but is also one of those subjects that is so subjective in nature (full of B.S.) that everyone who talks about member service is an expert because no one else knows what the hell they are talking about either. And in the real fitness world, it is much easier to talk about member service than it is to implement a truly outstanding program.

In the fitness industry, there is usually a large gap between understanding the importance of member service and implementing a member-focused quality program, or more simply put, learning how to understand and meet the needs of the members.

One of the hardest things to understand in the business is why reasonably competent owners who are honest and hardworking people with nice gyms in good towns still fail. Some folks believe that gyms fail because they are traditionally undercapitalized, while others believe that compared to most other types of small businesses, gyms cost too much to start and attract owners who are not business people but are merely passionate about their chosen lifestyle.

The real reasons why many fitness businesses crash are related to lack of balance. Good balance comes from understanding the relationship between getting new members and fighting just as hard, if not harder, to keep the ones already in the system.

New sales are easy to understand and most owners can figure out how to work that side of the formula. Member service is difficult and very few owners ever really understand or will do the necessary work and investment to keep the members who have already bought once.

The challenging question is how many members did your club lose last year to poor member service? How many members bought, believed in you and then left the gym or failed to renew because of the indifference showed toward them by you and your staff?

Before we discuss how to implement a member service program, let's first discuss what member service isn't. Owners define member service in many strange and wonderful ways, but seldom in specific acts that actually benefit the member and make them want to remain a long-term member.

Owners and their staffs are creative, but these following items define what service isn't more than what it is:
• A clean gym
• Giving the member three or four workouts and then expecting them to solo
    • Having sign-up sheets and time limits on your cardio equipment
    • Letting the staff take all the good parking places in front of the gym

- Four different types of leg extension machines
- Suggestion boxes
- Aerobics instructors screaming in a microphone when there are only four students in class
- Having items in the pro shop for sale that can only be mail-ordered
- Giving a good tour
- Forcing members to show their cards every time they come in to workout
- Putting ties on your salespeople

All these perceived methods of member service have one thing in common. They're all good for the club and the staff, and none of them are really aimed at finding out about what the members need or want. And none of these items actually benefit the member beyond what's expected from a normal business open to the public.

A clean gym, for example, isn't member service, it's necessary to run a business. The members don't get all excited about a clean gym. If you're open for business, they expect you to be clean. And suggestion boxes are just another way for the managing staff to avoid actually talking to a member face-to-face about what he or she wants to happen in the gym.

Implementing a member service program is extremely hard, and in some ways it's also very simple.

The hard part comes from trying to get past the thought that we are already doing great customer service in the gyms, when in reality what we are doing doesn't really qualify as member service at all.

The simple part is that it's easy to get started on the right program. We can do it by simply listening. Learn to listen and to understand what the members want. Fitness owners should define member service as paying attention to your members by listening to, understanding and meeting your member's and employee's wants and needs.

Member service can also be defined as asking the member what they want and need, listening to the answer and then responding the best way we can. Any good business can tell you that customer service is simply asking the customer what it takes to get and keep their business.

But most owners are afraid to listen to their members and employees, because they fear changing things in the business, and because a lot of what the member tells them goes against the owner's preconceived notions of what the business should be. It's hard to dream about opening a business for three years, finally get it open, and when you talk to the first five members about what they want, you find that they don't really like what you've created.

There is also the problem of "old-timers disease." This happens to owners who were fresh and innovative when they opened, and one year later it's hard for them to make change, because "that's the way we've always done it here."

What is the main reason for this resistance? It's simply that the known is preferred to the unknown. Until the discomfort level, or until pressure becomes too great or until the new idea is proven (often by your friends or com-

> **A clean gym, for example, isn't member service, it's necessary to run a business.**

petitors) to be significantly better, change won't occur. When most owners change their business plans, assuming they have a business plan, it's usually because they are forced to change and by then it's too late.

The truly great owners learn to make major changes in their businesses to keep them growing before it's necessary, and before their competitors catch up and copy what they are currently doing. A successful owner learns, often from their members, to anticipate trends and changes that will affect the future of their businesses.

Clubs that are in trouble, not as profitable as they would hope or are just plain flat, have everything they need to know to grow their businesses to the next level right in front of them. But to do this you have to ask the members, listen hard to the answers they give and be willing, after all, to change.

If you ask and then listen, the members will help you answer the following questions:

- What's wrong with your club?
- Why don't they refer their friends to the club?
- Who are your best staff members for delivering real member service?
- What could you do to make more money in the gym?
- What would they buy if you sold it?
- What do you sell that they won't buy?
- Who is really your competition, and why do people buy from them?
- What attracted them to the gym in the first place, and how can you use this information to attract other potential members?
- What would it take for them to keep paying you in the coming years?
- What's broken and what needs to be fixed in the facility?
- What kind of equipment do you need to buy in the next few years? Often their answers about equipment are completely inconsistent with an owner's buying equipment to fulfill his own personal equipment fantasies.
- Is there anything else of value you might need to know to save your business?

Understanding the member is right there for the asking, but few owners ask. We don't ask because we always seem to be too busy, it's too time-consuming, or the worst blunder is believing we already know what every member in the gym is already thinking. We always have enough time to sign up a new member, but we never seem to have enough time to ask current members what it would take to get them to stay awhile.

A hard lesson to learn is that *someone else* may pay attention to the member, ask them what they like and want and then do everything they can to make them happy. It's too bad when it's our competition who's doing the asking and the listening.

Implementing a member service program can be easily broken down into a few basic steps. These steps should be followed in exact order to be effective. The further you get in the steps, the more successful member service program you'll have in your business.

Understanding the member is right there for the asking, but few owners ask.

Remember that member service in our gyms is our future because good member service means good word-of-mouth. Good word-of-mouth means more renewals and more sales, the staff is happier and more motivated when the members are happy, the multiple profit centers are more productive because they are designed to the member's needs and wants, and overall profits increase.

A final point here is that you already may have instituted some member service concepts in your gym. You may, in fact, already be on the right track when it comes to listening to the members, but as the famous American humorist Will Rogers once said, "Even if you're on the right track, you still get run over by the train if you're standing still."

Step one: Make a total commitment to member service

Here is a sample mission statement from a club that will make money in the coming years:

**Never lose a good member
Never lose a good employee
Deliver more than is promised
Be No. 1 in all that we do**

If the owners don't believe in member service and taking the commitment to the next level, then they won't successfully implement a higher level of service. If the owner believes in member service, but the manager doesn't, then it won't work. If the senior management of the club believes in member service, but can't get the staff to buy in, then it won't work. Everyone on the staff, from the owner to the babysitters and janitors, has to be on a mission to make the club the No. 1 fitness business in the country when it comes to member service.

Your goal, your vision, building a business we'd all want to own and workout in, and one that all the members want to belong to, is a gym that:

• Commits to providing legendary member service in the club industry and refuses to be anything but No. 1 in everything it does

• Values its members and employees above all else

• Works harder every day to become better in its delivery of true member service

Your vision as an owner or senior manager has to be the driving force in member service, and it always has to come from the top down. A motivated employee can make a difference for a while, but she only has to hear, "Sure, we believe in member service, but you still have to tell the members that there are 20-minute limits on the treadmills on busy nights. That's our policy," from her boss and then she knows that the member is not really No. 1.

This is also the point where she realizes that what's convenient for the club is always going to take first place over the member's needs and wants. It's

If the senior management of the club believes in member service, but can't get the staff to buy in, then it won't work

a sad fact, but most gyms are still internally oriented, meaning they're focused on what's best or most convenient for them and not what will ultimately please the member enough to buy again.

But keep in mind that the member is not always right. That's not what's being said here. The person who wrote that the customer is always right died a very impoverished death, working at a fast food restaurant somewhere. A better way to think about it is that the member is always right, up till the time bad business begins.

For example, a member might request the owner add a neck machine to the club's equipment list. Neck machines are brutally dangerous and only an insane owner, or one that owned her own insurance company, would ever put a neck machine in the gym.

Sometimes the member is not right. But if a member complains that he has to wait for 30 minutes to get on a treadmill, and that the time limit is unfair to someone who pays $40 a month to work out here, then he is right. The club needs more treads and the time limit is not good member service, it's an owner's poor attempt at disguising poor member service.

BUILD COMMITMENT WITH THE TEAM BY DEVELOPING A MISSION STATEMENT

Building a mission statement for the gym is a group project and can take several hours or more. Therefore, it should be done outside the gym if possible. Building a mission statement is also part of the first step of building commitment, because it starts the whole team thinking about member service.

A mistake here would be to write a mission statement at the management level and then leave out the junior staff. Everyone on the staff should have a chance to contribute to a company statement which should then be prominently displayed near the front counter so all prospective members can see it as they enter the club.

The goal

To build a working mission statement in which every member of the staff gets to contribute to at least once.

Time required

It usually takes about two hours for a group of people to agree on a mission statement. The owner or manager should act as facilitator to keep the meeting moving.

Handouts

Use the following questions to build a handout for the meeting. The goal is to discuss the questions as a group, so the team can get a better idea of how everyone else views their jobs and the gym.

> **The person who wrote that the customer is always right died a very impoverished death, working at a fast food restaurant somewhere.**

Questions for the handout
- What kind of staff do we want to be known for having in this gym?
- How do you want the members to view you personally, and your job, at this gym?
- How would you wanted to be treated as a member of this gym?
- How should the members be treated? When you discuss this question, consider all aspects of the gym such as weight training, group exercise, front counter greetings and personal training.
- What kind of image should this gym strive for in the community?
- What kind of reputation do you think we have now?
- What kind of atmosphere do you think we should create in this club?
- What kind of results can we get for all the members?
- If we really want to be known for legendary service, what do we have to change from what we do now?

Sample missions statements from some working gyms

We are a high energy, always up, rock and roll jammin' type club that believes we give the best workouts, with the best attitude, of any other club in this state (This is from an Eastern licensed gym).

Everything we do is simply best for the member (This is from a Southern wellness center).

We believe we have the best fitness facility in the area, the most friendly and courteous staff, and make the hardest effort to provide quality service to all members. Everything we do starts and ends with the member (This is from an adult alternative club in the Northern Illinois area).

Step two: Set up a complaint system in the gym and learn to listen

By listening to our members and their complaints, and then responding to what they say, we give them reasons to keep doing business with us. Members hate change, but they love improvements to their facility in direct response to one of their suggestions.

Let the members know when we have listened and responded to what they had to say, and do it in ways they can't miss, such as creating a Member Service Board display and by listing the member suggestions and complaints in the newsletter with the club's response.

Without a system in place, we usually act incorrectly when a member complains. Unless we take a set specific action at the time of the complaint, the problem will grow bigger in the member's mind and they will tell everyone they can find, in the gym and at their place of work, about the bad experience they had in our club. We need, therefore, to create a system that handles all complaints quickly and efficiently each and every time.

Let the members know when we have listened and responded to what they had to say, and do it in ways they can't miss.

The following is a basic training guide for the staff. This information would be one of the first things a person learns when starting work in a fitness facility, and it should be reinforced on a regular basis.

1. STOP WHAT YOU'RE DOING AND LISTEN

Acknowledge the member in a sincere way even though the member may be worked-up at the time because of the negative experience they just had. Nothing seems more rude to the member than the staff person trying to do three things at once, while the member is trying to complain. Stop what you're doing, look up and give the member your full attention.

2. NEVER ARGUE WITH A MEMBER OVER THE COMPLAINT THEY ARE TRYING TO MAKE

Members need to vent. The problem obviously upset them enough to complain. Arguing or defending the club just irritates them more. Most young employees, however, feel the need to defend the club and end up arguing with the member that just makes the problem worse. Don't argue; learn to listen.

3. DON'T LET THE MEMBER GET YOU MAD

It's not the complaining member that's the problem; it's the problem that's the problem. Young, inexperienced staff often takes a complaining member personally and then gets mad. Teach the team to ignore the mannerisms of the messenger and get to the message, which is the problem we need to hear and fix.

4. LISTEN PATIENTLY UNTIL THE MEMBER DESCRIBES THE ENTIRE PROBLEM

If the member was inconvenienced by the problem, venting the story often helps to alleviate the problem for the member.

Most complaints are not that new or original. The staff has heard them before and therefore wants to finish the story once the member gets started. Resist the urge and let the member finish the story. If the member was inconvenienced by the problem, venting the story often helps to alleviate the problem for the member. There was one member, though, that got his tie stuck in the urinal handle machinery. This was a fresh and welcome change for the staff from the common run-of-the-mill treadmill or missing weight stack pin complaints. Learn not to interrupt, except where you need to guide the member to the end of the story. "What happened then?" or "How can we make this right for you today while you're here?" are sample ways to keep the member on track with the story.

5. LET THE MEMBER KNOW THAT WE ARE ON THEIR SIDE AND OUR JOB IS TO LISTEN AND THEN DO EVERYTHING WE CAN TO FIX THE PROBLEM

Simple comments such as, "Yes, I understand how you could be upset," are easy ways to let the member know we are on their side and that it's our job to help them solve their problem the best we can.

6. GET THEM TO FILL OUT A MEMBER COMPLAINT CARD

No matter how big or how small the problem is, if it's important enough for the member to complain, then it's important enough for us to get a card filled out. Be sure and get it filled out now, while the member is standing there ready to get it out of their system. It's another form of venting and also a written guide for problem solving for the management team. See Illustration A for a sample Member Complaint Card.

7. IF YOU CAN FIX THE PROBLEM, THEN DO IT IMMEDIATELY, WHILE THE MEMBER IS STILL IN THE CLUB

If it can't be fixed immediately, then tell the member what you plan to do to get some action started. For example, if the member is upset because there is no soap in the showers, then immediately go put some soap in the shower. If it's a problem we can't fix that easily, tell the member we will take the card and immediately turn it over to the manager for attention. But if it can be fixed by the staff, or by the manager immediately, then do it while it makes a positive impression on the member.

If it can't be fixed immediately, then tell the member what you plan to do to get some action started.

8. FOLLOW-UP WITH THE MEMBER

Personally send the member a postcard telling her the outcome of her complaint. If we could fix it, tell her what we did. If we are working on the problem tell her what we are doing, and what the expected outcome will be. If it can't be fixed, tell her as nicely as possible why. A card should go out within 24 hours of receiving a complaint.

9. POST THE MEMBER COMPLAINT CARD ON THE MEMBER SERVICE BOARD

The club should have a Member Service Board displayed somewhere in the main traffic flow so the members can stay in touch with what's being done to improve the member service in the club. Regardless of the outcome, post the Member Complaint Cards on the board and write in red ink in the action section what the club did in response. It would be great to see 20 to 30 of these up at one time. Keep them up for about 30 days and then replace an old card with a new one. Yes, it does encourage other members to fill out cards, which does nothing but improve the club and the member's perception of member service.

Step three: Interview the entire staff

The front-line staff members, such as the check-in staff and the counter people, are the only staff members in the club who really know everything. The owners and the managers are the last to know anything because the staff never really wants to pass bad news uphill.

If you want to know what's really wrong in a business, go to the folks who know the whole scoop. Front-line staff are the first to hear a complaint; they constantly chat with the members and catch everything that's wrong in the gym even if it's passed on to them in a very off-hand manner. And the members are more likely to complain to someone at the bottom of the food chain than at the top.

To stay in touch with the members' feelings about the staff and the club, try formally interviewing each staff member on a monthly basis. Here is a sample questionnaire that could be adapted to most clubs:

FRONT-LINE MEMBER SERVICE QUESTIONNAIRE

This questionnaire should be used by management as a technique to gain information from the front-line staff before implementing any member service program, and then monthly after that to keep in touch with the members' current impressions as to what's happening in the club.

Interview the staff in person and write down the answers yourself. Don't make this into a handout and just give it to the staff to fill out. You will learn more about your club and your staff by asking questions and then patiently listening to the answers without interrupting.

- What compliments do you most frequently hear about the gym?
- What do you think our members like best about doing business with us?
- Where and when do misunderstandings with members most frequently occur?
- What member problems do you encounter most frequently?
- What systems or policies do we currently maintain that need to be corrected to help the member?
- Where do you, the employee, feel you lack the authority to help the member? What is your recommendation to fix this problem?
- If you had to name one thing that would make the members happier in this gym, what would it be?

Listen just as hard to what makes the members happy, as well as unhappy. When we start these programs, we tune in only to the negative, but we also need to listen to our successes too, because what we do right may be our biggest edge in the marketplace.

To stay in touch with the members' feelings about the staff and the club, try formally interviewing each staff member on a monthly basis.

Step four: Interview members through surveys and individual key member interviews

Here's a classic quote from a frustrated member: "You were so busy selling me, you had no time left over to listen to what I really wanted from you in the first place."

The only way to get and stay close to what the members are thinking is by constantly getting in their faces, and we do that through surveys and individual key member interviews.

There are many ways to survey and interview, but all of our tools should be based on asking the same question in a number of different ways. This question is: "From your viewpoint as a member, what is truly great member service and performance?"

What do the members really consider to be great service? How would they define the service they desire? What would it take to keep them as members of the gym, and paying, for years into the future? What would a member feel is great performance from our staff? We have our own definition as fitness professionals, but it's possible that how we define performance and what we expect from staff actually gets in the way of good member service.

Obviously, gathering this type of information from the members gives us a tremendous advantage over the gyms that don't take the time to do this vital task. A lot of owners don't like to ask these questions because they don't like to get any type of bad news. But when you're developing a member service program, sometimes the bad news is the good news since we may learn something that will help our businesses grow in the future.

If we ask, listen and respond to our members through surveys and individual member interviews, we should be able to spot the bad trends happening in the club before they become a big problem. We should also be able to capitalize on the good trends, know what actions we need to do and in what order, and be able to set short-term and long-term goals for the gym, our staffs and ourselves.

> **We have our own definition as fitness professionals, but it's possible that how we define performance and what we expect from staff actually gets in the way of good member service.**

SAMPLE QUESTIONS FOR PUTTING TOGETHER A MEMBER QUESTIONNAIRE

Clubs with 800 or fewer members should try to get out about 100 questionnaires a month. If there are more than 800 members in the facility, try to get out about 200 surveys a month. This is enough to get a real pulse check on what's happening in the business. Be sure to make the surveys available at various times of the day so you can get a thorough cross-section of the members. Useful survey questions include:

1. What equipment would you like to see us add to the gym? Your list could include new equipment or duplicates of what we already have in the facility.
2. What do you think our biggest weakness is when it comes to equipment?
3. What services or amenities would you like the gym to offer? Don't

forget the little things we can do to keep you happy as a member.

4. Please list three things you believe the gym does well and should do more of in the future.

5. Please list three things the gym could do better.

6. What new products would you like us to add to the pro shop?

7. What drinks could we sell that we currently don't?

8. What new trends or programs have you read about or seen that could be added to the gym?

9. Your guests are very important to us. What could the gym do better to attract and service your special guests? Please check all the points that you think are important.

    __Free T-shirt for you for bringing a guest in to the gym

    __Free gift certificate for bringing in a guest

    __Three free personal training sessions

    __One free month added on to your membership for every guest that joins

    __More guest passes available to you on a regular basis

10. Please give us your thoughts on guest incentives for you and your guests. How can we better attract and serve your friends?

11. Please rate how our staff treats you during your visits to the gym?

          Fair   Good   Excellent

          1.....2.....3.....4.....5.....6.....7

12. How would you rate the club on cleanliness?

          Fair   Good   Excellent

          1.....2.....3.....4.....5.....6.....7

13. We want to continually improve our customer service to you. How can we improve our service to you personally in this gym?

14. Your comments are important to us. Please take a few moments and give us your thoughts on any aspect of the gym you feel is important.

15. What were the three most important factors to you in your final decision to join this gym?

16. What are the strongest points in our marketing that appealed to you as a potential member?

17. What turned you off about our advertising or might have made you hesitate in becoming a member of this club?

18. Was there anything that surprised you about the gym once you became a member? For example, did our gym match your preconceived ideas about the business either positively or negatively?

Owners and senior managers should do at least 25 key one-on-one personal interviews a month asking the members these questions.

These survey questions should also be used to do individual key member surveys on a monthly basis. Every club has that core membership that's been there since the facility opened, attend regularly, support the profit centers and care deeply about "their" gym.

Owners and senior managers should do at least 25 key one-on-one personal interviews a month asking the members these questions. The manager interviews a member and then writes down the answer as the member gives it. These interviews allow you to stray from the questionnaire if a good topic comes up, and it lets the member know their opinion is important to the club. Interviewing also allows whoever is giving the interview a chance to watch the expression on the member's face, in case there is more to an answer and it needs to be drawn out of the member.

Step five: Have a third party call and interview at least 25 former members every month

These are members who are at the end of their memberships and decided not to renew with us. We need to know why we had them and now we don't. You would expect to hear a lot of bad news from this group, but most of them are already into something else in their lives and won't give you much except non-threatening answers.

Every once in a while, however, you'll get that rare opportunity to talk with a member who was unhappy with the gym. That's what you're looking for in this survey: those one or two people who give you the real story and help the gym grow another notch.

We've found over the years that using a real, or pretend, third-party interviewer will get the best results. When you call as a club representative, no one really wants to unload and get into the real issues. But if you're calling as a third-party, a person that they don't know, their answers are usually better and more complete.

It does help to have someone that is at least somewhat familiar with your business do the interviews. If the member starts discussing a certain topic, a person who has an understanding of your business can talk the person further into the subject where the most helpful information usually lies.

> **That's what you're looking for in this survey: those one or two people that give you the real story and help the gym grow another notch.**

A SAMPLE FORMER MEMBER PHONE SURVEY

Use this survey to gather information from the past members. Don't bother sending anything; you seldom get anything back even with stamped, self-addressed envelopes.

If the former member takes the time to participate in the survey, offer him or her a free month to come and see the changes you've made since they've been gone, and to let them know that you've taken their suggestions seriously.

Greeting: Hello, my name is _____, I've been hired by _____ (gym name), to do a survey of former members. Would you please take a few minutes and answer a couple of questions for me?

1. Why are you no longer a member of the gym?
2. What three things could the gym do to improve its member service?
3. What did you like least about doing business with this club?
4. What one thing could the club do to significantly improve its product?
5. What did you like best about the club?

Closing comments: (Member's name), thank you for taking the time to answer my questions. Since you have been so helpful, may I send you a free month membership to the gym to come back and see the changes they have made since you've been gone?

Summary

Sales gets members. Service is what keeps them. For too many years, the industry has only practiced the sales part. For the industry to grow and mature, and to shake its high-pressured sleazy sales image, the growth must be toward providing the consumer a better level of customer service.

We are also stuck on the product quality, the "our gym is better than your gym" mentality. Product quality is what the member gets, how the product is delivered is service quality, and that's what will set us apart from our competitors in the coming years.

Member service doesn't just happen. It's not a spontaneous act by the staff. Member service has to be planned and developed over time. For most clubs, it will take at least a year to get a good member service program in place.

The steps listed in this section are a guide to help you think about the implementation of a plan and about how detailed you have to get to make member service work. Do the steps one at a time and once that step is part of your operational plan, move on to the next step. Take your time and do each step correctly.

As the overall quality of gyms improve in the coming years, due to the large investment needed to start one and the addition of real business people to the industry, member service will become even more important, because it will be all that separates one club from another. The perception of member service in your club by the prospective member will be all that separates you from everyone else in the market.

The perception of member service in your club by the prospective member will be all that separates you from everyone else in the market.

Things you can do to use this material

Teach your staff the Ten Points of Member Service their first day on the job, and make it a central part of their training from that point forward.

The Ten Points of Member Service
1) Greet the member by name every time.
2) Thank the member for coming into the gym today. They have a choice and we want to show our appreciation for the money and time they spend with us.
3) Deliver service when the member wants it, at their convenience, not just when it's convenient to us.
4) Be accessible at all times to the members.

5) Every gym has about the same equipment and services that we do. The difference is you and the way you treat the members each time they come into the club.

6) Answer all phone calls by the third ring with a positive, enthusiastic voice.

7) Greet everyone you don't know by asking them their name, giving them yours and welcoming them to the gym.

8) Make every member we have feel important, because they are important to the future of this business.

9) Members are not bothering us when they expect good service, it's our most important job to provide that service.

10) Do everything you do in this gym the best you can do it.

These points should be part of staff training and also displayed throughout the gym. Displaying them reminds the staff of what we're all about and also lets the members know we are trying to get it right.

Sample training games and meeting formats that raise member service awareness among the staff

Good news/bad news game: Give each staff member $10 to $25 in an envelope, depending on the size of your club and staff. Tell them there is good news and bad news. The good news is that the cash is a bonus for good performance in the club. The bad news is that they have to spend it by the next meeting and document the experience.

How were they treated in the store? Did they leave smiling after the sale, or did they feel they were imposing on the salesperson's time. Were people friendly and did they spend time, or were they rushing the person out of the store? The staff member then has to relate their adventure in the next meeting and how what they learned relates to the club and the member service the team is now offering.

Learning the competition game: Send each staff member to visit another club and get pitched. This is an old game but we probably never looked at it from the member service viewpoint. How does the competition present member service, if at all? Does what they claim in their tour match what the staff person sees in the club? For example, a club can talk about member service, but when you go into the locker room and it's dirty, then that's how that club and its staff really feels about customer service.

Learning the competition/team style: Try the team approach as an alternative for large staffs. Split the staff into member service teams and assign a team to one of the competitors in the area. One team member works out, one gets pitched, one makes a phone call as a prospective member, and then they all give an overall view of the visited club. The goal is to steal one good idea we can use on member service and to also prove that the competition isn't so tough after all.

Breakfast club game: A staff member is assigned to get bagels and coffee for the weekly staff meeting. The only rule is that the staff can never go back to the same place twice. Each meeting starts with a review of the buying experience and the customer service they received at that week's location. If

> **How does the competition present member service, if at all? Does what they claim in their tour match what the staff person sees in the club?**

the staff gets unusually good member service from someone, then steal them as an employee. This game keeps the team focused on customer service each week, and also is a good way to recruit new staff members who already understand the fundamentals of service.

Problem solving game: Ask the staff one tough question during the meeting, such as what new products could be added to the club that would improve member service, and give them one hour to come up with solutions. Be willing to let go here. Be willing to try strange suggestions if they won't hurt the business. Many of their suggestions will be positive and most will, at the worst, be neutral. By trying their suggestions, they begin to think like a team and they're a real part of the company.

Member Complaint Card sample

Member Complaint Card

The complaint: Date:

What needs to be done:

Suggestions for improvements in other
areas of the club:

Taken by:

Action by club:

The staff should be trained to hand a member a card every time the member has a complaint or even a strong suggestion.

How to use this card: These cards should be kept at the front desk at all times. The staff should be trained to hand a member a card every time the member has a complaint or even a strong suggestion.

SAMPLE SCRIPT A STAFF MEMBER WOULD USE WITH THE CARDS

The member: I really think you should do something about that leg press. It seems to be sticking even more than last week.

The staff person: Thank you for letting us know about that problem. To make sure it's taken care of properly and in a timely manner, could you please take a moment and fill out this card. It helps us serve you better and makes sure none of the member suggestions and ideas get lost.

SPECIAL NOTE

All problems should be addressed within 24 hours. The members will stop giving you realistic suggestions and complaints if they know you don't respond. If you have a newsletter in the club, list the suggestions for the month and the club's response or solutions.

The members will stop giving you realistic suggestions and complaints if they know you don't respond.

LESSONS FROM LIFE — #10

Hanging on to employees too long

THIS STORY COMES FROM one of our own businesses on the East Coast.

We had a manager who had been with the club for a number of years and wanted to pursue another career. She had done a great job for the club including developing an excellent assistant manager who was in charge of all production at the club. The assistant manager supervised the sales staff, the nutrition program and the trainers, and made a certain amount of sales each month herself.

When the manager left, the assistant moved up. After 15 months of consecutive profits, the club lost money four months in a row. The new manager had great excuses, including the fact that we were in the middle of a small construction project at the gym that involved closing down a pool area and covering it with a deck for a new cardio area in the club.

But at the same time, the new manager went from 45 to 30 hours a week. All the systems, such as the monthly goal setting with employees that she had done so well as an assistant, were discarded over the four-month period. She also had a hard time letting non-performing staff go, like a nutrition tech who was barely performing at a most basic level.

During her fifth month as manager she quit, which was during the second week of January. She sensed she was in

We failed to act, which in itself is making a decision that cost everyone a great deal of money

trouble and left before she was fired.

The moral of the story

We knew she was in over her head and needed to be replaced several months earlier. But because we felt obligated to give a loyal employee a chance, we stuck with her too long, therefore, severely hurting the business. In other words, we hired wrong the first time and then failed to rectify the mistake soon enough.

Sometimes an employee can move up to a level that is too high for them to handle it competently. In this case, the woman was successful as an assistant manager, where she received daily direction and had someone watch over her. When she advanced to a position of manager, however, her ego inflated and her work ethic was not strong enough without supervision.

Our mistake was that we didn't take action immediately to correct what we knew was a bad hiring decision. Because of the emotions involved with a long-term employee who had made the company money over the years, we failed to act, which in itself is making a decision that cost everyone a great deal of money.

11

Beware: The members have this secret urge to get even

It just doesn't make sense to the average owner. A guy joins the club, pays each month and then expects service for that money. When the member has the nerve to stand at the front counter complaining about something minor — minor from the owners viewpoint — the owner becomes stressed because all the damn members do is moan about the club.

What the owner has to learn is that the member paid for the right to moan, and most members aren't shy about exercising that right. If the member believes he didn't receive value for money spent, he will get even, often in a negative manner by withholding his financial referral support from the club.

Members expect and seek equity in their relationship with your business. The gym's staff has to understand the member's need for equity to provide a higher level of member service. Equity is achieved when the member is satisfied that they received equal or greater value for money spent. The staff also has to understand that unless they learn to exceed the member's base expectations of the business, they'll never be able to reap the benefits of this equity relationship.

Everyone in the fitness business talks about giving good member service. Everyone who owns a gym believes that they give the best member service of any of the competitors in the area. The sad point is that there is a huge difference between wanting to give great member service and actually delivering the product. We've all heard, "We have the best gym in town," or "We provide the best workouts." But the real management challenge is to translate these slogans into actions that the member will understand and that separate you from the competition.

To start this translation process, and to understand the equity relation-

> **What the owner has to learn is that the member paid for the right to moan, and most members aren't shy about exercising that right.**

ship, begin with a common premise: The No. 1 purpose of you, your employees and the services and amenities you offer, is to attract, satisfy and preserve customers. You are not there to provide a great, well-equipped gym, the best workout in town (which is not enough and usually not what the member is looking for from his purchase anyway) or a staff that smiles the most.

You are there to satisfy customers. Satisfied members are those who purchase and receive value from the service you offer. It's not what *you* want that satisfies the member, it's giving the member what *they* want. If they don't like what you offer, or the way you offer it, they can go elsewhere. But when they do, you and your organization suffer. Satisfied members create profits in your business. Dissatisfied members still spend the same amount of money, they simply spend it at one of your competitor's.

The average gym will lose between 60 to 80 percent of its current member base by the end of next year. For instance, if you have 1,000 members currently working out in the club, 12 months from now there will only be between 200 and 400 of them left. This represents the industry average. The majority will leave because of their personal perception that the equity relationship was in your favor, or that you were receiving more from the relationship than they were.

Member satisfaction is like an election that is held every day in your gym.

Member satisfaction is like an election that is held every day in your gym. In this case, the members vote on the member service they receive. If they believe it's poor, they vote with their feet by walking out the door. The sad thing is you may never know why they left.

For the gym business, member service needs to be defined as equaling renewals. Renewals will be the most important issue clubs have to face in the coming years. We are in an age of severe competition. Learning to satisfy and preserve the member base you fought so hard for in the first place is the key to your future business success.

But before you can jump in and start working on the equity position of your members, you need to first understand why they do what they do. Why do members behave in certain ways, and why do they sometimes choose to renew or sometimes simply disappear and end up elsewhere?

Understand why the members do what they do

Members are motivated to act in particular ways because their actions will either result in a gain (reward) or will avoid a loss (punishment). Members are rational people. If their experience in the gym is positive, they will probably come back; if it is negative, they will stop coming and disappear altogether.

Members first come to the gym with base expectations that need to be met at the very first level. Base expectations are the basic services and needs that the member expects to be met as part of doing business with you.

Members expect clean locker rooms, enough equipment so they don't have to wait an unreasonable amount of time, a friendly well-groomed staff, towels and enough help to be able to participate in a basic program. This is where the trouble occurs, however, because many gym owners confuse meeting basic expectations with providing member service.

A clean gym is not member service. It is a basic expectation you have to fulfill just to get into the game. Trainers who are available to help the member set up a program and who are around to help them with the mechanics and necessary changes is not member service. It is the very least the member expects from the club for the money that they spent with you.

The following chart explains how base expectations relate to member service:

	Not met	Met	Exceeded
Base expectations	————————————		
	(member feels indifference)	(member is committed to the club)	

For a member to renew, spend money in the profit centers and bring in guests, they have to be moved beyond base expectations being met. The member has to be moved into the area of commitment by having their base expectations exceeded.

In the chart, even if the member's base expectations are met, the member is still in the area where they feel indifference to the club. It's OK, meets their base needs, but if something better came along, they'd give it a try. Meeting the base expectations is no big deal; they expected that in the first place. The only way you impress the member is to move beyond base expectations being met to the expectations being exceeded.

We make our biggest mistake in member service by thinking we are providing great member service by meeting the member's base expectations. That still leaves the member in the area of indifference, where they have no commitment to the gym in the long run.

To really understand how the member thinks, we have to also take a look at the equity theory. The equity theory is just a fancy way of saying that as human beings, we work very hard to keep everything in balance in our lives. If you invite me to dinner, then I feel obligated to repay that kindness by inviting you to my house for dinner. If I don't, there is no balance or equity.

This theory is really the base for what happens to members in the gym. If the member joins, they feel they have already done you a favor by picking your gym. They had choices in the community but they picked you. They feel, therefore, that you owe them and it's up to you to balance. In other words, now it's your turn.

If the member doesn't feel you evened the score early, then the situation gets worse once they start making payments. Eventually the member will seek equity, meaning they will even the score on a negative point rather than a positive one.

For example, the member at this point feels that there is an inequity on their part. They put more in than they received. Once they feel this, they will either start ignoring you (stop coming or stop payment), demand attention (love me now or lose me forever), retaliate (bad word of mouth to every-

For a member to renew, spend money in the profit centers and bring in guests, they have to be moved beyond base expectations being met.

one that will listen) or withdraw from the situation altogether by cutting off all support, money and friends.

You can benefit from this theory though. If you exceed the member's expectations, meaning the member perceives that they are getting more from the gym than they are paying for in their membership, they will also seek balance.

In this case, they feel that they are getting more than they deserve so they feel that they owe you and the gym. This is called a positive imbalance for us. The member wants to pay you back by buying a product at a premium price, bringing in a friend or, most importantly, renewing when it is time.

The ultimate goal for member service, then, is to work toward creating positive imbalances by exceeding member expectations.

But again, the hardest part of member service is taking the concept and translating it so the members perceive you are exceeding their base expectations. Even if the owner makes a commitment to getting a real member service program started, it's the member contact people who actually deliver the service and ultimately do the translating.

You may build a $600,000 gym, but it's your lowest-paid front counter person and trainers who will determine your financial success by delivering member service. At McDonald's, it's not the president who demonstrates the service standard, it's the 15-year-old kid at the counter who smiled, showed courtesy and tried to get you to buy fries with that drink. McDonald's is known for their service, but it's not service from the corporate staff, it's from the training they put into their most inexperienced staff.

To members, the front-line people are the business. These are the people who the members come into contact every day, the ones that they perceive as the real gym. The front-line people, therefore, need to be the best trained and most service-oriented people you can put into the field. But what happens if they are not the best trained? How can a weak front-line person really affect you?

The following is a true story from a gym member. We call the member Joe Smith in the story and he is definitely in a negative equity position with the club:

> Joe Smith has been a member for two years. His dues are $40 per month. He's been on the same routine for a year, since no one at the gym has offered to review him and update his workout. He currently trains four days a week, has gone through the club's nutrition program and buys a drink every time he's in the club.
>
> During his last visit to the club, he stopped at the juice counter but the gym was out of his favorite drink. He also stopped in the pro shop to make a purchase of a ballcap for his brother-in-law's birthday, priced under $20.
>
> The new counter person didn't recognize him, so she asked him for an ID when he tried to pay by check. None of the staff said hello when he came

...the hardest part of member service is taking the concept and translating it so the members perceive you are exceeding their base expectations.

in and no one thanked him for his purchase at the counter.

Joe just received his renewal notice in the mail but decided to lay it aside on his desk and just try a few other gyms before he sent it back. He was a little upset with the notice, especially after his last visit to the gym, since it began, "Dear Valued Member."

Joe's thoughts were that after two years as a member, if they don't know me or care about me, then it's time to shop the other gyms in the area. In other words, Joe doesn't think he is getting $40 worth of value a month from his relationship with the gym, let alone the extra money he spends there every visit.

Was the situation that bad from the gym's viewpoint. After all, the gym was simply out of a drink and the counter person was only following procedure by asking for an ID. The club was open, clean and all he had to do was ask and a trainer would have helped him with a program. To the gym, member service was there and they thought they did a good job.

The important point, however, *is Joe's perception of what happened.* In his mind, he was rudely treated when he was asked for an ID. He's been a member for two years, paid each month as promised and was supporting the club by buying $20 worth of merchandise.

In his perception, the pro shop and juice counter people are the club, and they both treated him badly. Even his base expectations, getting a drink, being able to write a check and being served by friendly considerate people, were not met — let alone exceeded.

What did these two improperly trained front-line people really cost the club if they lose Joe?

Joe pays $40 a month, or $480 per year. Joe is a resident of the area and enjoyed the club. If he was a member for five years, and yes, we need to start thinking of members in the long-term, he would be worth $480 x 5 or $2,400.

Studies also show that an upset member tells, on an average, 11 other people about an unhappy experience. A very damaging number that we usually ignore altogether is who these 11 people tell.

This is called secondhand word of mouth or, "No, I've never really been in that gym but a friend of mine said...." These 11 will tell five others. So who is really unhappy and how far does the story go?

> Joe Smith starts out the bad word of mouth = 1 person
> This one person tells 11 = 11 new people in the word-of-mouth loop
> These 11 people each tell five others = 55 new people now have a
> negative image of the club

We have the potential here for 67 people to have a negative image of this gym. Why? Because two underpaid, undertrained counter people didn't correctly handle your most valuable asset, your long-term member.

"No, I've never really been in that gym but a friend of mine said...." These 11 will tell five others. So who is really unhappy and how far does the story go?

Even if only five of the 67 didn't come in, quit if they were members or drove off others, you still have a huge loss. Five times $2,400 is $12,000. Again, the $2,400 is from one member staying five years. This doesn't count other money they might have spent in the gym.

An important number here is that it costs the club six times as much to attract a new member than it does to keep one already in the system. The cost of advertising, commissions, staffing costs to get the new member in the system, and administrative costs are all more expensive than the service it would have taken to keep this guy around the gym. If those two counter people really cost the gym that much money, would it have been worth it to hire slightly better people, at a slightly higher rate, and then put more training into them?

One front counter person, in a bad mood, with bad breath or bad hair, or undertrained can do serious financial damage to the gym. What should those two counter people have done if they would have been properly trained?

What you could have done to deliver better service, for example, is simple. If you were out of a drink you normally carry, you could have given the member a discount toward another drink. Or you could have given a rain check discount toward the next purchase when you have the drink back in stock. You could have bought the member a drink if the owner or senior manager was present. You could have done any number of things except say no. It was not being out of the drink that was the problem. It was how the staff handled the situation that hurt the business.

> **It's the member's perception that you don't care about his experience in the club, you didn't care about his two years of support, and you didn't treat him as an individual.**

It's the member's perception that you don't care about his experience in the club, you didn't care about his two years of support, and you didn't treat him as an individual. And you certainly should have taken his check. By simply changing the club's current policy by asking only nonmembers for IDs for checks could have made a negative situation positive.

The most important issue is to properly arm the staff with enough information and training so they can provide member service far superior to the competition, and so we can every day exceed the expectations of the members. The following training points should be in the basic arsenal of every staff member and form the core of a good member service program:

Economical ways to arm your staff for member service

1. Greet everyone, every time, like it's their first visit to the gym

The regulars often get lost in the shuffle after they have been around for a while. The staff is always excited to see prospective members come through the door, but we seldom give the regular members that same enthusiastic greeting.

2. GREET EVERYONE, EVEN THE REGULARS PROMPTLY, MEANING WITHIN FOUR SECONDS

Waiting for service, even if it's only 10 to 15 seconds, seems like a long and frustrating time. Everyone coming through the door, whether the staff knows them yet or not, should be greeted or at least acknowledged in four seconds. The consumer often equates being made to wait with bad service.

3. MAINTAIN EYE CONTACT AND SMILE

After a while, we get into a routine at the front desk and forget to greet those coming in the door. Stop what you're doing, look up, make eye contact and smile. This simple ritual may set the club apart from every other business the customer has been in that day.

4. TEACH EVERYONE A WELCOME STATEMENT

"Hello, welcome to the gym today" is a safe, but friendly statement that should be the first thing out of everyone's mouth, including yours, who is standing behind the front desk. It may sound like this could get repetitious, but members like to be part of a routine that makes them feel comfortable coming into the gym each day.

5. TEACH A STRATEGY IF YOU HAVE TO MAKE SOMEONE WAIT

The staff members should have set procedures to handle and entertain potential members who have to wait. For example, if a guest has to wait more than five minutes for someone to show them the club, the staff should be able to escort the person to the juice counter and offer them a drink handled through a special owner's account.

The magic number is 3 to 5 minutes. Set a time and teach the staff to automatically go into their waiting strategy if someone is waiting for service, waiting for an appointment with a late staff person, or is a prospective member who is waiting for a tour.

6. START WITH PERSONAL APPEARANCE AND GROOMING

Remember that the member perceives the club through the staff members they most often come into contact with. The old saying "you only get one chance to make a good first impression" is especially true in our business, both for potential members and regular clients.

How your staff dresses, the uniforms, jewelry, hair and personal grooming directly affect our day-to-day business. The key word for dress and grooming is "appropriate." What is appropriate for your target market and atmosphere in your gym? Uniforms are highly recommended for everyone working in the gym. Uniforms give everyone a little more professionalism and allow the members to find someone quickly if they need help or service.

...if a guest has to wait more than five minutes for someone to show them the club, the staff should be able to escort the person to the juice counter and offer them a drink handled through a special owner's account.

139

7. CHECK THE APPEARANCE OF YOUR WORK AREA

Part of the member's daily perception of service and one of the biggest parts of the potential member's first impression is how clean and professional the front counter area and entrance areas are. Clutter seems to grow in these areas and hurts the appearance. These areas need to be cleared of all non-essential clutter at least on a quarterly basis.

8. STUDY GOOD TELEPHONE TECHNIQUE

We need to go beyond just role playing to get guests to come in to the gym. Part of member service is effective phone training to cover all calls besides just information ones. Here is a list of things to concentrate on to maintain good phone technique.

• Answer the phone by the third ring.

• Include the staff member's name as part of the greeting.

• Never, ever, put anyone on hold if it can be helped. If you have to put someone on hold, wait until the caller says yes before cutting them off.

• Smile into the phone. Callers expect a happy enthusiastic response from the people they call. Give it to them.

• Let the caller know what's going on. If you have to get someone else to help with the call, or if you need to get more information to answer the question, let the caller know what you are doing and when you will be back.

• Invite the caller to get to the point. Lead the caller to the point by asking, "How can I help you today?"

• Give specifics. If someone needs to return the call, give them a name and a time they can expect a call back.

• Thank the caller when the conversation is over.

• If you have to put someone on hold for more than a few minutes, get a number and call them back.

• Be proud of the gym, and always invite the guest callers to come in and see the place and meet the staff.

• Keep a pen and call message sheets by the phone. Nothing is more frustrating than when calling a business during regular business hours, the person taking the call doesn't have a pen handy to take a message.

• Return all calls within an hour.

• Take all calls. It is easier and more polite to take a call and simply say "no," than it is to blow off a message sheet altogether.

• Never, ever, say, "Let me see if he is in. Who's calling please?" If you are unavailable, then be totally unavailable. Screening your calls in such an obvious manner is rude to the caller and a waste of your time.

• Say "please" and "thank you."

• Good manners aren't dead, just severely wounded when it comes to the young people who work at our front counters. Every member should be thanked for their business every time they leave the club. Every time someone buys something, even something small, they should be thanked. Show appreciation for the member's business and they'll show loyalty to the club.

If you are unavailable, then be totally unavailable. Screening your calls in such an obvious manner is rude to the caller and a waste of your time.

10. LEARN AND CALL PEOPLE BY THEIR NAMES

This is the most important thing you can teach your staff. If they just make an effort to learn and use a member's name, you are already far ahead of the competition. Try using the Name Game as a way to train the staff. Stand by the staff member at the front counter and say, "Jane, I'll give you a dollar a name (or a free drink if you're thinking cheap) if you can greet the next 10 members by name without looking at the computer. Miss one and you're done."

Managers and senior staff are held to much higher standards. The manager should know just about every member in the club no matter how many members the club has. Remember that knowing the member's name is the cornerstone of member service, and all other service builds from this simple concept.

11. SEND A LOT OF THANK YOU CARDS

If a person becomes a member, send a thank-you card. If a member brings a guest that's thinking about joining, send the member a thank-you. If a member complains, send a thank-you. Thank-you notes are strong, and they are always perceived as exceeding a person's base expectations.

12. COVER BUYER'S REMORSE

We need to have a small list of positive things to say to someone who has just become a member and they are on their way out of the club. "Thank you for becoming a member. I look forward to seeing you tomorrow," would be an example.

13. TEACH THE STAFF WHAT UPSET MEMBERS REALLY WANT WHEN THEY ARE STANDING AT THE FRONT COUNTER READY TO KILL ANY STAFF PERSON IN THEIR WAY

A lot of our younger staff members take it personally when members complain. If a member is upset, a young staff person often feels that they did something wrong and that the member is really mad at them. Teach the staff early in their training what an upset member really wants:

> **If a member is upset, a young staff person often feels that they did something wrong and that the member is really mad at them.**

- To get the problem handled quickly
- To be listened to and taken seriously
- To have you understand the problem and the reason they are upset
- To receive compensation if there was a loss
- To avoid further inconvenience
- To be treated with respect
- To be assured that the problem won't happen again

To get the most out of these training guidelines, create a sample problem in the club for each of the points.

141

14. Explain the "Never Evers" and the "Laws" on the first day

There are certain rules tied to member service that can never be broken by the staff. Teach them these rules on their first day and enforce them strictly. Some samples might be:

- Never insult a member
- Never bad-mouth a competitor
- Never bad-mouth a fellow staff member in front of a member
- Never lose your temper with a member
- Never come to work under the influence of drugs or alcohol
- "On time" means 15 minutes early for their shift or appointment
- Treat members with respect even if they don't deserve it
- Take pride in yourself and your work environment

15. Give staff a few short breaks a day

Don't let the staff skip meals, and make sure they take a couple of short breaks each shift. Burned-out and grouchy employees never make anyone any money.

16. Revise all of your policies with member service in mind

Usually these policies begin because some bonehead wrote the club a bad check five years ago and the owner overreacted and has punished every member since.

Sometimes our policies prevent us from giving good member service, such as the previous example where the counter person asked a two-year member for an ID to write a check. It may have sounded good at the time, but it kills member service in the long run. Usually these policies begin because some bonehead wrote the club a bad check five years ago and the owner overreacted and has punished every member since.

17. Give the staff the right tools

It's hard to do a good job if you don't have the right stuff to do it with at the time, such as pens, information on the services, starter kits, message pads, towels, rental locks, phone numbers for who to call for help, and a procedures manual where the employee can look up sample forms and procedures if someone in management is not there at the time.

18. Bring up member service in every staff meeting

The following are some focus questions to keep the staff thinking about member service. Use one or two of these at every staff meeting and allow time for discussion:

- What three things have you seen this month that we could have done better?
- What three things have you seen this month that we really did well in the way of member service?
- What employee has really stood out in member service this month

and why?
- How was the club's member service this month?
- What comments did you hear about the club's equipment this month?
- What other products and services have the members requested that we don't currently offer?
- What's our biggest weakness when it comes to member service?
- What does the competition offer that you would like to see this club provide?

19. LET THE MEMBERS KNOW HOW TO BE A GOOD MEMBER

"How to be a good member" signs should be nicely framed and posted around the club. It reminds the members that we want them to tell us what they think. The signs also remind the staff that complaining members are what the club needs if it is to make improvements to keep the members happy.

How to be a good member:
- Complain: If you as a member don't, then who will? It takes only a minute, you will feel better and the gym will benefit from your observation.
- Praise: This is just as important to us as criticism. It lets us know when we are doing something you think is right, and it lets us reward creativity and good member service by the staff.
- Be articulate: You know what you want, the staff may not. Be as specific as you can about what you want, and spell it out simply and clearly.
- Demand quick service: There is no excuse in this business for slow or poor service. We are here to provide a service to you. Please let us know when we are living up to your expectations.
- Be quick yourself: If something is wrong, tell us now. Don't wait for five months, slowly seething over something we could have fixed when it happened.
- Be kind: Remember, we are human beings just like you. Give us a chance to have the pleasure of helping you meet your fitness needs and fixing the problems you may encounter.
- Be persistent: If necessary, go upstairs. Sometimes, the management has no idea what really happens on a day-to-day basis. Even though we would like to be on top of every little detail, sometimes we need your help in providing the best service possible.

> **"How to be a good member" signs should be nicely framed and posted around the club.**

Summary

When members join, most feel the membership is an investment. Because of the nature of the fitness business, and because of how memberships have been sold during the last 25 years in this industry, most owners forget about the relationship with the new member, and most are already looking for the next sale.

There is no actual value on a membership. A person may pay $40 a month and feel they get $20 worth of value, while another may pay $30 a month and feel they get $60 worth of value. The member's perception of value is what we are trying to influence toward a positive imbalance, where the member feels that there is far more value than price.

The confusion starts with the member's base expectations. Each member expects the club to provide basic services for the money paid. For example, each member expects the club to be clean, the staff to be friendly and courteous, to be able to get help whenever it's needed, and to be appreciated for giving the club their business.

Most owners don't understand that they need to learn to exceed these base expectations to keep a member long-term. Just meeting these basic needs doesn't qualify as member service. Exceeding these basic needs is where member service begins.

No matter how much the owners or an individual staff person believes in members service, it's the day-to-day people at the entry staff levels who have to deliver and who members identify with member service. And most of all, it's a team effort to provide member service. Every person on the team has to understand the member service function and how to deliver it in a way that separates you from the competition.

Every person on the team has to understand the member service function and how to deliver it in a way that separates you from the competition.

Things you can do to use this material

1) Staff training has to start at the bottom and work up. Most owners spend too much time training senior staff members and not enough training the entry level folks. A good sports example is the difference between a high school quarterback with a lot of talent and a pro quarterback. The raw talent kid would need a lot more coaching and support to bring him to the pro level, while the pro needs small tweaks and changes to get the most out of his game. Start your training with the rookies and give them the most time out of your training schedule.

2) Build added value into everything you do. It's the little things, such as knowing a member's name, that give the member the perception that there is real value in the membership. Review every policy in the gym, or create new ones, and make sure they work in the favor of the member. For example, the Joe Smith story, above, illustrates what happens when we create policies to cover bad behavior from one or two people, and how these reactionary rules punish the rest of the members. Someone probably did write a bad check years ago, and now the club has a policy that punishes every member for one person's error. You already have the person's membership information. How much more do you need to track a bad check writer?

3) Teach the members to be good members. We want them to complain. We want them to feel that they are part of the gym's family. We want them to feel ownership in the club. We want them to feel that throwing out

ideas is part of their responsibility as a member. Set up systems and post signs that open the door to members getting involved in the club.

4) Always remember that the member will get even. If we lose a member, it's for a very simple reason. They simply didn't perceive that they received enough value for the cost. If you lose a member, don't blame that person for not being serious, don't blame the competition and don't blame your location. Always start with the basic premise that the member just didn't get value for their investment. Thinking like this will help you improve your business by putting the responsibility for member service on yourself, where it should be.

If we lose a member, it's for a very simple reason. They simply didn't perceive that they received enough value for the cost.

Multiple profit centers lower the dependency on new sales while increasing a club's daily cash flow

Multiple profit centers decrease a club's vulnerability in the market place and also increase the perception of the club's ability to supply member service

Chapter 12

Competitors with gas station price war mentalities can be beaten with the use of multiple profit centers

Section Four

LESSONS FROM LIFE — #11

Maybe your standards are wrong

MANY PROBLEMS IN THE fitness business can be traced back to the old Burt Reynolds movie, *Deliverance*. These guys were in an area where there was simply too much inbreeding which made everyone stupid.

The gym business is much the same. When someone new opens a club, they usually spend a year observing other clubs and stealing their ideas. When they finally open, they often are a direct copy of all the mistakes other owners have made over the years, mistakes picked up by owners who stole ideas from someone else before them.

In the end, many fitness businesses turn out the same around the country. The colors, equipment placement, and business systems, right or wrong, are perpetuated year after year, as everyone keeps stealing from everyone else in the business.

This leads to a fitness business that truly may be better than a competitor's, but is still lousy because the standards they are comparing themselves to are set too low.

The moral of the story

Our standards are too low, because we've been comparing

In the end, many fitness businesses turn out the same

ourselves against each other for too long. To improve our standards, we need to look outside the industry for better role models.

For example, the main street in Pasadena, Calif., has a hundred or so businesses that could set the design standard for clubs around the country. There are small restaurants on this street that use light, color and sound better than 90 percent of all the clubs in the country. And these design techniques are usually simple and affordable, compared to what most owners spend to build the same old floor plans and colors.

If a novice owner wants to build something new and exciting, they might be better off not to look at any other clubs and just concentrate on the shops in Pasadena's old town instead. To raise our standards for the industry, we need to expand our role models and bring new blood into the gene pool, instead of continuing to fish in the shallow end of the current pool.

12

Competitors with gas station price war mentalities can be beaten with the use of multiple profit centers

As OWNERS, WE ARE operating in an era of intense competition, where member prices are insanely low — often below membership prices charged in the early '80s. Today's market is also negatively influenced by large chains with a gas station mentality, that have declared a price war using prices artificially supported by speculative money from outside the industry.

How can independent and small-group operators compete against mega-chains that strive to be the biggest ever, but are proud to be known as the cheapest players in the market?

Cheapest can't be the best

There is room to compete if owners and operators understand a simple rule from the real business world: If your competitor stakes out the "cheapest price in town" niche, this obviously opens up the "higher price quality" niche. A product can't be the cheapest and the best at the same time.

Wal-Mart is a successful chain, but so is Nordstrom. A Geo Metro is a nice entry-level car, but there is still room for upper-level automobiles too. In the fitness business, we all don't have to follow the chains that base their marketing strategy on price wars, and go after the cheapest people in the market.

We also forget that we are selling a service and not a commodity. If our

> **If your competitor stakes out the "cheapest price in town" niche, this obviously opens up the "higher price quality" niche.**

business and the competitor's are both selling shampoo, and the product is the same, then the lowest price makes sense to the consumer. But we are selling service, just like doctors, accountants and other professionals. In those fields, the lowest price equals the poorest service and the least experienced providers.

Most importantly, owners of fitness facilities need to understand the return-per-member concept of doing business. The return-per-member concept is simply defined as making more money from fewer members.

Endlessly chasing new members is not the answer

Chasing an endless supply of new members is a self-defeating business plan

Chasing an endless supply of new members is a self-defeating business plan. When a club lowers its membership price to an absurd number, such as $19 per month, it bases its business plan on pure volume.

The volume approach is costly to a club because of the costs of marketing, high pressure sales force and the extreme wear and tear on the facility as a result of trying to cram as many members in as possible (all paying the lowest dues possible) into the physical plant.

Member service also completely disappears, because the bulk of the payroll goes into the sales force. Staff divides into either highly paid salespeople or very expendable low-paid desk people. Few employees are left in the middle to provide member service as an ongoing aspect of the business.

When an owner seeks return per member, they base the business plan on going after fewer members — those willing to pay higher prices for less-crowded conditions, more personal attention and a cleaner, more functional physical plant. In other words, the plan is based on learning to make the same amount of money a volume gym makes or more, from fewer members.

The return-per-member approach drives down the cost of operations because sales and marketing costs are lower, and a facility used by people paying a higher price will usually take less of a beating. These folks show more respect for the club because they have more of a feeling of ownership than those members who pay cheap membership prices.

More money from fewer members

A key factor in the return-per-member strategy is the use of multiple profit centers (MPCs). Using MPCs allow the fitness operator to gross more money in the operation on a monthly basis, without signing up as many new sales. The additional cash flow comes from existing members who spend money on the club's services or amenities.

Introducing MPCs helps to eliminate one of the biggest conceptual errors gym owners make — becoming solely dependent on member dues, a single source of income, for their revenues. This is especially true in a high-pressure sales system where all company resources are dedicated to keeping sales flowing. One seldom sees a club with old-style sales offices, first-visit aggressive closers, cold calls and draw boxes, that also offers great member service and viable multiple profit centers. All resources in these clubs are dedicated to only one thing: keeping the sales volume alive.

Fitness businesses need daily cash flow to survive. In a gym totally dependent on sales, the cash flow is only as good as the sales made that day. If there aren't sales, the cash flow is still only as good as the sales made that day, which is nothing. If there aren't sales, then cash flow stops, especially in a gym going mostly for cash. Even a club that has developed a strong receivables base from monthly memberships won't have daily cash flow unless a sale is generated that day.

In a business with multiple profit centers, cash flow continues daily even if sales slow or temporarily cease. The business has a greater chance of surviving without dependency on just new sales alone. The club still has to generate sales, but the amount of sales can be fewer in number and at a higher price, therefore niching the business away from low-price competition.

Work to make your business less vulnerable

MPCs decrease your vulnerability in the marketplace. To decrease vulnerability and increase cash flow beyond new sales only, a fitness business should have at least four profit centers in place that are netting at least 20 percent profit on sales every month.

With operating expenses that increase yearly, and the cost of capitalization to get a new gym started, an operator can't afford to have any areas of the business not generating at least 20 percent.

To develop a business plan including MPCs, visualize the gym as a mall. The mall represents the gym and each store in the mall represents one of the multiple profit centers in the gym.

In the mall world, a store that consistently loses money eventually disappears. In the gym world, we often keep parts of the business operating long after the usefulness to profitability is past. This means that if one profit center is profitable, with a $500 net per month and a second profit center loses $500 per month, one cancels out the other's profit. In other words, the club has a total net profit of $0.

In real-life business, there is no such thing as zero. If two profit centers combine to equal zero, the real total is not zero but probably a loss of some amount. The process and management to manipulate the profit centers for the month has a cost and lost opportunity value that are usually not calculated in any formula.

Profit centers can be defined into two distinct categories. First are the service MPCs, such as a nutrition education system, a basic drink service or one-on-one training. This type of MPC is basic to a club's business plan. Other examples in the service category would be a juice bar, survival/impulse gear in the active wear store, and educational or specialty classes like a spin program.

A fitness business should have at least four profit centers in place that are netting at least 20 percent profit on sales every month.

The other MPC type includes club amenities, such as a day spa or child care. All are nice to have, but they are only profitable in the right populations and are not necessary for business survival.

For MPCs to be effective in a fitness business, certain principles have to be applied. Without the application of these concepts, or at least partial application, a profit center could go from successful to mediocre.

Create the impulse to buy

Profit centers work best when based on the impulse buying style. The impulse buying style simply means the member responds to certain stimuli, thus making an unplanned buying decision. If an owner doesn't understand that a large majority of retail sales are made on impulse and not by plan, the club's profit centers will not succeed.

Drink coolers are a great example of impulse. The traditional way to sell drinks in a club is to put a single cooler, handling only sports drinks, behind the check-in counter.

Applying the concept of impulse buying, drink sales from behind a counter should be pretty limited. When the drinks are behind the counter, the member needs to have a preconceived idea of wanting a drink, and then must seek service by telling a staff member what drink they want.

By putting the drinks on the member side of the counter, somewhere in the walkway where members checking in have immediate self-service access, the club creates an atmosphere for impulse sales or spontaneous buying decisions. The person may not intend to buy a drink, but as they pass the brightly-colored cooler by the counter advertising drinks on sale, the frost on a bottled beverage triggers the impulse to buy.

If you've ever gone to the grocery store for milk and come home with cookies and chips too, then you understand impulse buying. The vibrant display in front of you stimulated your attention and need to buy, and you bought on impulse.

One of the ironies surrounding drink coolers is that owners don't want to put them in the traffic flow area, because they worry about theft. But it's proven that employees thoughtlessly "steal" most of the profits from drink sales. Does it, therefore, make sense to keep drinks behind the counter close to the people who steal the largest amount of product?

Most gyms carry only sport-specific drinks with weird names like "Amino Thunder Killer" that usually apply only to a very specific target market.

Drinks also reveal another common mistake: the lack of selection in a specific profit area. Most gyms carry only sport-specific drinks with weird names like "Amino Thunder Killer" that usually apply only to a very specific target market. If a club offers these drinks, the assumption is made that the potential consumer needs and understands this type of drink.

But the club is made up of a variety of members who will buy water in various sizes, teas in different flavors and juices and soft drinks. They'll buy the same product in the gym that they will buy on the way home, if given the chance.

152

The arc of impulse and the arc of entry

The most valuable part of your gym is the first 35 to 50 feet from the door. The arc of impulse, approximately 35 to 50 feet in radius, stems from the entry door into the club. This is the most valuable real estate you rent or own, because every member has to pass through it every time they enter and leave the facility.

Every single profit center should be somehow placed or represented in the arc. The check-in counter should be partially included in the arc as well. You couldn't have one-on-one training situated in the arc, for example, but you could at least have a display promoting this profit center featured somewhere in the radius.

A secondary arc is the arc of entry and makes up the first 10 to 15 feet inside the doorway. Most entryways are too boring. We're not building churches where a quiet, discreet entryway is appropriate. Wild colors, crazy displays, stuff that moves, pictures, testimonials, things hanging off the ceiling, stuff you have to step around, staff working sample tables and anything else that creates impulse should be part of an exciting entry arc.

Going back to the mall example, think of a store like the new Eddie Bauer clothing stores. When you enter their stores, you usually have to walk around display tables and clothing racks. The walls are lined with stacks of clothing, some very brightly colored, and all very accessible to the impulse buying style. The check-out counter at the Eddie Bauer stores are toward the back of the building, forcing you to walk through a majority of the displays to pay, further increasing your chance of one last impulse purchase.

Promotion of the profit centers is an art form

Promotion is another key concept for successful profit centers. When we first think of promoting anything in the gym, we always think of signs. Signs are everywhere. Signs clutter the counters and locker rooms, and owners hang them in the stalls and on the mirrors. Signs in some gyms have reached epidemic proportions.

Putting a sign on the cooler for a drink sale is a form of passive promotion. Passive promotion is the least effective tool for developing your profit centers, or for bringing attention to any event in the club.

To further understand promoting in the gym, let's look a standard in-house member promotion that was popular a few years ago. Let's say we are offering a free mountain bike as a member referral promotion. If the member brings in two guests who become members, the member gets a free bike that cost the club about $100, because of a minimum guarantee to buy 10 from the local bike store and because of additional barter that brought the cost of the bikes down.

At the first level of passive promotion, based solely on the use of signs, the owner gets a picture of the bike and hangs it near the locker rooms, with a poster board sign announcing the promotion. A few owners would put up

The most valuable part of your gym is the first 35 to 50 feet from the door.

several posters around the club and a few of the more creative ones would add balloons or bright colors, but basically the sign and picture would constitute the entire promotion.

The next level up of promotion would be passive/physical representation. This is where the owner gets a bike and sets it on a table against the wall with signs. This is a step above a picture but it is still passive because there is no forced member interaction. The owner is using something (other than a sign) to draw the member's attention. However, this is still not enough to get very many people interested in what you are trying to accomplish.

The next level of promotion would be building a display, elevating the bike and placing it directly in the middle of the entryway. Members would have no choice but to walk around it each time they enter and leave the club. This is the first level of active promotion because members must physically react to the display by walking around it to enter the gym. This is the basic level we need to learn to promote successful profit centers in the gym.

The more advanced way to promote would be to suspend the bike from the ceiling on an electric fan motor. The bike could slowly spin, forcing the members to respond by giving it their attention. By alternating between an elevated display in the entryway and the ceiling display, more members would be forced to take notice. An alternative to the ceiling idea at this promotion level would be to have the staff take the bike onto the floor during prime times, ride it around if room permits, or give the members free, but cheap, certificates to the profit centers if they take the bike for a spin in the parking lot.

To be successful at building profit centers, you have to learn to promote on more sophisticated levels. If there is no active promotion, profit centers will never achieve their ultimate profit levels.

If there is no active promotion, profit centers will never achieve their ultimate profit levels.

Promote each profit center independently

For profit centers to be successful, again defined as a 20 percent net or better for each individual center, the MPCs need to be promoted independently. A sale should be in progress every day, supported by an active display. There should also be educational support tied to as many products as possible. For example, a weekly ab class on some sort of ab trainer would allow the club to sell the trainers in the pro shop. The educational aspect of the promotion would lead to the eventual sale.

A nutrition education program can be supported with cooking classes, a member happy hour where participants enjoy smoothies, and guest speakers on various aspects of training. Even something as simple as asking members (when they leave) if they'd like a drink for the ride home could add $100 or more to the gross revenues of the drinks profit centers each month.

A mistake many owners make with MPCs is failing to do year-round planning. Many moneymaking opportunities are lost because owners aren't proactive enough in their profit center planning.

For example, in many markets, April and May are pivotal months when members start shifting their interest toward summer. Two events allow clubs to use this time to develop profit center income if the events are promoted properly.

The first event would be a spring clothing sale. Most clubs put their spring wear out for sale as it arrives, with no promotion other than perhaps a sign announcing new arrivals in the pro shop. A better plan might be to store all spring clothing and have a one-week blowout sale supported by active promotion at the end of April.

An owner accidentally stumbled onto a very successful active promotion for pro shops. As the owner was driving home, he passed a women's clothing store that was going out of business. They had a sign in the window saying that all fixtures were for sale. The club owner purchased a bunch of chrome racks, and as he was leaving, the clothing store owner asked if he would like to buy the last large box of leftover fixtures for $10. He said fine, threw the box in the truck, and left for the gym.

The staff put the chrome fixtures in the pro shop, but left the box sitting unopened in the office for several days. The owner arrives one day and finds a male mannequin sitting in his office — wearing all of his workout clothes his staff had taken from his office. The owner thought it was funny, but it also raised an idea. In the box that no one had looked in, was also another male mannequin and one female.

The owner told the staff to have fun with the mannequins and use them as props for the pro shop. How they used them was their decision. He came in the next day and found the two male mannequins sitting in lawn chairs in the entryway with a cooler, beers in their hands and, most importantly, wearing stuff from the shop. The members loved it, and soon the mannequins had names.

The mannequins took on lives of their own. One day they were sitting in their chairs with binoculars watching the female mannequin work out on a stair machine. Each day they were up to something new as they traveled around the gym. The members began to look for them when they came in, and for about a year they became part of the gym staff, wearing nametags and uniforms when they weren't selling clothing.

Sound goofy? Of course it does. Did it work? It worked much better than cardboard signs with "Sale" written on them. By putting different clothes on them each day, they became active displays because they were constantly interacting with the members.

The second event most owners cover once a year has been done hundreds of times but seldom well. Everyone in the gym starts thinking about summer, and every person in the community starts thinking about swimsuit season. Yet most clubs don't get beyond a newspaper advertisement or paper sign talking about the coming swimsuit season.

An active promotion for the coming swimsuit season that worked rather well was also based on a mannequin. The same owner in the story above also purchased a female torso mannequin that was the mid-section only. It was just the upper legs, hips and buttocks. The interesting part was that is was from a section for women who were really pregnant and needed

The owner arrives one day and finds a male mannequin sitting in his office — wearing all of his workout clothes his staff had taken from his office.

larger clothing.

The owner put a string bikini on the female. If the dummy had been a real woman, she would have been at least 50 pounds overweight. The dummy with the string bikini was then placed in the entryway, bottom to the door, with a sign stating: "Eight weeks to swimsuit season — are you ready?"

The cure, of course, was the club's nutritional program for existing members or to simply join and get in shape for prospective members who were just coming in for the first time. The display attracted a lot of comments, some negative, but many thought it was very funny. But the club had a record month for its nutrition program. Keep in mind that this promotion was done several years ago, and probably isn't politically correct today, but it is still a great example of forcing members to pay attention.

Be selective when choosing MPCs

The final point when it comes to MPCs is choosing wisely. Not every profit center is for every club.

Under the service category, you could consider the following: drink coolers, a sports bar/espresso bar concept, a nutritional education system, one-on-one training as an educational program, an activewear store and spin classes. Amenity MPCs would be childcare, tanning, a day spa and massage.

Some MPCs, such as tanning, are starting to be phased out of many gyms. Childcare is another example of a giveaway that many clubs are finally admitting they don't do well with, lose money at and it really doesn't bring in the female clients they thought it would, therefore, they are getting rid of it and cutting their losses. Others, such as the day spa, are just starting to enter the market. To be successful, the MPC has to match the facility.

Summary

A fitness business should have at least four viable profit centers to take the pressure off new sales. Each profit center should net 20 percent or better on a monthly basis. Remember, in today's market, we can't afford to carry losers. If the profit center doesn't make money, then dump it. There are very few exceptions to this very basic business rule.

A mature gym can seek a 60:40 split in its revenues — a split between membership-related income and profit centers.

A mature gym can seek a 60:40 split in its revenues — a split between membership-related income and profit centers. This breaks down to 60 percent of the money the club brings in coming from membership/workout related income, including daily workout fees, cash sales, member dues, etc.

The other 40 percent of revenue should come from MPCs. A club that has a strong renewal base and 40 percent of its revenues coming from existing members already in the system would be hard to hurt, which allows the facility a greater chance to survive in a competitive market.

To develop a successful profit center program, you need to learn how to promote on a daily basis. Study great retailers like The Gap, Banana Republic and Eddie Bauer for ideas. They all have beautiful stores, and much of what they do can translate to the fitness business.

Things you can do to use this material

1) Most markets are open to a higher-priced quality club alternative. Never forget that not every member is driven by the cheapest price. There are just as many people who would rather pay more for a quality product as there are those who always want the cheapest. Start to position your club toward a narrower niche, servicing a more select market, and stay away from price wars. No one wins price wars, including the big chains who started them.

2) Learn what return per member means. Start to analyze your business, or build your new business plan toward doing everything you can to increase the return per member. This is nothing more than learning to make more money from fewer members.

3) Over the next year, try to add at least four profit centers in your club that each net a 20 percent minimum per month. Start with the basic service profit centers, and then add the amenity profit centers if they apply to your market. New clubs should add one at a time, learn to promote the profit center well and then move on to the next one. When you first open, start with a nutritional education program and drinks, and add one-on-one training slowly as your business builds. Add other profit centers as needed, once these are successful.

4) Learn to promote. Draw up a one-year promotion plan based on a week at a time, and plan to promote each profit center heavily during the coming year. Learn to promote at the active level, forcing needed interaction with the members, leading to increased sales.

5) Track the profit centers each month. If you can't make money at what should be a profitable area, such as childcare, consider getting rid of it. You don't have to be everything to everybody to be successful. Use the MPC Profit and Loss form (Figure 12.1) to track your centers each month.

6) Try to offer profit centers that no one else in your market does. Instead of always trying to have the same thing and improve it, try to offer different things and give the members, and potential members, a choice.

7) Analyze the 60:40 rule monthly. Work toward a lower dependency on new sales and more of your income coming from the profit centers. Once you start getting about 40 percent of all your revenues from inside your club, you're pretty hard to hurt by both competitors and outside market fluctuations.

8) Here is a checklist of some of the more common profit centers in use in the industry. Not all apply to every facility. Try to develop at least four different centers that net 20 percent each.

Start with the basic service profit centers, and then add the amenity profit centers if they apply to your market.

Drinks

• Put the drinks in the main traffic area near the front counter. Never put the drinks behind the counter, because it limits impulse sales.

• Start with at least one, two-door cooler and work your way up as needed. Clubs in the 8,000- to 15,000-foot range will probably need about six doors to offer the variety they should carry.

• Variety is the key that makes this profit center work. Members drink a lot of different drinks, besides a typical sports product. Copy the 7-Eleven style presentation, and talk to the local convenience store manager about what sells in that market.

• Unless you have a sophisticated software system available, avoid credit

Copy the 7-Eleven style presentation, and talk to the local convenience store manager about what sells in that market.

MPC profit and loss

Month_____

Profit center_____

Revenue

Program revenue	$_____
Product revenue	$_____
Other revenue related to this profit center	$_____
Total revenue for the MPC	$_____

Expenses

Product costs for the month	$_____
Support materials cost	$_____
Labor costs	$_____
Bonuses and commissions	$_____
Other related cost to this profit center	$_____
Total expenses for this MPC	$_____

Profit or loss for this MPC $_____

Adjustments for employee purchases

Revenue	$_____
Expense	$_____

Adjusted profit or loss for this MPC $_____

Figure 12.1. Multiple profit centers profit and loss calculations

for the members and the staff. The majority of the losses the club will incur from drinks will be from unpaid or lost credit purchases. Pay as you go is the rule for the members and staff.

• Set precedents by never ringing up your own drinks, and don't let the staff ring up theirs either.

• Always let the staff see you paying for your drinks. If you don't pay, then they too might not when you aren't looking.

• Put up a professional sign near the coolers that educates the members as to what drinks to drink, when and why. The sign should have a category for pre-workout drinks, drinks to use during the workout, after workout recovery drinks and drinks for the ride home such as water. List the drink, what it is for, when to drink it, the benefits you'll receive from that drink and the price.

• Have a featured drink of the week displayed on the counter with educational support material. Have a drink sale every day, and have an active weekly promotion based on drinks. If you consistently work the drink profit centers, sales will dramatically increase.

• Allow the members to have drinks on the floor. If you are that worried about spilled drinks, provide a quality screw-top water bottle at a cheap price to encourage the members to use drinks during their workouts.

• Round off the drinks to encourage impulse sales. For example, a can of soda pop should cost $1.00. It doesn't matter that they can get it for 80 cents somewhere else; they are standing in your gym looking into your cooler. A dollar is an impulse buy, whereas $1.10 would make the member search for change.

Nutrition education system

• A nutrition education system will be the most important profit center in the coming years. Depending on which expert you believe, working out is a small part of the total fitness formula. Nutrition and education about how you should approach working out are, by far, the greater part of the whole. As an industry, we need to learn how to give members the complete formula, so they can get the best results possible.

• If the members get results, they will stay longer and pay longer than those members who just approach fitness through a training-only system.

• A nutrition education program is a natural for a club. Every member in the gym will at one time or another be interested in losing weight or gaining more muscle, and will seek nutritional guidance as the solution.

• Your nutrition-education program should almost be a separate part of your business. If done correctly, it should be the centerpiece of the facility and all sales and training should revolve around the nutrition program.

• The fitness professional, or technician, is the key to making the program work. Dieticians and nutritionists seldom make good program directors because of their approach to fitness. The exception would be one of these people who is also a fitness enthusiast. The right tech should be someone who is into the fitness lifestyle, and who doesn't have too many preconceived ideas. Several of the professional programs, such as Apex Fitness, offer

> **Put up a professional sign near the coolers that educates the members as to what drinks to drink, when and why.**

week-long training for new techs, on-site support and backup training.

• The entire management team (including the owner, manager, assistant managers, lead trainer and lead fitness professional) for the education program should all go through training and be able to run a typical member through a program. They may never have to do it, but we can't sell it or control it if we don't understand it.

• Supplement sales are the desired outcome of any education program. A good program educates the member as to the proper approach to working out, and nutrition and supplements help the member achieve their goals. A key to supplements is to always mark them up at least 115 percent. There is little profit in any retail sales without at least that minimum level of markup.

• If you establish a good nutrition program, you can also build a good juice bar. We teach members what to eat and provide meal alternatives, such as shakes and snacks in the gym.

• A good nutrition program will help the members get results faster, which helps your member service, which ultimately keeps the member in the system longer.

• Try a two-tier pricing program featuring the most inclusive membership, and the highest priced, with the nutrition program included. The base or secondary program would assume the least amount of help, and the most expensive program would be built on the most help for the member, including nutrition and some basic training.

Childcare

• The basic rule of thumb is that male owners are horrible at making childcare work in the clubs. And since most owners are male, childcare is not usually very productive as a profit center.

• You do not need a childcare center in order for you to be successful in the business. It's an old habit we copy over and over from the competitors. They have it and lose money, so we offer it and lose money, and then the next club in the area offers it because the first two did.

• Childcare seems so logical. The women in the club are the right age. We offer the room at no charge. It should logically work. The disappointing thing is that less than 10 percent of an average club's members use childcare. There is always that core that uses it three or four times a week, but the majority of the members don't care and don't want it. A typical club with 1,500 to 1,800 members can lose $1,500 to 2,500 per month on childcare. Even if 10 percent of the members, or 150 in a club with 1,500, used the program, the average club would be better off to dump it and use the money to improve other areas of the club. If the members who used the program (and made sure the usage was documented) were offered three months free for the inconvenience of losing the program, the club would only lose 40 percent of the 150. This makes it worthwhile to shut down the program.

• The old logic that we offer it as a sales tool is also out of date. This logic states that a member sees childcare, joins and then never uses it, but we got the sale because we offered it. If you can't quantify it, then it isn't real. It's hard to make real business assumptions based on this logic. The only way

If you establish a good nutrition program, you can also build a good juice bar. We teach members what to eat and provide meal alternatives, such as shakes and snacks in the gym.

you can really quantify childcare is by the penetration rate, or the number of individuals using the program compared to the total gym population. The number of kids in childcare each day doesn't really tell you anything. The important numbers are how many different parents use childcare over a 30-day period, compared to the total number of members. If less than 10 percent of your population uses this program, there is a 95 percent chance or better that the gym is losing money each month by offering this service, even if it does charge a minimum per child.

• If you do offer childcare, keep in mind some basics that will help you minimize your losses. The room should be at least 300 square feet or larger and have its own bathroom facilities. Parents are not comfortable with teenage childcare providers in the gym. There should be a video camera in the room that has a monitor behind the front desk and also one in the cardio room. The smallest toy in the room should not fit through a toilet paper roll. Don't give it away free. You need to charge at least $3 per child per session to have a chance of breaking even. Analyze the program monthly, and consider dropping it if you continually run a negative cash flow.

The sports bar/juice bar/social area with espresso

• Juice bars work better if they have a sports bar theme rather than a café concept.

• The juice bar and the check-in counter should never be separate. Keep these areas combined to keep staffing costs down and available service up.

• Sports bars/juice bars don't work unless they are built into the club's traffic flow. A sports bar stuck in separate area without a view of the workout floor and entrance seldom if ever makes any money. The bar has to be where someone sitting at it can see people working out, people coming into the club, and probably the cardio area too if possible. If you're not sitting where the action is then you probably won't sit at all.

• Shakes and snacks that support your nutrition program will be your primary product sold at the bar, along with snack bars, bagels and other reasonably nutritious foods. The average shake should have about a $1 hard cost and range from $3.50 to $6 apiece, depending on the add-ons and extras.

• Espresso and coffee are becoming huge in the country; gyms need to be part of this trend. To make it work, however, you need to do it right. Use a commercial espresso machine, hang big menus from the ceiling and include all of the fluff that goes with selling premium coffee. Starbucks set the standard in the industry, and we need to copy as much as we can to make coffee a big part of the bar area. Do not, under any circumstances, even with a gun at your mother's head, give away free coffee. It's a rookie mistake that can cost the club hundreds of dollars a month. Remember that free isn't necessary member service. Good service might be several choices of coffee, served at a reasonable price in oversized cups.

• Racetrack style counters that stand free in the entryways are a popular design. Racetrack styles are giant ovals that have seating for the members on one side, and the check-in and entryway on the other. Wall-mounted designs also work if they have a bar style flavor to them with two or three tele-

Parents are not comfortable with teenage childcare providers in the gym.

visions mounted on the wall or hanging over the center. The TVs are close-captioned during the day, but the sound is turned on for a big game or sporting event.

• A good sports bar/juice bar also replaces a sales office. Most modern clubs no longer use a sales office, but do their sales at café tables around the bar or at the bar itself. The atmosphere is less threatening and more conducive to the sales effort.

• Pro shop items should also be displayed near the bar. If a member sits there long enough, staring at a bright shirt while sipping on a shake, somebody is going to buy something.

• Use dark, heavier colors for the bar area. It should also have its own lighting and atmosphere. Never light the bar area with halogen or fluorescent. Instead, go with warm bulb-style lights that make the area inviting.

Rental space

• Rental space means that we sublease space in the facility to other businesses.

• Always be a landlord, and never a percentage partner. There is implied ownership in a percentage interest and that means there is also liability to the owner. For example, charge a massage person a flat rent, and not a rent and a percentage of what that person generates. If the person is sued for hurting someone, and you are a percentage in their business, you too will be sued. Also make sure that the person has a valid insurance policy in place that holds you harmless.

• Be creative. There are many businesses that could do well in a fitness facility. For example, consider beauty shops, nail salons, massage, small insurance companies, chiropractors, physical therapists or any other small business that could thrive off of your members. Even a small dry cleaner could benefit from 50 square feet in the club simply by using a counter as a pick-up and drop-off site for the main business.

• Make sure that a condition of being a tenant is that the business co-ops in your advertising fees for the club.

Rental lockers

• It's estimated that at least 40 percent of a typical club's membership comes dressed and ready to work out. Rental lockers placed outside the locker rooms keep the traffic down in this already congested area, and offer additional income for the club.

Rental lockers placed outside the locker rooms keep the traffic down in this already congested area, and offer an additional income for the club.

• Use banks of lockers, usually six high by four wide, and place them around the edge of the workout floor, outside the locker rooms, near the cardio area, close to the spin room and, if you still have aerobics, put a bank in the back of the main room. Each locker is about 12 x 12 x 18 inches deep, or just the right size for a gym bag or coat.

• Rent the locker in six-month or one-year increments for about $10 to $15 per month, cheaper if they sign up for the year. Some clubs put small nameplates on the front of the lockers for members who pay for the year as a status item.

• A hint is to put an expiration sticker inside the locker for tracking, and keep a monthly file in the computer of whose time is up during that calendar month.

Day spa concept

• A day spa concept will work in most clubs, except an older style hard-core licensing gym. The day spa offers personal services for women, primarily, but many men do shop in that area and more are starting to use the services on a regular basis.

• A typical day spa will offer facials, waxing, spot massage, make-up consultation, personalized perfumes and other pampering services.

• An aesthetician works the program and can be hired from local beauty schools.

• While this position can be hired from the outside, most clubs are doing it in-house because the profit potential is so high. It doesn't make sense to give the bulk of the profit away for something most owners can learn to do and control themselves.

• It takes about $3,000 to start a program. You need a room that is about 8 x 10 feet and has a sink and water. The start-up cost is spread between equipment and the products needed to get going.

• As in the nutrition program that sells supplements, the day spa will sell a lot of products such as shampoos, body oils and lotions. There are several excellent national programs, and Aveda offers very good support on a local level.

• The club should be able to net from services and products about 40 percent on a monthly basis. One room can generate about $4,000 to $5,000 per month in total revenues for most clubs, with at least 500 members. Larger clubs may need more than one room.

Clothing and pro shop items

• Pro shops have become harder to operate over the years, as the margins have been cut by large retailers. Clubs used to be the sole source of most workout wear available to the consumer, but that has changed. KMart and Wal-Mart now carry clothing once found only in gyms, and they sell these items at a retail price, less than the wholesale price paid by most owners.

• The trend is moving away from setting up fully stocked pro shops with a variety of clothing lines. Most owners concentrate on what's called survival gear (basic workout clothing) and accessories that a member would most likely impulse buy while in the gym.

• For men, basic survival gear would include: basic white socks, black shorts with pockets or a short tight in a solid color, workout briefs, a basic non-logo T-shirt, a tank top if your gym allows them, a long-sleeved T-shirt, sweatshirts, baseball caps, gloves, water bottles, wraps, an economical gym bag and personal items such as razors, personal mouthwash and toothpaste, combs and other items a member would impulse buy, rather than miss a workout because he forgot an item.

• For women, basic survival gear would include: basic socks in two or

Most owners concentrate on what's called survival gear (basic workout clothing) and accessories that a member would most likely impulse buy while in the gym.

163

three neutral colors, black tights and leotards and one or two other basic solid colors, workout bras, overshirts and overshorts, and most of the same personal items as the guys would wear. Keep it simple and generic when you first start and remember the concept of impulse gear. A member is in the locker room, forgets a T-shirt, and has to make a decision to buy one from you or skip the workout. We want to stock the basic items, so the members will impulse buy from us.

• Go easy on your logos. Once the members have a collection of shirts with your company logo, they will be less likely to buy another on impulse. Offer a wide selection of shirts, either plain or with a different logo, that are sold cheaper than your regular shirt.

• Look for the special shirt or offer. If you can find a shirt or top that's not available in the local discount stores, buy a limited supply and do a one-time offering. If you're right, you'll make some quick money and be gone. If you're wrong, the damage will be limited.

• There is no rule that says pro shops have to have walls, be in a room or have any type of set structure. Think in terms of small islands with a center rack and stacks around it. Make sure there are displays in the walkways that force member interaction. There should also be an additional display with bright colors near the sports bar that changes daily.

• One of the future trends for fitness facility pro shops will be the entrance of the retailing pros such as Nike and Reebok. Consider a complete line of clothing from one of the majors. For example, you could offer a complete Reebok store that carries their central shirts and shorts line. You wouldn't have to worry about carrying a wide line of different colors and styles, just what's hot in the Reebok line that would limit your risk and exposure. To start a complete single line shop, budget about $7,500 for your first purchase.

Spin classes

• Spin classes [the trademarked "spinning" or other group cycling programs] will be a hot profit center for a limited period of time. As of this publication, the activity is still evolving with the non-aerobics class approach getting the most attention with the members. Non-traditional class groupings, such as a horseshoe-shaped presentation, are the most effective and popular with the members.

• Spin should be charged for and sold as a separate activity for the members. Don't give the program to the aerobics staff; that will lead to it becoming nothing more than another slide fiasco for owners.

• The program should not be taught on a regular aerobics floor. It should have its own room and identity in the club. Most clubs should start with 11 bikes and a 300- to 350-square-foot room that is specially decorated. Part of the image for the program is the black room, trick lighting and other add-ons that give spin its mystique.

• Bike enthusiasts are usually the best instructors. Avoid the traditional aerobics trappings, such as microphones that cancel the music and the instructor facing the class on a stage. The magic is that it's not the next step in aerobics but something totally different and new in group exercise.

There is no rule that says pro shops have to have walls, be in a room or have any type of set structure.

164

• Charge per class or use a punch card that offers a slight reduction in the per-class charge. Limit the classes to only about 12 per week when the program is first introduced. Overexposure will kill it quickly. Keep it limited in membership, resisting the urge to add bikes until it dies.

Staffing will be the most difficult issue you'll ever have to deal with in the fitness business

To achieve maximum success in the business, you'll have to master finding, educating and motivating your staff to work at their highest potential

Chapter 13

Why is that employee just standing there staring at you with nothing to do and no hope of ever finding the first clue?

Chapter 14

If your employees were as good as you are, they'd have your job

Chapter 15

Learning to live with a stranger in your business

Chapter 16

Staffing a fitness business is more complicated than seeing how many hours a week your relatives can work

Chapter 17

If it ain't in writing, it ain't real

It's the little things that will kill you

THERE WAS A NEIGHBORHOOD gym in the Chicago area that had a unique problem. No one could figure out how to get inside.

The gym had three doors on the front of the building. It was in a strip mall, and the owner had taken three bays and had left the doors in place from the old stores. He was only using one of the three. But the exciting part was that you couldn't tell which one was actually the working door if you were standing in the parking lot.

The first choice was the door on the left. A prospective member walked up to the door and pulled. It was locked. He peeked inside and saw a bunch of members in the free-weight area looking at him and waving back at him.

Door number two was in the center. The prospective tried the door, and it too was locked. He peeked inside and saw the members in the cardio area sitting on their workout pieces looking at him and waving. It was then that he realized that the closed doors were how the owner entertained the members in the club.

The third door was on the right and was the actual entrance into the club. But it wasn't really marked that well and didn't stand out from the other two choices.

It was then that he realized that the closed doors were how the owner entertained the members in the club

The moral of the story

It's the little things that can kill you in small business. How many prospective members drove into that parking lot and then didn't even try to get inside the business because the entryways were so confusing? It wouldn't take but a few a

months to affect the business' bottom line.

When most owners want to make changes in their business, they start with the big things: A new building, moving locations, all new equipment or a major name change. But it's the little things that can be easily changed where most owners should begin.

For example, how easy is it to find your location? Does your yellow pages ad have a map and does all of your marketing information have a map and landmarks to make it easier to find? Is your entrance inviting and well-marked? Does your parking lot have enough lighting at night to make your female clientele feel safe coming and going? Do you still have an old turnstile in your entryway that adds an extra barrier to the club and that can prevent sales?

All of these things can act as barriers to your sales effort and can hurt your business. If you're seeking change in your business, start with the small things and do them right first.

13

Why is that employee just standing there staring at you with nothing to do, and no hope of ever finding the first clue?

EVER WONDER WHY that employee is just standing there looking at you like you're an alien, or even worse, one of their parents? It's because you may have hired wrong in the first place. Our traditional system of finding and paying employees has led you to hire a person who is too young for the job, never worked before in their life, and can only communicate with Beavis and Butthead. In other words, you are suffering from the same staffing malady that all of your fellow owners and operators are suffering from — the "they're all boneheads" syndrome.

Staffing is one of those issues that raises a vast swing in emotions from a fitness facility owner. We can't live without staff, but we often lay awake at night wondering if we could get away with just killing a few chosen employees. Of course, this assumes that the employee in question is actually among the living.

You understand what I'm talking about here, the ones who really make us crazy, such as the counter guy who forgets to shave and always seems to have the wrong uniform top on when he comes to work. Nothing really serious here, but after a while he simply needs to be killed. But even our plans to kill them won't work because just when we set the trap, the employee doesn't show up to work due to a massive hangover or because of a "signifi-

> ...you are suffering from the same staffing malady that all of your fellow owners and operators are suffering from — the "they're all boneheads" syndrome.

169

cant other of the week" problem.

A typical owner will have to deal with the following important issues in the near future in the fitness industry: raising capital, increased operational costs and the endlessly stupid low pricing from the big chains. But the two most business threatening concerns will be staffing and renewals. These two key issues are directly dependent on each other, because a weak staff prohibits any type of member service and weak member service leads directly to poor member retention.

The traditional fitness staffing model doesn't work anymore

For our businesses to grow in the coming years, we need to reevaluate how we find, develop and motivate our employees. The reason staffing is such an issue for the typical fitness owner is that our traditional model of how we hire and pay employees no longer works. The fitness business has prospered over the years by depending on two distinct levels of staff: an elite high-paid sales staff and a very low level, undertrained and very expendable support staff.

But this system no longer works. Members are demanding more service and are supporting clubs that offer this service. As many of the big chains have proven over the past several decades, slick salesmanship is no longer the answer. The clubs actually have to produce a solid product after the sale to stay competitive.

As many of the big chains have proven over the past several decades, slick salesmanship is no longer the answer.

For example, many club systems are still based on high-pressure sales, but these same clubs are really in the business of just replacing the members they drive away each month because of poor member service. This opens the door to a competitor willing to develop a staff that can provide this service.

Low pay buys low service

The old model of good employees for $5 to $6 per hour is no longer valid in most parts of the country. These old style types of clubs can generate new business but they can't keep this business, because the support staff represents the lowest common denominator when it comes to hiring and training. Employees willing to work for $5 or $6 per hour in today's economy usually are too young, have little previous real-life work experience and have poor communication skills. These employees are not capable of delivering the kind of member service it takes to keep today's more sophisticated members happy and in the system.

Another way to look at it is that the clubs hire bodies and not talent. A body to fill that morning shift. A body to replace Jane who moved away, leaving a shift open. We hire bodies to fill slots, but there isn't usually a whole lot of talent at the lower end of the pay scale in a workers' market represented by the economy of the '90s.

Without a consistent well-trained staff, there can be no consistency in the delivery of member service. With competition developing at a near frantic pace, the only thing that will separate the good clubs from each other in the future will be delivery of the product, not the product itself. We'll all have decent physical plants and great equipment in the future. The winner in the gym wars will be the club businesses that understand long-term service is replacing traditional high-pressure sales as the central operating strategy for our business plans.

The major flaw in the theory of delivery of the product is that the owner doesn't have the final say in the matter. The owner may truly believe in customer service, but it's usually the lowest paid and most undertrained employee on the staff, such as the front counter person, that the members most associate with the club and its service image.

This person is the one who really has the responsibility for delivering the product and will do so according to the traits they bring to the job and the skills they possess. The flaw is that employees we now attract don't have the traits necessary for the club to be successful.

Traits in our business are defined as things the employee already possesses and can't usually be taught. Things that can be taught and developed are skills such as the ability to learn a sales pitch or a specific training routine. Enthusiasm, on the other hand, is something that can be inspired but seldom taught.

A caring, people-person attitude is an example of a trait and is also something that can't usually be taught. Running a cash register would be another example of a necessary skill for a club and is also something that can be taught. There was even a monkey at the St. Louis Zoo who could run a cash register. They got him a job at the zoo gift shop. He was bad at customer service, though, so they moved him to a convenience store.

A trait necessary for a front counter person, for example, would be the ability to communicate with a variety of people on a daily basis, not an ability most employees who work for $5 per hour possess. Hiring a quiet, fearful person because they are the only body that applied is the norm for most owners. We then throw them into the fracas at the front counter on a Monday night during primetime, after only three to four hours of training, and expect them to be competent performers. Of course if it were a new salesperson, we'd never let that person on the floor without *days* of training. We assume member service to be self-evident, but the sales skills have to be taught.

Before we discuss how to find an employee, we should first explore the traditional thinking concerning what we offer in the way of jobs. Owners think working in the gym business is one of the most desirable jobs any person could have. What could be better than working around a bunch of healthy, semi-naked people while you get to wear funny clothes and work out?

The truth, however, is employees no longer define our jobs as all that desirable. They have too many options in today's job market, many of which offer better training, benefits and a better starting wage. Let's look at what

The owner may truly believe in customer service, but it's usually the lowest paid and most undertrained employee on the staff, such as the front counter person, that the members most associate with the club and its service image.

we think is good and then look again from the employee's viewpoint.

The issue of how we pay

As owners, we want to pay the lowest wage for the best employees. We think the typical wages paid by the industry, usually a little above the local minimum, are enough and should allow us to get decent folks to work for us. It's the theory the business was built upon, and it should still work. But every business owner is thinking the same thing. They all want to pay $5 per hour (adjust this per region/substitute your local minimum wage) and get a dedicated employee. We, meaning all small businesses, are fighting for the same entry-level employee, especially in the service businesses.

What kind of employee will actually work for that much, or that little, money anymore? Our economy during the '90s is hotter than it has been during the entire 40-year history of our industry. This means the good employees are going out for a dollar or two higher than the local minimum wage, and they're going for the better jobs. Anyone left in today's market answering ads for minimum wage is probably a pretty lousy investment for the club.

Potential employees who are answering ads for minimum wage are probably too dumb to work or are using the club as their first work experience, neither of which situation is good for your business. Anybody who walks in and says, "Hi, I'm Johnny and I'm here for that minimum wage job in the paper," is most likely not going to be the person who can deliver legendary member service. Why wasn't he going for those $7 to $8 an hour jobs? Is it because he feels he is a minimum-wage type of guy, and is really proud of the fact that minimum wage is the maximum he aspires to?

Poor wages also means high turnover. Employees on the bottom rung of pay will quickly leave for a buck or two higher per hour once they gain practical work experience with you. If the employee has been somewhat trained and on the job for at least six months, it will cost you about ten times the employee's monthly salary to replace him or her.

For example, a well-trained counter person would know how to recognize potential business in the pro shop, be able to make a shake, answer some basic membership questions, and be able to competently handle the phone. They would also be able to recognize a potential member walking in the door and to promptly process that person.

The new person hired to replace the exiting one wouldn't have the experience and training necessary to step out on the floor and help a member put together an outfit in the pro shop. The new person might also put too much of the basic ingredients in the shake, therefore lowering the profit margin, and might initially mess up a lot of phone calls, some from potential members, before they are comfortable. The business they lose, or just don't see during their first six months, could easily cost the club 10 times the monthly salary of the trained and capable person.

It would have made more sense to have paid a dollar or two more an

Anybody who walks in and says, "Hi, I'm Johnny and I'm here for that minimum wage job in the paper," is most likely not going to be the person who can deliver legendary member service.

hour to keep the first employee once they are trained and productive, rather than to constantly lose and replace employees, let alone figuring the additional cost of hiring a new employee.

Another issue concerning pay relates to fishing. Lousy bait catches lousy fish, if any at all. The proper bait for the situation might get you the best fish. If we fish for employees with too low of an entry wage, we are only going to attract the most unskilled and weakest employees. By offering a better wage, usually a dollar or two over local minimum wage, we attract a better employee in the first place. If we train and develop properly, the employee is worth the extra salary anyway. Just be sure to hire all employees on a 90-day probationary period, so any mistakes can be rectified in a manner that won't hurt the club.

Poor working conditions

We think working in a gym is heaven on earth. Many of us have had real jobs and most agree that ties, offices and the other trappings of the real business world suck. But to our employees, the gym business offers less than ideal working conditions.

Long shifts, no breaks, no place to sit and enjoy a meal, constant stress from handling endless member service problems, and inconsistent leadership are just a few of the things employees have to deal with as part of their jobs. Throw in a lack of meaningful compensation and work, petty tasks and a cluttered, poorly lit workspace, all for a $5 to $6 per hour pay none of us would even think of living on in our own lives, and we end up with a frustrated, short-term job holder.

Imagine working in an environment where you stand behind a counter on a carpet over concrete floor without even a place to sit down between customers. Throw in a few pieces of broken equipment the members have to deal with, flooded toilets, a lack of training to handle complaints and a shortage of support staff during the busiest times. Don't forget to include a frustrating (if it's operating at all) computer system, and you have an exciting and glamorous front counter job in the gym business.

We think of gyms as a sort of glamour job, but working long hours on your feet, for low pay, and doing repetitive tasks can lead to a quick decision to change jobs. We should be thinking in terms of consistent breaks, say 15 minutes for every four hours worked, a regular lunch hour off premises, a break room with a locker and a decent wage for the work performed, or at least for the work expected.

We think of gyms as a sort of glamour job, but working long hours on your feet, for low pay, and doing repetitive tasks can lead to a quick decision to change jobs.

Poor training

In a recent survey among employees, we found that the majority of employees feel they are undertrained for the job they hold. On the other hand, the owners we surveyed felt they were giving adequate training for the employee and their job. This obviously leads to high expectations from the owners and managers, and poor performance and job frustration from the staff.

The lower the level of the employee, the more training they require. Front counter people, for example, probably need as many as four hours per week in training, in a combination of group and individual work. But it's usually the sales staff that gets the bulk of the training. These folks are sent to local sales seminars, role-play almost every day and get spot help any time they need it.

Front counter folks, though, are usually taught once and thrown to our mad dog members, the regulars who enjoy working over the new front counter targets. Most of the training the counter people need would be done on the basics, such as phone work, handling complaints, member service training and job essentials. The managers, senior employees and owners should do the bulk of this training. Again, four hours per week, every week, would be about right for developing a good counter staff.

The material covered should be a mix of the basics and the introduction of new material. Employees should also be cross-trained to all other jobs in the business. A front counter person may never sell a membership, but they should have sales training to better understand the goals of the team and the role the sales staff plays.

Lack of structure

Most owners hate structure. They are entrepreneurial types, which means operating according to the disaster at hand. Owners expect to have good employees, without setting a structure to ensure that it happens.

Employees, on the other hand, love structure. They seek leadership and guidance in the parameters of being able to do their own thing. Teach me, train me and then get the hell out of my way. But if I have a problem, I want someone to give guidance. Most employees also work better in a structured environment. Set rules, consistent follow-up, consistent enforcement of those rules, and an objective evaluation system all make for a better, more motivated employee.

A good way to create a sense of structure is to create a club procedure book. This is a master book kept at the front counter that has all of the club's procedures documented in simple, easy-to-follow terms. For example, there might be a section on how to close the club that includes lights, heating and air, alarms, a final club walk through and even where the emergency key is hidden.

Other examples would be to show how to fill out a contract and include a sample, how to send in a contract to the financial company, policies and procedures on renewals, how to make change and figure tax, and how to do a proper information call. Don't assume anything. Every single procedure in the club, no matter how small, should have a separate page or section in the book. Start with the basics and add to it as needed. It may take a year or more to build a complete book that documents everything in the club. Be

A front counter person may never sell a membership, but they should have sales training to better understand the goals of the team and the role the sales staff plays.

sure to keep a copy locked in the manager's office and another at home.

A complete procedure book is a great training tool. All of the entry-level training for new employees can be done with the book. Another benefit of having a compete procedures manual is that you don't have to do all of the training yourself from your head or by trying to reconstruct information from the daily tasks in the club. Anyone with any experience can show other employees how to do things by working though the procedure sheet for a job that's detailed in the book.

No employee benefits

We always hate it when a good employee comes in and says, "I have to quit. My mom says it's time to get a real job." Many clubs can't afford to put together a real benefits package, but every club should work toward a basic insurance and investment package for full-time employees as soon as the club can afford it. We want long-term folks, ones we can count on to help the business grow, but we are usually not willing to make it attractive enough for them to stay.

Using restrictive, old-style management principles

One of the biggest wastes in our payroll budgets is following the principles set down by our fathers. Everyone used to be a basic 9 to 5 guy. No one under 30 works like our fathers did in the '50s and '60s. Forty-hour workweeks are a thing of the past for Generation X.

We waste a big percentage of our payroll trying to give all of our full-timers 40-hour workweeks. Go to just about any gym on a weekday around two o'clock in the afternoon and you'll see what I mean. There are always at least three people standing around the front desk just waiting for something to do. They are there because we had to give them 40 hours.

Most would be happy working a 32-hour workweek, with bonuses and commissions, which should be considered full-time. This means an employee could work four, eight-hour days and be considered full-time. This could also mean one less person standing around on Friday afternoon burning up the payroll.

For example, most of us need our lead salesperson during primetime on Monday through Thursday. But we usually make that person come in on Friday because we need to give them full-time hours, meaning the traditional 40-hour workweek.

An option would be to give the person four eight-hour days and have them there Monday through Thursday, or give them four 10-hour days during the same time period and simply give them other tasks to do during slower afternoon hours. Either way, you save the cost of the clog on Friday afternoon. A note here, however, is that if the employees want to work four 10-hour days, they must sign away their rights to overtime on a document to be

> **Anyone with any experience can show other employees how to do things by working though the procedure sheet for a job that's detailed in the book.**

Having a job where you can make decent money and still have time off is one of the most desirable job requirements for most of our under-30 employees.

kept in their employee file.

In this example, you could keep a good salesperson from burning out by only working the key hours, and save wasted payroll on nonproductive days. Having a job where you can make decent money and still have time off is one of the most desirable job requirements for most of our under-30 employees.

The kiss of death in member service: hiring too young

Another negative byproduct of low wages is that it forces us to hire too young. Many of our front-line people, such as entry-level trainers, salespeople and most of our counter people, are simply too young and inexperienced for what we expect of them.

The problem with an employee who is too young is the lack of communication skills. A big part of member service is the ability to listen and understand what a disgruntled member is trying to get across to you. Once it's established what the member is trying to make us understand, the employee then has to rectify the situation or pacify the member until a solution can be found.

Often, simply listening well and then talking the member through the problem can settle the issue. Employees who are too young seldom have developed good communication skills. They don't know how to listen well, lack common ground with older members, and can't really talk the member through the problem.

We lose a lot of good members because they simply walk away frustrated over a problem that could have been simply handled by a sympathetic ear and a smile, instead of a shrug of the shoulders and an "It's not my job" attitude.

A prime example is the lead counter person. This is the person who is at the front counter during the busiest hours of the day until closing. This is the one person in the club who sees everything, is in contact with virtually every member who enters and leaves the club, and acts as the traffic cop for directing and leading the other staff members. In a club based on member service, this might be the most important job on the team, yet it is often one of the youngest and least-trained people we have in the system.

A perfect person for this job would be someone with good communications skills, a strong presence, the ability to work with a wide variety of members, and who could give some guidance and direction in the club to other staff as to what must happen at the moment.

The ideal person for this position would probably be a woman in her late '20s to whatever age, as long as she is a workout person. This person should also be a people person who has had some type of service experience. This type of person would probably have far better communication skills than your average 22-year-old male or female. Remember, "Yo dude" is not a standard club welcoming statement.

When all else fails, steal your staff from someone else

Finding a staff in today's market is tough. Everyone who is any good is probably already working for someone else. Traditional sources of employees, like help wanted ads, are useless. Again, in this hot economy, if you want to work, you probably are, which means you aren't home answering ads in the paper.

That leaves Plan B, or the "steal everyone you need" plan. If you can't find good employees because they are already employed, then we need to strongly invite those employees to change jobs. This has been going on for years in the real business world, but we've always had qualms in the fitness industry about such a sensitive subject.

We don't necessarily have to steal from local competitors, although any club over a couple of miles away is probably a fair target. They may, however, have just as lousy employees as you do. We do need to learn to steal from other types of service businesses, though.

Remember we are looking for strong traits, such as naturally good customer service, the ability to talk and to look you in the eye, a good work ethic, and a professional appearance. If the person has these traits, we can usually teach them the skills they need for their specific jobs. If the person doesn't naturally have these traits, all the training in the world won't make them much of an employee.

An example is an employee of a national chain of clothing stores who helped me at the mall. She was personable, had a strong sales presence, a professional attitude and look, and was about 25 years old. She was also making about $7 an hour after commissions. How do you find this out? You ask. If you've ever had anyone praise your work, then you know how flattering it would be to have a complete stranger offer you an interview after a brief encounter. A simple, "You're really good at your work — you're not looking for a different job, are you?" is all it takes.

This person had all the traits necessary for our type of work, and was susceptible to a steal because of the type of work she was doing and the pay she was currently receiving. To steal this person, you would have had to offer at least $8 per hour plus bonuses and commissions, but she would be worth it because she could be productive at a higher level with less training.

And the biggest plus is that she knows how to work. We didn't have to teach her how to show up, be on time and have a good work ethic. She learned that on someone else's payroll. Many of our potential employees who arrive fresh from college programs have never held a job in their lives. They want $40,000 a year a title, and yet have never worked toward anything, ever. You not only have to teach these people the job, you also have to teach them how to work too, something much more difficult than working with someone who has the basic traits.

Many owners, however, are afraid to steal employees because they're afraid someone will come back and steal theirs. If they steal yours, maybe it's because we aren't meeting the employees' needs as we discussed earlier. If

We didn't have to teach her how to show up, be on time and have a good work ethic. She learned that on someone else's payroll.

177

the employee is paid decently, works in a reasonable environment and has consistent training and support, they will probably be pretty hard to steal.

Hiring right the first time

It's been said thousands of times but it's still true. Most employee problems occur because the owner or manager hired wrong in the first place. They simply put the wrong person in the wrong job, and had to live with the results.

The first phase of your hiring process is to seek talent, which is something you're going to have to pay more than your competitors to get. Cheap employees may be a bargain for a week or two, but they shortly become more of a liability than an asset.

Offer base pay in your area high enough to get decent people to work for you. We also pay bonuses and commissions as part of the employee's incentive package. Every employee should have the chance to earn a little extra if they meet their goals for the month. Often commissions and bonuses are restricted solely for salespeople and managers. Every employee should have a chance to achieve an extra level of compensation no matter what their position. Goal setting and incentives are discussed in depth later in this section.

Your payroll may be slightly higher with this system, but not always. Better employees usually get more work done and achieve more than weaker people, and often cover the higher pay with increased production.

For example, let's say that you normally pay a front counter person $6 per hour with no additional bonuses. This time around you start the new counter person who is a little older, has more work experience and needs less training at $7.50 an hour plus small incentives from team bonuses. At 32 hours and $6 per hour, the first person would gross about $800 per month, or just enough to slowly frustrate them to either get a second job or eventually leave you for a higher paying one when they get some experience. Just when you get this person trained and productive, they leave you, burning up the training expense and with another rookie in a key production job.

At 32 hours per week and $7.50 per hour, the second person starts at about $1,000 per month. In this example, the second person would also have the opportunity to earn an additional $75 to 125 per month in team incentives from the multiple profit centers. Even if the second person hits all of the team goals in the profit centers, they're only getting an extra $300 per month.

But what type of person did the $7.50 per hour draw in comparison to the $6? In most markets where $6 per hour is normal service pay, the $7.50 per hour is a huge difference and would attract a much more sophisticated worker. If they produce, they are worth the extra money. If they don't, they are let go at the end of the 90-day probationary period, and the club is really not at much risk financially.

The $300 is big, only if all you want is a body to stand at the front desk. If not, an older and better qualified worker is worth the extra money when it

Every employee should have a chance to achieve an extra level of compensation no matter what their position.

comes to providing member service, working the profit centers and doing extra work generating extra revenue for the club.

Profiling our employees

When you hire for traits, not skills, you need to start with a basic profile of what you really want in your employee. Each position in the club should have a profile of the traits necessary to successfully do the job. If you already have a type of person in mind, written down on paper, then you'll have a much better chance of recognizing the real thing when it comes through the door.

The following is a profile of an entry-level (counter person, basic trainer and entry salesperson) position for the typical fitness facility. Use these points as a checklist for the hiring process, in addition to building a profile for the job itself.

The person has these traits:
• Generally enthusiastic and outgoing in personality.
• Makes eye contact easily, smiles often and is relaxed with other people.
• Interested in personal fitness as demonstrated by personal workout program and interest in other sports.
• Has held previous jobs that required customer service.
• Appears as a "people person" as demonstrated by activities enjoyed and jobs held.
• Demonstrates traits of a self-starter and hard worker.
• Held job at an early age.
• Wide range of interests and accomplishments.
• Held previous jobs that required being a self-starter (i.e., newspaper delivery person).

If a person has these traits, we could train them into most positions in a gym. Often we overlook these traits for skills, which may or may not prove to be valuable in the actual performance of work in your system. For example, a person may have had sales experience in another fitness facility, but has to be completely retrained because they don't fit in your current sales system.

Other jobs in the facility might require different traits. Managers need to be good with numbers. Salespeople need strong self-confidence and strong communication skills. By profiling each position, we concentrate on looking for the type of person we want in that job and then train them to the system they will work in at the club.

Each position in the club should have a profile of the traits necessary to successfully do the job.

Interviewing

Interviewing is a lost art dating back to pre-Columbian pottery and the early Elvis days. Very few people are good at it anymore, and even fewer care to learn. Most interviews in gyms consist of the owner begging the potential

Good interviewing for the gym business consists of three steps and a real understanding of the law.

employee to please take that morning shift starting tomorrow, so they don't have to open for the twentieth time in a row.

Good interviewing for the gym business consists of three steps and a real understanding of the law. We'll talk about the three steps here but you need to pick up a good interviewing book and start understanding what you can and cannot ask potential employees. For example, you can't ask age. You also can't ask any leading questions that try to determine age. You can ask how old a person was when they had their first job, one of my favorite interview questions. But you can't ask what year that was or who was president or any other trick questions that allow you to figure out their age.

Assuming you have read up on the legal aspects of interviewing, all interviews should be done in a three-step process.

Step one is simply a plus or minus on first impression and is a pre-screening for the next two steps. There is a sample hiring sheet at the end of this section that should be used during the first step.

Normally it's the assistant manager who's in charge of the staffing and also the one who would do the initial screening. In the smaller clubs, meaning fewer than 600 members, the manager or owner might do the first interview, but even these clubs should have an assistant who works with the staff, in addition to the manager.

The first impression is very important and is the key to the first step. If the person has grubby pants on, a hat on backwards, huge snake tattoos on both arms and hasn't shaved in several days, this is probably a person who won't fit into your uniform code. Is it fair to judge a person on their first look? Is it fair for an owner to have to interview someone who doesn't even know how to apply for a job?

We're not talking ties and dress shoes here. We're talking someone showing up for an interview with neat clean clothes, clean shaven, combed hair and a limited number of pierced body parts that are exposed. You have a right to wear what you want and dress as you please. We have the right to not hire you to work in a million-dollar professional fitness organization.

The first impression may be the deciding factor for a sale in the club. A potential member walks into several clubs in one day looking for a place to work out. The club with the staff that looks and acts professional and that can provide member service will most likely get that person as a member. The staff, therefore, needs to look and act professional and be able to communicate with a large number of people.

This is also a good time to discuss diversity. The best staffs are the ones that represent a wide range of cultures, colors and looks. The worst ones are the ones that all come out of the white bread mold of America. Many young owners in the country tend to hire people just like themselves.

A young single white male owner ends up hiring young single white guys to run the club. If there is a problem, the answer is always the one that a young single white male would come up with at the time. Diversity gives the club texture and feel and truly expands the member service and money-making potential of the business, because a variety of unique people combine to come up with solutions to the club's problems.

The same person who did the first interview (and the person who runs the department where the new hire will work) also performs the second step of the interview process.

Even in the smallest clubs that have only six to seven employees, it's good to have a manager, an assistant manager who works with the staff and sells, and someone in charge of the fitness programs and nutrition. This way you have back up if you lose the manager, or if you're the manager and want to take a vacation. You have multiple people in charge of training and working with newer team members.

The second interview is more indepth and structured. Keep in mind that we're trying to hire people we can train to be productive, and who can deliver outstanding member service. How they communicate in the second interview sets the tone for what they will do on the job. The second interview should also be based on a set series of questions that center on work history, personal interests and customer service situations they have faced elsewhere.

Some sample second interview questions:
• How old were you when you had your first job, and what did you do?
• Describe the last time you received bad service as a customer. What would you have done differently if you had been the employee?
• What's your idea of a great personal workout?
• What do you like to do when you aren't working?
• Tell me how you delivered customer service at your last job?

There are many possibilities, but stay consistent and keep the questions limited.

It's better to ask fewer questions; let the interviewee talk more about what they do and where they worked in the past.

The manager, or the onsite owner who is acting as the manager, always performs the third step in the interview process. This is the person ultimately responsible for the new hire and who should also have the final decision. The final step is more relaxed and is geared toward questions the potential hire may have about the company, the specific job or about the hiring process itself. If you're going to hire, always offer the job during the interview — unless you've lined up too many choices, which is unlikely if you've screened along the way.

We get into problems when we become desperate for help, and so we hire the first warm body, put it at the front desk, and then suffer because we find out this new front counter person is shy and quiet and has never used a computer. Try to stay one entry-level person ahead at all times. It's worth the extra money, and production doesn't stop if you lose someone.

Summary

Staffing will be the key issue in the coming years in the fitness industry. How you hire, train, motivate and develop your employees will be what sets you apart from the competition, and will ultimately become your competitive edge in the marketplace.

Try to stay one entry-level person ahead at all times. It's worth the extra money, and production doesn't stop if you lose someone.

The old model of hiring and staffing doesn't work anymore in the fitness business. In the past, we've followed the fast food model: Hire cheap, turnover often and keep payroll and benefits costs at the lowest possible level. This doesn't work in a thriving economy. The good people are already in the work force, leaving pretty weak candidates for the money we are accustomed to offering.

To grow our businesses, we need to hire a higher caliber of worker, one who we won't get unless we change our hiring and pay practices. The consumer expects a much higher level of member service for the money they pay, and this service can only be delivered by someone who can communicate and solve problems. This person is not the typical 19-year-old we traditionally place at the front desk.

The gyms are also switching to more multiple profit centers and these too require a more sophisticated worker to make them productive.

The gyms are also switching to more multiple profit centers and these too require a more sophisticated worker to make them productive. The days are gone where someone merely stands behind the desk and checks people into the club. Today's worker needs to understand our product, be able to sell and promote profit centers, and be cross-trained to handle other jobs in the facility as the need demands. Member service means being able to provide service where and when the member wants it; that takes a more sophisticated team than we've hired in the past decades in the gym business.

One of the primary problems is the pay itself. Minimum pay gets minimum, results and the people who work for the lowest pay need more training, more supervision and a lot more skill development than the older and more experienced worker. Better pay attracts better qualified people, who perform better sooner.

Another major issue is staff development. Most of our employees feel that they are undertrained for the position they hold. Training makes the employees feel better about themselves, perform better in their jobs, and makes them harder to steal from us in the long run. The prime trainer should be the manager.

A manager should devote about 50 percent of her time to staff training. If your manager spends most of her time on sales, then you don't really have a manager, you have a salesperson with a great title on their business card. Training makes the company more productive, and this vital task should be delegated to someone as part of their job. How they train and the results they get should determine how that person is paid.

Hiring is getting tougher all the time. The traditional methods of ads in the paper don't bring in the qualified candidates they used to in the earlier days of the industry. The best people are probably already working somewhere else, and these should be the ones we go after for our businesses. This is called stealing and it's perfectly legal and ethical in the business world.

When you hire, look for traits, which are the natural gifts someone brings to the table with them. An enthusiastic personality can't be taught. You either have it or you don't. Computer operation can be taught, if the person has at least seen one or is interested in one. Hire for traits, and teach the person your business. The person will stay longer and be more productive in most cases.

Things you can do to use this material

1) Hire the best people you can afford. Research your market, determine what the local minimum wage is and then go after people a level or two above that one.

2) Set up a recruitment system based on going after people who are already working. Carry cards and actively go after people who impress you with their professional look, customer service or just plain good attitude.

3) Set up a formal hiring system based on three interviews. Learn the law and make sure your interviews are clean and legal. Involve other members of your team in the hiring process, but reserve the final decision for yourself or manager.

4) Be creative in your hiring. A housewife returning to the work force would be a great lead counter person for 32 hours per week. A retiree might make a great club opener. What a concept! Why not hire a person who likes to get up at 4 a.m., instead of some young guy who usually gets in at 4 a.m. and then tries to make it to work.

5) It's almost impossible to overtrain someone. Start training aggressively on the first day a new employee starts working and continue with a consistent and intense training program. Also start the training at the bottom. Most clubs put their training into the higher level employees, such as salespeople, and neglect the entry-level folks. Think of training as a pro football team would. Who would need the most intense work — a seasoned pro quarterback or the rookie just out of college? The old pro may need a few reminders or help with a specific problem, but the rookie needs the most help and not just with being a quarterback, but how to adjust to the team's system. Your rookie employees are the same. They need job-specific training, as well as crosstraining in all areas of the club. They'll be better employees if they understand the entire system.

6) Set up a staff training schedule and make it mandatory for all full-time employees. Staff development meetings should be set weekly (on the same day and at the same time) so employees can make this part of their regular schedule. Keep the meeting to an hour only and structure it on a positive note. Chewing butts every week wears out the staff and decreases the team's moral. The following list is a sample of one-hour meetings focused on staff training:

- Answering the phone. This can be repeated every month for emphasis.
- Handling a complete phone inquiry.
- Greeting members and providing member service at the front counter.
- Efficient check-in procedures for the members.
- Focusing on one profit center and how to promote it.
- Working renewals in the club.
- The 30-minute club walk-through (including a quick clean in the locker room, the cardio area and the club's entryway).
- Education from a team leader, such as the nutrition tech, who educates the staff on a new product.
- Greeting the potential member.

Start training aggressively on the first day a new employee starts working and continue with a consistent and intense training program.

• Developing a wait policy for potential or regular members who have to wait more than five minutes for a tour or appointment.

• Working trial members using trial closes.

• Using the trial membership cards as a focus tool for the staff.

• Reviewing key procedures in the club such as teaching everyone how to make a shake, handle a renewal or do an info call.

• Member service for the trial members.

• How to handle member complaints and how to work the complaint card system.

• How to sell special club events and programming.

• Handling problem members.

These are just a few examples of one-hour training sessions. We do pay the staff to attend these meetings, even if they are not scheduled to be there at that time. Instead of their regular pay, we give them training pay, which is usually minimum wage. The best time for meetings is usually Tuesday, Wednesday or Thursday mornings. Mondays are bad for everyone and no one focuses on Fridays. All meeting times are posted 30 days in advance and are mandatory for full-time (over 32 hours per week) employees.

7) The following is a hiring sheet to be used for the first interview. It emphasizes the traits necessary to do the job and is designed for entry-level people in the company:

Hiring sheet

The person has or demonstrates the following traits:

__ Enthusiastic and outgoing.

__ Makes eye contact often.

__ Has a fitness look, is interested in fitness or is currently active in some type of program.

__ Has held some type of people job where customer service was part of their responsibility.

__ Has the traits of a hard worker or self-starter.

__ Self-motivated (advanced in other jobs or took on more responsibility).

__ Wide range of interests or accomplishments (Boy Scouts, active in church, ski team or soccer team as a youth).

__ Held previous jobs that would require being motivated or a self-starter (first job might have been as a paper delivery person at the age of nine).

__ Has strong communication skills demonstrated by speech, language and attitude.

__ Has the ability to relate to a large number of members and could provide member service in a patient and friendly manner.

The best time for meetings is usually Tuesday, Wednesday or Thursday mornings. Mondays are bad for everyone and no one focuses on Fridays.

Sample interview questions:

- Tell me about the last time you worked with a large number of people supplying member service. What did and didn't you enjoy about the situation?
- How old were you when you had your first job?
- Describe the last time you received bad service as a customer. What would you have done differently if you had been the employee?
- What do you like to do when you don't work? What kind of workout or physical activity do you like to do on your off hours?

Be sure to look for a professional dress and attitude. We're not necessarily looking for a shirt and tie or dress, but neat, clean and well-groomed is important. If someone shows up for an interview in ragged clothes, they are going to bring that same attitude to work.

Who is the most important person in the gym?

THERE IS ONE OWNER who built a beautiful club in New York that cost about a million and a half for a 23,000-square-foot facility. The club had the latest colors, newest equipment and a well-trained sales staff that was ready to do business.

The club's owners attended a business school to help them learn the business. All the trainers completed their updated certifications just prior to opening, and the nutrition people were trained and educated and ready to get their programs underway.

And there at the front counter was the club's receptionist. She was 21 years old, had no prior work experience and especially no member-service experience. She was hired because she was attractive and because the owner was a young male who thought she would look good up at the front counter.

The entire business was in the hands of the most undertrained and undereducated staff person on the team. The owner had made the fatal mistake of hiring from the top down instead of

who really most affects the business on a day-to-day basis.

The moral of the story

The most important person in the club is the one who most affects the level of member service and who has the most con-

She was hired because she was attractive and because the owner was a young male who thought she would look good up at the front counter

tact with the largest number of members. This person is the front counter person who works the front counter during the prime times, usually from around 4 to 9 p.m.

This person is your first line of defense between you and

everyone who comes into the club. A regular member may work out somewhere in the club and be in contact with a trainer. A prospective member may end up on a tour with a salesperson who may or may not get the sale.

But both of these people had to start with the front counter person. If that person can't provide a friendly and welcoming atmosphere, then the salesperson may have to overcome the prospect's first impression of the club to get the sale.

And if the regular member is not properly greeted and served each time they are in the club, then the club may not get that person's renewal when the time comes.

Again, the person who affects all of this is the front counter person. This person should be a little older, have great communication skills and be able to maturely deal with member-service situations that arise on a daily basis. In other words, the most important person in the club isn't you the owner, it's the person who has to deliver the great service you believe in as part of your business plan.

14

If your employees were as good as you are, they would have your job

MANY OWNERS EXPECT their employees to be as motivated and as skilled as they are at working in a fitness facility, but don't spend the effort to provide leadership and training that the employee needs to develop. Employees want to be led. They want you to show them how to do the job. They want you to provide the training they need to be effective. And they want the chance to fly and make mistakes on their own. They also want you to be there to guide and lead them.

Employees want to be led by a person with vision and leadership skills, not beaten into submission with a 1950's militaristic style of leadership. Leadership styles have changed over the past several decades, but most owners haven't adapted to these changes. Today's owners are entrepreneurs, which is a polite way of saying, "I'd rather do it myself," instead of learning to lead and develop others to do the job with them.

I once worked for a person who I thought was truly inspirational, a man with whom I thought I'd like to spend a great many of my working years. Ten years after I started, I walked out of my office completely beaten down and carrying a small box. I started as someone who had confidence, and ended up as a person who had little faith in myself or in my ability to work in the real world.

He managed by using fear and intimidation and by constantly making employees feel stupid. Years later, I realized that I'd let this happen and that it was my responsibility, but as a young and impressionable employee I didn't realize at the time what was happening.

Employees want to be led by a person with vision and leadership skills, not beaten into submission with a 1950's militaristic style of leadership.

There are many, many employees who want to be led, but not by people who manage out of their own insecurity and work to keep the employees in their place by fear. Today's more sophisticated employees want to work for a person who can provide inspiration, motivation and education, and who can create a vision the team can follow through the fire pits of hell and back, because the leader said, "Go and do the job I trained you for over the years."

Bill Gates leads this way. With his leadership skills, his vision and by creating an exciting company culture, he's created one of the most dynamic companies in recorded history.

Other great companies, like Apple in its early days or Nike, are defined by their style of leadership and the company's vision. These aren't just good places to work. These are places where the employees belong to something big and important, and that is changing how things are done in the marketplace.

Fitness facilities could be the same way. These facilities are staffed with young, gung-ho staffs that want to belong to something — to be part of an exciting business with direction. The driving force that makes this happen is the leadership style of the owner. The block that prevents this from happening in the club is that most owners instinctively end up following the old, authoritarian approach to leadership and to their businesses.

A simple definition of the authoritarian style is that the boss makes all the decisions. There is no team building. There is no discussion as to the way to do things. The manager makes the decision and the employee carries it out. The armed services are based on this system, with a very narrowly defined chain of command.

That's one of the downsides of being an entrepreneur. You took the risk, you started your own business because you were probably tired of working for someone else, or thought you could do it better than someone else, and now that you're on your own, you're going to do it your way.

The classic owner assumption under the authoritarian style is signified by how expendable the workers are. They don't make decisions; they don't have to think — they just do it the way you tell them and everything is fine. The trouble with this logic is that the employees of today are much more sophisticated, want to share in the decision-making process of the business, and seek more responsibility. In other words, good employees won't work under this type of leadership.

...the employees of today are much more sophisticated, want to share in the decision-making process of the business, and seek more responsibility.

Old-style management styles prevent growth in your business

Signs that your facility may be suffering from authoritarian suppression are pretty easy to spot. For example, does the club have a high turnover of employees at the lower levels? Are the employees working for minimum wage? Does the club not offer benefits for full-time employees? Is the club understaffed during key hours which leads to burnout for the ones you do have working? And are your producers working on commission only, high-pressure numbers and unrealistic quotas?

These are all signs that the staff is working under adverse management conditions. If the club has no benefits, is understaffed, puts salespeople on a chase after unrealistic numbers, and has a high turnover at the front desk, then the employee knows that they are expendable because everything in the club's system tells them that truth.

People want to be led by inspiration, not by intimidation. In your business, maybe the followers aren't following because the leaders aren't leading. And the results you seek from your business may be elusive, because the staff is not fully committed to your cause.

The search for good faith effort from our employees

When you impart an inspirational style of leadership, you get that extra effort from an employee that you can't force or can't just buy. This extra effort is called good faith effort. It means that the employee has the faith and trust in you to give you what they would normally hold back in other jobs.

A weakness in most small businesses is employees who are not totally committed to what they are doing and whom they are working for at the time. These are people who work for you, do their job, but never really give you their full potential.

For example, an employee at your front desk is on the clock and doing their job. A new member shows up at the front desk a little confused about their first visit to the club. The employee is courteous, tells the member where the locker room is, and tells the person that once he is dressed to come back to the front desk and he'll find the trainer waiting for him. Technically, the employee did the job we pay her for each week. She was friendly, helpful, and provided basic member service.

Our competitor, however, is faced with the same situation. Her employee walks the new member back to the locker room, shows him how to find the right locker and then finds the trainer and has her waiting for the new member when he comes out of the locker room. This club gave better member service, made a new member happier and opened the door wide for a member referral. Why? Because the staff gave more effort than was required, or good faith effort. You can't force it and you can't demand it, but it's what makes your business special and successful.

Many times a fitness business will fail because the owners create an organization that undermines motivation and discourages good faith effort. These clubs fail because of burnout among the producers, mistrust, missed opportunities and resistance to change. In other words, these organizations waste their most precious asset, which is the organization's human potential.

> A weakness in most small businesses is employees who are not totally committed to what they are doing and whom they are working for at the time.

The function of leadership

When you stray away from the basic functions of being a leader, your business and staff suffer.

It's easy to define the function of the leader. The leadership function is what the leader does, which is sort of their job description. When you stray away from the basic functions of being a leader, your business and staff suffer. The functions of a leader in the fitness business are:

• To build a pro-active business plan based on projecting the business three years into the future.

• Develop a marketing plan that leads to the sale of new memberships.

• Develop a mature and motivated employee base through strong and inspirational leadership.

• Learn to satisfy members, which leads to repeat business in the form of renewals.

• Work toward long-term profits for the business.

The key to good leadership is to balance these points. If the owner doesn't balance and understand all five areas, then the business doesn't grow.

Some examples of an unbalanced approach are:

• An owner who strongly believes in member service, but who under-trains the staff and will never be able to build a strong member service plan or have great member retention.

• An owner who is too nice to the employees and makes everyone a friend, but then doesn't have a strong business because there is no accountability from the employees.

• An owner who will do anything to get new sales, but puts all the money into the sales and marketing effort and doesn't put any into member service. The club will sign up new people, but won't keep any in the long run which puts even more stress on the sales effort.

LEADERSHIP STARTS WITH CORE ATTRIBUTES

Learning to be a good leader starts with understanding the basic attributes a leader might possess. These aren't all the attributes of good leadership, but are some that affect how we do business in the fitness industry.

• *A leader should have deeply held values about other people.*

There are basic core values a leader should have. Fairness, a sense of worth in others, a believe in the equality of people and a sense of right and wrong are all values necessary to lead a young staff into business battle. For example, would an owner who says he is fair aggressively drop close someone in a closed office? Would a respected leader refuse to hire blacks or women in the club? It's hard to follow someone who says one thing and then does something totally different in the workplace.

• *A leader has respect for an employee's unique talents and quirkiness.*

You come back from a trip and find one of your trainer/salespeople on the floor with a group of six women. You ask the manager what's going on and she tells you that they have a group tour and workout going on led by

190

the trainer. Your policy is that every potential member starts one-on-one with a sales person, so we don't lose the potential sale.

Out of the six women in the group, only two are actually members. The trainer/salesperson finishes the group, signs up two more new members and makes appointments for the other two to come back and work out again. Would you respect the employees' unique solutions or would you be upset and bring up the policy?

• *A leader has respect for a person's contribution on their behalf.*

Your front counter person calls off on short notice. Your other evening employees have a busy night with member visits, but they still manage to get four sales and they also do a respectable job in the multiple profit centers. You come in late in the evening and the first thing you see is how dirty the club is. Without knowing the situation, you immediately start chewing butt because the locker room is dirty, weights and dumbbells need to be put away, and the counter area is trashed. In this example, the owner showed poor leadership by not finding out the entire story and, most importantly, not respecting the job the remaining employees performed that night.

• *A leader has to be skilled at creating an environment that brings out excellence, accepts risk-taking, supports creativity and accepts mistakes from those who really are trying to do a good job.*

Your manager, who has been with you for several years and who does a good job, takes over the printing for your ad campaign. This is the first time she handled the entire project by herself with the printer. She orders 25,000 pieces at a cost of $1,500.

She made one small mistake though. When she and the printer proofed the piece, they overlooked the fact that the gym's phone number wasn't on it. The manager signs off on the piece and you have 25,000 cards with no phone number. Do you now do all future projects yourself? Do you yell and scream and try to blame the printer? Or do you calmly find a solution, such as getting stickers printed and attached, and write it off as an experience for the manager that probably won't be repeated?

• *A leader has to be patient.*

It took you many years to learn what you know about the business. Can you really pass this information along in just a few weeks of training? For example, you've been in the business for eight years running the club yourself. You hire your first manager and set about teaching her the basics. Even if you taught her full time for two months, she still is about eight years short of having your experience and knowledge.

And she still wouldn't have the most vital skill a manager needs, which is the experience from practicing and learning on the job from the decisions she makes. Until you make the big decisions, you don't really ever learn how to lead and manage. Being patient until a person has acquired some of this hands-on experience is very trying for an owner, but important while learning to be a leader.

> **It took you many years to learn what you know about the business. Can you really pass this information along in just a few weeks of training?**

• *A leader must have integrity.*

You hire an old sales dog as your sales manager who has had big-chain high-pressure experience. As the owner, you have established a policy that the club and the sales team have to get a consistent membership fee, meaning no deals for anyone. The new guy, however, will do anything to get a sale.

For example, he might give two women who come in together a two-for-one membership fee. The next guy might pay no membership fee in exchange for signing up today. An unsuspecting guy might actually pay a full membership fee because he joined, because his friend was already a member. This guy isn't following the club's rules, but he is selling a lot of memberships so you hate to say anything. What has the rest of the sales staff learned about you, your leadership style and your integrity? How do you now enforce other policies in the gym with the rest of the staff?

• *A leader must have trust.*

You hire a manager to start taking some responsibility in the club. After about six months of training, you feel somewhat comfortable with the person's progress so you decide to take a short vacation. While you're away, you call twice a day to see how things are going. What concept did you teach the new manager? Is there trust in the relationship or not? Will the person live up to the trust you have shown her, which is none, by not managing and waiting for you to make all of her decisions?

Common leadership mistakes gym owners make when it comes to running a fitness business

Leadership goes beyond just getting the staff to do what you want. Good leadership inspires a staff to go beyond your base expectations for them; it inspires your members to be a part of something special you create, and most importantly it allows you to reach levels of success very few people ever achieve in this industry.

Lack of leadership, on the other hand, affects your business way beyond the performance of your staff. Every aspect of leadership, no matter how small, affects your future as a business, as part of the community and as a money-making vehicle to enhance your life.

People like to be led, as was said earlier, but they like to be led by inspiration and not intimidation. If your staff is not giving you what you want, it's because you either made the wrong choice when hiring those people in the first place, or it's because you haven't yet learned leadership skills.

Leadership can be learned. You don't have to be a born leader. The skills are there to learn, but it does take time and experience. And extreme patience, too. You should also keep in mind that leadership makes a statement as to the kind of person you are, in the eyes of those you are trying to lead. What you are and what you believe in directly affect the type of leadership you will give.

Good leadership ... allows you to reach levels of success very few people ever achieve in this industry.

THE COMMON LEADERSHIP FAILURES AND MISTAKES

1) Failure to improve yourself personally.

Almost all business owners get to a point where they think they know everything there is to know about their chosen business. When this point arises, and it's usually about three to five years into the business, the business becomes stale due to a lack of new ideas and stimulation and it starts to decline. When you are not growing and developing personally, you run the risk that those around you might be moving forward and leaving you behind. It's hard to be a leader when you're more concerned about defending what you know than questioning what you don't know. To avoid this happening in your business, try to keep these growth points in mind:

• **Be open to change.** We are in the business of change. Trends in equipment force change. The sophistication of the members forces change. The central body of knowledge in the industry expands and forces change. Business methods change over the years to reflect the current level of owners in the field. Everything changes except the old entrenched gym operators who refuse to admit that what worked last year may not work this year.

• **Don't avoid the numbers side of the business.** Business people run fitness facilities better today than the old sales-driven owners from past decades. These new owners thrive on numbers and information. Many of the staff we hire today do a much better job when they understand what really happens in the business. The problem is that many of the old style of owners only know the sales side of the industry and don't learn the backside of the shop. Better leaders lead better when the troops have the right information.

• **Seek out advanced training.** The best business people in the world don't know everything. They do, however, ask the best questions. There is always education available, inside and outside the fitness industry, which can take you to the next level.

• **Cut down on time wasters in the business.** Many owners waste their days by doing work that could be farmed out to lower-level employees. This busy work prevents them from working on their business. In other words, eliminate the unnecessary and learn to work on your business, not always just in it.

• **Learn and practice time management.** Simple time-management techniques, such as learning to make a work list and set priorities, could greatly improve an owner or manager's production during the day. More efficient use of time means more time for training and staff development.

• **Set personal goals.** A good goal for most owners would be to write a 12-month self-improvement plan. For example, what five things could you learn in a short period of time that would improve your business? Once you achieve your basic goals, create a new list and move forward again.

> **It's hard to be a leader when you're more concerned about defending what you know than questioning what you don't know.**

2) Limiting yourself to only one part, or a very narrow part, of the business.

By limiting yourself to just specific parts of the business, you're setting yourself up for several costly mistakes. First of all, you make yourself vulnerable inside your business by letting someone else gain knowledge about your business you don't have, such as an owner who has a nutrition program but hasn't attended the school and doesn't really know how it works. If you create a new program, you and the entire management team should have a working understanding of the program and be able to maintain it at least at the minimum level.

For example, if you start a new nutrition program, you should go to school as should your manager, assistant manager and the person who will actually run the program on a daily basis. You can't lead if you don't understand what you own. Aerobics is a good example of a program that faded rapidly once the owners stopped taking classes and supporting the education function connected to staying current.

Secondly, you are also setting yourself up for burnout. Doing the same thing year after year will lead to a decline in your performance and eventually you will step away from the business which will lead to even a further loss of control. A typical scenario is an owner who becomes burned out, has a flat and unexciting business and then steps away to try to start another business. They hire a manager and then just leave that person on their own so they can concentrate on the new project. For a while, that project is fun and exciting, but eventually burnout sneaks in there, too. To stay fresh, stay current in all aspects of the business and keep learning.

3) Failure to accept responsibility for your own business.

If your business is not as successful as you wish, it's your fault. Leadership starts with accepting responsibility for your business, your staff and the decisions you make. That old saying, "What you are today is the result of all the decisions you made up to yesterday," is true. Some of the best excuses ever invented in the fitness business come from owners who refuse to start with themselves as the problem. For example:

• **The gym could make more money if only we could find good employees.** This means you don't know how to hire, lead or motivate employees. If they are truly rotten employees or, worse yet, truly rotten relative employees, who did the hiring? If you can't find good help, who set the pay scale and did the looking? If there aren't any good people in your town, who chose to open there in the first place?

• **No one came in today because the weather was rotten.** No one came into the gym yesterday because the weather was too good. You can't have it both ways.

• **My competition is underpricing me out of business.** Who set the focus and niche for your business? Who didn't establish more value in their product? Who hired lousy staff that brings you down to the competition's level (see above)?

• **No one is in my aerobics classes, and I hate childcare people.** Who

> **Doing the same thing year after year will lead to a decline in your performance, and eventually you will step away from the business which will lead to even a further loss of control.**

has failed to change their business to meet the changing demands of the consumer? Who made the decision to run programs that are out-of-date in your business? Who is losing money every month in their business, but refuses to deal with the issue?

A good exercise for this area is to list the five most glaring weaknesses in your business and who is responsible for these areas. Then list what needs to be done to improve these areas and in what time frame. Even the simple step of writing down the problems and accepting responsibility for them helps you move to the next level.

4) *Letting yourself become too successful and thinking it will last forever.*

Some owners actually become too successful. They hit a long streak, believe it will last forever and eventually hurt their businesses because they become too slow to react when adverse things negatively affect the strength they have come to rely upon over the years. In many ways, it's harder to lead a staff in times of success, than it is when the gym is in its lean and hungry years. The expenses slowly creep up, money is wasted and the staff and owner forget what it took to achieve that success in the first place.

When you lead from a position of success, you need to establish working goals for the business that keep the team moving forward. Protecting a profit margin is not a workable business plan. If you're not growing your business, then it is already in a state of decay — the rot just hasn't caught up with you yet.

Start with the desired profit margin for the business. How much is enough and when will it be there? If you are already at the desired profit level, list five ways you can grow the business in the next one-year, three-year, and five-year periods. List five things you can do to protect the margin while you're growing the business to the next level. Always remember the difference between growing the business and merely sitting in a defensive position trying to protect what everyone else wants to take away from you.

5) *Failure to make timely decisions.*

Fitness owners are notorious for putting off important decisions. They call all their friends, see if anyone else is facing the same problem in their club and what they are going to do about it, attend a seminar and look for solutions, call us and then just don't do anything and hope it will go away on its own.

Most major decisions should actually be made months before the owners get around to making them. For example, you get complaints about the gym being short of cardio equipment. A few of the regulars say something, then an employee notices a few aggravated members and then you start looking into the problem.

A few weeks later you admit there is a problem. This leads to a few weeks of research and negotiations that end up with an order that now takes four weeks to arrive. Instead of anticipating the shortage by watching the influx of new members, the time of year or the increased renewal rate in the gym, the owner waits until someone actually complains before doing any-

> **In many ways, it's harder to lead a staff in times of success, than it is when the gym is in its lean and hungry years.**

thing. By then it's too late.

The staff looks to management to make big decisions that will affect the club in a timely manner. It's hard to lead when most decisions are based on how best to scramble to cover the collective butts that week.

To test yourself in this area, list three decisions you avoided in the past that would have had better end results if you would have made them sooner. Then list three decisions you have to make in the club now, that you've been avoiding because you know they will be hard or unpopular choices.

6) Losing touch with the business.

A common disease in the fitness business is the "I finally made it" malady that affects so many owners of all walks of life.

A common disease in the fitness business is the "I finally made it" malady that affects so many owners of all walks of life. Once they start making a little money, the disease hits hard. Most stop working and just start dropping by for a few hours a day. They walk in, pick up all the cash, shake a few hands and then are off for the golf course. In their mind, they have paid their dues and they are ready to take it easy. In reality, this is when the club needs the most leadership, not the least. The business will start a slow decline once the owners lose the day-to-day touch to stay profitable.

The problem with getting out of touch with the business is that you're out of the leadership loop. Guiding your staff and making the hard growth decisions are hard enough anyway, and can worsen if you're not there enough to watch the details.

For example, one of the first things to go in the club is its atmosphere. If you were there, you'd quickly pick up that the music is on the wrong channel for that time of day, no one cleaned around the cardio area last night and the shades in the front windows are still down long after the sun left. Leadership is often compared to feeling the pulse of the business. It takes time and a practiced eye to stay on top of a constantly changing business.

7) Failure to control expenses.

One definition of profits is expenses we are able to cut. Most owners, because of their experience growing up in sales-driven clubs, only have a sales solution to the problems of the club. The only question they ask is: How can I generate more income through more sales volume?

Providing leadership in your business means growing and watching the business. You grow through the sales effort and the multiple profit centers, and you also grow by watching the expenses and keeping them in line.

Leading a staff requires the ability to do both. Just working on sales is a self-defeating business plan that eventually leads to a sales-driven environment short on member service and member retention.

8) Failure to make sure any job, assigned to any employee, is understood, supervised and completed.

The problem with being a leader for most people is that they don't have the patience to turn around and tell the people who are following them where they are going and what their role is going to be.

People will do their best for you when they know what their jobs are, and when they know exactly how you want them to do that specific task. We often assume that the employee has the same skills, cultural background and work experience we've had in our lives. When we tell a staff person to do something, we assume that person is operating with the same basic wiring we have. They aren't.

A key to leadership is understanding that the people who work for you learn and gather information in different ways. Some do best when you show them what to do, and they learn by watching. Some learn by having you explain in detail what you want them to accomplish. And some function best by doing the task while you watch and correct.

Failure to understand these different learning styles is a failure in leadership, because the employee will have a difficult time accomplishing what you want since they don't understand what you expect.

For example, I learn primarily by reading and secondarily by doing, and having someone correct me as I go along. If my employee learns by watching and doing, we are already off to a bad start. I want a specific task accomplished, put out a memo and expect the work to get done. The employee reads the memo and has no real idea how to complete the task.

Let's say I'm trying to get the staff to start cleaning under the treadmills once a week and checking if the belts are loose. I spell out all the directions clearly in the memo. The staff person who learns by seeing it done will have a hard time understanding and successfully completing the task, unless he first has someone take him through it once so he can watch. He then has to try it on his own with someone watching. Learning can only be accomplished in the mode one works best with in their own head.

This is a simplistic explanation of learning styles, but it does illustrate how a leader could fail because she simply doesn't understand that the followers don't understand what she wants.

Unclear instructions, indecisiveness on your part, vagueness and only partial information are often to blame for an employee's lack of performance and their failure to get the job done. It's up to you as an owner or manager to clearly tell your people what you expect, and in a way that makes sense to them, so that they understand what you're trying to accomplish.

Since you may never really understand how an employee internally processes information, try to cover all the learning styles each time you teach the crew something new. An easy way to make sure they are getting what you're saying is to use a notebook system.

Every employee has a notebook given to them when they start work. The notebook is kept at the gym, except when they are traveling to special educational events. Every time you teach the employee something new, they are expected to write out the procedures in their notebook. You explain the new task, the staff person tries it once in front of you for correction and then they write down the process in their notebook to make sure they have it.

You're covering all three parts of the learning process and now you have something in writing that you can refer back to when you check later for understanding.

Checking for understanding simply means: Does the employee under-

> **A key to leadership is understanding that the people who work for you learn and gather information in different ways.**

stand and is she able to do the task? If not, check back to her notebook and start again by telling, showing and having her correct her notes. This system also allows the staff that has been with you a while to start passing on information to more inexperienced staff members because now they have documented how things work.

For example, let's say you're trying to teach the employee to fill out a membership agreement for a new member. She brings her notebook to the training session and you start by verbally explaining how to fill out a contract. You then have her fill out a sample on her own with you looking over her shoulder and giving pointers. Finally, you have her write down the procedures in her notebook, and staple the sample to her page.

When she is on her own, she has something to refer back to if she is having trouble. If she still has difficulty, verbally review her mistakes, have her fill out a new sample concentrating on the parts she is having problems with, and have her update the notebook. This passes the burden of ownership of the material to her, since she is responsible for adding it to her book.

Leadership of a young staff is not an easy task. Make sure you can communicate your needs, before you expect your desired results.

Leadership of a young staff is not an easy task. Make sure you can communicate your needs, before you expect your desired results.

9) Wasting time doing work that should be delegated.

First master it, then delegate it. It's a simple premise of leadership. Much of the work that consumes a typical owner's day is work that does not grow the business. Collecting your own membership agreements, hand writing checks, paying bills every day instead of twice a month, giving workouts to your favorite members and taking a desk shift to save a few dollars are all examples of working *in* the business, not *on* the business.

To be an effective leader, you need to know when to work and when to let others do the work for you. We often confuse being busy with doing the important work of growing the business. You work all day, come home exhausted at night, put your feet up on the couch and wonder what in the hell you really got done that made a difference in your business. Part of leadership is learning to delegate and simplify most routine tasks in the gym.

A good rule of thumb is to remember that you or your manager's time is worth $250 an hour. Keeping a number like this in your head forces you to ask yourself this question: What is the best use of your time at any one period in the day? Are you doing $250-an-hour work growing the business, which means working on the marketing, training staff, selling a membership or working the profit centers? Or are you standing at the front counter filling a regular shift on the schedule that's worth $6 per hour? Before you do anything, always start with the concept of what the best use of your time is at this moment, and whether that task is worth $6 an hour or $250 an hour?

10) Failure to rethink your business.

You've had trouble with employees for years. They are always too young, they don't stay after you invest time training them, no one even applies themselves anymore, and yet you are still offering almost the same hourly wage you did several years ago. Maybe the wage is wrong? Maybe your area has changed? Maybe you need to rethink your hiring and compensation methods to attract and keep good people?

This is like trying to fix your bicycle with the same broken wrench. You try and try, and you just can't get that tire off the bike. You need to sit down and think about replacing that broken wrench with one that works.

In business, it's often the same. We try to fix problems with the same broken solutions we've used for years. We say to ourselves, "It can't be the pay system or training, it has to be the people who come in for a job."

Good leadership means supplying the team with the best solutions or tools for the job you expect. This means you have to sit down on a regular basis and analyze the tools you are using to accomplish the job at hand, which is to build a financially successful business.

Make every tool a suspect. Many of the things we do in this business are simply habits copied from other owners who stole that idea from someone else. Why do you charge the way you do? Why do you offer a set number of guided workouts for new members when common sense tells you it's not enough? Why do you pay, hire and train the way you do when you still don't get the results you want in your business?

11) Failure to keep your word.

This is probably better known as trying to be liked instead of working toward being respected. When you try to be liked, you'll tell the person what they want to hear, so they'll be pleased with you. It's easier than telling that person the truth, which may not make them happy at the time.

Are you the type of person who does what you say you will do, or are you the type of person who has a lot of excuses for not doing what you promised? Broken promises, such as "I'll drop the check in the mail today," and then you send it two days later, or "I'll call you Monday morning at 10 a.m.," and then you get busy and call on Tuesday, really make people question your integrity and leadership ability.

Staff promises that are given as encouragement but have no real substance can destroy a developing staff person. "You're doing a great job managing this club. I'm going to open a second club for you to manage, and give you some ownership as part of your incentive package. I should be able to get that done in the spring."

This promise may have been made with some sincere belief that it's going to happen. The owner may be thinking that this is a possibility in the future. But in the manager's mind, it's a promise. When you break this promise, even though there was no intent to do wrong, you are a leader who is no longer dependable or trustworthy.

People don't care why you didn't do what you said you were going to do. They only care that you didn't do what you promised. Once you break the faith with your staff (who follows your vision of what the business is going to be on blind trust), it's almost impossible to get it back. They trusted you as a leader and you failed.

Again, the promises don't have to be big ones. In fact, it's often the little ones that do the most damage. "Good job, let's talk about a raise at the

People don't care why you didn't do what you said you were going to do. They only care that you didn't do what you promised.

SECTION FIVE *Staffing Will Be the Most Difficult Issue You'll Ever Have to Deal with in the Fitness Business*

end of the month," or "You're doing a good job as a trainer. If Bill ever leaves, it's your job if you keep working the way you are," are innocent comments meant to motivate. But in the staff member's head, these are things their leader promised would happen. If they don't happen, you've completely de-motivated what might otherwise have been a good employee.

A development thought is to review your personal style. Do you promise everyone everything and are you trying to be liked, or do you only promise what you can really deliver and then work to gain a person's respect instead? Also, reflect back on a typical workweek. Did you deliver on what you promised, or did you have excuses for why they weren't fulfilled?

12) Failure to set a personal example.

As a leader, you want the young employees to look up to you and re-spect you, yet you date the members (or worse your staff) and are a legendary all-night party person. You want everyone in the community to support your business, yet you haven't given a dime's worth of time or money back to the community. You give a sales tour to a potential member about the benefits of working out, yet you're 15 pounds overweight. You want your employees to work hard for you, yet they are undertrained, yelled at in public, given wages lower than you could hire trained animals for, and their boss (you) is a moody SOB with irregular work hours, a bad attitude and no life outside the gym.

It seems we may have a leadership problem here. Leadership starts with the example you set for the staff. The old, "do what I say, don't do what I do" theory is not a form of leadership in a small business. If you can't live it your-self, it's hard to expect the staff to meet the standard. How you look, how you live and how you treat the staff are the pillars of leadership in a fitness business. Make sure your personal example is at a level that can stand scrutiny before you attempt to lead.

13) Failure to ask employees for their solutions and insights for club problems.

Gym owners are generally entrepreneurial by nature, meaning they do everything their way, whether they know anything about it or not. The prob-lem is that most fitness businesses are too complicated for a single person to control and understand every single component every single day.

Your employees, meaning the ones who actually do the work each day, often see creative solutions for the problems you face each business day. But as entrepreneurs, we always have to look good, so we try to come up with all the solutions ourselves, instead of including into the creative problem-solv-ing process the people who probably understand the problem better than we do.

Employees like to be challenged in their jobs and to feel part of the de-cision-making process in the business. Everyone likes to believe that they have good suggestions that could help solve a problem. Part of leadership is knowing when to let go and get your team involved in the business. There are four steps to keeping employees challenged and involved in the creative

You want everyone in the community to support your business, yet you haven't given a dime's worth of time or money back to the community.

200

problem-solving process:

• **Let the staff participate in some form of management.** Show them how the numbers work, let them help decide on uniforms and profit center items, and let them have some level of responsibility in their jobs. In other words, let them be in charge of something even if it's small.

• **Let them help make the rules concerning their work and how they do it.** You don't have to turn over your business, but the staff can participate in some of the rules that concern them. For example, what happens if someone on the team comes in late? They are usually harder on themselves than you would be in an employee manual.

• **Let them take part in the decision-making process.** The gym needs new treadmills. Let the staff try a few, let them work with the equipment reps, and let them have a vote in the final decision if possible.

• **Keep them informed about the details of the business.** Employees work better when they know what's going on in the business. They also like to feel like insiders. Sharing information keeps them in the loop and keeps them more involved in the outcome of your business.

Here's an example that illustrates getting the team involved in a small but important way. The club's drink sales are flat. You've tried every idea you could come up with to sell more drinks but nothing has worked. The problem is that the process usually stops there. You've tried everything you know, so there must not be any known solution to the problem.

Why not run a contest to see which employee can come up with the most innovative gimmick to sell drinks that month? The employee whose idea sells the most gets a $50 bonus, or something they want personally such as new shoes as a reward. The key to leadership in this example is that the owner sought and obtained involvement from the staff. Most owners complain that the staff just doesn't care about their businesses. Telling them to get involved doesn't work. Asking them to get involved by seeking their help immediately solves the problem.

14) Making decisions for your employees, instead of having set procedures or guidelines.

Every time you make an arbitrary decision concerning a business situation in the gym, you have taught your employees to be ineffective. You must have systems that force your employees to make their own decisions. Guidelines and procedures, in the form of a procedure manual, must be in place. These guidelines are where the employees look for guidance, instead of coming to you or the manager for decisions concerning a situation that you handle differently each time, depending on who's in front of you.

For example, the policy in your manual states very clearly that any member who is 30 days past expiration must renew at the current rates and fees. An old member is standing at the counter trying to get back into the club. You walk by, greet the member and then tell the staff person that she was a great member and let her in at her old rate and no additional membership fee.

Now what does that employee do the next time he is faced with a sim-

> **Employees work better when they know what's going on in the business.**

ilar situation? Does the employee give a deal and break the policy because he saw you do it, or does he follow the policy because he doesn't know if the former member standing in front of them was a "good" member, or a not so good member?

What will probably really happen is that the employee just comes to you to make the decision for them, since you just make things up as you go along anyway. By making the decision for the employee, you've taught him not to make any decisions for himself. When you ask yourself, "Can't anyone make any decisions around here except for me?" the answer is no, they can't because you taught them not to without you.

If an employee comes to you with a problem, learn to say, "What is the procedure on that?" or "What have I taught you previously about handling that type of problem?" Don't say, "Do it this way," which means don't worry about ever making a decision on your own, that's why I'm here so I can teach you to bring everything to me, so I'll never get anything done except handling routing, mundane questions all day that should be covered by my staff.

15) Failure to develop a second-in-command.

You're hurt in a car accident. Who is trained to run the business when you're not there every day? One-man shows are a sign of poor leadership. If the gym would suffer in its day-to-day business because you're not there, then you have signs of an immature leader who thinks giving up power and information undermines their leadership position.

But you've put off finding a second-in-command for years. Maybe it's because when it comes down to it, you won't give up the real power and authority to get the job done. Some people like having people come to them for every decision. But great businesses aren't built that way. You might be willing to give up the things you hate to do in the job, but not the things that are really important and that would allow someone to run the show when you're not there. This point is so important that there is a separate section dedicated to developing a second-in-command for your business.

> ... you've put off finding a second-in-command for years. Maybe it's because when it comes down to it, you won't give up the real power and authority to get the job done.

Summary

If you create an exciting vision of what your business can be, how it can help people improve and how important a fitness business can be, people will want to follow you.

Good employees will follow a strong leader, one who can make work seem important, fun and exciting all at the same time. Leadership can be learned and can be sifted down to a few key points:

• Leaders must have vision and the ability to set goals. Leaders must see the whole picture. If leaders have unclear goals and incomplete vision of what is going to come to pass and no plans in place, how can you lead if you don't know where you are going?

• Leaders must be trustworthy. Are you a trustworthy person? Is your word good? Do you deliver what you promise? Do you work to earn the respect of your employees, or do you try too hard to be liked?

• Leaders inspire participation. A poor leader can get people to work for a short while through intimidation. A good leader can get people to go beyond their basic job; that is where employee satisfaction begins and profits grow.

• Good leaders practice diversity. Good leaders are diverse in their personal interests, well-rounded in life and have an outside life beyond their businesses. Poor leaders are narrow in scope, and usually hire other people just like themselves. Practice diversity in your own life and in your hiring of the people who work for you.

• Leaders are big-picture people. Good leaders spend a great deal of time working *on* their businesses, not *in* them. Good leaders expect their people to have creative solutions and support that creativity even if it isn't right all the time.

• Leaders are high-integrity people. Good ethics is good business.

• Leaders making learning a lifetime passion. When you think you know it all is when you really don't know anything anymore. The business changes, the consumer changes, times change and so should you.

• Good leaders have a sense of community. We support the community and then the community supports us.

> **Good leaders are diverse in their personal interests, well-rounded in life, and have an outside life beyond their businesses.**

Things you can do to use this material

1) Start with you. Are you the leader you should be? Write out your five strongest gifts as a leader, and your five biggest weaknesses that you need to work on in the next six months.

2) Review your systems. Are your employee systems, such as pay, hours and incentives relics from some age-old club, or are they vital and current? Can an employee grow and thrive in the environment you've created in the business?

3) Especially review your hiring systems. If you're not getting the type of people you need to grow your business, this is the place to start.

4) Review your training strategy. Most owners don't understand the learning process. Institute the notebook system and slow down. Make sure your people truly understand their tasks and what you expect from them on a daily basis. Most employees like to do a good job — if they know what a good job is.

5) Leadership can be learned. Write out all of the things that you need to change before you can become the leader you want to be. Also write down the top 10 leadership mistakes you have made with your staff in the past and how you should have handled the situation.

6) Training is everything. Write out a 30-day training program for all key positions in the business. The program should:

• Outline what they should anticipate — both the good and the bad in whatever job they will fill in the gym.

• Explain how you will measure performance.

• Explain how you will recognize and reward good work.

• Start with member service on the first day.

• Create a detailed job description.

• Assign another employee as a big buddy.

• Spend at least two hours a day on the basics of working in a gym, such as phones, member service and basic sales information.

• Build working examples of member service situations that have occurred in the club, and let the employee work through the solutions. Build at least 10 different examples.

• Let the person follow a variety of employees around the gym, they will have more of a sense of teamwork and understanding of what everyone else does each day.

• Let the person try or tour every profit center and get started training, spinning and doing whatever other activities you offer.

• Review the employee manual in depth.

• Train from the procedure manual. The employee doesn't need to memorize every procedure, they just need to know where to find them.

• Try to not let the employee work alone during the first two weeks.

• During the third and fourth weeks, end each workday for the employee with a 30-minute training and review session of their work.

• Include a formal review at the end of the 30-day period.

7) Learn to delegate. Create a list of at least 10 things you do that could be delegated to someone. These items should free more of your time, and give the employees a sense of participation in the business.

Create a list of at least 10 things you do that could be delegated to someone.

LESSONS FROM LIFE — #14

You're part of the act

THEY DREAMED OF HANGING OUT with trim, in-shape people. They were also tired of working in offices, wearing dress clothes and working regular hours. Somewhere out there, they knew there was a business that was casual and must be so easy that anyone could do it. And as brother and sister they wanted to create a family business that they could do together. So they bought a licensed gym in Pennsylvania.

Besides being wrong about the business in general, they weren't workout people. He was round-shouldered, had never picked up a weight in his life and was about 40 pounds overweight. She was very short and very heavy at five-foot-three and 200 pounds. No, there is no reason they should have picked the fitness business.

He became the manager and trainer and she took charge of the nutrition program. A year after buying the gym, they still weren't even close to being in shape. He at least had started a fitness program. She hadn't because she was just too busy running the club and was still in the same condition. They had quite a bit of family money, but after a while they were going through that pretty quickly. It seems they had a hard time convincing people they could get into shape in their gym.

It seems they had a hard time convincing people they could get into shape in their gym

The moral of the story

You're more of a role model than you think. This doesn't mean that you have to take Arnold down in a one-on-one pose during his peak years, but you at least have to live the lifestyle.

Relating fitness to people is often having been there yourself. Salespeople who were out of shape are often more believable and convincing when it comes to selling a membership because they've been there themselves. The same goes for nutrition people or trainers who had to fight their genetics to achieve their level of fitness.

The owners and the management in a fitness club are part of the act and should look like they've seen a workout before today. They don't have to be a finished product, but they should be a work in progress.

For example, an often-asked question in seminars is: Should the owner hire someone who's out of shape? If the person has lost 30 pounds, and still has 30 to go but is working on it, then the answer would be yes. If the person is 30 pounds overweight but has never worked out, then the answer is no. Works in progress are more motivating than someone who hasn't yet seen the light.

Fitness isn't just vital for your health, it often can be vital for the survival of your business too.

15

Learning to live with a stranger in your business

IF YOU'RE SEEKING GROWTH and stabilization in your current business, or if you dream of adding a second or third unit, then hiring and developing a second-in-command may be the most important decision you make concerning the future of your business. For most owners who have raised their gyms from small baby businesses, it may be time to consider letting a stranger into your business.

By adding a No. 2, which may be a manager, assistant manager or just a strong administrative person, you free yourself to work on your business, not in it. A strong second gives you the freedom to expand your business beyond what you can accomplish yourself. In today's business world, and especially as it relates to the gym business, one person can't do it all. You have to shift the burden away from yourself and start relying on other people who are capable of taking responsibility to ensure the future success of your business.

A strong No. 2 person also provides additional stability in a business that has a higher-than-average employee turnover. The national average for employee turnover, according to the Bureau of National Affairs, is 1.9 percent monthly, or about 23 percent on an annual basis.

Our numbers in the fitness business often exceed 23 percent, and usually reach as high as 30 percent, which is the same as most financial institutions. Financial institutions encounter the same problems we do with young, low-paid, over-worked entry-level employees, that ultimately lead to a high turnover at the lower levels. By giving the senior management team some depth and stability with the addition of a No. 2, the employee loss numbers should drop. More trained management can provide more training and individual attention, two prime reasons that cause entry-level people to leave

> **A strong No. 2 person also provides additional stability in a business that has a higher-than-average employee turnover.**

207

if these things are missing from their jobs.

While every owner dreams of having a strong No. 2 who handles day-to-day operations, takes responsibility, runs the place when you're out of town, and does so in an honest, high integrity manner, these people seldom just drop in and ask for a job in real life. If they do, they seldom last very long because they are talented enough to move to better paying and higher image real life jobs. This means that probably the only way you're going to get a second leadership person is to find and develop your own.

With your No. 2, you are like the Lone Ranger and Tonto, Picard and Riker, or Yogi and Boo Boo; in other words, a team that is stronger than either one is alone.

With your No. 2, you are like the Lone Ranger and Tonto, Picard and Riker, or Yogi and Boo Boo; in other words, a team that is stronger than either one is alone.

Before we go any further, let's first define what's meant by a No. 2 or second in command. The No. 2 person in the business organization should be the owner's counterpart. He or she should cover the owner's weaknesses and bring other skills to the business that help to grow the facility beyond the owner's ability to do it on his own.

In other words, there should be some type of synergistic effect where one plus one equals something greater than two. If the magic is right, the owner and the No. 2 person should be able to combine forces and be more effective than both people working separately.

There are many reasons for never developing a strong management team, or for losing them when we do find them. But most of the time it comes down to just a few key errors by the owners.

First of all, employees usually can't follow us or perform on their own because we don't develop systems. Most fitness businesses are dependent on the owner's on-the-spot decision-making capabilities to survive. If the owner isn't on the spot, then they are calling in every few hours to check the numbers and to make those instant decisions no one else can make. This happens because there are no set systems to follow by the employees that could be substituted for the owner's presence.

There are hundreds of examples of situations where owners make instant and inconsistent decisions that drive the staff crazy. For instance, a salesperson is touring the brother of a long-term member. The owner just happens to walk by as the salesperson is explaining the prices to Joe, who is the guest, and to Bob, who is the member and who is sitting in on the presentation with his brother. Bob says to the salesperson, "Hey, can you give my brother the family deal? I know that Sue the owner is here. How about asking her if she'll give us some type of discount? " The salesperson asks Sue, who says, "Sure, Bob is a great member, go ahead and give his brother the family deal."

The club policy that the salesperson was trained on says that family deals are only for married couples. The owner made an on-the-spot, subjective decision for the employee. What does the employee do the next time a friend of the owner, a good member or anyone else asking for a deal comes into the gym?

How does the employee make a decision to act, since the club has a policy the owner ignores depending on the member and the situation? The next time, will the employee follow the policy or will they make a judgment decision, meaning a special deal in this case, based on whomever the member is talking to at the time?

The owner certainly has the right to give deals in her own club. But making these deals on a random basis in front of the staff destroys her ability to build a team of competent employees. Training employees to follow set procedures is relatively simple. Training them to interpret the procedures, so they know when to make deals and when not to is almost impossible on a staff-wide basis.

A sophisticated salesperson would use deal-making as a last ditch effort if they couldn't close the deal using normal techniques. A weak salesperson would use deal-making as a way to close every sale, therefore, lowering the yield and the return per member. In this example, a lack of a set structure hurts the return per sale and, therefore, lowers the income the club can expect.

This type of situation is why employees keep coming up to you all the time for answers, instead of making their own decisions. This happens because the owners of the club don't establish and follow consistent guidelines. In the example above, the employee should have known not to even ask the owner. They should have already known from the training they had received that there wasn't a deal possible, because these two brothers didn't qualify for the family plan. But since the owner has a history of making deals, the employee had to ask to see what the deal of the day was going to be.

It's hard for someone else to live up to your experience

The second issue when it comes to developing a No. 2 in your business is that employees go through stages of growth that often contrast with where you are as an owner today. We seldom find employees good enough to become key people because we are always comparing the employee's current stage of development against our own current stage.

A side issue here is that the longer an employee works for us, the better we get to know them. The better we get to know them, the more visible their weaknesses become over time. It's sort of like marriage. After a certain amount of time, we're more willing to hire someone outside our organization because that person is fresh, new and without visible flaws. This is why we're usually overcritical of employees (or spouses) who have been with us for a while, and have given us time to see their strengths and weaknesses.

For example, a promising employee has two years of experience working in the same gym. The employee has gone through several seminars, has taken minor responsibility (the owner won't give up any major responsibility) and has worked in several jobs in the gym after starting at the bottom as an entry-level person.

The owner has eight years of experience in the business and is looking for a strong No. 2 person to take some of the management load and to help grow the business to the next level. The owner says, however, that the

We seldom find employees good enough to become key people because we are always comparing the employee's current stage of development against our own current stage.

promising employee just won't work in the new position because she doesn't yet have the skills or experience to take a leadership role in the business.

What's happened here is that the owner is comparing the employee's current level of skill and experience against his own eight years, and the employee just doesn't stack up. The owner is also comparing the employee against his own current state of business understanding, which has taken eight years of on-the-job training and trial and error to develop.

The questions that should be asked instead are: where is the employee today, what is she capable of doing in the future, and what responsibility is she able to handle now and in the future after additional training? We know that in this industry, the majority of our employees are undertrained and very few of our developing people could ever live up to the high and often unrealistic standards we set for them.

Most owners forget the price they paid to get the knowledge they now have after years of experience. In this example, eight years of daily decision-making, right or wrong, has led to an experienced and capable gym owner. Two years of working for someone as a trainer or salesperson does not develop the decision-making process, nor does it prepare the person to take responsibility. Only taking responsibility prepares someone for more responsibility.

Most employees never have a chance to learn responsibility because they never have a chance to fail on their own, which is the way most owners learned the business in the first place. If we only give them minor-level responsibility, their failures will be of no consequence and they won't learn anything from the experience. But we won't give them any real responsibility because we're afraid they'll make major, business-threatening mistakes.

If it has taken a specific number of years for you to learn the business, how long would it take you to teach someone else? How much time do we really spend on education? Here is an example of a two-year employee who has worked up to manager:

> **The new employee starts by spending six months as a front counter person.**
>
> Training:

• Two eight-hour days of orientation	16 hours
• One staff meeting a week for 26 weeks	26 hours
• One two-day weekend training session	16 hours
• Sixteen hours of general staff training	<u>16 hours</u>
Total training for the first six months	74 hours

> **The employee is promoted to assistant manager, a job they hold for one year.**
>
> Training:

• Two hours a month special training	24 hours
• One hour staff meetings over the year	50 hours
• Attendance at one industry show/six seminars	6 hours
• Two two-day seminars	<u>32 hours</u>
Total training for the year	112 hours

The questions that should be asked instead are: where is the employee today, what is she capable of doing in the future, and what responsibility is she able to handle now and in the future after additional training?

The employee is then promoted to manager, a job they hold for six months.

   Training:

• One-hour staff meetings	26 hours
• One two-day seminar	<u>16 hours</u>
Total training over six months	**42 hours**

The employee has received 228 hours, or about four weeks, of training over two years of employment. The owner has had the business for eight years. Eight years equals 416 weeks of ownership, or taking full-time responsibility for the business every day it's opened.

The training for this employee is probably exaggerated for most fitness businesses. Yet we still feel that since this person has been there for two years, they should know the business simply by absorbing while they're on the job. In reality, the only way to learn most jobs is to simply do them, and to learn from your mistakes as they happen.

Another problem to consider when looking for a No. 2 is that we often hire people who are too much like ourselves. Even if they aren't at first, most owners slowly mold the person into their own likeness. Ever notice that dogs and their owners start to look alike after they've been together for years. It's the same in gyms. Most owners have strong personalities, and many of our new hires try to emulate them as their role models. After a while, the employee acquires your strengths and your weaknesses.

One of the biggest mistakes in the hiring process is failing to hire people who are smarter than ourselves. The opposite of this, of course, is that we constantly hire people who are dumber than we. It's like the intelligent woman who always dates dumb guys, because they make her look so much smarter in a crowd. She may never have great conversation, but she also doesn't have to worry about looking bad either. Some owners are like this. They don't ever want to be shown up or challenged, so they hire people with less talent. This leaves the owner with a loyal bunch of people who never run the business to its fullest potential.

In the club business, egos often dictate avoiding people who challenge us. For example, the No. 2 person in many gyms (owned by young males) is either an attractive, very young and usually very attentive female with little experience or education, or a young male who is a workout guy like the owner, but still without education or experience. Neither challenge the owner's image.

Even in the bigger fitness businesses, the No. 2 is often the loyal salesperson who has no real experience in actually running a gym as a business. This person is usually loyal and nonthreatening, but never develops into the kind of person who could be trusted running the business if you were gone for a month. You need to hire someone who will make you think, someone who can challenge the decisions you make out of habit, and someone who can stimulate new ideas from the rest of your staff.

When you try to build a strong organization, consider hiring a person who is a complete opposite of yourself. If you're strong on people skills but

> **One of the biggest mistakes in the hiring process is failing to hire people who are smarter than ourselves.**

211

When you try to build a strong organization, consider hiring a person who is a complete opposite of yourself.

weak on organization, look for someone with adequate people skills, but who can get you and the gym organized and ready for the next level of business. Most owners are good with people, but not good with details and organization. What many owners need is someone who can get them organized and structured enough to move to that next level.

Hiring someone just like you can also slow down the progress of your business. For example, a 28-year-old single male owner in the northeast has two licensed gyms. He's a serious workout guy and is in excellent shape. His management team is made up of all males, all about 25 to 30 years old, and all are workout guys who are also single. They work together, party together and chase women together on the weekends.

What kind of male to female mix do you think these clubs would have? The desired average is 55 percent female to 45 percent male. Their clubs are about 70 percent male. If the management team had to make major decisions, wouldn't their solutions all be somewhat alike, because of the lack of diversity among the team?

For example, the club needed some new equipment on the workout floor and on the cardio deck. As young males and serious workout guys, most of the money was spent on advanced weight training machines and very little on cardio. A different perspective might have sought more balance or at least equipment that would have attracted and supported a broader clientele.

There would also be issues of the club's atmosphere, colors and finish, music, uniforms and member service. All of these areas would end up with the same solution and same perspective, that of a single, white male who lifts a lot of weights. Women, older males and other gym populations would be ignored in this environment.

Before you can hire a No. 2 person who can perform, you have to take time to analyze yourself as a boss and as a person. What are your strengths and weaknesses, and what will you need from your second-in-command? Here are some starting points to help you understand yourself better and what you want from your chief assistant:

1. STAY IN TOUCH WITH YOUR EXPERTISE

You were the one who made the gym happen in the first place. For example, as an owner you were good in sales, but now that you're the boss you feel you should be active doing something boss-like, such as paperwork. Sometimes it's good to go with your strengths and find someone else to take care of your weaknesses.

In this case, once you understand and master the numbers and the back shop part of the business, you can still sell and handle production for the company and hire a No. 2 who takes over the paperwork, budgets, payroll and other management necessities. By doing it this way, you're still improving the business with the addition of the No. 2, but you are also working within your strengths to grow to the next level.

2. YOU CAN MANAGE MORE THAN YOU CAN DO YOURSELF

Streamline the business by farming out as much as you can. You could probably learn to do your own books and collect your own memberships, but one person can manage more than they could ever do alone.

Many owners consider giving up parts of the business as losing control. It's hard to understand, but the more you give up and then manage, the more control you'll have in the end.

Also streamline by creating set systems and procedures in the business. Training a No. 2 will be easier if you are teaching them how to follow a system, rather than how to freestyle the management decisions.

3. PROVIDE REAL EDUCATION

A classic owner quote: "It would take me five hours to teach this to someone, or five minutes to do it myself." This quote is the justification we use for still trying to do everything ourselves. The five hours of education, though, could save you hundreds of dollars and many, many hours of labor in the long run. Your people will be more loyal and become better performers if you spend the time and money to educate them.

4. LEAD BY EXAMPLE

If you don't do it and live it, then neither will your employees. For example, if you're 15 minutes late for an appointment with an employee, stop and consider the statement you have made about acceptable behavior in the business. That employee has an appointment with a member tomorrow for training. What happens if the employee is late for that appointment? Whose fault is it? Could you fault an employee who might have learned the behavior from you?

If you don't do it and live it, then neither will your employees.

5. SET CLEAR OBJECTIVES

People work better when they know what's expected of them. If an employee thinks he is doing a great job, and his boss thinks he is not, you are already in a no-win situation. If a situation occurs such as a potential raise review, where both sides argue their stance is correct, then the boss is to blame for not setting performance standards so the employees know how they are doing as they progress.

6. PRAISE AND RECOGNIZE

As bosses, we too often fail to say thanks or to recognize an employee who is getting the job done. Since we are paying them anyway, we expect them to do a good job. Therefore, we only get involved if they are not doing such a great job. But, since so few people do good jobs for the money they receive, we need to recognize effort that is ultimately in our behalf.

As owners, we too often reward the heroes and ignore the steady, dependable folks who are the heart of the business. For example, salespeople are always the stars, get the greatest pay and have the best perks. We then ignore those steady, always-there employees who get the job done every day.

The steady producers who understand other aspects of the gym besides sales often make good No. 2 people. This type of person needs to learn the role of sales in the business, and should be able to do enough sales to lead by example, but they don't always have to be the top sales producer in the business.

A good trainer or counter person can bring in renewals, handle complaints and help make a sale through good member service, and still not be recognized. These people are as important, if not more so, than some employees who constantly try to write new business at any cost.

7. TREAT EMPLOYEES AS INDIVIDUALS

No two employees are alike. The management techniques you use on one may not work on another. We need to develop techniques that can be adapted to individual employees. For example, a young employee who is chronically late may respond better to a stern warning that is written up and put in the file, along with a serious parent-to-child talk. An older employee with the same problem might respond better to a sit-down talk about their role in the gym, and how their behavior lets down the rest of the team.

Once you understand what it takes to be a good boss (and for many people this process takes years of self-review and awareness), you then become ready to hire and start developing a good No. 2 person.

A No. 2 person has a unique position in the company when it comes to their relationship with the other staff and with the owner. Most people in the world either like to give orders or they are more comfortable taking direction and working under a strong leader. The No. 2 in most fitness facilities has to do both; take charge when you're off the property and defer to your authority when you're onsite. This means that the person has to have a certain degree of maturity to be functional in your organization.

The search for the perfect No. 2

The search for the perfect No. 2 in your organization begins with avoiding the biggest mistake you can make, which is to hire too young. Hiring the youngest and, therefore, the cheapest employees we can find has forever been a tradition in the industry. But this practice is especially counterproductive when you're trying to develop your business by adding a strong assistant who must have working leadership characteristics. Here are a few reasons not to hire too young:

• It takes more work to keep an employee who's too young. Many of our young employees have not yet developed a real work ethic or have enough experience in other businesses to carry over to ours.

• They are less dependable than more established workers, meaning they're often still searching for the perfect job,.

Once you understand what it takes to be a good boss (and for many people this process takes years of self-review and awareness), you then become ready to hire and start developing a good No. 2 person.

• They have lifestyles that can be met by most any job. With what we pay entry-level workers, their average lifestyle is pretty basic and can be replaced with almost any other entry-level job.

• Most of our younger employees are undertrained and underexperienced in work that relates to making money in the fitness industry, such as customer service or sales.

• Weak communication skills are common among the younger workers. It usually takes a number of years in the workplace to develop competent communication skills, especially when it comes to dealing with a wide variety of clients.

• As a group, they may be young and not properly prepared, but most employees in this group want responsibility quickly. As owners, being aware of their age, we confuse more responsibility with the assignment of menial tasks. For example, we have a front counter person who's assigned to stocking the coolers, not an exciting job but one that has to be done. An owner might consider this responsibility, but the employee considers it a low-level task.

To challenge the employee, we still might assign the task of stocking, but that person is also on the drink team for drink sales and is responsible for one drink promotion per week, under supervision of course. The difference is in the perception of what responsibility is and who has it· The owner, who usually sets up all drink specials, or now the staff person, whose first responsibility in the gym is running a weekly profit center promotion.

> **It usually takes a number of years in the workplace to develop competent communication skills, especially when it comes to dealing with a wide variety of clients.**

Guidelines for hiring and developing a second-in-command

1. MAKE SURE YOU ARE READY TO DELEGATE AUTHORITY

Many owners never develop a No. 2, because all they are really looking for is someone to do grunt work and menial tasks. No. 2 people, to be effective and grow the business in tandem with the owner, have to have the responsibility and authority to make real decisions, especially when you're not there.

For example, you're at a seminar in Las Vegas for the weekend. You either call the gym 3 to 4 times a day and end up handling the same problems you would have while you're at home, or you relax and enjoy the pool knowing that the club is in good hands and you can review the paperwork when you return.

If you're more likely to be running your club from the road, then your business won't grow because you aren't comfortable giving up partial control while you're there, and still need total control when you're not. Remember that your job is to grow the business, and to do so you have to pass along some of the responsibility so others can help you.

2. MAKE SURE YOU HAVE A CLEAR IDEA OF THE TRAITS AND SKILLS YOU'RE LOOKING FOR IN A NO. 2

Your No. 2 should complement you, not be a clone. Analyze your own strengths and weaknesses first; then create a description of someone who is opposite and adds to the mix, instead of adding to the weaknesses that already exist.

3. ASK YOURSELF WHAT YOU REALLY WANT THIS PERSON TO DO IN YOUR ORGANIZATION

Before you hire a chief assistant, write a job description that describes specific responsibilities and the authority the person would need to do the job. Include the duties you see this person handling for you as you continue to grow. For example, your second-in-command might handle one or more of these responsibilities:

• Take over the entire staffing function including staffing, staff training, monthly goal setting and teams (discussed in a later section), staff disciplinary action and files, and scheduling. This might allow the owner to concentrate on the marketing and sales function of the business.

• Take over the development and promotion of the multiple profit centers including the daily promotions, monthly analysis of each center, teams and incentives, and ordering and stocking.

• Take over the marketing including the direct mail campaigns, newspapers, public relations, handling the club charity, and setting up and promoting club events and programming.

• Take over the sales and training functions including training all the salespeople, training the trainers to work in conjunction with sales, develop and stock sales materials, and work with the head trainer, head nutrition tech and lead salespeople to develop a consistent team sales approach.

• Development and implementation of a procedure manual and staff training program including all staff meetings, new-hire training and the coordination of outside training events.

These are not all the possibilities, but in most fitness businesses, the owner is currently doing all of this stuff and more by herself. You're better off to follow the old adage of doing fewer things but doing them better, and giving some of these tasks to your new No. 2.

4. CONDUCT AN EFFICIENT SEARCH

Once you have a description, where would you find this person? We often make the mistake of hiring someone we already know just because we are familiar with that person. This is opposite of not hiring someone because we know them too well and already know their quirks. The important part to remember is that the best person for the job may not be in your organization.

A common mistake is limiting your search to someone already in the fitness business. A fitness enthusiast with business experience or a customer

You're better off to follow the old adage of doing fewer things but doing them better, and giving some of these tasks to your new No. 2.

service background might be a great candidate. Again, look for the traits and not necessarily the skills we value in the fitness industry such as training or sales experience. If the traits exist, then business experience or real-life service experience is more important, and we can teach the fitness functions later.

5. Pay equals performance

To keep a key person, we need to learn to break their lifestyle pattern in order to move them ahead in their careers. Many of our key people become too comfortable in their jobs because we have let them become too comfortable in their lifestyles. This means that we have trouble moving these people up because it's too easy to go back to their old comfort level they have been getting by on for years.

Here's another real-life gym story that illustrates this point. One owner was going to open a second unit in a town about an hour from his first business. He wanted to promote a female in her mid-20s who had been with him for about two years as manager of the existing facility. The manager would be responsible for all of the day-to-day transactions in the gym, hiring and firing and for meeting goals. The owner was most concerned that he would train this person, start the second unit and then she would quit for some reason.

The owner's original plan was to give her a raise and put her on probation for 90 days to see if she could do the job. He was going to train her for about 60 days on the daily operations and procedures she hadn't had experience with yet, before he left for the other project.

This woman was ideal for the job and had been a loyal employee for a long time working at most of the various jobs in the gym. She also had many of the skills necessary in business, such as organizational skills, that the owner didn't have. This hiring plan, however, didn't meet the situation and might actually cause the new manager to leave because the changes only affected her job and not her lifestyle.

In other words, there was no risk for her to try because she could always go back to her other job or find an equivalent somewhere else in town. Her current compensation paid enough to cover her bills, pay for a nice little older model car, and let her live fairly comfortably for someone her age by sharing expenses with one other roommate.

The revised hiring plan was to change her lifestyle in conjunction with her new job. Upon interviewing the woman, it was found that her personal goals were to have her own place and to get a new car. She was also concerned that even a management job at the gym was no guarantee of a long-term career.

The final hiring plan, that she participated in, gave her a small raise, a small loan for a deposit on her own place, and a new company car which only cost the club $149 a month on a lease. Also, if she managed the gym successfully for one year, meeting goals and growing the business, she would be vested with 5 percent of the gym's stock in an equity-only position with an option to buy 5 percent more if she wanted.

> **To keep a key person, we need to learn to break their lifestyle pattern in order to move them ahead in their careers.**

The revised plan changed her lifestyle, making it hard for her to go back to what she had in the past after she had gotten into the new job.

The revised plan changed her lifestyle, making it hard for her to go back to what she had in the past after she had gotten into the new job. There were no other jobs in town that would give her those perks and future, so it would be unlikely for her to want to jump to something else.

If the owner had left her in her old lifestyle, meaning just a raise and the same old car and apartment, he would have created a situation where failure would not have been costly to the new manager. In her situation, failure means giving up an awful lot compared to where she had been in the past.

She was still hired under the 90-day probation for the new job, received more training than she anticipated, including business schools and a trip to a national trade convention, which made her feel ready to accept the responsibility to take on the new job.

6. SOMETIMES, IT MAY TAKE TWO

We sometimes need more than one No. 2. High-volume clubs, or multiple units, may need more than one No. 2. Two people may be needed but they may have completely different job descriptions and have different functions in the business.

Review the possible responsibilities that were listed earlier. In a high-volume club with 2,000 members or more, you may need two second-in-commands. Their tasks may be such that any of the responsibilities on the list may be enough to keep a full-time person busy, in conjunction with assuming some of the staff management areas. If you're looking for two people, however, start with one only and concentrate on getting the best you can the first time. Then move on to the second.

7. CREATE A SYSTEMS-DEPENDENT BUSINESS, NOT A PEOPLE-DEPENDENT BUSINESS

Every procedure you have in your business should be documented so any employee faced with that situation can look it up. All new staff should be trained the same each and every time through their initial stages. For example, you hire someone new, someone you think may fit well into your system. During their training, could you show them:

• A set procedure manual for every basic function in the gym such as cleaning and maintaining equipment?

• Working samples of every piece of paper generated in the business?

• Procedures for every phase of the business, such as opening, closing, handling renewals, personnel policies and daily business reporting?

• Policies to handle common situations in the gym, such as cancellations, problems and complaints?

Many businesses could not produce all these things in written form in manuals that are easily accessible to the staff. Most owners would have to talk the person through everything because nothing is in writing and everything they do in the business is situational, which means every problem that arises is handled individually, as it occurs. In other words, do you limit, or leave open, operating discretion for your people? The more open the discretion, the more mistakes and less money you will make.

This lack of real, working information is partially why we lose key people. They are eventually given responsibility toward making the business work, but they never really gain an understanding of our business on the backside. Your second person will do a better job if they have enough information to relate the task at hand to the bottom line, and then is able to share that information with the staff.

The concept of sharing information with your people is new to most owners who grew up in systems and worked under owners who tried very hard to conceal every number. The basic idea of sharing information is to make sure everyone on the team understands why their job is important with regard to the bottom line of the company. If they are asked to do something, even something that seems menial at the time, they have an understanding that this job affects the bottom line in some particular way.

For example, if you or your No. 2 is working with the staff on the importance of walking through each locker room every 30 minutes and shutting doors, replacing toilet paper, wiping off the sinks and generally doing some basic cleaning, how would you make this job seem important enough to do without question?

One way might be to show the staff the revenue generated by the sales team. Then relate these numbers to the overall financial picture of the club. From here it would be a short walk to the payroll section. If sales go down because potential members see a dirty locker room, revenues go down, and eventually the payroll would have to be decreased to compensate. Even the lowest level counter person will do a better job if they know why they are doing certain things.

> **Even the lowest level counter person will do a better job if they know why they are doing certain things.**

8. KEEP THE PAY COMPETITIVE FOR YOUR AREA

Another major consideration in keeping your No. 2 is to find out if the salary you're paying is competitive for the area, but not restricted just to other fitness facilities. It's helpful to find out what equivalent jobs, such as retail shop managers, get paid in your market. When comparing, include all the perks such as health insurance, days of paid vacation and other benefits we can offer to make the job more valuable.

Incentives for your No. 2 person can be a combination of money and other specific things of interest to the individual. The following survey might give you an idea of other incentives that employees are interested in (besides money):

Out of the employees surveyed:

• 87 percent viewed special training, such as a paid trip to a certification school or educational event, as a positive reward.

• 85 percent considered stock options or the ability to participate in the company as important.

• 77 percent said a trip to a desirable destination with a spouse or guest would be an appealing reward.

• 76 percent valued recognition at a company meeting or event.

• 63 percent ranked gifts and a pat on the back as very desirable.

What this says it that it doesn't always have to be money. Your compensation package for your employees, including your No. 2, can be based on a combination of things, such as the car for the young manager who was mentioned earlier. Remember that it's not money, but what the car represented. We could have paid her enough to get her own car. But for her, in a small town and being in her mid-20s, the recognition and status of having a company car was far more important as an incentive than giving her the $149.

As a final note, it's usually a sign of poor management when a good employee leaves to take another job. If you lose several key people in a relatively short period of time, it's usually your fault, despite the stories they give you.

If they liked working for you, and liked the job, they would go out of their way to keep it instead of going out of their way to find another job. They may give you a lot of great stories and excuses as to why they are leaving, but if they really wanted to stay, they'd find a way. It's hard to change a job and for most people it's even somewhat scary. Once someone gets a job they like, they usually like to settle in and stick with it for a while, until either a better opportunity comes along, which still should be from you, or until you force them out with bad management, which we need to correct.

If you lose several key people in a relatively short period of time, it's usually your fault, despite the stories they give you.

Summary

Even the smallest business can usually improve with the addition of a strong teammate for the owner, someone who can carry more responsibility and increase the workload beyond what one person can handle. An easy summary for creating a No. 2 spot, and for staffing in general, can be simplified in some straightforward points:

1) Avoid drastic overstaffing and understaffing.

2) Clearly spell out, in writing, what you expect from your No. 2.

3) Delegate major, not just minor, responsibility.

4) Encourage ideas, even if they are different from your own.

5) Visualize, using visual management techniques, every staff member's goals, including your No. 2's and your own contributions.

6) Visualize your team's goals, so everyone has the same basic information about the business.

7) Promote from within if possible.

8) Set a realistic leadership example.

9) Rotate job responsibility with your No. 2 on the really ugly jobs. You know, she fires one and then you fire one.

10) Use positive incentives, goals and performance standards to motivate.

11) Give the low-level folks challenging assignments.

12) Accept mistakes.

13) Establish reasonable deadlines.

14) Be liberal with praise on even the little things you expect anyway.

15) Criticize with tact. "Bonehead" is not an acceptable staff name.

16) Tell the truth even when it makes you or the business look bad.

17) Say "no" tactfully, and only for good cause.

18) Set up long-term incentive programs for your senior people.

19) The more training and education, the better. You can't overtrain a staff person.

20) Don't downplay bad assignments.

21) Don't work with idiots. Don't expect your No. 2 to do so either.

22) Teach everyone time management.

23) Meet and exchange information often with the entire team.

24) Be consistent in your treatment of your No. 2 and the entire staff.

25) Show personal interest in your management team.

26) Learn from the employees who quit. When good employees quit, they are telling you something.

27) Admit mistakes.

28) Share the inside information.

29) Build systems-dependent businesses.

30) Inspect everyone's work often.

31) Share the profits of the business with those who make them.

32) Give constant feedback on individual performance.

Things you can do to use this material

1) Project your business three years into the future. Where do you want to be? How successful do you want your business to have become by that time? Now figure out what type of person, with what skills and knowledge, you need to reach those goals.

2) Build a model of the pay, incentives and a job description before you begin your search for a No. 2.

3) Build a systems-based business that is not dependent on any one person to succeed. If your business is truly a systems business, you should be able to interchange staff without seeing a decline.

4) Hire a No. 2 who has practical business skills, instead of fitness experience.

5) Review the incentives you are currently using with your staff. Could you improve performance by changing incentives? Keep in mind that it's not always money that motivates people. Start with recognition as your prime motivator.

6) Protect the key people you already have in your business. Learning to change their lifestyle to match their position makes it hard to leave you for another job that may not have all the great extras.

7) Study your work style. Most owners and managers are doers. Remember that you can manage much more than you can physically do yourself.

Remember that you can manage much more than you can physically do yourself.

221

LESSONS FROM LIFE — #15

Everybody does everything

DURING A TOUR OF A fitness facility, the potential member asked the salesperson how the aerobics classes were at that club. The salesperson said she didn't know since she never took aerobics classes herself.

When cardio came out, many of the owners in the club business shifted away from classes to doing machines. It was simply a matter of time usage. A busy owner may have to jump onto a bike or step machine when they have time, and not when a class is scheduled.

Over the years, most owners dropped out of aerobics altogether and shifted their workouts to other parts of the gym. During a survey of owners in 1997, only three owners out of the 100 surveyed had done aerobics classes at least four times in the past 30-day period.

Aerobics as a club activity also started to decline during the mid-'90s. A two-year survey of

200 clubs showed member participation in aerobics dropped from a high of 22 percent to an average of 6 percent.

The moral of the story

Is there a correlation between owner support and member

The salesperson said she didn't know since she never took aerobics classes herself

participation? Yes, because if you don't do it, you can't sell it and probably don't support it as well either.

In the fitness business, everyone on the staff needs to

participate in every program the gym offers. Owners especially need to be regulars in everything they own so they can better understand what the members go through as they participate in the various club programs and offerings.

The staff should be encouraged to participate in everything, including the services and amenities the club has for sale. For example, if the club has a nutrition program, everyone on the staff should complete the program at least once so they can competently answer questions for prospective and regular members, too.

There is a relationship to the success of a program in a club and whether or not the staff supports it through their participation. If the staff has a hard time taking part in a club activity, then it won't be long, as in the aerobics example, until the program itself starts to decline.

16

Staffing a fitness business is more complicated than seeing how many hours a week your relatives can work

STAFFING A BUSINESS is almost more of an art form than a science for most fitness businesses. Learning to staff by creating the key positions, learning to use a staffing budget plan, and learning to hire by levels are all part of an advanced approach to running your business.

Of course, you could still use the system many owners use when they first get started. Figure out how many hours you're going to be open, total up all relatives and divide. This is OK when you first start, but eventually you're going to need something more comprehensive to make your business grow.

Before we discuss staffing basics, first look at how staffing budgets affect the overall business. For many years, most owners in the business looked at what staffing cost, as a percentage of sales, or in other words, a percentage of the total money the business brought in that month.

The problem with this system is that the staff expanded as revenues increased. This continually drove up expenses as the revenues grew, and also left the business severely overstaffed when revenues dropped.

A more advanced way to look at your staffing budget is to compare cost to staff in relationship to the monthly base operating expense (BOE). This percentage ratio also has changed over the years. During the '80s and early '90s, a financially sound fitness business would have its BOE divided into these percentages:

A more advanced way to look at your staffing budget is to compare cost to staff in relationship to the monthly base operating expense (BOE).

**Rent/mortgage and any additional landlord add-on charge (triple net) =
33 percent of BOE**

**Payroll and payroll taxes and any commissions or bonuses =
33 percent of BOE**

**General operating expense such as supplies, repairs
and maintenance, phones, etc. =
33 percent of BOE**

The club's monthly expenses were divided into three distinct areas, each of which equaled a third of the club's operating expense. These numbers were a good starting place for analyzing a business as a start to the problem-solving process. For example, it's common for club that overstaffs or makes other staffing mistakes to have a staff percentage that's way over an acceptable percentage.

The percentages above have changed dramatically, however, starting in the mid-'90s. The cost of payroll and related payroll expense, such as commissions, bonuses and other basic business expenses have risen faster, in comparison to increases in rent or the cost of owning a building. A properly balanced club now looks like this:

**Rent/mortgage and any additional landlord add-on charge (triple net) =
20 percent of BOE**

**Payroll and payroll taxes and any commissions or bonuses =
40 percent of BOE**

**General operating expense such as supplies, repairs
and maintenance, phones, etc. =
40 percent of BOE**

Payroll and other payroll costs are now 40 percent of most fitness facilities' operating budgets.

Payroll and other payroll costs are now 40 percent of most fitness facilities' operating budgets. Again, this is a good place to start analyzing a business and the problems it might be having. If payroll costs are higher than 40 percent, the club might be wasting payroll dollars. Keep in mind this 40 percent of BOE target as you try to improve an existing facility or start a new one.

If payroll expense is more than 40 percent, then most clubs are wasting money, usually by making some basic staffing mistakes. A few common mistakes include trying to give everyone 40 hours a week, having a sales system that is too complicated and forces up the cost per sale, simple overstaffing, giving everyone titles and the associated costs that go with them, and rewarding longevity instead of performance.

Save money by redefining full-time work and allowing flex time

Two basic concepts that are somewhat new to most operators could save you a very large percentage of your payroll. The first is reconsidering what's considered full-time employment, and the second is the use of what's called flex-time hiring.

Three o'clock in the afternoon is the kiss of death for owners trying to keep the payroll under control. There, standing at the front counter, are a small herd of staff all bored to tears waiting for the evening rush to begin.

Most of these folks are there because we're still trying to apply 1950s work theory to Generation X-ers. No one works like our fathers used to. Gone are the days of straight 8-to-5, 40-hour workweeks, working for the same company your entire career, and endless overtime in the name of the company. Also included here is the end of the authoritarian period of management discussed in other sections.

Employees in the gyms now (and they all don't have to be in their 20s to feel this way) want more free time, participation in their jobs and the decision-making process, opportunity to grow through education and advanced training, and work schedules that fit their lifestyles.

At the base of many of these problems is the full-time issue. Except for several key people on the management staff that will be discussed later in this section, full time should be defined as 32 hours of work (or more) per week. By setting full time at 32 hours, you'll eliminate a lot of wasted payroll by trying to find busy work to fill 40 hours for all of your full-timers.

Being full time should have a great deal of status in the gym. Full-timers should receive the most education and training, get the most perks and be treated like the serious investment they are in your business. Most clubs need that central core of full-timers who carry the load for the business, and who are supported by a cast of part-timers that changes depending on the age of the club, time of year and needs of the club's target population.

Full-timers are the kings and queens of the business, and the part-timers are the scourge of the earth barely fit for the consumption of good food. Full-timers should have a status in the club that makes becoming one desirable, especially if you're a low-life part-timer. For example, full-timers might have a free membership for their spouse or significant other, 30 percent off all clothing, supplements and programs offered, such as nutrition, vacation time and other perks which separate them from part-time people.

Hand in hand with declaring full time at 32 hours is the use of flex time for scheduling. For example, a full-time salesperson might only work Monday through Thursday, from 1 to 9 p.m., and still receive all the benefits and perks of being full time at 32 hours.

This person might be the lead salesperson, and still have the chance to achieve all the bonuses and commissions a salesperson would get but would only work four days a week instead of five. This would be a very desirable job for someone, save you the additional eight hours on Friday when sales are traditionally slow anyway, and still provide the person a decent living since

Hand in hand with declaring full time at 32 hours is the use of flex time for scheduling.

225

they have a 32-hour base and commissions from the prime sales times.

Flex time simply means that not everyone has to work five-day weeks. Another example might be a weekend person who also supervises the club on Saturday and Sunday. That person might work Saturday, Sunday and Monday and still get in 32 hours. The same person could also work four days of 10 hours each and still be full time.

The consideration here is overtime. If an employee is working a 40-hour week and he or she voluntarily decides to accept four 10-hour days, then that person needs to sign a simple form giving up the right for overtime for those additional two hours a day over eight, depending on your state laws. You don't want someone coming back years after they have left, looking for overtime pay for something they wanted to do at the time.

What are the key jobs and responsibilities in the fitness business?

It's easy to overstaff when we hire two or three people to do parts of what one person should be in charge of in the business.

When you're restructuring an existing club or starting a new one, always go back to the key positions in the club and what they should be doing. It's easy to overstaff when we hire two or three people to do parts of what one person should be in charge of in the business. Unclear expectations by senior management also drives up the cost of staffing because we have no clear concept of what one person could or should do as part of their job.

Here are the key jobs in a club, the hours needed to get that job accomplished, and what these people should be doing. There are variations, of course, but this should give you a good starting point. Salaries for these people will be discussed in the next section.

1. THE MANAGER

The manager is the one ultimately responsible for the club's financial position. If the owner is onsite and filling the manager's position, then they are the manager and you should have an assistant manager to help. Avoid the confusion for the lower staff of having the owner onsite and someone using the manager's title. It's hard to work for more than one boss at a time; having an owner and a manager onsite makes it difficult.

The manager should be the chief watcher of the business. Whoever has the manager's job, whether it is a separate person who works for an offsite owner, or the owner onsite acting as manager, should be responsible for most of the tasks listed below:

• Establishes the base operating expense for the business and is responsible for bringing the club in under budget.

• Writes all checks and generates reports based on the club's computerized check writing system, and takes care of all deposits and banking concerns.

• Is in charge of daily production reports and tracking.

• Works with the third-party financial company on problems and reporting.

• Leads sales by example. The manager should do at least 10 to 20 percent of all sales to set the pace and stay in touch with the problems encountered by the salespeople. In the smaller club (meaning less than 600 members), the manager may do more of the sales load. In clubs with more than 2,000 members, managers may not get to do many sales, but should still turn in a few a month to keep their finger on the club's sales pulse.

• Responsible for the monthly tracking of the multiple profit centers, including a profit and loss sheet on each profit center in the club.

• Staff training is a major part of the manager's job. The manager should coordinate all training in conjunction with the assistant manager, including weekly group training sessions, weekly one-on-one training with each full-time staffer, and other special training such as bringing in outside speakers.

• Responsible for any other numbers reporting and financial analysis, such as tracking sales per square foot, cost-per-sale, cost-per-lead or renewal percentages.

• All marketing is handled by the manager, including working with the ad people, supervising distribution and managing ad budgets.

• The condition of the club is also the responsibility of the manager, including scheduling cleaning service, repairs and maintenance and the club's atmosphere during working hours, which includes music, staff uniforms and club cleanliness for the sales effort.

• Daily promotions of the profit centers are split between the manager and the No. 2 person in the club.

• Interpretation of the club's policies including disciplinary action against the staff, handling of all cancellations of memberships and the final action in all member service problems that may arise.

• The manager also supervises all other management staff including the lead trainer and lead nutrition professional. The assistant manager would co-manage these people, in reference to expected production and goal setting.

• When all else is accomplished, the manager should be on the floor most evenings helping generate business. Production is still part of the manager's job, along with the watching function, but the manager is not the prime producer.

These aren't all of the possible duties for the manager. If you have others, however, consider that the manager is usually the watcher of the business. The assistant manager is considered the doer, or the person who is in charge of generating the business for the club. One creates the business, the other watches the back shop to keep expenses under control and guide the business for long-term growth.

The hours a manager should work have always been somewhat controversial. Some old style owners believe nothing short of seven days a week will do. Some managers think they're in power positions and as soon as they get the job, they start leaving the club at 5 p.m., just when the real work begins.

The manager's job is 45 to 50 hours a week. The manager should be in the club Monday through Thursday to do whatever it takes to get the job

The manager should do at least 10 to 20 percent of all sales to set the pace and stay in touch with the problems encountered by the salespeople.

done. Paperwork is usually done during daytime hours; once prime time begins, the manager should be out on the floor. After about 4:30 p.m., we don't make money in the office. The action is at the counter and on the floor, and that's where the manager should be acting as traffic cop to keep everyone focused on the money-making aspects of the business.

On Fridays, the manager should be in the club from about 9 a.m. to 3 p.m. to finish paperwork for the week and then be gone. The assistant manager can finish the day, and the weekend supervisor can handle the weekend. Managers who are good are very valuable assets, and shouldn't be worked until severe burnout sets in and kills their productivity.

2. THE ASSISTANT MANAGER OR NO. 2 PERSON IN THE CLUB

As was said above, the assistant manager is the generator of business for the club. They are the ones who deal with most of the staffing, goal setting and generation of business in sales and profit centers.

It's important, however, to make sure the top two people are interchangeable. They should have the same education and training, and should be cross-trained in each other's jobs and responsibilities. Listed here are some of the responsibilities the assistant manager or No. 2 person would have in the club. Keep in mind that in small clubs, the manager might fulfill many of the functions of the assistant manager, too. In this case, the No. 2 might be a strong administrative assistant:

• Responsible for staffing, including initial hiring screening, staff scheduling, pay review and evaluations in conjunction with the manager, and implementation of the employee manuals with each staff member.

• Conducting individual goal setting with each staff member.

• Establishing and supervising teams and goals for the profit centers on a monthly basis.

• Responsible for about 30 to 40 percent of the sales in most clubs in the 600 to 1,500 member range. The club would also have a lead salesperson that works prime time that should generate another 30 to 40 percent of the sales load. Prime time is usually considered from about 4 to 4:30 p.m. to 9 or 10 p.m. from Monday through Thursday nights. Many clubs will do 60 percent or more of their business during these times, which vary depending on the area. Saturday morning is also considered a key time for sales and profit centers for most clubs.

The No. 2 person ...takes charge of special events and daily promotions that push the profit centers in the club.

• Takes charge of special events and daily promotions that push the profit centers in the club. This is done in conjunction with the manager. The assistant would generate the idea and an expected profit and loss, and the manager would handle budget considerations.

• Has charge of the entire sales team. Even in the larger clubs that have a sales manager, the assistant manager is in charge of that person and of the entire production of that department.

• Responsible for submitting all ordering of supplies and merchandise for the profit centers to the manager for final budget approval.

The hours for the assistant manager are almost the same as the manager. Both need to be involved in the action during prime time, and both should be out of the club Friday evenings, although the assistant manager should stay later and have a floor presence until early evening. The total hours would also be about the same in the 45- to 50-per-week range.

3. THE LEAD COUNTER PERSON

Who runs the counter in the prime time hours in most clubs? A very young and very inexperienced person is working a position that has the highest turnover in the club. Most club owners consider front counter people as strictly entry-level folks who are expendable — just bodies to be replaced as the next one leaves us for a better job.

The lead front counter person, which is the person who works from about 4 to 9 p.m. Monday through Friday, is the most important person in the club.

Your lead counter person is the first and last person every member sees coming and going from the club. The lead counter person is the standard for the club's member service image. The lead counter person is the one who can make or break your profit centers because of her presence at the counter during prime time.

In other words, this shouldn't be the weakest and youngest person in the club; it should be the best communicator and one of the most mature people you have who can deliver member service.

Over the years we have hired women employees for all of the key jobs in the club including manager. Women in our businesses have demonstrated better communication skills across a wider range of people, better member service skills in the form of an empathetic attitude, have been more dependable, and respond more sincerely to recognition for the work they do.

Women often have been given a bad rap in the business world. They are not the hormonal ones. From my experience, it's always the young males who come running into the office shouting, "I quit. I met a new girl! We're moving to Miami tomorrow. Gotta go." No female employee (in more than 20 years of the club business) has ever done that to any of our managers. The list of male employees, however, who have left for a new girl, gone back to the old girl, gotten married and now has to get a real job, been busted and has to join the Army, or just can't do the job because of too much partying, is very long.

Anyone could be a front counter leader, as long as they are mature, can communicate, are outgoing caring people, love to be in the center of action, can manage other front counter people and love to help people figure out solutions to their problems. If you notice, we're not talking about the typical 22-year-old male here. We're probably talking about a female in her late 20s with great communication skills and a little practical customer service experience.

Here are some of the responsibilities a front counter person might have:
• Supervises other front counter people during their shift.
• Works the profit centers.

> **The lead counter person is the one who can make or break your profit centers because of her presence at the counter during primetime.**

- Greets and settles in all potential members.
- Is team captain of most of the counter-related profit centers such as drinks.
- Is the first stop for all member service problems such as late appointments or dirty locker rooms.
- Stocks and keeps the counter ready for business.
- Works the cash register and is in charge of money at the front counter.
- Has the authority to compensate member-service problems such as a trainer who runs over on his prior appointment. The front counter person can give away drinks, discount pro shop items and give away free tans and childcare or other similar items to help compensate members for bad service elsewhere in the club.
- Is responsible for the promotion of the day in the profit centers, in conjunction with the assistant manager.

These are some but not all of the front counter lead person's responsibilities. In smaller clubs, this person might take on a bigger role and do sales or even help train. Once the club gets more than 600 to 700 members, however, the club needs a dedicated counter person at prime time hours who can set a standard for member service.

The hours for this person are about 32 to 35 hours per week. This would be a great job for a housewife returning to the workforce or a person who wants free time during the day.

4. THE WEEKEND SUPERVISOR

Most clubs operate with an eclectic group of weekenders, usually chosen by their low status on the totem pole or by their inability to find other work.

This would be somewhat of a new job for most club owners to create. Most clubs operate with an eclectic group of weekenders, usually chosen by their low status on the totem pole or by their inability to find other work.

This too is a key job in the gym. From our research over the last decade, we've found that most clubs are simply giving away potential weekend business with their unwillingness to staff properly. Saturdays have always been strong, but the inexperience of the weekend crew usually restricts the revenue potential.

Sundays have always been dead, but is that because Sundays are dead or because we create a self-fulfilling prophecy and put the weakest staff on the weekends and kill it anyway? With a little work and creativity, such as opening Sunday up to any member guest without a pass or without paying, Sundays can be developed into a fair sales day and a strong profit center day.

If you're in a competitive area, try opening Sunday up to members from any other club in the area if they have a current membership card. They get to see your club and get a chance to spend money in your profit centers.

Your new weekend supervisor is the person to start making these things happen. This person is part of the management team, and is usually sort of a trainee manager who gains experience by taking over the club on the weekends. Some possible responsibilities for this job might be:

- Has charge of the weekend staff team.
- Opens and closes the club on Saturday and Sunday.

• Is the lead salesperson on both these days.

• Is responsible for the profit center income on the weekends, including running profit center promotions with the assistant manager's direction.

• Is in charge of special events such as Guest Sunday, Super Bowl parties, member lifting contests or anything else that will develop a consistent weekend traffic.

This person should be in the same training program as the rest of the management team. Think of the weekend manager as part of your farm team or as a future manager in training. Give them the same sales, numbers and production training that you would give your manager and assistant manager.

This person could get all of their hours done in three or four workdays. It might be better to have the person work Saturday, Sunday and Monday, instead of Fridays. No one will really give up those three days on a consistent basis.

If the person is there on Monday, traditionally one of the busiest days, they could handle some of the floor action and also be part of the backup sales team. In smaller clubs, the person might have to work four days to make enough hours. Hours for this job would be 32 to 35, although a smaller club might need a 40-hour person over a four-day period.

5. THE LEAD SALESPERSON

The lead salesperson should be the one who generates the most sales in the club. This person works the best selling hours, which again are usually Monday through Thursday nights, and is the one who has first up at any prospective members. Larger clubs with high volume would need more than one during the heavy hours, and everyone on the team needs to be cross-trained to do sales.

For example, if the lead salesperson were on a club tour and a second prospect came into the club, the assistant manager would take the tour. If the lead salesperson and assistant manager are on tour, then the manager goes.

However, if there are no tours, but the counter is packed with members buying things, then the lead salesperson needs to be trained to step in to make some shakes or do whatever else is needed.

In large volume clubs with a membership of about 1,800 members or more, the club might need a sales manager. This person would also be the lead salesperson whenever they are on the job, and would also be responsible for sales training the rest of the staff.

The lead salesperson may or may not be on the management team. Over the years, it seems that good salespeople are not always good managers. Many productive club salespeople do their jobs with a lot of natural ability and instincts, something that is hard to teach to those who aren't naturally born sales killers.

If your salesperson is a good teacher and can relate to a staff that may not have the same natural traits and skills, then that person may have man-

> **Think of the weekend manager as part of your farm team or as a future manager in training.**

agement potential. This person would also have the ability to be a good assistant manager who could lead by example and still teach. A few responsibilities the lead salesperson might have would be:

• Responsible for 30 to 40 percent of the sales goal, depending on the size of the club.

• In charge of training every member of the staff in basic sales.

• Responsible for follow-up training and review of the staff on a monthly basis.

• Responsible for keeping all sales supplies stocked and ordered through the direction of the assistant manager.

• Expected to assist in any stressed area in the club at any time, if there are no sales tours going on in the club.

The hours would vary according to the club size. A lead salesperson in a smaller club would probably have a larger variety of duties and would most likely work 40 hours a week. In the 600 to 1,800 member clubs, the lead salesperson could work 32 to 35 hours per week over four days.

6. THE MORNING PERSON

This is not a management person, but it is a very key job. Good morning people — those who show up 30 minutes before the club is to open, have everything ready before the members arrive, never miss a day and even get a few sales now and then — are not just good employees, they are the acts of a divine being.

The morning crowds in most fitness facilities are usually a hardcore group of regulars who get to know each other, have regular routines which they hate to have disrupted, and expect to get through their workouts with minimal fuss. The morning person is the one who supplies the glue that holds the whole morning ritual together.

We normally look for students or someone else who has little experience in the fitness business, but who is willing to work hours that for most people are not very desirable.

The morning person is the one who supplies the glue that holds the whole morning ritual together.

Maybe we're looking in the wrong place. My mother would be a great morning employee. She's retired as a real estate broker, thinks getting up at 4 a.m. is fun and does it anyway every morning, is a great people person who would know everyone and their dog in a week, and would be extremely consistent. She would also work for $7 to $8 per hour just to keep busy.

Instead of someone like her, we historically look for someone who by their choice of lifestyle is just getting in at 4 a.m. — instead of just getting up. After a while, these folks leave us for other less disrupting jobs for their way of life. Replace these folks with an older, more dependable person, and your morning business should increase.

Some responsibilities for the morning person might be:

• Be at the club 30 minutes before the shift starts in order to have the club ready when the members arrive. Don't get into the habit of letting the members in as they arrive just because the morning person is already there.

• Serve as a multiple-purpose person. This person should be able to sell, work people out, run the front counter and provide member service all at the same time. The morning person is usually solo for the first several hours of their shift. A suggestion here is to go mobile with the phone in the morning. Many clubs unplug their regular multi-line phone and replace it with a single-line wireless during the time the morning person is solo. Make sure you have a holster for the phone so the person can wander the club and service instead of being tied to the desk or running for the phone.

• Perhaps be able to do some basic service on the equipment during the slower mornings.

The morning job is in the 32- to 35-hour range over five days. It's good to have the same person during every weekday to build consistency with morning members. Morning people usually receive a shift deferential that is added to their base pay.

7. LEAD NUTRITION TECHNICIAN

Nutrition centers in clubs will be one of the more exciting profit centers in the coming years. Giving nutrition information and education on the relationship between the results you can expect in the gym and what goes into your body, has covered a wide range in fitness facilities over the years.

Some clubs have formal programs with offices, fitness professionals running them and complete supplement lines to back them up. Others still write diets on clipboards based on something somebody read in a magazine. As clubs move more toward the professional approach, the fitness professional in charge of the program becomes more important.

Since the nutrition program is so important for the club's financial future, the fitness professional in charge of that area is considered part of the management team. Members who get better results in a shorter period of time will stay longer and pay longer in the gym. The fitness technician is the person who makes this happen by direct contact with the members and by educating the entire staff that then aids in the support of these members.

Some responsibilities of the nutrition education fitness professional are:

• Set up an office and establish a program based on selling an education program to the members.

• Educate and train the staff on how the program affects members and how to sell it, and on the supplements sold within the program.

• Stay current in the chosen education program, and obtain and stay current in a training certification. For example, one of the most professional nutrition education programs in the business is the Apex Fitness program that offers a one-week school for new technicians and also supports the National Academy of Sports Medicine. A tech should repeat the school on a yearly basis to stay current and obtain and maintain a certification in training.

• Be responsible for member education in the form of monthly workshops that discuss key issues in diet or training.

• Take responsibility, in conjunction with the assistant manager, for running weekly supplement promotions, monthly program promotions and

Since the nutrition program is so important for the club's financial future, the fitness professional in charge of that area is considered part of the management team.

for selling a certain number of programs per month if the sales staff does not do it at point of sale. For example, a fitness professional in the Apex program can run about seven new programs per week and still have time to do the follow-up needed for the 12-week program that is sold. If the staff does not generate 28 to 30 programs a month for the tech to service, then the tech is responsible for developing sales and education events that can lead to program sales.

The nutrition technician job is about 45 hours per week with evening times, several mornings a week and possibly Saturdays. This person should also receive much of the sales training with the rest of the management team, including numbers and sales.

In smaller clubs with fewer than 600 to 700 members, the lead nutrition person and the lead trainer can be the same person. Once the club gets to 600 or so members, the technician should be too busy handling the programs to properly supervise the training staff.

8. The lead trainer

Because of the issue of control, most clubs have eliminated outside trainers and have gone with all in-house staffs.

Because of the issue of control, most clubs have eliminated outside trainers and have gone with all in-house staffs. In the past, when trainers were hard to come by, many clubs let the trainers pay rent to use their facilities. The problem was the control issue. The trainers sold their own clothing and supplements, did their own diets and worked when and if they chose, therefore bypassing the club programs and profit centers.

In recent years, most owners have started to develop their own training staffs as part of the employee base. This gives the owners more control and a greater share of the overall revenues generated by the training programs.

The lead trainer is the person who sets the training standard for the club and is the one who should have the best credentials and the most training experience. This person is in charge of finding and developing a group of trainers who sell elite one-on-one training, who run the club's educational programs and who set up programs for the club's trial members.

Some of the responsibilities for the lead trainer are:

• Find and train a training staff for the club.

• Run quarterly two-day mandatory training sessions for all trainers on the staff, and issue certificates of education from the club for those who compete each session. All new hires from all departments are to attend the first available session after they are hired so they will better understand the training function of the gym and what the trainers are trying to accomplish.

• Handle the hours and scheduling, in conjunction with the assistant manager, for the training staff.

• Complete advanced education, such as the NASM-certification programs, on a yearly basis or as needed.

• Create all training support materials, in conjunction with the rest of the management team.

• Set up workout programs for the entire staff as they are hired.

• Complete the nutrition education support school and training.

The lead trainer needs to be in the gym about 45 hours per week over five days. The trainer also needs to make sure everyone on the staff is cross-trained enough to at least give the club's basic workout program. This way, there is always someone on duty who can at least answer a member's basic questions.

These are core jobs for almost any gym. If you're restructuring an existing gym or building a new one, start with these positions and the responsibilities, and then expand as needed. Most facilities farm out their membership payment collections, thus eliminating an office staff of any kind, although large clubs still need a liaison between the financial company and the club who can also function as a general purpose paperwork person.

Hiring by levels cuts staffing costs and motivates employees

We once had an employee who had been with the company for five years. She worked from 9 a.m. to 3 p.m. Monday through Friday. She was very loyal, never missed a day and would do just about anything you wanted done, although she wasn't very good at sales and avoided doing them unless we were desperate.

Each year she received her annual review, where she told us how good she was with the members, how dependable she was, and how much we benefited from her presence in the gym. She started at $7.50 per hour, and was now at $10 and due for her review.

As she started this year's story about her worth, we realized that we were going to start paying someone $10.50 an hour for a position that we could fill for $7.50. This also made us realize that we were paying for longevity, not performance. She didn't sell, didn't train anyone or work the floor. She was just a great personal assistant who could do almost anything, except make the club money.

From this came the level system of hiring and placing employees. Each employee is hired at a certain level. Each level has a pay range that is capped. For example, you may be hired at Level One, which in this example has a range of $6 to $7 per hour, plus the appropriate commissions or bonuses for whatever job that person holds.

If the employee stays with the company for 10 years, and if they never complete the necessary requirements to move up to Level Two, they will never make more than $7 per hour, unless the cap should happen to be adjusted. The salaries below are for illustration and may not reflect your market.

This level system described here is an actual one, but you may substitute your own requirements to make it fit your organization. The levels and core requirements for each level are:

Each employee is hired at a certain level. Each level has a pay range that is capped.

LEVEL ONE (ALL EMPLOYEES/ENTRY-LEVEL)

The basics

• Pay range of $6 to $7 per hour.

• Hired on a 90-day probationary basis. The employee has 90 days to complete the training and programs, or at least start programs that can't be finished in 90 days, or lose their job.

Making the grade

The employee must complete each of these training areas, or at least get started, to keep a Level One status.

• Complete two days of in-house management training done by the manager, assistant manager, lead salesperson, lead trainer and lead nutrition technician. General training is done from the procedure and employee manual discussed in an earlier chapter.

• Start and complete the gym's nutrition program. In the Apex example, which is a 12-week program, the new hire has to complete the program and go through the same things a member would. They only have to do it once, but they do have to complete the program to keep their job. This program should be such a big part of your revenue stream, that every employee needs to be able to explain it to any potentially interested member.

• Get set up on and start a workout program under the direction of the lead trainer. Fitness is part of the business, and we expect everyone to participate in every program the gym offers. If we have weights, everyone does weights; if we have nutrition, everyone goes through the program.

• The new hire is also expected to try the spin program, aerobics if you have it and any activities or programs that the gym sells. We can't really fire someone for not participating, but we always find a way to get rid of that person anyway. If you don't do it or understand it, you can't sell or service it. The person is also expected to complete the first available two-day workshop the lead trainer gives. This person may not ever be a trainer but they have to understand the training function.

• Complete any job-specific training. For example, if the new hire is going to work in sales, they are expected to complete all of the above, as well as specific sales training from the lead salesperson or assistant manager. The training should be done by a wide variety of staff. Even in the smallest club, the new hires could be trained by as many as three different people. All training at Level One is done in-house by the management team. Level Two is where the employees start to go outside for their formal training. The new hire is on the clock for all training, if it is scheduled during their regular hours. If they are off the clock, they receive training pay, which is minimum wage.

LEVEL TWO

If the employee completes all the listed material for Level Two, they may move up. At this level, they are eligible for higher pay and higher com-

Fitness is part of the business, and we expect everyone to participate in every program the gym offers.

missions and bonuses. For example, a Level One salesperson may make $20 per sale. A Level Two salesperson may make $30 per sale for the same membership. The Level Two person is worth more to the company, and should be more likely to get the sale, because they have had more training.

A good employee manual should state some type of policy for who pays for training. For example, we recommend a policy that states, "We may reimburse any employee for up to $100 of approved training costs that will be paid within 90 days after the employee completes the training."

This allows the club not to have to pay for all training for employees to change levels. It does allow, however, for the club to pay more if it desires. An employee who has been with the company for a few months, and wants to move up to another level, is still an unknown. That's the employee who falls under the strict interpretation of the policy.

A second employee has been with the company for two years and now wants to move up. This employee has proved herself, and as such, the owner or manager may desire to pay for the entire training cost since a better-educated employee helps the company. The management team has a pretty good idea that the employee will be around long enough to justify the training cost.

The basics
- Pay range of $7 to %9 per hour.
- If the employee changes jobs due to the level change, they go back onto a 90-day probationary status. The club should always have a legal way to correct its mistakes when it comes to hiring.

Making the grade
The employee must complete each one of these steps to qualify for Level Two status. We are using the Apex Fitness program and the National Academy of Sports Medicine, two long-term standards in the industry, as the example here. Substitute whatever systems you are personally subscribing to at your club.
- Completion of the two-day National Academy of Sports Medicine.
- Completion of the five-day Apex School.
- Completion of the Thomas Plummer & Associates two-day business management seminar.
- Job-specific training.

The requirements for this level are broken down into three distinct divisions: the training function, which is taught through NASM, the nutrition/education function, which is supplied through Apex, and the management/business function, which is supplied through our own business seminars. You may substitute here by creating your own management training course out of the material in this book that is taught and applied by the management team.

The job-specific requirements would differ from employee to employee, and should reflect management's attempt to cover weaknesses the employee may have. For example, a trainer moving up to Level Two may not have any

A good employee manual should state some type of policy for who pays for training.

237

spin experience, therefore part of their training might be a spin certification program.

LEVEL THREE (MANAGEMENT LEVEL)

This is the beginning of the two management levels and includes the assistant manager, the lead nutrition person, the lead trainer, the weekend supervisor and any other managers you might have on your organizational chart. If you are a multi-unit operator, you may have people who oversee the same area in several clubs, such as a nutrition person who runs all the techs in those units. These folks would be classified here.

This is also the start of salaried positions. Usually, for positions to be salaried (and "exempt" from certain requirements) they must meet tests set by the labor boards and the IRS. One such test is whether the person supervises at least two people and it's documented in the personnel file. Check the legal requirements in your state. Salaries will be discussed in the next section.

If you are a multi-unit operator, you may have people who oversee the same area in several clubs, such as a nutrition person who runs all the techs in those units.

The basics
• Each person at Level Three is on a salary and commissions or bonuses, depending on the individual's job.
• If the person changes jobs to move to this level, the person goes back on the 90-day probationary period.

Making the grade
The employee must complete each of these steps to move up to a management job. The employee may complete the steps, however, and not be automatically given a job when it's open. This is different from the first two levels where an employee may automatically move up once the level requirements are completed.
• Completion of the four-day NASM program.
• Must complete the Apex School again (all managers must complete the school once a year to stay current).
• Must complete the Thomas Plummer & Associates five-day resident business school.
• Job-specific training.

The requirements for this level are again broken down into the three basic functions of being in the fitness business. You need to understand how the training, nutrition and business areas of the club work. The club pays for all training at levels three and above.

Once we start investing in employees at this level, they should be part of your long-term management plan. And again, you can create your own management/business training requirements that can be taught at the club by your own staff.

LEVEL FOUR

This is your manager, or if you're in multiple clubs, your managers. To protect the stability of your business, all assistant managers and managers should go through the same training. In this system, if something happened to the manager, the assistant should have the necessary training in all aspects of the club to step up and take over without disrupting the business.

The basics

• This is a salaried position on a base salary and bonuses for total production of the company.

• All new managers should go on a new 90-day probation once they accept the job.

Making the grade

The employee has to complete all of these steps to be considered for a manager's job. You may grandfather the person in at this and the other levels, however, and then require that the person complete the requirements for that level in a fixed time period, such as six months.

For example, a seasoned salesperson from another club may join your staff. This person may be too experienced for a Level One status, but may not have the training required in your club. This person can be grandfathered in at Level Two and be given six months to complete the requirements.

• All training for this level is the same for Level Three, except that it must be repeated on a yearly basis to get and keep a manager's job.

These are the core requirements that cover the basic functions of the club. It would be easy to start with these and then add club specific requirements for each level. Clubs with aerobics could require aerobics certification at Level Two. Clubs that have complicated computer systems and collection procedures might require a working knowledge of the systems at Level Two and above. Start with these and adapt as needed.

LEVEL FIVE (FOR MULTIPLE CLUB OWNERS)

This level is for multiple club owners who use a general manager (GM) to oversee their businesses. The requirements here would be much the same as those for a manager except that more business skills would be required. Here are a few of the skills a GM might need to run more than one business.

• Extremely organized. This person needs to be organized and able to create a solid paper trail as to what's happening in each unit. There are business courses that center on using a laptop, cell phone and fax units to stay in touch with different locations. This should be a requirement for this level.

• A time-management expert. A time-management course, repeated yearly, would also be a set requirement for this job.

• Basic accounting and the ability to read financial statements.

• One or two marketing and advertising courses that include public relations work.

• Labor laws and information on hiring, firing and disciplining employees.

• Education on sexual harassment, wrongful termination and drugs and

Clubs that have complicated computer systems and collection procedures might require a working knowledge of the systems at Level Two and above.

alcohol.
- Computer classes of almost any kind.
- Customer service training such as the Disney Institute or Dale Carnegie.

Any or all of these would also be good education for managers too, not to mention the owners of any small business. Specific requirements for a general manager have to be tailored to the club, but these would be the basics you'd want anyone interested in the job to have or obtain in a short period of time.

Specific requirements for a general manager have to be tailored to the club...

Staffing budget sheet

Day _____ Club _____

Total hourly expense   _____

Total salary expense   _____

Bonuses/commissions   _____

Payroll taxes   _____

Name:	Joe	Sue	Jan	Fred	Bill	Ann	Beth
Position:	MP*	FC	MAN	AM	LT	LFC	AT
5:00	H						
6:00	H						
7:00	H						
8:00	H	H					
9:00	H	H					S
10:00	H	H					S
11:00	H	H		S			S
Noon		H	S	S			
1:00		H	S	S			
2:00		H	S	S			
3:00			S	S			
4:00			S	S	S	H	
5:00			S	S	S	H	S
6:00			S	S	S	H	S
7:00			S	S	S	H	S
8:00			S	S	S	H	S
9:00			S		S	H	S
10:00							
Direct Costs:	$7x7hr= $49	$6x7hr= $42	$2,000/ 20=$100	$1,600/ 20=$80	$1,400/ 20=$70	$8x6hr= $48	$1,600/ 20=$80

*The key:
Joe is the morning person. Sue is the front counter person.
Jan is the manager. Fred is the assistant manager. Bill is the lead trainer.
Ann is the lead front counter person. Beth is the Apex nutrition tech.

Figure 16.1. Staffing budget sheet

Using a staff budgeting sheet

All staffing should work off of a budget. A common mistake for many owners is staffing by personality, instead of what is actually needed in the club. For example, your loyal employee Joe has worked 20 hours a week putting himself through school. He is now getting married in a few months, and wants to go to 25 hours. Normally, most owners would simply expand his hours to meet his request.

Another hazard is staffing by employee quirks. Mary can open on Monday and Tuesday, but she volunteers at her son's school on Wednesday and she can't come in on Thursday until 9 p.m. Add four or five other employees to a schedule with the same quirks, and you have a complicated piece of work that forces you to redo the entire schedule every time someone leaves or wants to change hours.

The way to avoid this is to staff by using a block system. A block system is creating a set job on a set schedule, and then hiring for that specific block. Managers should also do a staff budget once a month based on the block system and expected needs for the time of year. A budget sheet would look like Figure 16.1.

A block system is creating a set job on a set schedule, and then hiring for that specific block.

A filled-out sheet might contain this information:

Day: Today's date

Club: The Gym (more for multiple clubs)

Total hourly expense: $139

Total salary expense: $320

Bonuses and commissions: 4 sales @ $25 = $100
(there would be other bonuses)

Payroll taxes: $139 + $320 + $100 = $559, and
$559 x .13 (worst-case tax scenario) = $72.67

Total payroll for the day = $631.67

The illustration above is a one-day sample and doesn't have an entire staff listed. To use these effectively, do one for each day of a typical month. Some days may be redundant, but it's still a good learning tool to do an entire month the first time. Redo the budget sheets each time you lose an employee or there are other major staff changes.

Summary

Mistakes in staffing can increase a typical club's payroll by at least 10 percent over what it should be under normal conditions. The rules in staffing have also changed over years, and could add even more waste to the club's budget. For example, keeping staff costs as a percentage of total revenues (sales) continually adds to the expense side of the club without necessarily adding to the net.

Payroll and related payroll expenses should be about 40 percent of the club's monthly base operating costs. If the club's percentage climbs above this number, the club needs to analyze the waste and start cost-saving controls to bring that percentage down.

Clubs can save payroll expense by defining today's worker and what they want from their jobs. Flex time, full-time status at 32 hours and staff budgeting can all help reduce the cost of employees in your business.

Instituting a level system can also help reduce the payroll cost, since it eliminates those automatic yearly raises. Instead of paying for longevity, the club now shifts its emphasis to paying for employees who learn more, and therefore bring more to the business.

When starting a new business, or restructuring an existing one for more profits, start with the actual staff structure. If jobs aren't narrowly defined, the club ends up with more employees than it needs, because the owner ends up hiring people for specific tasks that arise, instead of redefining who should really be doing that work. Create the structure first and the responsibilities for each position, before adding random jobs that could be done by someone else.

Another starting point is the use of staff budgets. By setting staffing budgets and by working off a budget sheet, you can get away from staffing by personality or availability and shift toward a block system. A block system allows the club to create a set period of time over set days for the job. The employee either accepts the block offered or not. If an employee wants to add hours, it is done so only if there is a block of time open on the budget sheet.

Instead of paying for longevity, the club now shifts its emphasis to paying for employees who learn more, and therefore bring more to the business.

Things you can do to use this material

1) Create a management team with defined tasks and responsibilities.

2) Switch to flex time, meaning work doesn't have to be over five days, and redefine your full-time status down to 32 hours a week.

3) Start a staffing budget. Do one entire month the first time, even if some of the days are redundant. Change as needed to reflect staff changes in the business.

4) Create a level system. Grandfather in existing staff at their approximate level and then give them six months to complete the steps. The step level in this section is to be used as an example, and you may need to add extra requirements to meet the specific circumstances of your club.

LESSONS FROM LIFE — #16

There is no right answer to the music issue

A CLUB IN DALLAS WAS SO frustrated with their members constantly complaining about the music in the club that they ran a survey of 100 members, and then said they would play music according to the responses they received.

The 100 members listed 46 different music choices that they wished to play in the club. The survey turned up everything from country to rap to reggae to Cajun.

The moral of the story

As a club owner, you'll never win in the music war by leaving it up to the members. The music in the club needs to reflect the target market of the club, the time of day and the region of the country. The music is selected not because of who is in the club at the time, but because of the desired target market the club wishes to attract.

For example, a club that caters to a target market of adults in the 25- to 45-year-old category

The 100 members listed 46 different music choices that they wished to play in the club

might play music on a schedule like this:
• 5:00-9:00 a.m. — Contemporary or classic rock
• 9:00 a.m.-4:00 p.m. — Contemporary or alternative rock
• 4:00-9:00 p.m. — The place should rock with classic or alternative rock
• 9:00-10:45 p.m. — Contemporary or alternative rock
• 10:45-11:00 p.m. — Classical, because it can clear a gym faster than the trainers!

Also, use a music system that can be controlled through a flipper type of remote and avoid a radio altogether. Radios disrupt the energy in the club and also play too many ads during the prime time hours when we need the clubs to pick up their energy and pace.

17

If it ain't in writing,
it ain't real

MOST SUCCESSFUL GYM BUSINESSES are totally goal-driven. Every employee should have individual goals and accountability, and every profit center in the gym should be part of a team goal. Employees work better when they understand what's expected of them on an individual basis, and when they have a standard of performance to compare their daily performance against.

Motivating a staff to achieve high individual performance is indeed the most difficult job in the gym business. The fitness business can be very frustrating at times. Equipment breaks, competitors are crazy and a strange run of weather can shut down your entire sales production. But the biggest frustration voiced by owners over the years is how to find, and then motivate, people to do their best on a daily basis.

In the early days of the gym business, staffing was not so difficult. There weren't as many service businesses competing for the same type of staff we need, and the minimum wage was much more in line with what it really cost to live. Now, we have to compete against a zillion other service companies from Wal-Mart to McDonald's that are scouring the undergrowth for the same type of young service people we need in the gyms. And don't forget all the young salespeople we used to attract who are now choosing to sell cell phones and copiers.

Now it seems almost unbelievable, but when the early guys first figured out how to staff their clubs, Wal-Mart, McDonald's, K-Mart, Wendy's and all the rest of the fast-food and discount stores didn't exist. And in today's extremely competitive market, with our strong emphasis on member service, the clubs need highly productive and highly motivated people more than ever.

> **Motivating a staff to achieve high individual performance is indeed the most difficult job in the gym business.**

SECTION FIVE   *Staffing Will Be the Most Difficult Issue You'll Ever Have to Deal with in the Fitness Business*

Today, any gym, including every competitor you have, can run any programs you run and, in a sense, duplicate your entire business plan and operation.

The real difference in the future between you and your competitors, and the difference between merely staying alive and being a financially successful business, will be made by your people. If your people are better educated by you, better trained by you, and better managed and motivated, again by you, you will win.

Putting a Cardio Theater system in for example, which is an entertainment profit center usually tied to the cardio area, gives you a technological advantage. At best, it's a temporary advantage, but it also increases the stakes to play the game. The competition now has to at least invest in the same tech to stay even in the consumer's mind. In the end, it'll come down to one simple concept: The person with the best-trained and motivated staff will be financially successful and the others won't.

In the end, it'll come down to one simple concept: The person with the best-trained and motivated staff will be financially successful and the others won't.

Before looking at employees and how to motivate them, we have to back up a step and discuss basic pay issues. Although pay ranges widely around the country, we can set some base guidelines that will at least start the discussion.

Basic pay issues

Whenever you have a group of at least three fitness facility owners sitting around talking about business, inevitably the discussion turns to what everyone is paying their employees. Most owners are in that constant search for the perfect pay system that will make employees get naked and run through the club selling everyone in their path a membership or something from a profit center. But there is no magic pay formula. Each employee is an individual and needs to be motivated by what's important to that person.

To attract an employee, you have to start with their base pay. Base pay gets the employee to work but also gets base performance. Extraordinary performance comes from incentives beyond the base pay package, but, as we'll discuss later, these incentives don't always have to be money.

Paying people by the hour is the most elementary form of base pay. To attract higher potential employees, you need to offer at least $1 more per hour than the local minimum wage in your area. For example, in the Denver market, real minimum wage is about $6 per hour. This will get you a very entry-level employee without much experience or training. To start attracting employees that can be trained and make a difference in your business, you need to start shopping in the $7 to $7.50 range.

Each area of the country is different, but the system still applies. To get a better quality employee, the opening wage has to be slightly stronger than the market demands. The club could probably survive with the cheaper employees, but it could be more successful with the higher caliber people. The extra dollar or more an hour should be made up by the production and performance we can expect from hiring a better person in the first place.

There is also the issue of true hourly wages. The employee's base wage might be $7 per hour, but the same person also makes an additional $200 per month in commissions. For example:

$7 per hour x 32 hours per week = $224 per week

32 hours per week x 4.2 weeks per month = 134.4 hours per month worked

$224 per week x 4.2 weeks = $940.80 per month

$940.80 per month base pay + $200 in commissions = $1,140.80

$1,140.80 divided by 134.40 hours per month = $8.48 true hourly wages

In this example, the employee thinks he is working for $7 per hour but, in reality, he is earning $8.48 per hour. Most employees really don't understand what they are actually making. They may leave for a job that pays only slightly more when they have actually been making more per hour than they realize.

The true hourly compensation should be written out as part of each employee's pay package each month and included with their checks. Other employee costs that are related to each employee should also be listed with each check.

For example, if you are spending $150 per month for insurance for that person, that amount should be listed, too, so the employee understands what they are really earning from you.

Salaried employees should be only those who actually supervise other people on the staff. It's not only old style to pay employees salary in order to beat overtime, but it's also something that a pissed-off ex-employee can use against you with labor boards and the tax people.

Salaried staff usually has a base salary plus bonuses on performance. Most salaried people shouldn't collect individual commissions but rather be paid on the total performance of the employees they are in charge of at the gym.

For example, if the lead sales person is acting as sales manager in the club and supervises several other salespeople, then she should have a base salary and be paid a bonus on the total production of the sales department and not on her individual performance.

There are two issues here; what should her base be and what should her bonus include. Let's look at the base numbers first.

THE MANAGER

The ranges are so varied that it's hard to give specific numbers. In the South, in the smaller clubs, managers can be found for $1,200 a month, total pay package. In the Northeast, the pay might be as high as $5,000 to $7,000 per month for a manager who has profit-and-loss responsibility in a club. A manager earning this much would be operating a club that might have an overhead of $90,000 per month and do sales of $1.3 million or above.

Somewhere in the middle is the answer to most managers' salaries. A more typical starting reference point might be a base salary of $2,000 to

The true hourly compensation should be written out as part of each employee's pay package each month and included with their checks.

$2,500 per month and bonuses that would bring the total package up to $40,000 per year. Exceptional managers who can net 20 percent or more in the clubs might be worth up to $50,000 per year. How these bonuses are figured will be discussed later in this section.

There is a point of no return, however, where you're paying the manager so much that it might be worth replacing that person with a cheaper employee. In other words, the job is only worth so much and then you're overpaying for the same results someone else can produce at a cheaper rate.

ASSISTANT MANAGERS

Assistant managers can be found in most markets in the $1,500- to $1,800-a-month range, plus bonuses. The combination of bonuses and base would bring their total package up to between $25,000 to $30,000 per year.

THE LEAD COUNTER PERSON

This could be a salaried position or it may be hourly, depending on whether the person is supervising anyone. If you're introducing a level system (discussed in Chapter 16), this person should be a Level Two employee. The hourly for this person should be in the $8 range for most markets, plus additional commissions and bonuses that would add another $100 to $150 per month to the package.

THE WEEKEND SUPERVISOR

This also might be a salaried or hourly position, depending on whether there are enough weekend employees to supervise. But most likely, this person would be hourly since they would also be doing regular hours on other days.

In the level system, this person should definitely be a Level Two. The hourly wage for this person would be similar to the lead counter person's wage and be in the $8 range in most markets, plus another $100 to $150 per month performance-based incentives.

THE LEAD SALESPERSON

If the person is supervising a sales team, the position would be salaried in the $1,200- to $1,600-a-month range, plus bonuses based on the total production of the department. For example, if the sales goal were 60 new memberships for the club, the lead salesperson would receive her base and a bonus if the team hits the goal.

Motivation is personal, and money is not the prime motivator for most people.

How much bonus is right? As we'll discuss later, most owners would set a cash value on the sales and offer a cash incentive if she and the team hit the goal. The question, though, is what does *the person* want for hitting the goal? Motivation is personal, and money is not the prime motivator for most people.

If the lead salesperson is not responsible for the team and, instead, the assistant manager is in charge of total production, then the lead salesperson would be paid hourly and a commission on sold memberships.

The hourly rate depends on the level. Level One employees, which might be the lead in a smaller club, would be paid lower commissions on sales since they have less education and probably aren't as productive as higher level people. For example, the club only has one membership based on a 12-month contract. A Level One salesperson might make $7 per hour, plus $20 per written contract. A Level Two salesperson might make $9 per hour, plus $30 per written contract.

Sales bonuses should be flat amounts for contracts produced. It's better to avoid paying a percentage of the contract, because the salespeople start thinking like used car guys and you'll eventually end up paying a higher cost per sale. A flat fee based on a signed contract keeps the sales costs down and the team focused.

> **A flat fee based on a signed contract keeps the sales costs down and the team focused.**

THE MORNING PERSON

This is an hourly job based on the level. The national average might be $7 per hour, plus another $75 to $125 per month based on individual production incentives. This job is also worth an extra 50 cents to $1 per hour as a shift deferential, since the morning person usually has less traffic to work with than the evening crew.

THE LEAD NUTRITION TECHNICIAN

This is a salaried position with bonuses and commissions. For example, the tech might be on a base of $1,200 to $1,400. They would also receive an additional $30 to $50 per program run, depending on time on the job and the area of the country.

The average nutrition tech using the Apex 12-week program can do about 28 programs per month. The tech would also receive an additional 10 percent of the total supplements they personally sold, as well as a secondary cash bonus for total supplement sales for the month if the trainers and front counter people are selling too.

The total pay for a productive tech would average between $20,000 and $30,000 on a national average. The wide range would be dependent on the area of the country, what the nutrition program sells for and the number of programs the tech can handle each month.

THE LEAD TRAINER

In a small club, the lead trainer would be hourly and definitely a Level Two person. The national average would be $8 to $9 per hour, plus bonuses for programs sold. There are so many personal training systems in use in the country that it would be hard to describe an accurate bonus system. The end result, however, is that a lead trainer in a small club should be able to make between $20,000 and $25,000 per year depending on production.

If the lead trainer is supervising other trainers, then they should be on a base salary similar to the nutrition tech, or about $1,200 to $1,500 per month plus bonuses based on the total production of the department. For example, the trainer might be at the $1,500-a-month level and also receive a bonus of $400 if the team can hit $8,000 in total one-on-one training sales.

Right now as you are reading this, you may be having one of two reactions: "This is crazy, I could never hire anyone that cheap in my area," or "This is crazy, I would never pay people that much in my area."

Both are right. These are national averages that throw out the extremes on either end. Lead trainers in California might be more expensive, and salespeople in Alabama may not make $30 per sale. Use these numbers as starting points when you put together your budget, or if you're creating new positions and don't know where to begin.

Motivation and bonuses through individual and team goal setting

In most of the examples, bonuses are mentioned as part of the pay packages. Most everyone always asks, "How much should I give that person for a bonus for the job they do?" This is the wrong question. They should be asking, "As an employee, what do you want to reach that goal, beyond all pay and commissions?"

Motivating employees is answering the basic question of, "What's in it for me?" not, "What do you think I should have?" Learning to answer this question and then getting employees to move beyond their minimum level of output is based on several key concepts that are easy to learn and easy to put into practice.

> **Motivating employees is answering the basic question of, "What's in it for me?" not, "What do you think I should have?"**

1. CREATE A VISION THAT WILL KEEP YOU AND YOUR STAFF EXCITED ABOUT COMING TO WORK

Big visions generate excitement and enthusiasm. To be big and to get big results, you have to think big. Explain your goal to everyone who'll listen: You want to be the best gym in sales, with truly legendary service, and your goal is not just to be as good as other gyms, but you want to set the standard for the industry.

Where are you going? Where is the gym headed? How will you know when you get there? These are all the basics of goal setting for your business and your staff. In other words, how can you motivate your staff to move forward if you don't know where forward is?

But the vision you create has to be something they can all share in. Telling your staff that you were named the No. 1 gym at your license national meeting, for example, may get you excited, but it doesn't affect their productivity.

On the other hand, telling the staff that our goal is to be named No. 1

gym in the country, then working toward that vision all year with motivational meetings, using it as your meeting theme, and getting shirts made that say "We're the No. 1 gym in America," is something they can buy into because it's part of their work environment. Then taking as many of your staff as possible to your national meeting in hopes of getting the reward is the proof that you feel your team is the best.

There are three reasons staff fails to perform up to a minimum level of performance:
- Deficiency of skill
- Lack of desire
- Poor leadership

Poor leadership is usually the reason most staff doesn't perform. Deficiency of skill is simply a lack of training, which brings us back to leadership, and lack of desire is lack of a leader who can motivate the troops to the next level. Poor leadership starts with a lack of a clear vision of what you expect from the club, yourself and, finally, how you expect the team to help you reach those goals.

One employee-based survey concluded that uncertainty is the prime reason the staff loses their motivation over time. Constantly tell your staff where they are going and define their goals so they know when they are there. But you can only do this if you first create a vision large enough and strong enough to carry the team along with you.

2. Understand the concept of gamesmanship

It's not the money, it's the game that's important.

This is a simple statement but very important when you are trying to motivate employees. Work is not always pleasant. Work is basically work, at one time or another. To stay constantly up and excited about a job is tough and it's an unrealistic expectation from an owner.

Money, except with young males in the age range of 18 to 25, is not always the stimulant we expect it to be for the staff. After a while, money as a motivator loses its impact. At that point, you need to apply gamesmanship.

For example, I once had a manager who was a golf fanatic. He was paid well, had time to play in the mornings, and was usually very motivated to work.

His pay was based on a base salary and bonuses for the total production of the company. The club was netting a steady 20 percent over monthly operating expenses and his first job was to maintain that spread. The second part of his job was to steadily increase total monthly production by 3 to 5 percent over the same month last year.

If he netted 20 percent, he received one bonus, and if he grew the business by 3 percent over the same month last year, he received a second. The gamesmanship comes in at these two goals. Instead of telling him what he was going to get for hitting the goals, we sat down each month and negotiated for that particular month. Each month was different, so there was a new prize to shoot for during that period.

> **To stay constantly up and excited about a job is tough and it's an unrealistic expectation from an owner.**

251

During one month, he set two goals. For holding net, he wanted a brand new golf bag, and if he hit the 3 percent increase, he wanted a new driver. The bag he picked out was $200 and the driver was about $300.

It wasn't the money, it was the game. He could have asked for the same amounts of bonus and bought his own stuff but that's not as important as beating me, the owner, out of free stuff. The game was the motivator, or trying to win the prize.

Each week, we would review goals and see where we were. I would also bring golf magazines to the meetings, and at mid-month I took him out for a round of golf and set up a demo with the club pro, so he could use the same type of driver he wanted for the entire round. We made it fun and a game for the entire month.

At the end of the month, he hit both goals. I had to make a big show of taking him to the golf store and buying the stuff on the company credit card. He actually hit 5 percent over last year, so I threw in another free round of golf as a thank you for the additional work.

In this example, the motivation came from having something fun to look forward to, something exciting to work for this month, the idea of being in a game of trying to beat the boss out of something, and the base motivator of working for something you want instead of someone telling you what you're going to get.

3. ESTABLISH A LEVEL OF EXPECTATION FOR THE JOB

Employees work better when they know what's expected of them. Goal setting is the foundation for establishing this expectation. Employees should know what's expected from their work today, this week, this month and this year in their job. These goals should be tangible, meaning that we can quantify them at any given time.

To motivate the staff, you must learn to understand and then practice visual management techniques.

Our main tool for laying out exactly what we expect in the goal setting from individuals and from the team is visual management. To motivate the staff, you must learn to understand and then practice visual management techniques. Employees are more productive when they know exactly what's expected from them that month and what the consequences are for not reaching the minimum performance levels, which are also spelled out in terms that can be quantified.

Visual management simply means establishing and displaying goals of performance for all aspects of the club, and then breaking these goals down into individual and team goals. The visual part means that we constantly share all information with the team as to how everyone is doing. You do this by posting all of the daily results on a wall in the manager's office. By the way, this is no longer "the office," it's the war room where you track the progress of the business on a daily basis.

Setting individual goals

Most employees in the gym business are rewarded for working hard, instead of getting paid for getting the right things done. They come to us several times a year asking for more money stating what a good job they've done this year. They say they're hard workers, good with the members, put in a lot of hours and are extremely loyal, therefore, "Give me more money."

In most cases, we don't really have any way of telling if they really are doing a good job. For example, a salesperson says she is doing well and had 25 sales last month. Is that number good or bad? Without some type of number to compare it against, such as a goal that was agreed upon between the manager and the salesperson, we don't really know if this number by itself is an outstanding performance or extremely poor work.

THERE HAS TO BE A STANDARD TO COMPARE ONE'S PERFORMANCE AGAINST

The salesperson may think that she did a great job for hitting 25 sales that month. Last year during the same month, she only hit 22. The owner, though, thought she should have done better. He started a new marketing campaign, there was an extra Monday in the month this year, and he'd put a new cardio area in the club. By his expectation, she should have done better.

To avoid a conflict and keep the employee motivated, the owner and the salesperson should have sat down and established a goal for her to work against. The key here is that the owner or manager and the salesperson have to mutually establish the goal. It's a very common mistake for the owner to set the goal for the salesperson and to also set the bonus for achieving the goal.

THE EMPLOYEE HAS TO PARTICIPATE IN THEIR OWN GOAL SETTING

For example, the manager sits down with the person during the last week of the month and has the following conversation to set a goal for the coming month:

> **Manager:** Joan, you did a great job by hitting 22 sales during this month last year. And you wrote 20 memberships last month. Thank you for the great job. Now for the coming month, we have to set a new goal. And don't forget that we've started that new marketing and that there is an extra Monday in the month this year. So how many do you think you can do?
>
> **Joan:** Well, based on those things, I think I can write 25 memberships next month.
>
> **Manager:** Thank you, that's a great increase over last year. Now, besides your normal bonuses and commission, what would you like to shoot for this month?
>
> **Joan:** Well, I'd like a new pair of workout shoes. The ones I've been

It's a very common mistake for the owner to set the goal for the salesperson and to also set the bonus for achieving the goal.

When the person participates in the process and sets their own goals, there is a transfer of ownership of the goal that takes place.

thinking about are about $125.

Manager: That's a lot of money. But I'll tell you what I'll do. The club will pay half at 25 sales and the full amount at 27. I think we're going to have a good month with the new marketing, and I think you can hit those two extra sales. Does that sound fair?

Joan: Sure, let's go for it.

Manager: Put it on your goal sheet [see Figure 17.1], hang it on the wall and be sure to sign it. And, don't forget to fill out your performance contract for the file.

A lot of good things happened here. First of all, the employee was in-

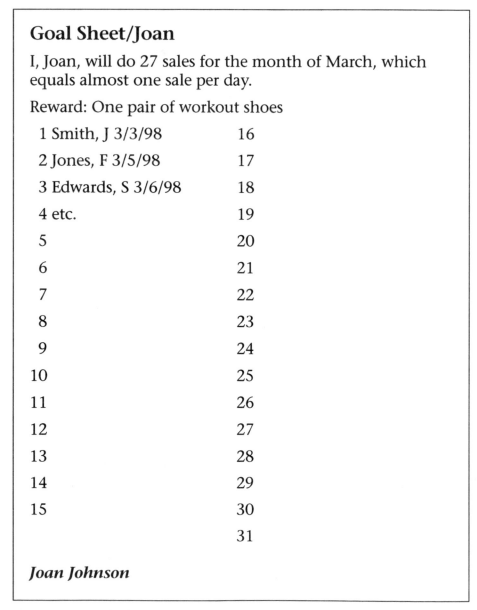

Goal Sheet/Joan

I, Joan, will do 27 sales for the month of March, which equals almost one sale per day.

Reward: One pair of workout shoes

1 Smith, J 3/3/98	16
2 Jones, F 3/5/98	17
3 Edwards, S 3/6/98	18
4 etc.	19
5	20
6	21
7	22
8	23
9	24
10	25
11	26
12	27
13	28
14	29
15	30
	31

Joan Johnson

Figure 17.1. Goal sheet for Joan

volved in the process. She was allowed to participate in the goal setting for the month and actually made the final decision on what she could produce. When the person participates in the process and sets their own goals, there is a transfer of ownership of the goal that takes place. It's no longer the manager giving the employee a mythical number to chase. It's the employee setting their own goal. If they don't hit it, it's their responsibility since they set it themselves.

Secondly, the employee was allowed to determine what's in it for her if she reaches the goal. This is the gamesmanship aspect of goal setting. The employee has set a goal that reflects a reasonable sales goal for the time of year and her current skill level (her previous record was 22 sales). If she reaches this goal, she receives the regular pay and any commissions she would normally be paid for each sale. The shoes reflect an additional motivator that keeps the employee personally involved in the month's outcome.

Thirdly, there was a formal transfer of ownership. The employee is expected to hang a display on the wall that lets everyone including the manager know how she is doing each day. There are no rules except that the manager needs to be able to figure out the number of sales the person has, who they were made to, and that the employee has to sign the display.

The employee also has to sign a performance contract (Figure 17.2). This is a simple form that formally transfers ownership of the goal to the employee. These are signed by the employee and put into their file each month.

If the employee doesn't hit the goal for several months, or has other problems in the club, the performance contracts are a good record of the person's performance over time.

The displays are as varied as the employees themselves. Some will simply hang up a piece of flipchart paper, write their name on it and then write the name of each sale and the date they made it. The manager then knows by the number and the date if the employee is on track to meet the goal that month.

Other employees are more creative. One tropical fish fanatic put up the outline of an aquarium each month on her spot on the wall. She represented each sale with a tropical fish that was a representation of a real-life saltwater fish. Alongside her display, she would put up an index card telling the rest of the staff what kind of fish it was and where it could be found.

At the end of the month, if she hit her goal, the club would have a complete and very colorful aquarium on the wall. The manager could tell how she was doing in sales by counting fish and comparing the total against the day of the month.

> **She represented each sale with a tropical fish that was a representation of a real-life saltwater fish.**

EVERYONE ON THE STAFF HAS INDIVIDUAL GOALS

Everyone on the staff, from the salespeople to the front counter person, has to have individual goals that they are accountable for each month. Individual goals may be as standard as the number of sales each person has to do, or as simple as the front counter person's being responsible for sending out a minimum of 100 postcards to members we haven't seen in a few weeks. (See

Figure 17.3.) But everyone has to have a goal and, in most cases more than one goal, that they are expected to meet each month.

Don't forget to extend goal setting to the entire staff. For example, counter people may have personal goals concerning selling profit center items. Trainers may have a goal centered on their personal programs sold. The club's maintenance person may have a five-point cleanliness standard they have to hit each week. Everyone should have a goal and every goal should be documented on the wall in the war room.

There are a few hints that help the management team start goal setting. When the employees first start choosing their own rewards, they always start with money because they don't really know what else to choose. Develop a

Everyone should have a goal and every goal should be documented on the wall in the war room.

Employee Performance Contract

I, _____, agree to meet the following goal for the month of _____, 1999.

Goal:
If I meet the agreed upon goals, I will receive the following, in addition to normal bonuses and commissions for the work performed:

Additional incentives:

I also understand that I am accountable for a minimum level of performance based on the following numbers. If I do not reach the minimum level, I understand that I'll be written up according to the company's policies as listed in the Employee Manual.

Minimum level of performance:

Staff member _____
Date _____
Team leader _____

Figure 17.2. Sample employee performance contract

list for each job in the club and items that fit that level. For example, a front counter person who sends out 2,000 direct mail marketing pieces a week isn't going to get a new golf club. The prize has to match the job.

Some generic examples might be:
- Movie tickets
- Concert tickets
- Dinner for two
- Supplements
- Clothing from the pro shop
- Day off
- Money for an educational event or training session

The prize has to match the job.

Goal Sheet/Sue

I, Sue, will get out 10,000 marketing pieces this month and 200 "I miss you" postcards for the members.

Marketing pieces = 2,500 per week

Reward: Dinner for two at Red Lobster

	Marketing pieces	Cards
Week 1		
Week 2		
Week 3		
Week 4		

Sue Smith

Figure 17.3. Goal sheet for Sue

- Gift certificates
- Short-term memberships for relatives
- Going to a trade show
- Ice cream

Start goal setting with one goal per person. Make sure the goals reflect what's happening in the business at the time. Goals have to reflect something that is possible to do, not something that is a far-and-away dream by the owner or, worse, a goal set too high on purpose so the club doesn't have to pay. Unrealistic goals can be just as harmful as no goals at all. It's up to you and the management team to set clear, reachable standards of performance.

Unrealistic goals can be just as harmful as no goals at all.

Team goals

Team goals are something that the whole team, or sometimes just specific groups, share in each month. For example, the entire staff might be part of the drink team that has a goal of selling $3,000 worth of drinks in the club this month. This is a goal the entire staff should be a part of, since everyone on the staff can influence a member to buy a drink. A team sales goal, on the other hand, would be just for those who sell memberships in the club.

There should be a team goal established for every profit center in the gym and for the other major profit areas such as sales and renewals. For example, these areas would make for good team goal setting:

- Sales
- Renewals
- Drinks (e.g., see Figure 17.4)
- Tanning
- People in guided exercise classes
- Personal training totals
- Total supplements sold
- Shakes sold
- Total number of members and guests who attend an event in the club

It's easy to set up team goal setting. First of all, start by selecting the team. Each person on the team should be someone who affects the outcome of the profit center. For example, if you're putting together a team for supplements, everyone on the team should influence supplement sales. The front counter people and the trainers might be the base of the team, along with any salespeople who also do workouts.

The manager and the assistant manager aren't part of the teams since they are usually paid for the total production of the company. The working concept behind the teams is to keep the lower-level employees aware of the need to sell other things besides memberships, and to keep them motivated by having the chance to earn extra money beyond their base pay.

MONEY IS NO. 5 ON THE EMPLOYEE MOTIVATION LIST

But remember it's not just the money that motivates them. A survey done a number of years ago, called "What do people want from their jobs?" asked employers and their employees to rank a list of 10 items in order of importance to them. Employers ranked the top three things they thought employees wanted from their job as 1) high wages, 2) job security and 3) promotion in the company.

The employees didn't agree with that order. Their top three were 1) recognition/appreciation of work done, 2) feeling in on things and 3) help on personal problems. Job security was fourth on the list and money/high wages was a distant fifth.

But remember it's not just the money that motivates them.

Goal Sheet: Drinks

Team goal $3,000/We need $100 per day

On the team: Dave (captain), Fred, Kathleen, Sarah

Day/Total/Over or under for month

(On the 3rd of the month, the club should be at $300, or $100 per day. It's at $340, or $40 over goal for the month so far.)

1	$120 + $20	16
2	$90 + $10	17
3	$130 + $40	18
4		19
5		20
6		21
7		22
8		23
9		24
10		25
11		26
12		27
13		28
14		29
15		30

Dave, Fred, Kathleen, Sarah all sign

Figure 17.4. Goal sheet: Drinks

Employees want to be motivated. Employers that throw money at the employees expect them to get excited, and as owners they get frustrated when money doesn't work. Employees don't always want money as the No. 1 motivator. In their minds, the thing that really gets them motivated to do a good job is recognition for the work that they do.

Team bonuses should be a form of recognition. The most important staff meeting of the month should be held during the last week of the month. This is usually an evening meeting that is mandatory for the entire staff. It's not, however, hard to get the staff to attend since this is where the bonus checks for the preceding month are handed out.

For example, if the meeting is held in the last week of March, the bonus checks should be for the month of February. Bonus checks should be separate from the regular paychecks because they lose their value if they just become part of the pay.

The meeting should be fun, should last about an hour and should recognize those who have met their goals for the preceding month. The owner or manager calls the person up, says something nice about the work they did that month, and everyone claps. Birthdays, weddings or other special occasions are remembered during the meeting, too, with small gifts or flowers.

Make a big deal about the success of the individual and of the teams if they hit goal. This gives the people the recognition they want and need to stay motivated.

The key is not the check; it's how it's presented. Make a big deal about the success of the individual and of the teams if they hit goal. This gives the people the recognition they want and need to stay motivated. One side rule is to always praise in public and chew ass in private. This meeting is to build up the staff, not to tear down the individuals on the team in front of their peers.

SMALL BONUSES DISRUPT THEIR LIFESTYLE

If our trainer makes $7 per hour, most of his friends probably make the same. People tend to hang around with people like themselves. The difference in working for you is the extra $75 to $125 per month that separates the trainer from his friends.

This money is most likely not saved but becomes part of the employee's lifestyle. If he is looking for other work, it's going to be hard to leave the gym for another $7 an hour job, especially since he gets a sheet each month with his check showing that his true hourly wage is a little more than $8.

These small bonuses can make your business a lot more attractive than the jobs his friends might have in the same pay category. They just get paychecks. Your staff member gets special checks handed out in front of his peers where he is formally recognized for the work he is doing. And keep in mind, you didn't pay these bonuses unless you hit goal and the business made money too.

One of the most important business quotes concerning small businesses (such as those in the fitness industry) came from the retail mogul, Sam Walton. He said, "The hardest thing I ever learned was to share the profits of the business with those who made them." He didn't mean to give all the net away. He did mean to learn to give a little extra back to the people who made your club successful: the employees.

BUILDING TEAMS THAT WORK

Once you pick a key area and select the team that influences that area, you need to pick a team captain. The captain can be the senior person on the team, or the leadership can rotate on a month-to-month basis to let everyone have a chance. The captain is the one who keeps score on a daily basis for the rest of the team and keeps the wall display up to date.

For example, the owner/manager sets the team goal based on sales expectations for that profit center in conjunction with the assistant manager, who is the one in charge of teams. If you have a 12-month history, the number can be based on a 3 to 5 percent increase over the same month last year. If there is no history, then base it on growth from the last month. When you first start, you may be wildly off, but after a month or two you should start to become more accurate.

Let's say the team is centered on drinks. The owner looks at the same-month-last-year's numbers, which were $2,800, and then sets this year's goal at $3,000. The owner gives this number to the assistant manager, who then gives it to the team. Each day, the assistant manager gives the captain the daily sales total for drinks and the captain adds this number to the visual management display.

The team gets a bonus if they hit $3,000 or more in drink sales during that month. The owner can give between 3 and 5 percent of the goal, or between $90 and $150 to the team if they hit goal. The money is then divided as a percentage of hours worked that month.

For example, let's say there are three employees on the team and they worked a total of 1,000 hours for the month. If they all worked an equal third of the hours, then they would each get a third of the bonus.

If the bonus was $150, then they would each receive a third, or $50 each. If they were on more teams that hit bonuses, then their total check would be bigger at the end of the month.

Team bonuses are just another form of positive reinforcement, rather than the negative reinforcement that most inexperienced owners use on their staffs. Positive reinforcement might be giving an employee who went over the goal by five sales a surprise afternoon off with pay.

A negative reinforcement is when the team is threatened with their jobs unless somebody starts making some sales around here. There is an old saying that the carrot catches more rabbits than beating them with the stick. The same is true of motivating employees.

BEING HELD ACCOUNTABLE

In goal setting, we pay for results not efforts. Good effort and good intentions didn't get the job done unless there was money made somewhere at some time. At this end of the scale is the fact that we also have to set a minimum level of performance that is acceptable so we can hold staff members

Team bonuses are just another form of positive reinforcement, rather than the negative reinforcement that most inexperienced owners use on their staffs.

accountable for at least a basic level of performance.

With every goal to be achieved, there should be a minimum level that is acceptable. For example, a salesperson agrees to do 20 sales for the month. The marketing is right, the person is trained and has performed at that level before, and they should be able to write 20 memberships.

The minimum acceptable number would be 60 percent of that number, or 12 sales. The employee may not make the goal, which means they did not live up to their performance contract. For example, the salesperson only made 18 sales, but was sick for the last three days of the month. The assistant manager and manager can choose to give the person the benefit of the doubt and give the goal reward.

On the other hand, if the salesperson came in hung over, called off sick one day and basically just went out of control at the end of the month, then 18 sales is not the goal and there is no reward.

The minimum number, or about 60 percent of the goal, is where the employee is written up and then undergoes whatever remedial training or work is necessary to get them back on track. There is a goal to achieve, but the person still has to be held accountable for basic production in their job.

Everyone on the staff should have minimum levels as part of their goal setting, even those folks who aren't in sales. This performance level should also be part of their performance contract (Figure 17.2) .

Everyone on the staff should have minimum levels as part of their goal setting, even those folks who aren't in sales.

INSTITUTING CHANGE IN THE STAFF

There are two ways you could start goal setting with your staff: the slow easy "one step at a time" method or the "walk in Monday and get started" method. Try the more aggressive second approach. Change is good and there is sometimes motivation in the change itself.

As you grow as a manager and leader, some of the staff will have a hard time moving up to the next level. It's much the same when you take over a gym that's having problems. The staff is used to doing it one way, and to start with another method is difficult. That staff hasn't had any leadership or direction and they will be very resistant to change. It'll be the same with your staff when you're ready to implement a somewhat drastic change such as goal setting.

Change for the staff is a matter of refocusing their efforts. Here are a few ways to work with a problem or transitional staff. Start with letting them know:

• Change is going to happen. What we did before is no longer acceptable.

• Expectations are set. You now have a base level of performance to live up to, starting today.

• Nonsense is out. The days of back stabbing, in it for yourself, member bitching, late for work, I overslept and it's not my job are over.

• A good work ethic and putting the customer back where he belongs are in.

• We will be tough but we will be fair. You'll know what's expected of you, how you can earn more money, how you are doing at any given time of the month, and exactly what it takes to get ahead in this job.

Set the tone early and hard. When you're going to change, get a fast start. Once you start, some people will move and some won't. Reward the ones who do and give extra help to those who are having trouble. If they can't change in 90 days, change them in for new ones. As you get better, you may need to surround yourself with better people.

Summary

We need to buy better talent with our payroll dollars, educate and train them better than any other gym in the country, then learn to motivate them so they can achieve their maximum performance.

It sounds simple, and if you could actually accomplish this, the things listed above are some of the real secrets of running a successful small business of any kind. These three points are also the ones most often broken because they are the ones that require the most from the owners. Most owners simply aren't yet up to the task. They'd much rather run the same old ads, put most of their time and energy into training the sales guys, and expect the entry-level people to come and go through the employee revolving door.

If you buy better talent up front, you can get a higher level of production sooner. Paying is actually pretty simple if you keep in mind the three basic parts: the base pay, commissions or bonuses and the extras that come from introducing gamesmanship into the formula. For example:

> We hire a front counter person who works 32 hours per week, which is full time, at $7 per hour starting pay, which is $1 more an hour than the normal local minimum wage. For this, we get a slightly more experienced person who brings stronger traits to the job because she is also a little bit older than we normally hire. Her pay might look like this:
> - Base pay is $7 per hour @ 32 hours per week = $940 per month
> - She earns an additional $75 to $125 per month from her individual and team bonuses.
> - Using the $125 number, her true hourly wage is $7.95 per hour.
> - She's a workout person so she wanted a bottle of supplements for hitting her personal goal for the month, which was handling and preparing 10,000 pieces of direct mail.

Paying is actually pretty simple if you keep in mind the three basic parts: the base pay, commissions or bonuses, and the extras that come from introducing gamesmanship into the formula.

You could have probably replaced this person for $6 per hour, eliminated the team bonuses and saved the money, and skipped the extra bonus altogether. But the team she was on met its goal of increasing the club's profit centers and she did take the responsibility for the marketing, which she completed under the supervision of the assistant manager. Would you have gotten the same performance out of the $6-an-hour person?

Goal setting can have instant success in the club, but it does take work. Study and implement slowly, using one individual goal for each person and only one or two profit centers.

Putting outrageous displays on the walls has far more power then most owners would believe, especially if the management uses progress on the charts to work with the employees.

Also, don't lose track of the visual management techniques. Putting outrageous displays on the walls has far more power then most owners would believe, especially if the management uses progress on the charts to work with the employees. You can now ask questions such as:

• You're slightly behind your goal. Do we need to review your training for the job?

• What are you doing today to reach your goal?

• What have you done today to help the team reach its goals?

• We're behind on the drink goal. Give me one idea we can do tonight to increase sales before we close. Good idea! You do it.

• Do you understand what I expect from you this month?

These questions are the ones that can lead to performance improvement because they keep everyone focused on the goals set for the month. "What are you doing right now to reach your goals?" is a powerful focus question to get people moving.

Included are sample goal sheets and a sample performance contract. Feel free to modify them as needed for your business.

Things you can do to use this material

1) Evaluate your base pay system to see if what you offer attracts the traits and skills you need to grow your business.

2) Switch your management team away from individual commissions to bonuses based on the production of the team they supervise.

3) Start every employee on individual goals. Goals are negotiated during the last week of the month and must be posted on the war room wall no later than the fifth of the month, or the employee does not have an opportunity to receive additional incentives. The employee would also be written up for not having the goal sheets displayed on time.

4) Introduce team bonuses for each profit center in the facility. Start slowly with only one or two and add more as you get experience.

5) Add performance contracts for each employee that transfers the ownership of their job and goals to them. All future pay increases are based on whether the employee hit the goal or not during the preceding months.

6) Put everything in writing. If it's in writing and hanging on the wall, it becomes real. Make it a formal structure that's based on written contracts, visual goals displayed on the wall, and formal write-ups for nonperformers.

7) Develop lists that encourage the employees to choose other things besides money. Add the employees' own choices to the list over the year and learn to guide them into the fun things that eventually motivate them to perform.

8) Learn to negotiate. If they set a goal, add a second tier. If they set too low of a goal, let them have it but add a second higher level of achievement. If they ask for goofy things like cars, rent them a car for the weekend based on a higher goal. And remember that you only have to pay if they hit the goal, which means you won too.

9) Goal setting may be the most important thing you do for staff motivation. Master it and practice it every month.

Marketing is a learned skill based on a few easy-to-acquire concepts

Traditional fitness industry marketing can't attract the people we would really like as members

Chapter 18

There is a naked fat person out there who would just love to meet you

Chapter 19

You don't have to be a marketing dummy just because you're in the fitness business

section six

Sign-up sheets and time limits on cardio

DURING A SEMINAR FILLED with numerous speakers, one really stood out from the rest. He was selling a machine similar to those found in busy ice cream stores where you take a number and wait for the counter person to call you to order ice cream.

His idea was to take the same type of machine and use it for clubs that didn't have enough cardio. As a member came in, he or she would grab a number and then head in to change. After they were dressed, they were supposed to hang around until their number was called and then they took their turn on an open piece of cardio.

The machine also had the capacity to time stamp the slips. This meant that as the person came up to take his turn, a staff member could time stamp the member's slip in the machine so that person couldn't stay on the cardio over the club's 30-minute time limit.

The moral of the story

Sign-up sheets and time limits are not providing member

Member service is not telling a member paying $40 a month that they can only stay on the cardio for 30 minutes at a time

service. In fact, these methods do nothing but highlight just how bad that club's member service is.

Member service would be having enough cardio to provide a minimum wait except for those two or three busy weeks a year in January. Member service is not telling a member paying $40 a month that they can only stay on the cardio for 30 minutes at a time.

Member service is another one of those things that we do out of habit. Sign-up sheets and time limits are a logical solution to the problem of having too many members and too little cardio, but it is not a member service solution that satisfies the members.

Your gym may be filled with these old habits. Once a year, you need to do a spring cleaning and question whether you are doing what you're doing because it's convenient to you, instead of what might be good for the member and member service in the club.

18

There is a naked fat person out there who would just love to meet you

THE LARGEST newspaper in the country estimated that 92 percent of Americans have never set foot in a health club. This seems absurd until you take the time to think about it. There are almost 300 million people in this country and only about 15,000 fitness facilities, including Ys and recreation centers. How many of your members have had memberships at some other facility before joining yours?

Most owners spend their marketing dollars fighting their competitors for the 8 percent of people who drift from club to club over the years. The important question they should be asking is, "What is it about the clubs in this country that would prevent the other 92 percent of the population from ever trying a fitness center?"

Why can't gyms attract a wider market?

The Surgeon General has threatened people with death. The major chain clubs run ads that scare them by using supermodels with ripped bodies. We've begged them to come in, we've offered ridiculously low prices, and we've even given the clubs away free. And yet we still haven't been able to pry large numbers of these folks off their couches. Something must still be a scary enough barrier to prevent them from responding.

There are many reasons this mysterious group doesn't frequent health clubs. Maybe one of the biggest is that we're using technology that is too many years out of date.

...we still haven't been able to pry large numbers of these folks off their couches. Something must still be a scary enough barrier to prevent them from responding.

269

How willing would you be to use equipment from the 1960s in your current facilities? Chrome selectorized equipment, limited black free weights, mechanical bikes and tons of passive equipment such as pony rollers and electric butt shakers were all part of the early '60s in the club business.

Most owners wouldn't even dream of trying to operate a modern facility using equipment technology from the 1960s. Yet many of today's owners still operate on marketing and sales principles that actually predate that era.

Much of what the club industry uses to attract new members was developed in the late '50s and early '60s in the dance studio industry, the life insurance business and through door-to-door sales concepts invented by guys who sold vacuums and siding for your house.

Drop closes, handling endless objections, high-pressure sales and lengthy, memorized pitches were all part of the old sales concept from that era. Along with those were loss-leader pricing, unbelievable sale prices, cash discounting and the first offerings of credit, which eventually became part of the marketing system that many clubs still use today.

Increased competition, the need for higher pricing for memberships and a more resistant and sophisticated consumer all force us to re-examine our current marketing practices.

Increased competition, the need for higher pricing for memberships and a more resistant and sophisticated consumer all force us to re-examine our current marketing practices.

Advanced marketing skills

To gain an understanding of marketing, you first need to understand the difference between marketing and advertising. Most people interchange the two words because they don't really know how to make a distinction. Instead they end up using the word "advertising" as the generic word for everything that concerns bringing potential members to the club.

For our purposes as gym owners, we use the following definition:

Marketing = the combination of advertising and events

To further define the term, marketing is everything you do in and outside your gym to bring potential members to the door. Marketing can be broken down into two distinct parts: advertising, which is what you do to get your message to the public, and events, which are what you do to enhance your name and to expose your gym to member's friends in a nonthreatening way.

In advertising, there are two completely opposing theories fitness business owners can pick from to entice potential members to their doors. The first is price, such as listing some type of discount, price special or price gimmick, like a sale.

The second method is exposure-type advertising, which uses a system that is nonthreatening or, more properly called "low consumer risk," to attract new members.

Research from clipping services that tracked the ads in the 100 largest newspapers in the country for six months demonstrated that 99 percent of all fitness facilities use price as their main method to attract potential members.

PRICE-DRIVEN ADS DON'T WORK TO ATTRACT NEW MARKETS BECAUSE THEY ARE BASED ON THE WRONG ASSUMPTIONS

Price-driven marketing does not work to attract a wider market because it does nothing to break down entry barriers. Entry barriers are things that prevent people from becoming members once they are in your club, or they might be things that prevent people from ever coming into your club in the first place. Many of our potential members don't respond to typical price-driven ads because they do nothing to eliminate their fears or doubts about health clubs.

To the average person, a gym or fitness facility is a scary thing. The person knows that they will not fit in because of their present fitness level, that they will have to make a very expensive buying decision based on a short, high-pressured selling situation, and that they'll have to make that decision during their first visit to the business.

These potential members also believe that they will have a hard time sticking with a program once they start because there will be no service after the sale. And, secretly, they are really afraid to go at all because they know that everyone in the gym is already fit and beautiful and they simply don't want to be embarrassed.

WHERE DID THEY GET SUCH NONSENSE?

They believe these crazy things because we have taught them that these things are true.

Look at typical ads run by the two biggest chains in the country. One uses supermodels with big hair, big chests, 23-inch waists and a lot of gold jewelry as the centerpieces of their ads. The other uses television ads that should really be classified as soft porn and be kept out of reach of teenage boys. They're just 60 seconds of beautiful, scantily clad women walking in front of the camera. Are these women role models or are they everything that's wrong with the fitness business today?

We showed the ad in question to 200 women currently working out as members in clubs in three different states. Out of this pool of women members, 93 percent of them found the ad to be offensive. One of the great comments from a woman who was surveyed summed it up very well. "There are only nine or 10 supermodels in the world. What about running ads that appeal to the other two billion women in the world?"

This ad is not featuring a role model for women. It's creating an entry barrier that is preventing the typical woman from responding because she feels she won't fit in at that facility.

Another example of what we have taught the average consumer over the years is that they will be pressured into a sale that they may later regret. Keep in mind that the people we are trying to attract may never have been in a club and don't really know if they want to join or not — let alone be forced

"There are only nine or 10 supermodels in the world. What about running ads that appeal to the other two billion women in the world?"

271

to sign a two- or three-year contract during their first visit.

Where would they learn this? One example is from one of the large chains that made the regional television news in the Northeast of the country. It seems that the club fired its manager, but since they were desperate for help they kept him on for three extra weeks. During this period, he had time to think and he got pretty mad at the club. He went to the local television station, found a sympathetic young female reporter and told her about the high-pressure sales tactics the club was using.

He and the reporter sneaked into the club after hours, which was easy to do since he was manager and had the key, and placed a hidden camera into a vent in the sales office. The next day, the reporter was to come into the club as a potential member and get the pitch.

The first salesperson who brought her into the office was about six feet tall, a bodybuilder who weighed about 230 pounds, and who had on a short-sleeved very tight shirt with a tie. The reporter was in her late 20s and in very good shape. The sales guy kept working her and you could tell that he was getting frustrated because she wouldn't sign but kept asking questions. Finally, he had had enough and leaned forward and hit the old hidden button under the desk. The door then opened and the manager walked into the room. He made the first guy look tiny at about six foot four and 260 pounds. The following is the conversation they had with the reporter/potential member that was shown on television across a multistate area:

> **The manager:** So Billy, what's the problem here?
>
> **The sales guy:** I don't know, I think she's just here to waste my time.
>
> **The manager:** So what do you want lady? If you're not serious, we're going to have to get you out of here. My man is busy and there are other people he could be selling that really want to join this club.
>
> **The manager** (then looks over the desk at the reporter's body and says): Gee lady, I don't know why you're having such a hard time making up your mind. You obviously need this. What are you, 10 to 15 pounds overweight? Just how big does your butt have to get before you're willing to make up your mind? Come on, what's your load limit, 20, 30 or 40 pounds overweight? Are you going to wait until your butt gets so big that you can't get through the door? Obviously you need this, but if you can't make up your mind then it's time to leave.

This was on television as an investigative report. Thousands of potential members in the area saw this report on their nightly news show. To the average consumer in the Northeast, all gyms must sell this way. This will be their perception of the gym business and what's going to happen to them if they inquire.

PRICE-DRIVEN ADS ADD TO THE NEGATIVE IMAGE

Price marketing makes a fundamental assumption that is wrong from the start. Running a price-driven ad assumes that the person is already fa-

The sales guy kept working her and you could tell that he was getting frustrated because she wouldn't sign but kept asking questions.

miliar with your product. If you understand the product, then you know whether the price is a good value for what's being offered. If you're not familiar with the product, then how do you know if the price is any good?

For example, let's assume that you've never snow skied in your life. Listed in the newspaper is an ad that offers a pair of skis, Atomic Beta Carve 928s with EssVar bindings for $500. Is this price good or bad for this pair of skis? If you don't ski, you have no idea whatsoever. Even if you do ski, you may not have enough experience to know if there is any value in this deal.

If you've never been in a gym, or if you've had a bad experience, been in a low-quality facility or just don't understand what working out is all about, then a price ad that states, "Summer special: Three months for $99," doesn't mean anything to you as a consumer. How would you know whether this is good or bad if you aren't even really sure you want what they have for sale?

In other words, price-driven ads assume that you have already made up your mind that you want to join this particular facility, and the last remaining barrier is the price. The overall assumption is that if the gym has a sale, you'll buy because you have already made a decision that you want the product.

In these examples, price-driven ads may actually limit your ability to attract new members because they only appeal to potential members who have a previous interest and experience with your business, which is probably a very limited segment of most markets. These ads do nothing to develop a wider market because of their limited appeal and the requirement of prior knowledge.

Again, any ad or marketing piece that mentions a price is defined as a price-driven ad, or an ad that hopes to attract members by having some type of sale. Examples might be: one year for $249, 50 percent off the membership fee for July only, one month for $19, or get started for just $25; these are all price-driven ads. Each one is offering some type of discount off of regular membership prices.

> **...price-driven ads assume that you have already made up your mind that you want to join this particular facility, and the last remaining barrier is the price.**

OTHER ASSUMPTIONS ABOUT PRICE-DRIVEN ADS

• Price-driven ads will eventually shrink your potential marketplace because of their limited appeal. The longer you run price-driven ads, the harder it will be to attract new members, because you're fighting for the 8 percent instead of trying to develop a market in the other 92 percent.

• Price-driven ads lump you into the same category as your competitors. You work your entire career to separate your business from that lousy competitor down the street, and the second you run a price-driven ad you become exactly like him in the consumer's mind. If you run a price-driven ad, and your competitor runs one, you are the same no matter how different you are, because the consumer may not have enough experience to tell the difference. You, as an owner, may know that the other guy has a dirty club and doesn't really service anyone, but you're not the one who has to make a buying decision. It's the uneducated consumer who is doing the comparison shopping.

• Price-driven ads teach the consumer to never again buy at full price. If you own a gym and have taken a call from a prospective member who asked when you're running your next sale, then you know what this really means. Why should a consumer pay full price for a membership when all they have to do is wait for the next sale?

• Price-driven ads tell the public that you couldn't sell your product at full price in the first place. Consumers are not stupid, nor are they unsophisticated. When the big chains run ads for absolutely stupid prices, such as $19 per month, the average consumer knows that they couldn't sell it at full price so they had to have a sale. They also know from this sale that they're lying. How can a club claim to give great service after the sale for a $19-a-month fee? It's not logical in the consumer's head that you can be so cheap and yet claim to be so good. Remember that we aren't selling a commodity, such as toothpaste, we are selling a service. In the real world (outside of gyms), the higher the price, the better the service will be from that provider. For example, is the lawyer who charges $100 per hour better than a lawyer fresh out of school who charges only $40? Which of the two would you bet your divorce on, your ability to drive for the next year or even your life? The consumer understands that they are buying a service, not a product, and that good service comes with a corresponding price.

• Price-driven ads lower the perceived value of your business. You may list your prices at $39 per month, but if you run a three-month-for-$99 sale, you are now a $99 club in the consumer's head. In effect, you've lowered the perceived value of your business by running a sale.

• Price-driven ads attract members who we may not want in the first place, meaning those attracted by the cheapest prices. An owner says, "Come on in and meet my members. That guy over there is Joe and he brings his own milk jug with him every day because he's too cheap to buy one of my sports drinks. And that is Fred over there. He wants to be a bodybuilder, but he signed up for one year for $249 because he's cheap — too cheap to buy supplements from me. He takes Flintstones One-A-Days from Wal-Mart. And don't forget Beth. She'll drive seven miles to a convenience store because they sell Diet Cokes for 10 cents less than I do. Yep, these are my members, the cheapest people on the planet, and they're all here because of all those cheap specials I keep running." A gym full of cheap people who respond to price-driven ads will not support your profit centers. Therefore, you can never decrease your dependency on new sales by developing a strong profit center base.

• Most importantly, price-driven ads do nothing to attract deconditioned people, those who have had a bad experience with other clubs, those afraid of getting pitched too hard on their first visit, or those who would really like to try a fitness club but really don't have enough experience to make up their mind after only one visit. In other words, price-driven ads only attract those who are already fitness-experienced and who also are looking for the cheapest deal. Sophisticated workout people might be looking for the best equipment and service, but not necessarily for the lowest rate.

When the big chains run ads for absolutely stupid prices, such as $19 per month, the average consumer knows that they couldn't sell it at full price so they had to have a sale.

PRICE-DRIVEN ADS ALSO LEAD TO THE WRONG FOCUS IN THE CLUB

In a typical price-driven environment, the entire staff becomes sales-driven. Since price-driven ads eventually shrink your potential market, the staff has to spend more of its time trying to bring in enough potential members to satisfy the needs of the business by doing such things as lead boxes and cold calling.

This external focus forces the club to put most of its resources into getting members and very little into keeping the ones it already has. Most price-driven clubs have very few service people because of the cost of maintaining the sales effort.

Price-driven ads also eliminate the ability to add multiple profit centers to the club. Without service people, it's impossible to properly develop and sustain profit centers in the gym.

This system eventually forces the club into dependency on only one source of income — income related to memberships and monthly member payments. If new sales slow down, then the club hurts financially because it has no ability to generate any money from other sources; therefore, it is forced to run more drastic price-driven ads that further lower the value of the club and the return per member.

PRICE-DRIVEN ADS ARE JUST ONE OF MANY ENTRY BARRIERS

Entry barriers are things that prevent potential members from becoming part of your business. All of your marketing should be aimed at eliminating as many of these barriers as you can from a prospective member's mind. But all entry barriers are not in your marketing and ads.

A barrier might be something as simple as an unattractive entryway or as damaging as an ad with a semi-naked model that offends the majority of your female clientele. Again, all of your marketing has to focus on bringing these barriers down, or you'll never get the sales you want. Here are the seven most common barriers you'll have to deal with in a typical fitness business:

1. Is this going to be convenient to my lifestyle?

The No. 1 reason we find from our own research that people join a gym is that it's close to their home. This is why many downtown corporate locations don't seem to do as well as they should. The typical working person will sit in traffic and suffer until they get to the gym that is close to their home, instead of the logical choice of working out near their business and avoiding the commuter traffic.

Then there is the member who comes into the gym mad because the parking spaces near the door were full. "You have to do something about this parking problem. I had to walk all the way across the parking lot to get here. Now tell the manager I want to see her. I'll be over there on the treadmill for the next hour." Is this logical? No. But people hate inconvenience, and that's one of the key barriers they look for when they consider a gym.

Always have a map on every marketing piece showing how easy it is to

> **...all of your marketing has to focus on bringing these barriers down, or you'll never get the sales you want.**

get to your business. If there is a parking problem, always show additional parking on the map, have a huge sign near the door directing people to the other spaces, and have a special sign somewhere on your sales tour showing people how easy it is to get in and out of the facility's property.

Hours and accessibility are also barriers. Make sure your hours reflect the market's workforce and that your schedule is included in all of your member information.

2. Has someone "real" joined this gym before me?

We highly recommend testimonial ads that feature real members telling their stories.

Supermodels are not real people. Besides the obvious sexist barrier these ads create, they also don't kill the barrier of not knowing that someone in the community has joined before them. We highly recommend testimonial ads that feature real members telling their stories. This type of ad lets the potential member know that they won't be the first to consider buying a membership at your business. Very few people like to pioneer anything, but everyone likes to jump on the proverbial bandwagon as it goes by loaded with other people in their community.

3. Will I fit in?

One of the most renowned excuses used by prospects when asked to join a club is, "Yeah, I'd love to join your place, but I'm working out at home first because I want to get in shape before I join."

People don't want to look bad in front of anyone, especially strangers. Joining a club is scary to most people because they think that everyone in the gym is already in shape. And we didn't do anything to change this perception. Running ads with glamorous models only makes this image worse in the marketplace. These women and these ads aren't role models, they are barriers that prevent people from wanting to do business with us.

Imagine a 30-year-old mother of two who after having kids is maybe 10 to 15 pounds overweight. She used to be in great shape, but hasn't worked out in at least five years. She might not be feeling really good about her body, and might be a little nervous about coming back to working out. Then she picks up the evening paper and sees an ad featuring a very in-shape woman who's about 22 years old with a flat, rippled stomach.

Is that model in the ad a reason to join? Or does the woman at home secretly, deep down inside, really absolutely hate that bitch, and the last thing in the world she really wants to happen is to join a gym where she might have to work out next to someone who looks like that. In her mind, most of the people in the gym are already in shape. She doesn't feel she will fit in at this club. And she most likely won't want her husband to work out there either.

The other side is the 40-year-old business guy who decides that it's finally time to get back into shape. His pants are too tight, his wife is trying to help him eat better, and his friends are kidding him about the old beer belly. He calls a gym, makes an appointment and then never shows. Why? Because he has nowhere to start and no reference point to go off of when he gets ready to come down.

The guy looks in the closet and doesn't have any workout clothes from this decade. In fact, he doesn't even have anything to carry them in if he did have them. He has visions of everyone being in shape, dressed in cool clothes, laughing at him in his white T-shirt and black socks. And he knows that his trainer is going to be a 20-year-old woman named Heather who will kill him after only a few exercises. He doesn't show because he knows already that he doesn't fit in at that club.

The ads might be a barrier because they show unrealistic people. Your staff may be a barrier because they are too young to know what it's like to be out of shape. Your handouts may be a barrier because they show a whole lot of equipment that may scare people with no recent fitness experience.

Something as simple as faxing over a confirmation to the guest may help break down this barrier. For example, it could mention suggested clothing and that we expect you to be nervous so please call so we can talk you through your first visit over the phone before you get here.

This may be the hardest barrier to deal with, because the staff forgets what it's like to be a beginner again and to have that feeling of not fitting into something that they might have been doing their whole life.

Testimonials that show other real people, and support materials that tell the person how to dress, what to bring and how to fit in help eliminate this barrier by giving the guests at least a clue as to what to expect.

4. Is there a risk to joining here?

Risk means that money has to change hands before the person actually knows if they really want to buy a membership. This is why money-back guarantees don't have the impact that they used to, because there is still risk in the consumer's mind. They still have to hand over the money first; how do they really know that they'll get it back if they're unhappy?

This problem is compounded if the person doesn't have any prior fitness club experience. Not only does the person have to make up his mind during the first visit to most clubs, but also he has to do so after only a 20 to 30 minute sales tour of the business. In the salesperson's mind, she learns how to handle objections so she can overcome this fear of risk in the prospect. In the prospect's mind, one visit simply isn't enough to settle the risk aspect of buying a membership.

True trial memberships are the only way you can ever break down any of these entry barriers. This is called exposure marketing or simply giving the consumer the chance to try before they buy. The premise behind this type of philosophy is to break down the entry barriers by letting a prospective member actually try the club for a reasonable amount of time before being asked to make any type of buying decision. Short-term memberships, such as one month for $19, don't fulfill the requirements of being a true try-before-you-buy concept. Money still has to change hands; therefore, there is still risk involved to the potential member because they never had a chance to experience the club before being forced to sign a membership.

Trial memberships are not an ad gimmick. Over time, the try-before-you-buy membership philosophy becomes the method of operation for the

In the prospect's mind, one visit simply isn't enough to settle the risk aspect of buying a membership.

club and governs the way member service is delivered, how the staff is trained and how the club is positioned in the marketplace. The staff begins to believe that this club is the best and that it's the only one willing to back it up by letting a member try before they buy.

The five-workout trial membership is the tool of choice for clubs that are in their first 90 days of operation. After that, 14-day trial memberships would be the next step. Many clubs will never have to move beyond a 14-day trial, because their competitor uses a price-driven marketing approach or because of the lack of competition in the area.

The 30-day trial is the working tool for a mature club that has a solid, well-trained staff. When you use the 30-day trial, you're making a statement to the community that you have to be able to back up.

The philosophy behind a trial membership is that this is the best club in the area, with the best staff and best equipment, and that the owner is so proud of this club that they are willing to let anyone in the community try this business absolutely free, with no obligation and without paying any money.

If a potential person is reluctant to try a fitness facility, which of the following two concepts would be most appealing: an ad that features young, good-looking models and a sale price, such as a two-for-one summer membership fee, or a testimonial ad featuring a person in the community that tells her story and how non-threatening and risk-free it was to try this other club by using a try-before-you-buy membership?

5. I don't want to make an error.

People like to believe they made the best choice out of what was available, and they don't like to make an error that will waste their money. A typical club sales scenario leaves the new member with a feeling that, since they were rushed and were forced to make a decision in just a few minutes, that maybe they made the wrong choice.

Many potential members choose not to become members because the salesperson tried to force them to make a decision in too short a period of time. The person then feels they made the only decision they could in the time available to them, which was not making a decision.

This barrier should be one of the easiest to remove. But 30 years of sales history and theory in this industry that stresses the importance of trying to close during the first visit often gets in the way. You still have to sell; it's *when* you go after the sale that causes the problems.

Trial memberships allow you to get the potential member into the system in a non-threatening manner, and then allow you to close them slowly and at the prospect's own pace. Some are happy and ready to go after one visit; others may need the full trial membership to be comfortable. But few are ready to make a major commitment to buy a club membership 20 minutes after meeting a complete stranger.

6. Will there be service after the sale?

Every gym that has ever opened, except for one crazy guy in Texas who

The philosophy behind a trial membership is that this is the best club in the area, with the best staff and best equipment, and that the owner is so proud of this club that they are willing to let anyone in the community try this business absolutely free, with no obligation and without paying any money.

claimed to have cheap prices like Wal-Mart but no service at all, advertises that they have the best service. This guy did Wal-Mart a disservice. Wal-Mart has great service. In fact, have you ever seen any business that claims to have lousy service?

All businesses claim great service. This is just one of those things that people stop responding to as buyers, because it would be so stupid to claim the opposite. Talk is cheap and this is the ultimate form of cheap promotion.

The consumer says, don't tell me about your service, prove it to me. Let me try your business, and let me hang around here long enough to see if I'm going to get service after the sale. Everyone promises everything before the sale, but what is really going to happen to me after I'm here for a while?

No form of advertising can handle this barrier. The person has to experience the service before they will believe it. Trial memberships allow the consumer to get a feel for what is really going to happen to them once they become a member of your gym.

7. But I didn't like this place even before I tried it.

Any aspect of your business could be an entry barrier that prevents a person from trying you at all. Here are a few possible barriers that may prevent a potential member from considering you as their gym of choice:

• Dirty or poorly lit parking lots.
• Intimidating staff uniforms or an unprofessional look because of no uniforms.
• People screaming or dropping weights.
• Not giving the prices over the phone to a sophisticated buyer.
• A cluttered entryway into the club.
• Ads featuring semi-naked models.
• Bullet points in your ads that list the names of equipment that mean nothing to the average consumer.
• Sales offices, which always have a very negative connotation for all consumers except car guys.
• Out-of-order signs on any equipment.
• Cheap informational or sales materials.
• Bad mouthing other clubs in the area.

These are just a few of the more common entry barriers that guests to the clubs cite as intimidating or unprofessional. Every single aspect of your business, from a beer can laying in the parking lot to the choice of picture you make for your ads, can affect your ability to do business.

Summary

A large majority of the people in this country have never set foot in a fitness facility. The traditional marketing approaches that we have used in the industry for the past 30 years or so do nothing to develop a wider market.

In fact, much of the price-driven and model-based advertising that is the center of most marketing plans actually limits our ability to attract mem-

Every single aspect of your business, from a beer can laying in the parking lot to the choice of picture you make for your ads, can affect your ability to do business

279

bers, because its appeal is so limited to such a narrow part of the potential member base.

Entry barriers are a part of every fitness business to some degree or another. The goal of a broad-based marketing plan should be to eliminate as many of these as possible in order to make it easier for potential members to try us.

The two most important barriers to deal with, which are risk and the potential member's feeling that they may not fit into our clubs, can only be eliminated by the use of try-before-you-buy memberships. Traditional advertising in the fitness industry does nothing to bring down these barriers.

In normal application, these ads may actually add to the barriers because of the need to buy a membership before you get to use the facility, and because of the choice of the type of people who are usually featured in fitness ads.

The type of advertising you run dictates the type of sales you have to do. For example, if you run ads based on price and strong first-visit incentives (drop closing with price), then you are forced to use high-pressure sales.

Price-driven ads are just no longer effective over a long period of time. This type of advertising lowers the perceived value of the club, lowers the return per member and forces external focus, which therefore lowers the club's ability to provide member service and to develop multiple profit centers.

Trial memberships, or try-before-you-buy marketing, allows you to raise your prices, because after a trial period of being serviced in your club and meeting your staff, price will not be the deciding factor. Trial memberships also allow you to develop multiple profit centers, and to attract a wider and almost endless stream of potential members that clubs which run price ads don't get.

If you use a try-before-you-buy system of getting potential members into the club, you will be able to use a different, less-pressured sales approach. The important point to remember is that sales are still important to the club's financial future. Good salesmanship still needs to be learned and practiced, but it's when and how you sell that gives the potential member a different impression about your gym than about the others in your area they may have visited.

Most importantly to the member is *when* the sale is asked for by the salesperson. In a trial membership, the potential member does understand that eventually someone will ask them to join the club. It's *when* you ask that makes a difference to the member.

Do you ask before the person has a chance to get to know you and your staff, and to get a feel for the club? Or is it after the person has had a chance to get to know you and the quality of service you can deliver? If you develop a system to ask after the person gains trust in your business, then the price will not be the deciding factor as is when a high-pressure salesperson tries to close a sale in 30 minutes.

> **The two most important barriers to deal with, which are risk and the potential member's feeling that they may not fit into our clubs, can only be eliminated by the use of try-before-you-buy memberships.**

Things you can do to use this material

1) Switch to a try-before-you-buy membership as the heart of your marketing plan. Remember that allowing the member to try before they buy is not just another ad gimmick, but an operational philosophy of really proving that yours is the best club in your area.

2) The try-before-you-buy membership would be the tool you use. The testimonial ads would become your vehicle to get the message out. Testimonial ads eliminate many of the barriers potential members encounter, such as proving that there are other non-model-type people in the gym, that not everyone was in shape before joining the gym and that there will be service and help after the sale.

3) Start with the outside of your building and do a tour of the entire facility, trying to recognize and then eliminate entry barriers. Keep in mind that you may be part of the problem and not necessarily part of the solution.

Start with the outside of your building and do a tour of the entire facility, trying to recognize and then eliminate entry barriers.

When does the relationship with the member really begin?

THERE IS A CARTOON THAT seems like it runs every year in *Playboy* magazine. It shows a man and woman standing in front of a minister getting married with the balloons over their heads that reflect what they're thinking at the time.

Over the man's head he is thinking, "Oh boy, I'm going to have sex every night for the rest of my life." Over the woman's head she is thinking, "Thank God I never have to do that again."

The moral of the story

Our relationship with our members is often thought of in the same way as these two cartoon characters. To most owners who are heavy sales-driven operators, the relationship with the member is over once he or she signs the contract. Then it's "get the hell out of the way, and let me get to the next new person through the door."

To the member, once he or she signs that contract, the

To the member, once he or she signs that contract, the relationship just begins

relationship just begins. When they come in for their first workout, they expect everyone to be happy they are there and give them the help and support this relationship needs to bloom over the years.

The differing opinions as to just where the relationship with the member begins and ends, is the difference between a club that offers great member service and one that has little to offer the member after the sale.

Businesses that want to grow in the future need to understand that the member is right. Once he or she signs a contract, our relationship, and responsibility to provide real member service has just begun.

19

You don't have to be a marketing dummy just because you're in the fitness business

MARKETING IS A SKILL EVERY small business owner needs to learn in order to protect his or her business. Much of the waste in small fitness businesses comes from owners giving away the control of areas that they don't take the time to learn. Again, the two most important things an owner should be doing are building a proactive business plan and creating a marketing program that ultimately leads to sales. Luckily, the basics of fitness marketing can be reduced into a few key points called the Plummer rules of marketing.

Know the true boundaries of your marketplace

Most owners spend marketing dollars to buy coverage way beyond the true geographic area that the majority of their members actually come from to visit their businesses. The basic rule to follow is that 80 percent of your members will have a 15-minute drive time from the gym. This equates to a three-mile ring for most fitness facilities in the metro areas and a five-mile ring for those who have clubs in the rural markets.

This rule is important to follow because money spent outside these rings seldom, if ever, brings in a consistent amount of traffic. For example, radio is not effective in most markets because it is one of the more costly media to use and because you have to pay for coverage that goes way beyond

> **Most owners spend marketing dollars to buy coverage way beyond the true geographic area that the majority of their members actually come from to visit their businesses.**

283

your drawing area. There are a few exceptions to this rule for radio, as when you have multiple clubs in the same town or are in a very small town, but you would still have to decide which stations would be most likely to hit your target market.

To get the most out of your marketing program, you should spend 100 percent of your marketing dollars chasing potential members in the ring appropriate for your area.

Be consistent

If I say Pillsbury, you say Doughboy. You say that not because the name of the company is the Pillsbury Doughboy Company, but because you have never seen a Pillsbury ad in your life that didn't have the Doughboy in it. When you say Doughboy, you're repeating the company's "hook."

Your goal in marketing is to develop a positive, recognizable hook.

Your goal in marketing is to develop a positive, recognizable hook. Most fitness businesses never develop a hook because they change their marketing theme and look too often, or because they start and stop marketing programs too many times a year.

Some hooks are very recognizable but are not always positive. Nautilus, for example, is one of the better known names by the consumer in the fitness world, but the image associated with the name is not always positive. The early marketing of Nautilus equipment was so dramatic and so penetrating in the marketplace that many of today's consumers can't shake the old images.

One of the hardest tasks the current management team at Nautilus will have to overcome with today's owners is the marketing image left from the early days. When asked in our seminars about the first thing that pops into their heads when we say Nautilus, their reactions vary along the lines of the way the equipment was years ago. Blue and black color, chain drive, and out-of-date equipment are some of the standard answers, although the company has progressed tremendously over the years and now makes competitive equipment. Their own hook, (that founder Arthur Jones paid millions of dollars to own and develop with his marketing when he first introduced the equipment in the late '60s) is now the company's own worst enemy.

A hook is developed by being consistent in the marketplace with a consistent look and theme over the years, and being out in the market every week, every month, every year for as long as you own your business.

Consistent marketing buys you name recognition, as in the Pillsbury example. Inconsistent marketing destroys your name recognition and lets your competitors run uncontested in the marketplace. Many consumers are confused by your image if you run a certain look and theme one week, and then next week you have a whole new look and identity in your marketing pieces.

When you change your ad theme and identity often, the consumer can't really get you in focus and then have the image of your business stick in their minds. This only happens when the same ads, again like Pillsbury which runs hundreds of different ads (but all with the same theme and identity), are run consistently enough that they begin to connect that image to your business.

Build from the foundation up to develop a solid marketing plan

The foundation of your marketing plan should be a level of advertising that consistently appears in media and that is cost-effective and consistent with the image of your business.

The current trend in marketing is toward target-specific marketing and away from the old shotgun approach. Target-specific means that you try and get a specific piece into an individual's hand. Direct mail would be an example of this approach.

The shotgun approach is an older style of marketing based on broad appeal media such as newspapers. The shotgun approach means that you run an ad and hope that your message is seen by somehow standing out amongst the other advertisers.

The problem with this approach, and with newspapers as an example, is that newspaper production costs have risen significantly over the past decade and the newspaper owners have met that increase by cutting the editorial to ad ratio.

A number of years back this ratio used to be a 50:50 split between the two. Now in some papers it's as high as 70:30 in favor of the ads. This means that your message is lost among the other ads, and that it's harder than ever to stand out.

Direct mail is a perfect foundation marketing tool for most fitness facilities because it is so easy to maintain and so cost-effective. A typical club that has 1,500 members with a base monthly operating expense of $50,000 and a strong profit center program may need to do 60 new sales a month to keep the cash flow coming.

If you know a few specifics about your business you can determine exactly how many pieces to mail each week for your budget. For example:

> **Direct mail is a perfect foundation marketing tool for most fitness facilities because it is so easy to maintain and so cost-effective.**

- The club would like to do 60 new memberships a month.
- The club is running a trial membership program and closes 40 percent of the trial members.
- The club is using direct mail and expects a one-percent response rate.
- The club is using a direct mail specialist and is paying $.26 per piece that includes postage, printing and labels.

To figure out how much the club needs to budget each month for a basic direct mail program, start with how many leads it will take to get 60 new sales. To figure that:

Divide 60 by .40 = 150

Now, to figure out how many pieces that club needs to mail each month:

Multiply 150 by 100 = 15,000
This is the number of pieces the club needs to mail
to get 150 people in the door.
It assumes a one-percent response rate from the marketing piece.

A one-percent response rate is considered good in today's direct mail market. Many of the old textbooks on marketing talk about a 2 percent response rate, but most of those books date back to the era before the consumer was overwhelmed with as much target mail a single individual now receives.

Now, figure out the cost of the monthly direct mail budget by:

Multiplying 15,000 pieces by $.26 each = $3,900 for the month

The club could lower the cost of its program by either increasing the response rate, therefore, lowering the need for so many pieces or by better staff training that would increase the closing rate.

Foundation marketing means that you do this as your primary marketing for the business. This is where the consistency part comes into play. Even mediocre marketing works if it is done over and over again. You may end up doing other target-specific marketing, such as newspaper inserts, but don't do those in lieu of your foundational direct mail campaign.

Also keep in mind that where you advertise is as important as the message itself. Advertising in low rent shoppers or in cheap coupon books gives the image of a discount or low-quality business. Stuck in a bunch of ads in a shopper between discount muffler guy and a mom and pop pizza place does not enhance your professional image in the community.

You may end up doing other target-specific marketing, such as newspaper inserts, but don't do those in lieu of your foundational direct mail campaign.

Each testimonial campaign has a six-week life span

A testimonial ad has about a six-week life span and then it needs to be changed. The theme is always the same and the trial offer is consistent as the main tool, but the person or people in the ad need to be recycled every six weeks.

Educate the staff

Part of any marketing program should be staff education. When surveyed, the majority of staff members could not fully explain the promotions being run by the club at the time.

There should be a staff meeting before any new promotion is kicked off. You should have samples of what is going to be mailed or distributed in the paper so the staff has an idea of what the potential member is reacting to when they come in the door.

There should also be a procedure folder kept at the front counter that reviews what is supposed to happen to the potential members as they arrive to take part in the club as trial members. For example, when using a trial membership, how would you track that member, how would the staff be expected to follow-up, what information or materials do you give the new person, and how does the staff know when and how to ask for the sale?

Never run price

Exposure advertising allows you sell the quality of the club, your member service, the real differences between you and your competition and, most importantly, it allows you to get a higher price. Your entire marketing program should be based on how you can get potential members in to try what you offer so they can see the differences and quality for themselves.

Running price in your ads brings you down to the competitor's level. Trial memberships will bring in more potential business in the long run and separate you from the other clubs in your market. To develop this separation and an image as the try-before-you-buy leader in the market, never run price in your ads.

Spend enough to make it happen

Money spent consistently over time is the formula for a good marketing program. Most owners consistently underspend, which prevents the accumulation effect from happening, and prevents the marketing program from being effective.

A good marketing program is based on two parts: offensive, which means the ability to generate leads that end as new sales, and defensive, which means you are protecting your market against competitors.

A long-term program must be based on tapping into the cumulative effect that a consistent theme and budget develops. The cumulative effect means momentum: If you run a program long enough, it picks up speed and starts carrying along everything in its path. The old example is rolling a big round rock down the side of mountain in Colorado. If you roll it from 20 yards up the hill, it picks up a little speed and then crashes at the bottom — then you have to carry it up and start over again.

If you roll the rock from the top of the peak, it will start out slowly and then build up speed as it races downhill. Along the way it picks up a strong momentum and starts to break other rocks, shrubs and small trees loose and then these things start downhill, too. As it bounds through the trees, it knocks down two deer, which start doing cartwheels down the slope following the thundering boulder.

All of a sudden, the boulder soars over a little rise and crashes into the middle of a Boy Scout Troop, and then they all start tumbling downhill along

> To develop this separation and an image as the try-before-you-buy leader in the market, never run price in your ads.

with the boulder, a sea of green shirts and shorts careening off huge immobile trees. Soon it's a full-scale rockslide that wipes out everything on the side of the mountain and the new open space ends up as a new ski slope, all because of someone pushing one boulder down the hill. The boulder ended up out of control, like this story, because it had enough time to build up momentum.

The first example is what happens in most clubs. The owner gets a new promotion going, but before it can build up any momentum in the marketplace, he stops it and starts a new look and new theme. This too dies because it didn't run long enough to gain that much-needed momentum.

The owner gets a new promotion going, but before it can build up any momentum in the marketplace, he stops it and starts a new look and new theme.

Marketing takes time to gain its own identity. In some ways, it's almost naive to think that by running just one ad you'll improve your business. It's a pretty overoptimistic assumption that enough people will first of all see the one ad, and then enough of those who saw it actually recognize who you are and what you sell.

For consumers to understand your hook (again the ultimate goal of marketing is name recognition and identity that leads to sales), they need to have your message waved in their faces about nine times before the hook catches them. The problem is that the average person only connects with your message one out of the three times they see it.

For example, you might send the person three different pieces of direct mail over six weeks but they will only see it once. It may be part of a stack of bills one time and get tossed, a color that doesn't catch the eye the second time, and the third time there is just a utility bill and your piece in a color that snaps attention to the piece. Following these numbers, the average person needs 27 times (3 x 9) before they get the hook.

This is why consistency is so important. It takes about four months for your program to start gaining recognition in the market. Most owners would have changed their theme, ads, colors and special at least four times during that time period. Go back to the Pillsbury Doughboy ads. The same theme, same character, year after year.

Another way to think of consistent marketing is to seek a compounding effect. The longer you're out there, the more overlap you'll have from people seeing your message last week, last year or even several years ago. By using the same message and theme, the ads compound their effect over the years you are out there with your program.

It should be the same with your testimonial ads and your try-before-you-buy campaign. The same vehicle and the same theme year after year. Will the consumer get tired of it? No, because the consumer may see it and recognize it, but not yet be ready to inquire about a club. When that consumer is ready, the first thing they do is scan their heads for some kind of recognition factor concerning their knowledge of a fitness facility.

She has seen your ad for years (consistency builds trust), she remembers the testimonial format (the most recognized and read ads in marketing), and most of all she remembers the key words that have been in your ads for years (only club in the area where you can try before you buy, no risk, no obligation, we're the best and we'll prove it).

How much should you spend to make this happen? If your club is a start-up or less than 13 months old, you should budget 7 percent of the monthly base operating expense (BOE) toward advertising. For example:

The club's BOE is $50,000 per month
$50,000 x 7 percent = $3,500
The club has a $3,500-per-month advertising budget

If your club is over 13 months old, you should budget 10 percent of last year's gross revenues split each month between advertising and events. For example:

Last year, the club had gross revenues of $600,000
$600,000 x 10 percent = $60,000
$60,000 divided by 12 months = $5,000-per-month marketing budget
$5,000 x 70 percent = $3,500-per-month advertising budget
$5,000 x 30 percent = $1,500-per-month events budget

Remember that events are a less threatening way to get buddy referrals. For example, you can hound your members into them giving you the names and numbers of their friends, or you can have an event or programming offering on Sunday and invite the members and their guests, who of course, can come for free.

Defensive marketing means that you spend the marketing money every month just like it was your rent or mortgage money. For example, if you spend $4,000 a month every month of the year, you'll not only have a good chance of bringing in traffic on a regular basis due to the compounding effect of the marketing, but you'll force your competitors to at least spend that amount to stay in the game. In other words, you're forcing them to react to your business plan.

It's like the Coke and Pepsi wars. Coke has led for years and spends enormous amounts of money to develop image ads. If they would stop for four or five months, most of that name recognition would erode, giving Pepsi a chance to challenge. Coke spends the money to get new business and to keep Pepsi from ever having a chance at being No. 1.

> **Defensive marketing means that you spend the marketing money every month just like it was your rent or mortgage money.**

Attack the weaknesses of the competition

Every competitor has weaknesses. Those weaknesses may be obvious to you, but not so obvious to the consumer who may be shopping several clubs at one time. They may sense that something is wrong but they may already make a buying decision at that club before they realize it's too late.

These weaknesses need to be exploited through the use of testimonial ads. We can't badmouth our competitors, because we're the ones who end up looking bad in the end. But our members can raise hell in our name through the stories in testimonial ads.

Through the years, we've found that certain types of members in the gym have more credibility talking about one specific problem over another. For example, if your competitor is a high-pressure sales guy, a businessperson in their early 40s is very believable attacking this issue:

> **Joe Jones**
> **Age 42**
> **Father of three**
> **Member of the Chamber of Commerce**
> Joe says: "I've been a businessperson my entire life and have been working out in area clubs for over 10 years. I found other clubs in the area very insulting with their pressure sales techniques. It's almost as if they have something to hide and they have to get you signed up as a member before you discover their secret.
>
> Ed and his staff at the Frisco Gym were truly different. They gave me a chance to try before I made up my mind with no pressure and no obligation. Ed said he had the best club in the area and he'd prove it to me with the trial membership. He was right. Frisco Gym is the best club in the area and they stood behind that with a 30-day trial membership, something no one else in town was willing to do."

Another example might be the issue of cleanliness. Every club owner claims to have a clean club, but many times their standards are just too low. We've found that a mother/daughter combo has worked well to attack the issue of cleanliness in the competitor's facilities. For example:

We've found that a mother/daughter combo has worked well to attack the issue of cleanliness in the competitor's facilities.

> **Ellen Smith**
> **Age 25**
> **Single**
> **School teacher**
> **June Smith**
> **Age 45**
> **Married/Ellen's mother**
> **Real estate broker**
> Ellen says: "I'm a workout person and have belonged to gyms since I was old enough to join. The Frisco Gym has great equipment and their trainers have taught me everything I needed to get the most out of my workouts.
>
> Last year I wanted to get my mother involved in working out, but I knew she was going to be particular with what she wanted. She would need help getting started. Someone to talk nutrition with and most of all she wouldn't workout in any club that wasn't up to her personal cleanliness standards. After belonging to other gyms in the area over the years, I knew that that the Frisco Gym was the only one clean enough to bring my mother to as a member."
> June says: "Ellen talking me into working out was the best thing that ever happened to me but I was skeptical at first. The Frisco Gym gave me

time to try a fitness program before I had to sign anything, and a chance to see what their service was going to be like. After years as a real estate broker, I'm pretty picky about a business being clean and giving good service. They proved both to me with their 30-day trial membership.

There are other issues you can bring up in your testimonials that high-light the strengths of your business and the weaknesses of the others in town. Some of these might be:

• Service before and after the sale: A housewife or business owner would work for this issue.

• Not a meat market or singles bar: Use a young couple in their late '20s.

• Not just a boring gym but the place to be: Use two or three workout partners that meet at the gym several times a week.

• My time and my place, no spouse, no kids, no bosses, just my time to relax: Use a professional businesswoman who uses the gym as her escape time.

A reminder on using testimonials is to change the ad every six weeks. You might have the businessman talking about high-pressure sales for six weeks, and then switch to the young couple talking about how comfortable he is bringing her into the gym with her saying how safe she feels not getting hit on all the time.

Take the cream out of the market

Any good marketing program should hurt your competition by taking the cream, meaning the easy sales, out of the market. You can hurt most of your competitors by just taking 10 percent of their sales over a year's time. This 10 percent often translates into a big part, if not all, of the club's profit margin.

We can do this in two ways. First of all, we run only trial membership ads. By doing this, we keep the potential members from price shopping off of our ads that would allow the competitors to further discount our published price or sale. A trial membership kills the famous "be-backs." These are the folks who are looking for a club and then shop two or three, before they meet the salesman of the day who may talk them into signing something.

The reality of business is that we may not always have the best sales-person on duty that day, but we can still take that person out of the market for up to 30 days at a time with a trial membership program. First of all, they stopped shopping because why make a decision at another club when they can hang out with us for 30 days with no risk or cost? Secondly, if we don't get them, then probably no one will. They tried it, they didn't like it and they most likely won't continue to shop again.

The second way we aggressively go after competitors is to run a heavier marketing campaign during our competitor's weakest time of the year. If our competitor is a cash club, for example, we would want to spend our biggest

> **Any good marketing program should hurt your competition by taking the cream, meaning the easy sales, out of the market.**

Refuse to feed your competition by allowing them to prosper during certain times of the year and by living off of our "be-backs."

marketing dollars of the year during September and October, just when the competitor is hoping that the fall influx of new members will save them.

Remember that if we don't get them, no one will. Refuse to feed your competition by allowing them to prosper during certain times of the year and by living off of our "be-backs."

Plan 12 months in advance

A good marketing plan has to be budgeted and planned carefully to be cost-effective and to be successful at bringing in potential business. Plus it takes at least four months to lay the foundation that leads to momentum and the compounding effect.

To accomplish this, you need to budget and plan 12 months in advance. This plan should tell you what marketing you will run for the next 12 months, when and where it will appear and the cost per week. For example, a sample plan might look like this:

The month of _____

- **The week of (Monday's date)**
  Advertising/Direct mail/3,000 pieces to zip code 12345
  @ 26 cents each = $780

- **The week of (Monday's date)**
  Advertising/Direct mail/3,000 pieces to zip code 12345
  @ 26 cents each = $780

- **The week of (Monday's date)**
  Advertising/Direct mail/3,000 pieces to zip code 12345
  @ 26 cents each = $780

- **The week of (Monday's date)**
  Advertising/Flyer inserts in the newspaper/5,000 inserts
  @ $50 per 1,000 = $500

In this example, the club could save a great deal of money by contracting the flyer inserts with the newspaper for 12 months at a time. Often you can save 30 percent or more by signing a contract instead of placing the ads in shorter time periods.

If you don't have a marketing plan, this is a sign that you are running your business as a reactive owner instead of being proactive. Reactive means your decision making is dictated by the moment, by what your competitors are doing that week or by a fast-talking sales kid from the high school yearbook who catches you on a slow day.

By being proactive, we can plan in advance for the key times of the year, keep the summers from being a sales death and also force our competitors to react to us and the consistency of our marketing plan.

Build your member referral program on events and programming

One of those things that members universally hate is the traditional buddy referral program. The club's salesperson asks, "Can you give me the names of four of your friends so we can give them a call and invite them in as your guest?" The member hears, "You want me to give you the private numbers of four of my friends so you can cold call them at home. They'll kill me if I do that."

Events and programming in the club are nonthreatening ways for the member to bring guests into the club. An event refers to mass happenings open to all members and their guests.

An example of this might be the annual summer bash party in the club's parking lot with a band, contests, a sidewalk sale, a basketball tournament and dunk contest, and special entertainment guests such as Ms. Fitness contestants.

Programming, on the other hand, is very specific and usually only appeals to limited groups in the club. An example of programming might be a stop-smoking class or a cooking class that supports the people who are participating in the club's nutrition program.

Events are usually scheduled on a more limited basis and are often considered another form of a member appreciation activity. No matter if it is an event or some type of programming, the key is to make sure the members are able to bring guests.

Some typical events are:

• The annual Christmas party. There are two versions of this, depending on if you allow alcohol on the premises. The majority of the clubs give away drinks (with controls) as part of their parties. Make sure your insurance allows you to give away alcoholic beverages as part of the events held in the club. The party should be held during the first two weeks of December and open to members and their guests. The party should be held in the club, and members are requested to dress in their holiday best. You can have contests, dancing, open bar, valet service and, of course, food. Most of the needed supplies can be bartered if you start in the spring for the December party. The second version is the family-style buffet with soft drinks, and your out-of-work brother-in-law comes and terrorizes the children dressed as Santa. Both work, and the one you choose should match the style of the club you own.

• The annual summer bash/member appreciation party. This works best if it is held during the last two weeks of July or the first two weeks of August. Hold it in your parking lot if possible, and have as many events as you can think of that would fit the occasion. If possible, sell small booth space to shoe companies, chiropractors or anyone else who will pay for access to your members.

• Holiday theme parties.

> **The member hears, "You want me to give you the private numbers of four of my friends so you can cold call them at home. They'll kill me if I do that."**

• Sports theme parties such as Super Bowl or the World Series. Rent a big screen television, give away free beer and open the gym up to members and any of their guests with no extra fee. Women's gyms have done well with anti-Super Bowl parties over the years that counter with chick flicks and wine. Again, pick your own style that matches the type of club you own.

Programming is virtually unlimited. Some clubs may have to charge for or let the members share in the cost, such as the ski trips. Most should be free and open to all guests, if possible. Some examples are:

• Special speakers such as tax planning, giving up smoking or dealing with back problems.

• Ski trips, trips to the beach, mass shopping trips to the nearest giant mall where the members split the costs.

• Weekly or monthly workout seminars, offered by the lead trainer, that include handouts, an hour of working out on that special muscle group learning new exercises and other training tips.

• Cooking classes.

• Short-term programming such as yoga, women's self-defense classes, t'ai chi, stretching, country line dancing or any other short-term course people might be interested in at your club. Pricing is easy if you think of one week for $19, two weeks for $29, three weeks for $39, etc. Most owners give away these things instead of charging for them and making them available to the nonmember guests of our members. In the past, if a club added yoga, for example, it put it on the aerobics schedule and became stuck with it. By using the short-term concept, if it doesn't work you are only stuck with it for a short period of time. If it does work, you can repeat it. Either way, you will probably make more money than adding it to the schedule and giving it away for free. It would make it perfect if the club had a 600-square-foot multipurpose room for these events. Consider putting an end to that old aerobics program — that is most likely losing you money.

• Weird events such as group bowling, mountain bike trips or just an expedition to a new bar in the area.

Again, the reason we would offer something every month is to encourage members to bring their guests. The best promotion is the simplest: Get in the member's face and personally promote the coming activity. Do the invitations and displays in the club too, but the best way to promote anything is one member at a time and by having the member sign a sign-up sheet guaranteeing they will be there on the scheduled date.

...the reason we would offer something every month is to encourage members to bring their guests.

Be first, not better

Better is not a definable or defensible business plan. Trying to be better than someone else just points out their strengths and, after a while, two businesses trying to be better than each other end up exactly the same in the consumer's head. For example, which is better, AT&T or MCI, or does anyone care after years of bashing each other on television?

First or only — this is the only position you can really hold in a consumer's mind. For example, who was the first person to fly across the Atlantic solo? Everyone knows it was Charles Lindbergh. Who was No. 2? No one really cares who No. 2 was because he wasn't first. Who was third and why do we remember her? Because she wasn't the third man who crossed, she was the first woman.

It's very easy in the fitness business to get into the "better than the other guy" syndrome. I'll open a bigger aerobics floor, put in more spin bikes, have more free weights or do something else the same as our competitors, but supposedly better.

We need to concentrate on positioning our business as the first or only club that does something. For example, we have the best club in the area and we'll prove it with our 30-day trial. We are the first club in the state to run a 30-day trial membership. We're the only club in the county that offers a 30-day unconditional money-back guarantee. All these statements are based on first or only, and should be part of all your marketing material.

Other examples might be the first club in the area, the oldest club in the state, the only adult alternative club in the city, the only licensed gym in town or the only gym just for families in the county. All of these are statements that make you different from a competitor, and are more likely to stick in the consumer's head than trying to make them think you are "better." When it comes to better, the consumer thinks, "If you are trying to be better than that guy, then he must already be the best and the one who set the standard for you to compare yourself against. I might as well go there instead."

Blast the market several times a year

You want to break up the natural rhythm in the marketplace by blasting the area several times a year outside of the normal cycles. Over the years, we have all started following the same dogma in the fitness business. January is a great month, summer sucks and fall is OK, but it's just the turning month for our real season. Why do you believe this and then market accordingly? Where is it written that it has to be this way?

There is no reason that April and May, followed by September and October, couldn't be very substantial months financially in the fitness industry. For example, potential members start thinking hard about what they're going to look like in the summer as early as March, yet most owners seldom hit the spring hard because they are either fat and happy from January and February or they are just burned out from the selling season. Why couldn't we run some of the biggest marketing dollars of the year during these two spring months and buy the start of a big summer?

The same applies for the fall season. In most markets, after the September holiday, everyone is done with summer and ready to head inside. Why not make that a huge splash time with advertising, and also severely hurt the competition by taking all of the cream out of the market?

Blast the market several times a year, but don't always make it in January. Change the rules by changing the way you look at what you are try-

> **All of these are statements that make you different from a competitor, and are more likely to stick in the consumer's head than trying to make them think you are "better."**

ing to accomplish with your advertising.

Own your own "word"

If you say the name of your gym, what one or two word description does the consumer say back to you?

What is your business known for in the community? If you say the name of your gym, what one or two word description does the consumer say back to you?

In the corporate business world, companies spend millions of dollars honing their image down to one or two key words that stick in the customer's mind. For example, if you say Federal Express, the normal customer response is "overnight." If you say Volvo, the customer usually says, "safety."

In the fitness business, most gyms have too broad of an image, which prevents the consumer from understanding your business in a narrow focus. The typical club might run five or six different ads over a year's time. This means the consumer has five or six different images floating in their minds which makes it hard for your community to identify with you.

Your job as a budding marketing genius is to burn your word into the potential member's head so that if someone says the name of your facility, the customer has a specific, predetermined image pop into their head. For example, a women's club might use the word "elite" to separate it from other women's clubs in the area. Elite is also a word that conjures up a positive image in most people's head, especially when it's applied to a service business.

A club that uses "elite" as its major focus word has a certain image to maintain in the market. The club would have to be a little nicer than the competition, and it would have to have better services because of what the word implies. It would also have to have the best equipment, the most current cardio and all of the support services too that let it live up to the word "elite."

Finding and using a word helps the staff better understand what kind of club they work in, how they are supposed to represent the club to the public, and how their work is supposed to fit into the image of the club.

The following categories represent four basic parts of the business, and suggest sample words that may fit your business. As you review these ideas, don't forget that your entire business should be able to be shrunk down to just one word:

• Benefit-related words. This answers the question: What's in it for the member? Samples of the words in this category are "results," "convenient," "total support" or possibly "caring."

• Service-related words. This is a category that can be used to separate you from the competition. Sample words or simple phrases in this category are "never a wait," "individual attention" or the word "service" itself.

• Audience-related words. Words from this category can be used if you are trying to appeal to a certain segment of the market. For example, "elite," "serious," "where the bodybuilders train" or "we understand beginners" are all words or phrases that appeal to specific audiences.

• Sales-related words. This is a category you should stay away from al-together. Being known as the "cheapest," "always a sale" or as the "cash club" is not a reputation that will take you long-term.

No matter how complicated you think your business is, nor how wide a range you appeal to now, you need to focus your image down to one word or benefit, rather than three or four different ideas that confuse the consumer as to your true identity.

Another way to look at finding a key word and then using it in every piece of marketing you ever put out is to find the one thing you do, and then claim to do it better than anyone else in your market. If you were the serious gym in your area, then everything from the front door to the staff uniforms all would have to support that concept. Find a word and make it yours.

It's hard to get prior images out of their heads

Once people get a word or image in their heads, it's hard to change. For example, Gold's Gyms started out in their early years with a bodybuilding orientation. Now, as their new generation of owners and their parent organization have matured over the years, most of their gyms have a wider appeal, are very nicely designed, and offer a much wider selection of equipment and programs for the members.

But even though their gyms have changed, many consumers still have a hard time with the older image. Remember that when Gold's started, their focus was narrower than it is now and they spent a lot of money in those days building a successful company.

But some consumers still think of the Gold's name as being a little more hardcore than the gyms really are after years of growing and developing. It's hard to change the image. The only thing that will probably work is to give the consumer something new to think about and focus on instead of the old focus.

So instead of changing the consumer's mind, change their focus. For example, Gold's owners could use a series of testimonial ads that have people saying how surprised they were that there were people like them working out in the gym. A key word for a Gold's owner might be "service," "elite" or "lifestyle." They might use a support phrase such as, "If your lifestyle is fitness, Gold's is your gym." Then all of the club's programs and services would be designed to support the fitness lifestyle focus.

In this example, we haven't changed the consumer's mind, just let them know that the early Gold's Gym has changed to meet the demands of the marketplace, and maybe you, the consumer, don't know how good we really are now. By taking this track, you ignore any preconceptions and replace them with what we now want them to know.

...you need to focus your image down to one word or benefit, rather than three or four different ideas that confuse the consumer as to your true identity.

Keep the faith

Most owners change their ads just to change them. They give their ads a whole new image, look, theme, special, and even a new logo sometimes — just to run something different. The best way to consistent presence and position in the marketplace is to *not* change your theme.

Midas Muffler is a perfect example of a company that sticks to a consistent theme year after year. The ads may vary slightly, but the theme is always the same: good service, we won't rip you off and professional-looking people in nice clean shops.

Give the consumers a consistent look, even if you, your membership and your family are all bored with it. In the fitness business, we never really know what day of the year the potential member will decide that it's time to get started. That consistent ad or theme you've been running for years may be old to you, but the potential member who decides "today is the day" is reacting to the image you have built up over time.

This potential sale may have seen your ads for years, and by now has built up a recognition factor in their head. The ads have been different each time, but always with the same testimonial theme and trial membership offer. The person wasn't interested in fitness at the time, but they have glanced at the ads enough to have an image form of the focus word or phrase that has been part of your marketing for years.

Now that they are ready to buy, they look for that old familiar ad, get the phone number, and then respond to an image that may have been established in their head several years ago.

If the club has run four or five different theme ads over that same time period, then when the potential member is ready to buy, the image of your club doesn't automatically pop into their head. Because there were too many different looks and themes, the potential member never really understood your focus nor were they able to capture the image we wanted them to have.

But if you were the club that ran testimonials for years, and is still the only club in the community that gives everyone a 30-day trial membership to try the club before they buy, then you have a consistent image and a focus. This consistency might have changed the negative outcome, where the member is confused and has no association with your business.

Because there were too many different looks and themes, the potential member never really understood your focus...

Summary

Most people make marketing harder than it has to be for a small business. By following just a few key points, you can simplify this chore and become more effective at attracting new members:

• Be consistent. Have some type of direct mail campaign, newspaper insert or other target-specific ad get into someone's hand each week. Do this every week, every month, forever.

• Use a trial membership. Go after a market seldom tapped by typical health club advertising. Use a trial as the basis for all your marketing (we're the best in the area and we'll prove it) and as the basis for your staff training.

• Use testimonial ads that let you prove that real people use your gym. Testimonials also allow you to attack some of a potential member's preconceptions, such as "clubs are dirty" or "all clubs use high-pressure sales tactics."

• Spend enough on a monthly basis to develop a long-term compounding effect with your marketing.

• Plan 12 months in advance so you drive the market, instead of being driven by the competition.

• Have some type of nonthreatening event or programming every month so the members can bring in their guests to experience the club.

• Find and then own a word or phrase that becomes part of your ongoing marketing plan. For example, "try before you buy" is a phrase that could be placed six or seven times in every advertising and marketing piece.

• Be patient. It takes at least four months to start reaping the rewards of a good marketing program.

Things you can do to use this material

1) Create a 12-month marketing plan.

2) Develop a testimonial campaign based on the weaknesses of the competition and the things that attracted your current members. Shoot four or five member pictures at a time, all in your target market, and plan for the next year. Use smiling head shots or tight family shots, and avoid lining the person up against a wall 52 feet from the camera.

3) Start with a simple programming activity at least once a month, such as your lead trainer directing an educational session for your members and guests. Don't forget to apply the rules of promotion that we use for the profit centers for your events.

4) Build an ongoing marketing cost into your budget starting next month, and add to it until you reach the right percentage for your business.

Develop a testimonial campaign based on the weaknesses of the competition and the things that attracted your current members.

Sales in the fitness industry are based on 20 years of bad habits

There is a better way to sell than the traditional slam method — it's based on trial memberships

Chapter 20

When they take you into the office, you know the bad news is coming

Chapter 21

You can't sell a million-dollar gym with a six-cent brochure

Chapter 22

Even if you give it away free you still have to have a system

Men running women's clubs

THE THEORY JUST ISN'T SOUND. A male owner opens a women's-only club dedicated to providing an atmosphere where women can work out in a nonthreatening atmosphere, without men staring at them or trying to pick them up.

And then the male owner works in the club himself selling memberships and working at the front counter canceling the atmosphere he has worked to create.

The moral of the story

Women's clubs are women's clubs. They are based on providing a nonthreatening atmosphere where women can work out

without feeling the need to dress up, get hit on or just avoid getting rated as they walk from one part of the club to the other.

There is also the privacy issue that is part of women's clubs, and male-only clubs, too. Many

And then the male owner works in the club himself selling memberships and working at the front counter canceling the atmosphere he has worked to create

of these women's clubs around the country attract women who, because of religious reasons, don't want to work out in co-ed clubs. They join a women's-only facility because they don't expect to see men working in the club.

Is this discrimination or is it a right to privacy? Courts in some states have decided in favor of privacy, while the question is open elsewhere.

But men working in women's clubs is counterproductive to grow the club financially. These clubs will never be as productive as they would be if they were staffed with all women.

20

When they take you into the office, you know the bad news is coming

AH, THE GOOD OLD DAYS in sales: aggressive sales people, unsophisticated buyers, loose laws and no stinking attorney's general. A prospect would call the club and you actually laugh when they asked for prices over the phone since no one ever gave out prices. If the prospect showed, you could take him into an office and ruthlessly drop-close him until he cried for his mother and still you didn't have to let him out; then it was time for the double team.

And the prospect actually believed the drop-close in those early days of the club business. Can you imagine a club's salesperson telling you that if you don't sign today, the same membership will cost you $150 more tomorrow, and you were such a hick that you believed it. And don't forget cold calling, draw boxes and relentless in-your-face buddy referral systems that made new members wish they'd never seen the club.

Ah yes, the good old days. And no one is happier these days are gone more than a typical prospect in almost any club in the country. The business culture has changed, the consumer has become more sophisticated, but the old-style sales gimmicks that should have died a quiet death years ago are still alive, clung to by a few tenacious owners who still live in the past.

The consumer doesn't want to be sold the way they were 30 years ago, because the consumer has changed. The new generation of membership buyers is more sales-experienced and sales-resistant, more business-sophisticated and now understands that the buyer is in the driver's seat. What worked then, in the days of the aggressive sales systems, doesn't work in great enough

...the old-style sales gimmicks that should have died a quiet death years ago are still alive, clung to by a few tenacious owners who still live in the past.

numbers now to keep a gym growing.

The contradiction to this change in the consumer is the gym person who keeps the old ways alive, accompanied by the new breed of owner who claims to be totally different in philosophy and then still does the same thing. For example, one of the large chains has gone to all open-end, month-to-month memberships in their ads. Then when the prospective member comes in, the salespeople still slam them. The only thing different is the length of the membership; the old-style aggressive sales techniques are still the same.

Don't think you still use any of the old sales techniques that have given this industry such a bad name with the consumer? See if any of these remnants are still lying about your club:

Sales offices

Name one experience in your life that has been positive and that has taken place in an office across a desk from someone. Even when you inherited all that money and the lawyer told you about it in their office, someone still had to die first for you to get the money. And let's not forget your visits to your lawyer, doctor and your banker, all usually very nerve-wracking events that all end up in an office.

Sales offices have been standard for more than 30 years, but the consumer has grown past being sold in an office. Most even find it offensive, and associate it with the stereotypical used-car salesperson.

And why would a salesperson take a person out of the energy and excitement of the club and then try to close the person in a closed office across a desk? Wouldn't it be more logical and less threatening to try to close the person at the bar area or on the workout floor, and keep them in the action that made them excited about joining a club in the first place?

Closing on the first visit

Closing on the first visit still works fine if the price of the membership is about $250 or less. The higher the price of the membership, however, the more difficult closing on the first visit becomes for the salesperson.

Yes, some of the old techniques still work and there are still a few people making money by drop-closing everyone on the first visit, using price ads and doing it in a sales office. But owners still supporting these practices can't normally sell enough members to support a major fitness business on a year-to-year basis.

It's like aerobics programs in most clubs; there are still enough students to have classes and programs but there aren't enough participants to make money doing it. But because the classes still attract some students, the owner doesn't want to give up the program.

In sales, you can still close some people on the first visit, but not

Name one experience in your life that has been positive and that has taken place in an office across a desk from someone.

304

enough to warrant using a system entirely dedicated to first-visit closes. You need an alternative that lets you close some on the first visit and still get another chance at the people who opt not to start right away as members, rather than anger the ones who don't sign.

As to the price, once you get to a certain price, depending on the area of the country and the market, the consumer will shop or at least go home and think about the decision. This decision point is different for each individual and you'll never really know what that number is, but you should be aware it exists and allow for it in your sales presentations.

For example, where would you have to stop and think about a buying decision?

- **A pack of gum that costs $1.**
- **A ball cap that sells for $15.**
- **A sweatshirt for the gym that costs $50.**
- **New workout shoes that go for $100.**
- **A sport coat or dress that sells for $250.**
- **A television that costs $500.**
- **A stereo that sells for $750.**

Somewhere around the television is where most consumers get nervous and may need to go home and think about the buying decision by themselves or by including their significant other. The sad point for most fitness owners is that around $500 is where we want our memberships to be on the minimum level, or about $35 a month for 12 months with an $80 membership fee. Just when we get our prices right, the member has to go home and dwell on the decision.

Let's look at this another way:

- **A gym membership at $99 a year.**
- **A gym membership at $249 a year.**
- **A gym membership at $35 a month with an $80 membership fee, or $500 total.**
- **A gym membership at $50 per month with a $90 membership fee, or $690 total.**

The lower two probably don't need much thought for a potential member, but you can't sign up enough volume to make those numbers work. Most of the more sophisticated owners seek a higher return per member and go after more money per member but fewer members. The problem with this, however, is now the membership price is too big to depend on a sales system based on closing everyone on the first visit.

The answer to this problem, of course, is the trial membership. By using trial memberships, you can still expect to close about 30 percent of all sales during the member's first visit. For example, a woman who has been a member for three years brings her sister into the club to join. That guest will sign during her first visit, as will about 30 percent of all your sales.

Just when we get our prices right, the member has to go home and dwell on the decision.

305

In the old-style first-visit-based sales systems, you still can close people on the first visit but two problems arise. First of all, you get false numbers because a large percentage of the first-visit sales will sign because of the pressure and then not pay. Remember that the higher the pressure, the higher the losses.

The second reason is that a system that puts so much emphasis on the first visit will alienate those who don't sign. In other words, once you miss those people, you also make sure that they will never come back because they were so pressured.

...once you miss those people, you also make sure that they will never come back because they were so pressured.

Draw boxes and cold calling

Put your name in the box and win something free. Give away something free, but small, and then call everyone else and tell them they were the runners-up and won two weeks at the gym. They come in and you slam them into a full membership.

Sounds easy. It was, about 30 years ago. Now, the names in the draw box are like a "Who's Who in Trailer Park Living," not the names of people you'd really want in your business as members.

Cold calling is just another version of the draw box. Call someone at home and give them a free membership of some type, and then go for the big close when they come in to check out what they won. The problem with cold calling is that it irritates the consumers in your area, and there are at least 100 phone companies already doing the same thing to them.

Both of these concepts were invented because traditional price-driven marketing could never bring in enough prospects to feed a sales-driven business. This meant the sales staff had to make up for the deficiency by developing their own leads, neither of which should be a part of a more sophisticated marketing plan in today's market.

Drop closing

There are two types of drop closing: a take-away or negative close where the potential member loses something if they don't buy, and a positive where the prospect gains if they buy today. The problem is that almost all owners only practice the negative version.

Taking away used to work beyond belief in the early days of the business. The consumers were not sales-experienced and they really believed that they would lose money by having to pay more if they waited until tomorrow to make up their minds.

Now the consumer understands that if the membership is $100 off today, and today only, if they come back tomorrow they will get the same deal. And many consumers revolt against the pressure the drop close implies. If this gym is really this good, why do I have to make up my mind now, instead of being able to think about it for a while? The now-or-never approach doesn't work as well with a more sophisticated clientele.

There is also the integrity issue that this type of deal-making states to the buyer. How does the consumer know that the guy before him didn't get a better deal by holding out longer, since you're obviously making a deal by dropping the price? If you're going to knock this much off, why not a little more if the prospect hits you up for the additional deal.

Selling off a trial membership system allows you to use a positive first-visit incentive, based on giving the prospect something additional if they sign today. This protects the integrity factor, because everyone who joins pays the same price but if they signed today they might have received an extra month on their membership or a small gift certificate to the pro shop.

The trend away from the old sales days

Potential members don't hate contracts; they hate the way contracts are sold and the length of the membership. Prospective members don't hate fitness clubs; they hate the way they are treated when they try to buy a membership from one of them. And they don't hate having to buy a membership to the club; they hate the old sales dog that sits across a desk in an office, writes upside down and practices door-to-door 1950s sales techniques on them.

Several of the big chains are trying to capitalize on this consumer frustration by coming up with gimmicks instead of fixing the problem. One group advertises $19 a month as a no-brainer decision in their ads and then slams people in offices for a much higher priced membership.

Another advertises no contract, just pay-as-you-go month-to-month memberships and then applies the same old techniques for the first-visit hard sell. These groups are aware of the consumer's frustration with fitness facilities; they just can't get past the old technology to find their solutions.

The solution is to develop a system that is fair and not insulting to the consumer, and that allows the club to do enough business to survive and even thrive if they do it right. Obviously, as has been said throughout this entire book, trial memberships are the solution because they solve all of these old sales problems.

A trial can still close people on the first visit, but doesn't alienate those who don't sign. A trial allows the salesperson to use better sales techniques than relying on a drop close to get the job done. And a trial treats the consumer with respect, something that adds to the word of mouth for the business. But most importantly, trial memberships allow the club to get a higher price for its memberships.

In most clubs that use a traditional pressured first-visit close, it all comes down to price, not because that's all the prospect is interested in, but because that's all the salesperson can talk about in a 30-minute sales close. You can talk about service but you can't prove it in 30 minutes. You can talk about how great the club is and how up-to-date the equipment is, but again, you can do nothing but talk about it in a 30-minute pitch.

The solution is to develop a system that is fair and not insulting to the consumer, and that allows the club to do enough business to survive and even thrive if they do it right.

In a trial system, the member has 14 or 30 days to find out how good the club is, and to experience the service they will receive. Then the final decision will not be price, it will be the quality and training of the staff, how clean the club is and how good an operation the owner runs.

First-visit high-pressure closes and drop closing don't allow this to happen, because these tools force a 30-minute buying decision, which forces the discussion to price, which is the only common ground that can be covered in such a short period of time.

Summary

The club still needs new members to survive. It's when and how the sale takes place that's important to today's consumer.

The potential buyer is aware of the reputation clubs have earned, and what some of the chains are still perpetuating around the country, and they don't try us. What we need to do is learn to give the member a different view. Instead of price-driven ads, we use a nonthreatening trial membership. Instead of slamming the first visit, we offer to sign them up during their initial stop, but if they don't we will still try to sell them as they become more comfortable with the staff and the facility. In other words, they are sold over time — as they are ready to be sold.

There are still hundreds of consultants teaching people how to sell with the old techniques. Before you create a sales system for your business, think about whether you need to build upon the old ideas mentioned here, or if you can build a system upon giving the potential member a different look at what a club can be, compared to those old dinosaurs.

Things you can do to use this material

You still have to sell, but take the emphasis off of the first-visit pressured close

1) You still have to sell, but take the emphasis off of the first-visit pressured close. Build a system that allows you more than one chance to close, as the member becomes more comfortable with the club.

2) Eliminate those old sales tools, such as offices, that make the member uncomfortable.

3) Let your marketing do the work and keep the sales staff focused internally, not externally. Trial membership marketing should bring in enough prospects to keep the sales staff busy. Their job would then be to concentrate on the service and training we give these prospects and to close them as they come in to use their trial memberships. In other words, we want the staff totally focused on the people in the gym, not in offices trying to bring prospects to the gym.

LESSONS FROM LIFE — #20

Honoring your mistakes

AN OWNER WHO STARTED OUT six years ago was naive when he first got underway, and he priced his early memberships too cheap. Coupled with this was the fact that he gave a discounted renewal, in this case, only $149 per year.

This owner has since grown in the business and now charges $40 per month for new members. He also guarantees the renewal rate at the same price, meaning that no matter what the club's prices climb to, the member's renewal rate will never go up if they renew within 30 days of expiration of this year's membership.

It irritated him that these early members were still renewing each year in significant numbers, which meant that he had to accept these lower rates. He wanted to change the old member's rates just one time, to bring them closer to the prices he is charging today.

The moral of the story

He set the prices and made those deals with the early members, and he should honor

It irritated him that these early members were still renewing each year in significant numbers, which meant that he had to accept these lower rates

his mistakes.

The members have lived up to their end of the bargain by renewing every year within the 30-day period. Some of his early members have renewed every year right on schedule for the entire six years he has been open. That means that they have supported his business without fail all those years.

As the old saying goes, integrity is like virginity, you can only lose it once. If this owner would go back and cancel the deals he made with those early members, his word would no longer be any good in the business and word of what he did would spread to the new members too. He could probably justify his actions because of the increase in the cost of doing business, but he still went back on a deal he made, which would upset a very large percentage of his members.

21

You can't sell a million-dollar gym with a six-cent brochure

YOU SPEND BIG MONEY TO BUILD a beautiful facility, develop a consistent and productive marketing campaign that gets people in the door, and then you send your prospects home with a price sheet and a six-cent threefold brochure in their hand. These cheap and incomplete support materials are what the person will base their final buying decision on when it comes to choosing a place to workout.

In a typical club that runs a trial membership as its prime marketing tool, about 30 percent of all the club's sales will take place during a member's first visit to the club. The other 70 percent will go home, pop open a beer, put their feet up and discuss which club to join with their significant other. The support materials you give the person to take home after their sales tour may be the only thing they have on which to make that final buying decision.

Most clubs don't give support materials that live up to the club's image. Your club may be beautiful, but you may be replacing that image in the prospect's head with brochures, price sheets and other handouts that don't live up to the rest of your presentation.

An example of the low-quality handouts a typical club uses are demonstrated by a tour of four clubs in the Hartford, Conn., area:

• The first club was a 45,000-square-foot national chain facility. The club's salesperson didn't have any paper or a pen to write the prices on after the tour. He had to borrow a sheet of legal paper and the prospect's pen in order to write down what a membership would cost.

• The second stop on the tour was an approximately 60,000-square-foot racquet facility that gave each person who toured a threefold brochure that probably cost about 10 cents each.

> **The support materials you give the person to take home after their sales tour may be the only thing they have on which to make that final buying decision.**

• The third facility was a licensed gym that gave each person a single price sheet.

• The fourth club didn't have any price sheets or brochures available at the time, but they would have some new ones from their printer in a day or two.

A prospect tours these four fitness businesses, goes home and sits on the couch to discuss the decision with the spouse. Based on this person's tour, what did they have to share with the other person and which facility would they choose?

These clubs all spent real money on marketing and had salespeople on duty to close a membership, but none of them spent that extra money needed on support materials that might have closed the sale while the person was sitting at home discussing options with their spouse.

You need a starter kit

One of the key pieces of your marketing and sales programs is a starter kit

One of the key pieces of your marketing and sales programs is a starter kit. A starter kit is a notebook with a really nice cover containing everything a potential member would need to make an intelligent decision about joining your club.

For example, the kit might contain a section on how to join the club, detailing the basics: hours and schedules, information on how to get the most of the first 30 days of their membership, who to call for help, what's fashionable in gymwear and a possible section on gym etiquette.

Mechanically, the starter kit would be a half-inch three ring binder with five tabbed sections inside. Different styles of starter kits were researched including stack brochures, plastic comb bound notebooks, and other cheaper methods to bind the materials together. The half-inch binder, while the most expensive, had at least a 7 percent better closing rate than the other methods.

The starter kit would be handed to the potential member early in the tour. Remember that during this person's stops at the other competitors, they were probably toured, taken into an office, worked over by a salesperson, and then sent home with one or two sheets of paper. By handing the person a substantial starter kit as soon as they walk into your place of business, you mess with their heads. Instead of being defensive on the tour because of their prior experience at the other clubs, they should be more open because of the gift you gave them before you even asked them for anything.

Now let's return to the example above, where the person toured four clubs. During the tour they received a threefold brochure, a single piece of paper, their own paper given back with handwritten prices on it and nothing from the last club. Let's add a fifth stop on the tour, your gym, and you give the person a notebook packed full of useful information on your gym and how to get started working out.

The person is sitting at home with the spouse talking about the gyms they visited, and they are reviewing all of the support materials including your notebook. Now which one of these clubs has the best chance of getting the member, and which one already has given more service than the other four?

As the person sits and considers their options, they have a chance to compare your materials against those from the other clubs in the area. When they discuss options with their spouse or friend, who hasn't yet been in the facility, the starter kit will speak for the service and support they can expect from your club, as well as demonstrate an understanding of how hard it is to make a decision to pick a gym.

A good starter kit should contain the following items:

1. AN INTRODUCTORY LETTER FROM THE OWNER

Welcome the person as a guest and explain why this club is different from the rest of the clubs in the area. Stay away from demonstrating why you are better, and concentrate on why you are different. A sample letter might look like this:

Welcome the person as a guest and explain why this club is different from the rest of the clubs in the area.

Dear New Member,

Welcome to our club.

We realize that you have other choices when it comes to fitness and we'd like to thank you for choosing our business as your place to work out.

We believe we have the best club around, meaning the most attentive and knowledgeable staff, a variety of the most current workout equipment, and a clean and comfortable physical plant. Talk is cheap, though, and every owner will tell you that they are proud of the gyms they own.

What makes us truly different is that we are the only fitness facility in the area that will let you try the gym before you make a commitment. Not just for a single workout, or for even a week, but for a full 30 days. We feel we are the best, but the only way you will know for sure is by trying us absolutely free for 30 days. Meet our staff, try our equipment and see what kind of service we offer. If we're not up to your standards, then don't become a member. It's that simple.

Making a decision to commit to working out is difficult. Will I like the other members? Will the staff appreciate my business after the sale? Are there things I don't see that later make me wish I didn't buy here? These are fair questions that can only be answered by trying before you buy. It's hard to hide bad service or poor equipment if you have a chance to see us doing business for up to 30 days.

We stand behind our business and we're proud of what we do here, and we feel that if we're given a chance, you'll want to do business with us. To help make that decision easier, we've included a gift certificate for discounts and gifts that you will receive if you decide to join any time during the first half of your trial membership. We do understand that some people need a full 30 days to decide and to be fair to them, we also have a package for those folks. Contact any staff person for more information on the certificates.

We also realize that we are one of the more expensive gyms in town. We do this by choice. Waiting in line for equipment, poor service and poor amenities are all part of being cheap. We feel that we can't be the best and be the cheapest at the same time. This also means that this gym is not for everyone.

If you appreciate quality, then we're for you. If price is your deciding factor, you won't be happy with us. We're better, and we're worth it. And please remember, we are the only gym in this area that will stand behind our business by letting you try before you buy.

I look forward to seeing you work out soon.

Sincerely,

Susan Smith
Owner and Operator

2. DESCRIBE THE FACILITY'S OFFERINGS

This includes a page or two describing the services and amenities, their costs and the hours they are offered.

3. INCLUDE A CURRENT INFORMATION PAGE

A basic information page lists the club's hours, class schedules, up-and-coming events and any special closings such as holidays.

4. DEVOTE AN ENTIRE SECTION ON PROPER GYM ETIQUETTE

Many people don't really know how to fit into a gym or understand the secret rituals that most workout people take for granted. For example, how would you work in with someone using free weights? How would you know when it's your turn to use the cardio piece you want? How do you get into a class without embarrassing yourself?

The No. 1 fear prospective members had when surveyed about joining a gym was that they felt they wouldn't fit into the club's routine, or that they wouldn't fit in because they would be the only one out of shape. This section should be used to quell their fear of not understanding how to make themselves comfortable with the club's routines. For example, this section might cover:

This section should be used to quell their fear of not understanding how to make themselves comfortable with the club's routines.

The gym can be a confusing place when you first start.
It's not unusual to be concerned about learning to fit into the gym environment. How do I share machines with someone? How do I know

314

when it's my turn to use a treadmill? How do I get help if I need it? All of these are common questions members ask during their first month or two with us. The following guide should help you get started, or simply ask the first staff member you see if your question is not included here.

How do I get a locker or towel when I visit the gym?

Lockers are first come, first serve, but we have plenty available. You need to bring your own lock and we recommend a lock that has a key instead of the old style combination lock. If you forget your lock, we can rent you a lock on a per-visit basis.

Most of our members bring a towel from home. If you prefer, however, the club can rent you a towel for your visit for $1. Towels and locks are available at the front desk from any staff person. We also have rental locks available if you forget yours.

How do I set an appointment for my first few workouts?

We want you to get started properly by having a trainer set you up on your own program. The club has individual and group workouts available to help you learn the basics of doing your first workout program. Everyone has different degrees of experience, so we tailor your workouts and the number you need according to your individual needs. Most new members start in the group workouts, but individual help is also available. To schedule your workouts and to find out what help you may need, ask any trainer or stop by the front desk. Please try to keep the appointments you set, since last-minute cancellations or no-shows are hard on staff scheduling and your fellow members who desire help.

"Everyone has different degrees of experience so we tailor your workouts and the number you need according to your individual needs."

How do I work in on the gym floor?

If you wish to share equipment with another member, simply ask, "May I work in?" When you take your turn, finish your set or exercise in a timely manner and then allow others to share. A common rookie mistake is to use a piece of equipment and then rest on it between sets. This doesn't allow others to share and slows down the pace of the gym. To rest, remove yourself from the piece you are using and be aware that others may wish to use the piece or bench you are happily resting on between sets.

When do I know it's my turn to use a piece of cardio equipment?

We recommend that you match your use to the time of day and the piece you want to use. Our busiest times are usually in the early evening after work. If you're one of those members who wants a fast 30 minutes and then go home, you'll be fine. If you're one of those who like a long hour walk on the treadmill, we suggest you come a little before or a little after the rush hour. We don't set time limits on the equipment, but we do recommend that the members use a little common sense when it comes to setting their workout time.

We also do not use sign-up sheets for equipment since we usually have enough of everything available. If you are waiting for a specific piece, however, simply let the person currently on the machine know that you wish to go next.

What is that piece of equipment?

It takes a while to learn all the pieces of equipment and what each one does. If you have a question about any piece we have and what it does, ask a staff member to show you how it works. Any trainer on the floor can tell you if that piece makes sense for the workout you are doing.

How to complain?

We love complaints and even have a system set up so you can feel comfortable about complaining. If you didn't care, then you wouldn't take the time to let us know. If you have a suggestion or complaint, stop by the front desk and ask for a complaint card. Fill it out and we'll address it as soon as possible. If it's something that you feel is too serious for a complaint card, see one of the managers immediately and let us know what you need.

5. What to wear in the gym and where to buy it

Many of your potential members who haven't been into a gym in the last several years really don't have a clue about current gym wear. When that guest shows up for his first workout wearing black socks, funny shorts and your basic white T-shirt, he will likely be embarrassed about not fitting in, and embarrassed people don't come back to try again.

Make sure to give them a list of what's fashionable in your facility and a second list of things suggested not to wear (so they won't make a spectacle like the middle-aged guys with big stomachs who love to wear split up-the-side running shorts).

Also let them know the types of things you have for sale in your shop, about other shops in the areas that carry workout clothes, and that your staff will certainly answer any questions they have about buying their first workout clothes.

6. Gym rules and procedures

Here is a sample of some possible rules and procedures you can adapt to your facility:

Club policies and guidelines

You, as a member or guest, acknowledge that you are physically able to engage in any activity, program or training provided, and agree that all exercises and use of this facility are taken at your sole risk. You also agree to accept full responsibility for all personal belongings. Derogatory remarks involving any other member of the club or club personnel will not

Make sure to give them a list of what's fashionable in your facility and a second list of things suggested not to wear...

be permitted.

General guidelines:
- To guarantee a training session focused on your individual needs and goals, please make sure you have had your group workout before you meet with your trainer. This gives you the foundation from which your trainer will build.
- Make sure you always have an adequate warm-up prior to beginning your workout. Warming up your muscles before exercising increases the quality and effectiveness of your workout and minimizes the risk of injury. Stretching helps control the adjustment between the muscles and connective tissue, which enables the body to meet the increased demands of a workout routine.
- For your safety and the safety of other members, our staff may make occasional recommendations on proper equipment usage and general exercise technique.

General club policies:
- No solicitation by members or guests is permitted in the facility without prior written approval by the management.
- It is important that members are out of the facility by closing time because the club's insurance does not cover members beyond regular business hours.
- Please remember to bring your membership card each and every visit to the club. There is a $10 replacement fee for lost or damaged cards.

Proper clothing and hygiene:
- Appropriate athletic shoes only. No street shoes, boots or sandals are allowed in workout areas.
- Clean workout clothes are required. The management will address any unsatisfactory hygiene condition, and corrective action may be required.
- All other clothing and shoes must be kept in lockers. Please keep all valuables at home. We are not responsible for lost or stolen items.
- Please avoid the use of heavy perfume or cologne.
- Please, no belt buckles, blue jeans or loose jewelry items can be worn in the workout area because these items may damage the equipment or cause you injury.

Equipment and cardiovascular training areas:
- Please be courteous at all times.
- Allow others to share the equipment while you're resting between sets.
- Keep hands and feet away from all moving parts and weight stacks.
- Do not attempt to repair or adjust any equipment that has malfunctioned.
- Report any equipment problems immediately to the staff.
- Use your workout towel to wipe off equipment and benches after use.
- Rack all weights and dumbbells after each use.

> *"For your safety and the safety of other members, our staff may make occasional recommendations on proper equipment usage and general exercise technique."*

- If dumbbells appear loose or cracked, report the matter to the staff immediately.
- Always use a spotter when attempting maximum weights.
- Collars and clips are to be used for "free bar" lifting.
- Screaming during lifting is a safety issue for other members and is not allowed.
- Please do not use chalk on any equipment in this gym.
- Dropping or the slamming down of weights may injure you or the other members and will not be tolerated.
- Profanity is not allowed in the gym.

Food and drink:
- Bottled plastic drink containers are allowed anywhere in the club. Due to safety concerns, glass bottles are not allowed.
- Please consume all food items and shakes at the bar area.

"Three strikes and you're out" policy:
- The club has a "three strikes and you're out" policy. If any of the above guidelines or policies are violated by a member, the manager reserves the right to write up an incident report about the violation, which will be kept on file indefinitely.
- If a member receives three of these incident reports, they will be asked to leave the club therefore terminating their membership.
- The club is especially concerned about guidelines that concern safety in the club, such as dropping dumbbells. A member will first be gently warned, but if that person continues to endanger themselves, they will be asked to leave.

General information:
- A $30 service fee will be attached to any returned checks or drafts.
- Should you have any questions or concerns about your membership, please contact the manager on duty or call 555-1234.
- Should you have any questions or concerns about your membership payments, please contact ABC Financial Services at 1-800-622-6390.
- If you refer either a family member or guest who joins the club, we will thank you by adding a free month to the end of your membership.

Guest fees:
- Out-of-town guests pay $15 for a single workout.
- Guests or family from out of the area who are accompanied by a member will pay $7.50.
- Area residents with a valid local ID may try the club once a year on a 30-day trial membership.

7. WHO TO CALL IF THEY NEED HELP

Contact people and phone numbers should be listed to help with every-

> "If a member receives three of these incident reports, they will be asked to leave the club therefore terminating their membership."

thing from babysitting to one-on-one training. Even though the phone number may be the same, give the members several different categories of help to choose from in the directory.

8. How to bring a guest and your guest policy

One of the biggest complaints found on member surveys year after year is that the members don't know how to bring their guests to the club and they are unsure of the club's guest policy. List the club's standard guest policy, how to get guest passes if you use them and any special guest events and programming that allows the members to bring in friends for special club activities.

9. Coupons for discounts and gifts in all of the profit centers

There should be at least 8 to 10 coupons that serve as an introduction to all of the club's services and profit centers. For example, you could include free childcare visits, free tans, one free workout drink, a free snack bar, 20 percent off of your first pro shop purchase, one free spin class and a free water bottle. These are just some of the ideas that are possible. Keep in mind that you are trying to introduce them to all aspects of your business and the services that you provide.

> **There should be at least 8 to 10 coupons that serve as an introduction to all of the club's services and profit centers.**

10. How to get the best results during the first 30 days

Many of our members are in the club not because they want to live longer or enjoy better health in their future years. Most are much more short-term than that in their thinking. For these new members, they want to know how to get into the best shape of their life sometime in the next 30 days.

Most new members are inspired to work out by something major and ego-threatening in their lives, such as a class reunion, being in a wedding or perhaps just dating someone new in their life. Their deadlines may not be reasonable, but that doesn't diminish what they expect from you in the way of education and training assistance.

This section should describe how to work out to get the best results you can in your first 30 days as a member. They may never admit that they have a secret agenda to meet, but this section just might be what closes them, because the club is showing it understands their need to move quickly once they get started.

Some sample topics that should be addressed in this section are:
• The basics of stretching and warming up.
• Why you should consider resistance training.
• How many days a week should you work out?
• The benefits of cardiovascular training.
• Cardiovascular versus resistance training: Which should you do first?
• Fat loss or weight loss, and what happens to your body when you first start a training program.

...it will help the club reduce its labor costs if the member already has a basic idea of what's happening and is more open to help and guidance.

• Considering a nutrition program to go along with your training.
• Do you need supplements?

Fatten up this section because it may be the first one the potential member reads, and it will help the club reduce its labor costs if the member already has a basic idea of what's happening and is more open to help and guidance.

11. THE CLUB'S NUTRITION PROGRAM

This is so important to the club's profits and to the member's first 30 days that it should have a separate section detailing how the club's program works and what it costs. A key line to open this section with is one that the Apex Education program uses in its materials: "Diets don't work and never will." Many of the prospects sitting home reading this material and trying to choose a club are frustrated diet people who might have tried everything and never got the results they desired. By addressing this issue strongly, we may convince them that we have an alternative to their problem.

12. INCLUDE A MISSION STATEMENT AS THE LAST PAGE

A good mission statement personalizes your club in the prospect's mind, especially if the entire working staff signs the page. An example might be:

> **We believe we have the best facility in the area with the most supportive and caring staff, and we're the only club that will prove this 365 days a year with our 30-day trial membership. Let us prove to you that we're the best and that we really do believe that everything starts and ends with the member.**

The staff should each sign this sheet with a personalized note. For example, "See me if you need help with your training goals," signed Ed, your head trainer.

13. YOUR OWN CLUB-SPECIFIC MATERIAL

This is definitely a more-is-better case. Be sure to include any club-specific information they may need, as well and any training and member-service support materials.

Summary

Most of our prospective members don't make up their mind during their first visit to the club. They go home, think about what they saw, and then compare their experiences at the clubs they visited. It will seldom be your equipment or club that really gets them excited enough to join. Often, it will be how friendly your front counter person was, how knowledgeable and caring their salesperson was, or maybe how good the support materials were that they were able to take home.

The starter kit is a tool that helps close more sales. Most clubs are willing to spend $3,000 to $4,000 per month or more in marketing to get some business. Would you be willing to substantially increase your closing rate by giving each person a $3 to $4 book once they are actually in the door?

You may have a beautiful club and a well-trained staff, but you may be missing that small but very important piece of the sales puzzle — the starter kit that they take home and compare against the other clubs and what they received from them.

The kit is also important because many members have those hidden fears of fitting into a new situation. Some of these fears are strong enough to prevent them from actually making a decision to join a club. The starter kit should eliminate as many of these fears as possible by giving the prospects detailed and informative materials that they can read and apply before they set foot in the gym.

> **The starter kit is a tool that helps close more sales.**

Things you can do to use this material

1) Build a starter kit using the notebook format. Spend a little extra money on the quality, including the cover.

2) Track the returns of your folks that have to go home and think about it. The number of people who come back should increase if the starter kit is good enough.

3) Don't cheapen out. You'll spend a lot of money to get people in the door. Why not spend a little more to increase your closing rate?

LESSONS FROM LIFE — #21

The 99 to 1 rule

AN OWNER IN A COLLEGE TOWN caught several of his members sharing their membership cards with their roommates. This was before the era of computer-generated pictures, so the non-members simply handed the card to whomever was at the front desk and came into the club.

The owner finally caught on and reacted by buying a camera, getting a machine that laminated the cards, and switched to a new card so everyone would have to turn in their old ones and have new ones issued. When he issued a new membership card, it was complete with a member picture laminated on the back.

This new procedure increased the cost of the card from $0.69 each to $2.50 each, but it did temporarily stop people from sharing a card.

The moral of the story

The owner should have applied the 99 to 1 rule instead of overreacting to the situation. The 99 to 1 rule states that we overreact to the 1 percent by punishing the other 99 percent.

Another example of an owner overreacting is when a member

Is this policy needed for the 99 percent, or am I overreacting to just the 1 percent that is causing the problem?

writes the club a bad check in the pro shop. Because the owner feels betrayed and pissed-off, he now institutes a new policy that forces all of the front counter

people to get picture IDs from every member who wants to write a check in the club.

One or two members wrote bad checks. Now the club is asking for IDs from members who have paid their memberships regularly for years. These same members are now getting carded for buying $20 worth of supplements with a check.

A compromise policy for the club that received a bad check might have been to only ask for ID if the person is not a member. This shows trust in the club's members, and the club does have information on the person's membership in case someone did write a bad check.

The 99 to 1 rule is a question you should ask yourself before you enact club-wide policies that affect the members. Is this policy needed for the 99 percent, or am I overreacting to just the 1 percent that is causing the problem?

22

Even if you give it away free, you still have to have a system

USING A TRIAL MEMBERSHIP doesn't mean that you just open the doors and let everyone try it until they turn themselves in at the front counter with their checkbooks in their hands. You still have to sell with a trial membership, and this type of try-before-you-buy method of selling still has to have systems in place that allow these sales to happen. The trial membership system is based on 5-day, 14-day and 30-day trial periods. During this time, the trial member has to be entered into a system, trained as we would a real member, followed up on to get the sale and finally converted into a regular member.

With a trial membership, the potential members are looking for a period of time to get to know the staff, see what kind of service the club has to offer, meet the other members and grow comfortable to the point that they are ready to commit to a regular membership. These prospective members may reach this comfort level at any time during their trial periods. And sometime during the trial period, they expect the club's salesperson to ask them if they'd like to join.

In other words, they understand that we are just letting them try it in hope that they will like it enough to buy it. If you're an old sales dog, this is just another version of the puppy dog close, where the pet store owner lets the family take the little puppy home for a couple of days to see if everyone likes it. No one ever brings back a used puppy.

We're doing the same thing. Try us for free and see if you like us, and of course, trying the club free for 30 days does build up a little obligation

...the trial member has to be entered into a system, trained as we would a real member, followed up on to get the sale and finally converted into a regular member.

toward us in the trial member's head.

Treat them like a member and they will become a member

Trial members should be treated like members because they are members, although they're just short-term members.

Your trial members may have visited other clubs before they found you. If this is the case, they are probably battle weary against salespeople. One of the keys to making trial memberships successful is to change their orientation. We do this by using starter kits that were discussed earlier and by using the strategy of touring the potential member on a trial membership, as if they were already a member and not as a guest.

When they first come in to inquire about the trial membership, sit them down, register the person as a new trial member and then tour that person as a member. This changes the orientation because instead of showing the club as if we're trying to sell them, we're showing them the club they now belong to as a member.

For example, instead of showing them the cardio area and pitching them on the number of pieces or brands the club has, you tell them that this is where they'll be doing their cardio work, here's how to use the machines and, by the way, this is Ann, she's one of the trainers and she'll be the one who shows you how to get the most out of your cardio workouts.

By touring as a member, the prospect loses much defensiveness usually felt around salespeople and is much more likely to come back and use the trial membership.

By touring as a member, the prospect loses much defensiveness usually felt around salespeople and is much more likely to come back and use the trial membership.

Trial membership procedures

The steps can be adapted to any length of trial membership. For sake of example, we're using the 30-day trial throughout the steps. When someone presents the advertising piece, or as they inquire about the trial memberships they heard about from a friend, take these four steps:

1. REGISTER THE PERSON IMMEDIATELY AS A 30-DAY TRIAL MEMBER

The registration is important for future tracking. Most clubs get the same information you would need to fill out a membership contract. Then as you trial close, later during the member's trial, you'll already have the information you need to get the person converted. Don't forget to have the person sign a liability disclaimer since they will be working out in the club.

2. GIVE THE PERSON A TEMPORARY MEMBERSHIP CARD
AND THE STARTER KIT

The membership card should be a bright, somewhat obnoxious color that works in the club's computer system. For example, if you were using the ABC Financial Services system, you would take the person's picture with the system's camera and give them a membership card that activates the computer system when they come in each time.

The card and the picture on the screen each time they use the card already makes them feel that the trial membership is a serious thing instead of a low-rent giveaway. The card system also allows them to get that comfort level to start growing by understanding one of the club's procedures that every member must use.

The starter kit that was discussed in an earlier section is a tool that helps close the member at home, which is where the majority of the prospects decide to invest in your club. The starter kit is also a tool that helps break down many of the barriers potential members encounter when starting at a new club, or at their first club. Before the member is toured, the salesperson should go through the starter kit with the new trial member.

For example, a prospect may feel nervous that they won't fit in at the club. By letting that person read about club etiquette and club procedures before they actually come in, you help them feel more comfortable about joining your facility.

3. TOUR THE NEW PERSON AS A MEMBER, NOT A GUEST

Again, this gives the staff a position of power when they tour the person as a new member instead of as a guest. By touring as a member, the person loses much of their defensiveness since they now don't expect to get pitched. For example, "As a new member Joe, let me show you your locker room and how you get a key and a towel when you come in to work out." We still have to tour, but from a different frame of mind and from a position of power now that the person is already a trial member.

4. AFTER THE TOUR, GIVE THEM THE GIFT CERTIFICATE
AND PRESENT THE PRICES

To give the member added value on their membership, and to help the salespeople get the sale, use a gift certificate that gives the person additional incentives if they join before their trial is up. For example, if the person joins as a regular member by the 15th day of the 30-day trial, they would receive everything on the certificate. This additional incentive package gives the salesperson an angle to work and a reason to keep approaching the person.

For example, the salesperson could say, "Now Joe, don't forget that you only have three days left before you'll lose everything on the certificate. Can I get the paperwork started today while you're getting your shower?"

A sample of the copy that would be on a certificate is shown in Figure

The membership card should be a bright, somewhat obnoxious color that works in the club's computer system.

Make sure to make the certificate a nice piece of work that implies value.

22.1. Make sure to make the certificate a nice piece of work that implies value.

Still try to close on the first visit. With a trial membership system' you can still expect to write about 30 percent of your business during the prospective member's first visit to the gym. To help close during the first visit, try offering additional first-visit incentives such as those listed as part of the certificate.

The two examples above, which were the additional month and an additional gift certificate to any of the club's services or programs, would be in addition to everything else listed on the certificate.

If the person converts to a regular membership any time during their

Membership Certificate
The Frisco Gym

Dear special guest,

We just wanted to say thank you for expressing an interest in our gym.

We are proud of our gym, and we believe that once you get a chance to try it, you'll agree we're the best gym in the Frisco area.

But talk is cheap, so we'll prove it to you with our 30-day trial membership.

We understand that making a decision to commit to a gym is difficult. We'll help make that decision easier because if you decide to join the gym sometime during your first two weeks as our guest, here's what you'll receive from us as **special gifts** for becoming a member of the best gym in the area:

• $25 off the club's membership fee
• The full 30-day trial time added to the end of your membership
• 20 percent off your first pro shop visit
• 20 percent of your first supplement purchase and a
   free starter supply of supplements
• A free Frisco Gym tee shirt
• Three free tanning sessions
• Three free childcare visits
• A free keychain from the club
• A free water bottle
• Two free shakes from the juice bar

Additional first-visit incentives:

• An additional month, valued at $40, added to the end of your membership
• An additional $25 gift certificate for the pro shop or any service the club offers.

Guest name _____

Date issued _____

Club representative _____

Date member must join or forfeit the gifts on this certificate _____

Figure 22.1. Membership Certificate, The Frisco Gym

first 15 days of their 30-day trial, they would receive everything on the certificate. If they convert to a regular membership after their 15 days are up, but before their 30-day trial expires, they can have any one thing on the list.

5. SET A FIXED APPOINTMENT AND GIVE THE PERSON AN APPOINTMENT CARD

It's not unusual for a club to have 40 percent or more of their trial members not show for their first workout after being set up as a trial member. There are several reasons why this might happen, but two important ones to consider are closing too hard during the first visit, which cancels out what the trial membership was designed to do in the first place, and letting the member leave without a clear idea of what's supposed to happen next.

Slamming too hard on the first visit sends a mixed message to the guest. They came in because they were responding to an ad and offer that made trying your club feel safe and different from the other clubs in the area. We have in essence lied to the person when we use a trial to bring them in and then do a negative drop close during their first visit.

The second reason is that they leave without a clear idea of what's supposed to come next and what will happen to them once they're in the gym. Many also find that the gym was more frightening than they anticipated. If they don't come back, it's because they may have seen something that scared them out of their comfort zone.

For example, a male in his 40s is interested in joining a gym but it's been at least 10 years since he's worked out and it shows. He's there but he's not comfortable with the way he looks, and he's nervous about getting started. You try to make him feel at ease by introducing him to his female 19-year-old hard-butt trainer who will be taking him through his first workout. He never shows again because he was intimidated at the thought of working out with someone like your trainer.

When they leave the club after their initial inquiry about the trial membership, they need to be well-armed with information as to what comes next. The starter kit helps to eliminate many of the fears they might have about fitting in at the club, but they need more than that to get them back in for that first workout.

Set a real appointment at the front counter using a large appointment sheet that the member sees you entering their name on before they leave. Give the person a formal appointment card that would be the same style as on you'd get from your doctor. Introduce the person to as many staff people as possible so they know a few people before they leave. And try to match the trainer to the member as closely as possible, keeping in mind that hard-body trainers are not necessarily role models for our trial members.

An important point here is to understand that the trial memberships often bring in a type of member that other clubs don't get and that you might never have had in large numbers in your business. These are the folks who would never consider even inquiring at your competition, but felt safe checking you out because of the trial memberships. These folks need differ-

> **Set a real appointment at the front counter using a large appointment sheet that the member sees you entering their name on before they leave.**

ent handling than your regular workout people who have belonged to other gyms or clubs, and they need a lot more personal attention during their first few weeks before they can be converted to a regular membership.

6. WORK THE TEMPORARY MEMBERSHIP CARDS

The brightly colored trial membership card is a focus tool and also a training tool for the staff. If there are trial membership cards in the club, the staff needs to be trained to understand that there is possible business on the floor and there are also people who need extra service.

The most efficient way to use the trial cards is to hang a rack similar to a message rack for a large office behind the front counter. As the trial members come in to work out, the staff takes the card and places it on the rack. The staff needs to be trained that if there is a card on the rack, there is work to be done.

The trial members can be trial closed throughout their memberships by referring to the expiration date on the bottom of the card. If the member is getting close to the deadline of losing the items on the certificate, any member of the staff can ask if they would like to see a salesperson about getting started during today's visit.

If there are trial membership cards in the club, the staff needs to be trained to understand that there is possible business on the floor and there are also people who need extra service.

Summary

The trial membership system requires that you modify how you sell in the club. You still have to sell, but it's when the sale takes place that becomes more important in this system.

Most clubs, because of the extreme pressure to close the first visit, risk their entire chance to get a new member on a single encounter between a salesperson and the prospect. If the salesperson is that good, wouldn't they be more effective if they had a possible 15 chances to close instead of just one?

The trial memberships simply decrease the emphasis on the first visit by giving the salesperson more than one chance to close the member. To do this, you need to modify your sales system to one that has much more follow-up than a traditional first-visit system.

First-visit-oriented salespeople do follow-up but, because of the nature of the pressure needed to close during the first visit, many of the prospects they talk to never will come back no matter how many times you call.

The trial memberships are weighted more toward a consistent follow-up and toward looking for that point where the member is comfortable with the club and staff and ready to commit to a membership.

Another key point for trial memberships is that you need to offer them to everyone who comes into the club. There will be a temptation to not tell a prospect who walks in off the street about the trial memberships until after you try to close them with the conventional methods. Tell them all up front and then rely on the additional first-visit incentives and the power and image of the trial memberships to close the person anyway. It just might not always happen during the first visit however.

Things you can do to use this material

1) Create a system that follows the trial member all the way through their membership. Most systems are based on only one chance to close. Modify your system to follow the trial member during their entire stay at the gym.

2) Develop a temporary membership card system that teaches the staff to focus on those trial members in the gym. The card should be brightly colored and tied to the computer system. If a salesperson comes on duty and notices five cards on the rack, then they should be able to run the card through the computer, see a picture of the trial member on the screen, and then know where all of the potential business in the club is at that time.

3) Develop a certificate that helps the staff convert the trial members to regular memberships. Use at least 10 items on the certificate. From research over the years on trial memberships, the two most important items on the certificates are the full trial time added to the end of the membership and the discount off the membership fee if they sign early. The trial time has a lot more value than most owners realize, and the member wants to use that time until the last day before making up their mind. By giving the full trial time back at the end (no matter when the person becomes a regular member), they are more likely to sign earlier rather than waiting until the last day.

> ...the two most important items on the certificates are the full trial time added to the end of the membership and the discount off the membership fee if they sign early.

A final thought

At the time this book was written, the industry was again under siege by another chain of the decade. The scenario was the same as it had been for the past three decades. Venture money looking for an easy kill meets lousy operators.

The damage done by these types of operators goes way beyond what they do to themselves. Most of you who read this book are independent operators in the business because you love it and, like me, probably couldn't work anymore in the real world, anyway. When clubs run ridiculously low prices, sexist ads and then high-pressure people into hating the industry and all fitness clubs in general, then all of our businesses suffer.

The information in this book is extensive and no single operator can do it all. Some things, such as the financial structure of your business, should be changed immediately. Others, such as the implementation of a good member service program, may take several years to achieve the results you want.

The key is to start to change now, one thing at a time. There is an old saying that success is not possible without action. Good business is the process of change, which means that you must learn, change, revise, learn again and then change again for as long as you're in business. If you're not changing, then your business will end — it's as simple as that.

There has never been a better time to be in the fitness business, and there has never been a worse time either. For those who refuse to grow and still try to copy systems that have proved unsuccessful for almost two decades, then this business will be tough. If you're the type of owner who wants to join the modern business world, forsake many of the old habits of the industry and move to and operate at a higher level, then you will be successful against any competitor.

Making money in the fitness industry is, in a way, relatively easy. Find

> **Good business is the process of change, which means that you must learn, change, revise, learn again and then change again for as long as you're in business.**

331

a niche you want to build from, lay a solid financial foundation, offer current programming and equipment, understand the numbers and don't be afraid to charge what you're worth.

The other option you have, of course, is to be a generalist, copy someone else's financial system and then offer programming that's 10 years out-of-date. Then enter into a price war with a competitor who has deep pockets and whose only interest is in going public and then raping the industry like so many clubs and owners before them. Do this and you have a typical owner's business plan for the '90s and beyond. The choice is yours.

You can make money in the fitness industry, but you have to follow a different path than we have ever followed before in this business. Good business is good business, and principles from the real world do apply to us. Study this book, practice good business and run your business for the long run, with integrity and passion, and you'll be successful.

Good business is good business, and principles from the real world do apply to us.

pay-as-you-go memberships, 78, 307
paychecks, 260
payments, 71-73, 76, 81, 84, 87, 91-93, 102-103, 108-109, 135, 275, 318
payroll expenses, 116, 241
payroll taxes, 15, 224, 241
payroll waste, 175
payroll, 15, 46, 61, 70-71, 78, 150, 175-178, 182, 212, 219, 224-225, 241-242, 263
people person, 171
people-dependent vs. systems-dependent, 218
perception of quality, 35-38, 40
performance contract, 254-256, 262, 264
performance standards, 213, 220
performance-based, 248
perks, 214, 218-219, 225
personal appearance, 139
personal attention, 36, 63-64, 150, 328
personal example, 200
personal interviews, 126
personnel policies, 218
personnel, 218, 316
philosophy, 61-63, 96, 277-278, 281, 304
plan, financial, 12
plan, five-year, 12, 15-18, 44, 109-110, 195
plan, long-term, 10
plan, marketing, 12-month, 9-10, 14, 16, 299
plan, member service, 9, 15-16, 54, 190
plan, one-year promotion, 157
plan, one-year, 10, 16
plan, prospectus, 12-13, 17-18
plan, three-year, 15-17, 44, 195
plans/planning, 9-10, 12, 15-18, 21, 32, 34, 39-40, 43, 47, 70, 109, 118, 148, 154, 169, 171, 202, 279, 294
Plummer rules of marketing, 283
point-of-sale, 45, 100, 234
policies, 11, 33, 124, 142, 144, 174, 192, 218, 227, 256, 316-318, 322
pools, 22-23
poor training, 173
positioning, 32-34, 295
postcards, 123, 255, 257
posters, 153-154
potential members, 4, 7, 10, 14, 31, 35-36, 40, 46, 55, 60, 62-63, 75, 79-80, 82, 85, 118, 126, 139, 140, 157, 172, 180, 183, 191, 200, 219, 222, 230, 270-273, 275-281, 284, 286-287, 291, 295-296, 298-299, 305-308, 312, 320, 323-325
praise, 143, 177, 213, 221, 260, see also recognition
pre-tax, 69
preconceptions, 297, 299
prepaid memberships, 99, 104
price war, 59, 147, 149, 151, 153, 155, 157, 159, 161, 163, 165, 332
price-driven ads/marketing, 62, 66, 271-275, 278-280, 306, 308
price-driven members, 60
pricing strategy, 6-7, 31, 59-63, 66, 83-85, 100-102, 104-105, 149-150, 160, 170, 208, 269-270, 273-274, 279-280, 294, 303, 305, 310-312, 325, 331
primetime, 171, 175, 229

priorities, 193
privacy, 106, 302
prize, 251-252, 257
pro shop, 30, 36, 48, 53, 100-101, 117, 126, 136-137, 154-155, 162-163, 172, 230, 257, 307, 319, 322, 326
proactive, 9, 11-12, 15, 17-18, 39, 154, 190, 283, 292
probation, employee, 173, 178, 217-218, 236-239
problem-solving, 200-201, 224
procedure manual, 201, 204, 216, 218
procedures, 15, 58, 139, 142, 174-175, 183-184, 197-198, 201, 209, 213, 217-218, 239, 316, 324-325
product, 6, 22, 24, 28, 32-33, 52, 63, 80, 84, 90, 126-128, 130, 133, 136, 143, 149-150, 152, 154, 157-158, 161, 163, 170-171, 182-183, 194, 206, 272-274
production, 68, 114, 132, 178, 181, 193, 212, 226-228, 231, 239, 245-251, 258, 262-264, 285
productivity, 228, 250
profiling employees, 179
profit centers, 14-16, 53, 55, 60, 62-66, 71, 119, 126, 135, 147-165, 178-179, 182, 191, 196, 198, 216, 227-230, 233-234, 263-264, 274-275, 280, 299, 319
profit margin, 172, 195, 291
profit-and-loss, 247
profitability of the fitness business, 12, 34, 40, 58, 60, 69-71, 92, 98, 111, 118-119, 132, 134, 151-152, 157, 190, 196, 203, 221, 242, 260, 320
programming, 7, 21, 27, 36, 40, 184, 216, 289, 293-294, 299, 319, 332
projections, 12, 14-16, 18, 77
projects, 14, 17, 34, 191
promotion, 286, 288, 299
promotion, active, 154-155
promotion, employee, 259
promotion, event, 294
promotion, member referral, 153
promotion, member sales, 288
promotion, passive, 153
promotion, profit centers, 153-159, 228, 230-231, 233
promotion, program, 233
proper clothing, 317
prospective members, 33, 62, 107, 109, 128-129, 139, 168, 186, 231, 274-278, 303-304, 306-308, 311-312, 320-321, 324-325, 328, see also potential members
punch pass, 85
purchases, 27, 53, 99, 109, 111, 158-159

Q

quarterly, 93, 140, 234
questionnaires, 124-126
quotas, 9, 62, 80, 189

R

racetrack juice counter, 161
racks, 153, 155
racquetball, 21, 23
radio, 244, 283-284
range of members, 35, 37, 75
rates, 10, 38, 50, 73, 77-79, 81-82, 86, 91-93, 201, 310
ratios, 69, 72-73, 104, 110-111, 223, 285
razors, 163
reactionary management, 9-12, 17, 144, 292

receivables base/assets, 70, 74, 88-90, 137, 178, 189, 228
receivables, 101-104, 151
receptionist, 186
recognition, 220-221, 229, 259-260, 284, 288-289, 298, see also praise
records, 115
recreation, 3, 36-37, 39, 269
recruitment, 130, 183
referrals, 53, 133, 153, 189, 289, 293, 303
refinance, 16, 110-111
refocusing, 262
reinforcement, 261
reinvestment, 22, 26, 45, 49, 50, 52, 54, 71, 81, 102, 108-110
relatives, 58, 167, 223, 225, 227, 229, 231, 233, 235, 237, 239, 241, 258
renewals, 16, 44-54, 63-64, 84, 93, 101-103, 116, 134-137, 156, 184, 186, 195, 201, 227, 310
rent factors, 70
rent, 16, 18, 70-71, 153, 162, 224, 234, 264, 286, 289, 294, 315
rental lockers, 162
rental locks, 142, 315
rental space/subleasing, 162
repair and maintenance, 49, 54, 224, 227, 256, 317
reports, daily business, 218, 226
reports/reporting, 227
reputation, 5, 81, 106, 121, 297, 308
reserves, 13-14, 73, 108, 110-111, 183, 318
resources, 46, 61, 78, 91, 93, 150-151, 275
response rate, 10, 16, 285-286
responsibilities, 216, 218, 226, 228-230, 232-235, 242
restructuring, 93, 111, 226, 235, 242
retail, 38, 63, 152, 160, 163-164, 219, 260
retention, 170, 190, 196
return on collections, 87-88
return on investment, 13-14, 99
return on profit center, 15
return per member, 45, 60, 63-66, 73, 76-77, 82, 89, 91, 99-100, 104, 150, 157, 209, 275, 280, 305
return per sale, 209
returning calls, 140
revenue, 14, 44, 46, 50, 53, 62, 65, 77, 85, 87, 94, 103, 111, 150, 154, 156-158, 163, 179, 219, 223, 230, 234, 236, 241, 289
rights, 175
risk to joining, 277
risk, 20, 64-65, 88, 164, 178, 188, 191, 193, 217, 277, 280, 288, 291, 316-317, 328
risk-free, 64, 278
role play, 174
rule breaking, 11
rules, 20, 54, 83, 86-87, 142, 144, 174, 192, 201, 241, 255, 283, 296, 299, 316
rumors, 106
running price in ads, 287
rural markets, 36, 92, 283

S

salary, 15, 68, 70-71, 172-173, 219, 226, 235, 238-239, 241, 247-249, 250-251
sales bonuses, 249
sales gimmicks, 303

sales leads, 46, 285, 287, 306
sales offices, 5, 7, 33, 61, 151, 162, 272, 279, 304
sales staff/training, 43, 80, 85, 132, 170, 174, 186, 192, 231, 234, 236, 306, 308
sales-driven, 61, 63-65, 80-81, 93, 193, 196, 275, 282, 306
sales-experienced, 303, 306
sales-related words, 297
sales-resistant, 303
salesdog types, 80
salesmanship, 79, 170, 280
salespeople, 6, 9, 20, 35, 46, 57, 61, 65, 70, 79-80, 82, 107, 109, 111, 117, 150, 176, 178-179, 183, 189-191, 206, 214, 216, 227, 231, 245, 247, 249-250, 255, 258, 291, 303-304, 312, 324-325, 328
salons, 162
same-month-last-year comparison, 26
savings, 10, 16, 27, 55, 74-75, 102, 242
scheduling, 216, 225, 227-228, 234, 315
seasonal market conditions, 84
second-in-command, 68, 202, 207-209, 211-216, 218-221, 227-228, 295
security, 98, 250
sectorized, 270
self-improvement, 193
self-motivated employee, 179, 184
self-review, 214
self-service, 152
semi-naked models, 4, 171, 275, 279
seminar, 23, 49, 174, 195, 206, 209-211, 215, 237, 268, 284, 294, see also workshop
senior manager, 87, 119, 138
service businesses, 6, 32, 172, 177, 245
service profit centers, 157
service, xiii-xiv
service-driven club, 61, 63
service-limited staff, 47
service-oriented staff, 62, 136
service-related words, 296
services, 7, 32, 39-40, 63, 77, 80, 82, 90-91, 125, 128, 134, 142-144, 150, 163, 188, 222, 270, 296-297, 314, 318-319, 325-326
sexual harassment, 239
shakes, 128, 160-162, 172, 184, 196, 231, 258, 284, 318, 326
shampoo, 150, 163
shift, 170, 173, 180, 198, 229, 232-233, 249
shopping, 246, 273, 289, 291, 294
short-term debt, 17, 57, 89, 107-111
short-term goals, 125
short-term greed, 42
short-term job holder, 173
short-term market conditions, 9
short-term memberships, 85, 258, 277, 324
short-term plans, see plans, short-term
short-term programming, 294
short-term sales goal, 10
short-term solution, 73
showers, 34, 45, 76, 123, 325
sign-up, 24, 78, 116, 294, 315
signs, 50-51, 101, 143, 145, 153-155, 188-189, 191, 202, 279, 282, 320
skills, 17, 35, 54, 107, 170-171, 176-177, 179, 184, 186-188, 192, 197, 208, 210, 212, 215-217, 221, 229,